REHABILITATION MEDICINE AND PSYCHIATRY

REHABILITATION MEDICINE AND PSYCHIATRY

By

JACK MEISLIN, M.D., F.A.C.P., F.A.P.A., F.A.A.P.M.&R.

Diplomate of the American Board of Psychiatry
and Neurology (in Psychiatry) and of the American
Board of Physical Medicine and Rehabilitation
Assistant Clinical Professor, Department of Rehabilitation Medicine
Albert Einstein College of Medicine,
Consultant, Rehabilitation Medicine Service
Veterans Administration Central Office,
Senior Psychiatrist, Rockland Psychiatric Center
Orangeburg, New York. Formerly,
Chief of Staff and Chief of Physical Medicine and Rehabilitation Service
Veterans Administration Hospital, Montrose, New York,
Consultant, Social Rehabilitation Service
Department of Health, Education and Welfare, Washington, D.C.,
Clinical Assistant Professor of Psychiatry,
Cornell University Medical College.

With 28 Specialists
in Mental Health and Rehabilitation

With a Foreword by

Walter E. Barton, M.D., F.A.P.A

Professor of Psychiatry, Dartmouth Medical College
Senior Staff Physician, Veterans Administration Center
White River Junction, Vermont
Past President and former Medical Director,
American Psychiatric Association

CHARLES C THOMAS • PUBLISHER
Springfield • Illinois • U.S.A.

WILLIAM MADISON RANDALL LIBRARY UNC AT WILMINGTON

Published and Distributed Throughout the World by
CHARLES C THOMAS • PUBLISHER
BANNERSTONE HOUSE
301-327 East Lawrence Avenue, Springfield, Illinois, U.S.A.

This book is protected by copyright. No part of it may be reproduced in any manner without written permission from the publisher.

© *1976, by* CHARLES C THOMAS • PUBLISHER
ISBN 0-398-03432-X
Library of Congress Catalog Card Number: 74 12598

With THOMAS BOOKS *careful attention is given to all details of manufacturing and design. It is the Publisher's desire to present books that are satisfactory as to their physical qualities and artistic possibilities and appropriate for their particular use.* THOMAS BOOKS *will be true to those laws of quality that assure a good name and good will.*

Printed in the United States of America
N-1

Library of Congress Cataloging in Publication Data

Meislin, Jack.
Rehabilitation medicine and psychiatry.

Bibliography: p.
Includes index.
1. Mentally ill—Rehabilitation. I. Title. [DNLM: 1. Mental disorders—Rehabilitation. WM30 M515r]
RC576.M4 362.2'04'25 75-12598
ISBN 0-398-03432-X

RC576
.M4

To my beloved wife Mildred and children Jay, Allan, Robert, Marcia, Arleen, her husband Melvyn and of course, our grandson Elliot.
In memory of my parents whose sacrifices made my professional career possible.
To those who are dedicated to helping the emotionally disadvantaged to achieve the dignity of self-sufficiency and who will hopefully be assisted in their efforts by the publication of this volume.

164492

CONTRIBUTORS

ABRAMSON, ARTHUR S., M.D., F.A.C.P., F.A.A.P.M.&R: Professor and Chairman, Department of Rehabilitation Medicine, Albert Einstein College of Medicine, Yeshiva University, Bronx New York; Diplomate, American Board of Physical Medicine and Rehabilitation; Visiting Professor, Ithaca College; Director and Visiting Physician, Rehabilitation Medicine, Bronx Municipal Hospital Center, Lubin Rehabilitation Center Hospital of the Albert Einstein College of Medicine; Medical Director, Division of Physical Therapy, Ithaca College, Ithaca, New York; Consultant, V.A. Hospitals, Bronx, New York, East Orange, New Jersey, Montrose, New York, Montefiore Hospital, Kessler Institute for Rehabilitation. *Partial list of former honors and affiliations:* President, American Academy of Physical Medicine and Rehabilitation; President, New York Society of Physical Medicine; on President's Committee on Employment of the Physically Handicapped; Governor's Committee on Employment of the Physically Handicapped; Chairman, Committee on Advances in Education, American Congress of Physical Medicine and Rehabilitation; Governor Rockefeller's Council on Rehabilitation; National Advisory Council, Vocational Rehabilitation Administration; President, Section on Physical Medicine and Rehabilitation, New York Academy of Medicine; Mayor's Advisory Committee on the Handicapped; American Board of Physical Medicine and Rehabilitation (Vice-chairman); Medical Research Study Section SRS-HEW; Medical Research Study Section, Vocation Rehabilitation Administration, Health, Education and Welfare; Clinical Professor, Physical Medicine and Rehabilitation, New York Medical College; Special Lecturer, Columbia University, New York City; Member, Harry S. Truman's Committee on Veteran Medical Services; Board of Directors, American Board of Physical Medicine and Rehabilitation. Recipient of eighteen awards including Gold Key Award, Congress of Physical Medicine and Rehabilitation. Author of over sixty publications. Military Service: Major, Purple Heart and Oak Leaf Cluster.

AYLLON, TEODORO, Ph.D.: Professor, Psychology Department and Special Education, Georgia State University, Atlanta, Georgia; Fellow, Division 25 of the American Psychological Association; Member of the New York Academy of Sciences, of the Inter-American Society of Psychology; of the Board of Directors of the Society for the Experimental Analysis of Behavior; of the Editorial Board, Journal of Behavior Research and Therapy; of the Editorial Board, Journal of Behavior Therapy and Experimental Psychiatry; Associate Editor, Journal of Applied Behavior Analysis. Formerly: Director of Clinical Research, Behavior Research Laboratory, Anna State Hospital, Anna, Illinois; Associate Professor, Rehabilitation Institute and Educational Psychology, Southern Illinois University; Associate Professor, Psychology Department, Southern Illinois University, Carbondale, Illinois; Associate Research Professor, Department of Psychiatry, University of Pennsylvania; Associate Director of Training, West Philadelphia Community Mental Health Consortium. Author of fifty publications.

BAER, LESLIE, M.D.: Diplomate, American Board of Internal Medicine; Assistant Professor of Medicine, Columbia Univ. Coll. of Phys. and Surg.; Assistant Attending Physician, Presbyterian Hospital; Assistant Attending Physician, Harlem Hospital; Associate Research Scientist, N.Y. State Psychiatric Institute; Diplomate, National Board of Medical Examiners; Member, Phi Kappa Phi, Alpha Omega Alpha, and Phi Beta Kappa. Dr. Baer has to his credit numerous publications and presentations, and among his special interest is the subject of electrolyte pathophysiology in psychiatric illness.

BAKER, JOSEPH J., M.D., F.A.C.P., F.A.P.A.: Diplomate in Psychiatry, American Board of Psychiatry and Neurology; Director, Mental Health and Behavioral Sciences Service, Veterans Administration Central Office; Associate Clinical Professor of Psychiatry, George Washington University Medical School; Member, National Advisory Mental Health Council, National Institute of Mental Health; Member, Council on Accreditation of Psychiatric

Facilities, Joint Commission on Accreditation of Hospitals; Fellow, American College of Psychiatrists; Formerly Commissioner, Tennessee Department of Mental Health; Superintendent and Physician-in-Chief. Butler Hospital, Province, R.I.; Superintendent, Davidson County Hospital, Nashville, Tennessee; Associate Clinical Professor of Psychiatry, Vanderbilt University Medical School; Chairman, APA Committee on Standards of Psychiatric Facilities; President, Tennessee District Branch, A.P.A. Dr. Baker has published extensively on the subject of mental health.

BARTON, WALTER E., M.D., F.A.C.P., F.A.P.A., F.A.M.A.: Diplomate of the American Board of Psychiatry and Neurology; Certified in Mental Hospital Administration, American Psychiatric Association; Professor Emeritus, Department of Psychiatry, Dartmouth Medical College; Senior Staff Physician, Veterans Administration General Hospital, White River Junction, Vermont; Adviser, VA Mental Health and Behavioral Science Service, Washington, D.C.; Member, Editorial Advisory Board, Administration in Mental Health; Member, Editorial Board of the Annual, Social Psychiatry. His previous prestigious positions are too numerous to mention, among them: Superintendent, Boston State Hospital; Medical Director, American Psychiatric Association, Washington, D.C.; Director and President, American Board of Psychiatry and Neurology. He is Past President of the American Psychiatric Association and had been for years until recently its Medical Director. He has just been designated as the recipient of the Salman Medal and previously had been honored with the Nolan Lewis and E. B. Bowis Awards. Dr. Barton is the author of five books and over 140 articles in the fields of hospital administration, clinical topics, and rehabilitation.

BEARD, JOHN H., M.S.W.: Executive Director of Fountain House since 1955. He received his Bachelor of Arts degree and his Master's of Social Work degree from Wayne State University. He serves as a consultant in psychiatric rehabilitation to the Social and Rehabilitation Service (Department of Health, Education and Welfare) and to the World Rehabilitation Fund. He has published a number of articles on rehabilitation of psychiatric patients.

BLACK, BERTRAM, J., M.S.W.: Professor of Psychiatry (Rehabilitation), Albert Einstein College of Medicine, New York; Director of Mental Health Rehabilitation Services, Bronx State Hospital, Bronx, New York; Professional Lecturer, New York School of Psychiatry, New York, New York; Special Executive Assistant to the Commissioner of Mental Hygiene; Formerly Director of the Comprehensive Health Planning Agency for New York City; Executive Director and President, Altro Health and Rehabilitation Services; Chairman, Mental Health Projects Grants Committee, National Institute of Mental Health, National Institutes of Health, Department of Health, Education and Welfare; Chairman, Delinquency Grants Committee, NIMH, DHEW; Member, Advisory Grants Committee, Training Division, Office of Vocational Rehabilitation, DHEW, Assistant Professor, School of Applied Social Sciences, University of Pittsburgh; Instructor, School of Social Work, Carnegie Institute of Technology; Lecturer, Department of City Planning, Carnegie Institute of Technology, Pittsburgh, Pennsylvania. He is Fellow, American Association for the Advancement of Science, American Public Health Association, American Orthopsychiatric Association, and a member of numerous professional organizations and an active participant in many National, State, and Local agencies and of a number of honorary societies (Alpha Kappa Delta, Pi Mu Epsilon, and others). Mr. Black has published fifty articles dealing mostly with rehabilitation of psychiatric patients and has served as consultant to many agencies (Chairman, Rehabilitation Committee, N.Y.S. Dept. of Mental Hygiene; Mayor's Task Force on Health Planning; and consultant to NIMH).

BUSSE, EWALD W., M.D., Sc.D.(Hon), F.A.C.P., F.A.P.A.: Diplomate of the American Board of Psychiatry and Neurology, (Psychiatry); J. P. Gibbons Professor of Psychiatry and Chairman, Department of Psychiatry, Duke University School of Medicine; Founding Director, Duke University Center for the Study of Aging and Human Development; Certified by American Board of Qualification in Electroencephalography; Director, Geriatric Society. Dr. Busse is a recipient of numerous research and professional awards and is a member of many honorary societies. He is consultant to the V.A., U.S. Army, Navy, and N.I.M.H. Past President of The American Psychiatric Association. Formerly Professor, University of Colorado School of Medicine, among other faculty appointments; and Director, American Board of Psychiatry and Neurology. His numerous professional affiliations in international and national societies include a number of geriatric organizations, a field of his special interest. He is the author of several books and of over 150 articles.

CIRCHIO, VINCENT T., M.A.: Coordinator, Rehabilitation Medicine Service V.A. Hospital, Montrose, N.Y. He received his B.S. degree from Rutgers University and M.A. degree from Columbia University with post-graduate work towards a Doctorate degree in Remedial Education at New York University. Certified Medical Rehabilitation Director and Coordinator, Association of Medical Rehabilitation Directors and Coordinators; (Chairman, Professional Liaison Committee) and recipient of its Professional Achievement Award, and Life Membership Award. Mr. Circhio has had extensive experience as a rehabilitation therapist and for many years as Coordinator of Rehabilitation Departments with various administrative responsibilities in the Armed Forces. He recently retired from the Air Force Reserve with the rank of Lt. Colonel.

DAVIS, SR., JOHN E., ScD.: Executive Director, National Rehabilitation Training Institute; Author of Play and Mental Health, Principles and Practices of Rehabilitation, Principles and Practices of Recreational Therapy, Clinical Applications of Recreational Therapy; Fullbright Scholar; Visiting Professor at Oslo University, Oslo, Norway; Lectured on Psychiatric Rehabilitation at The Karolinski Institute, Stockholm, Sweden, Columbia University, New York University, Springfield College, Washington College; Consultant in Rehabilitation, Veterans Administration, Department of Health, Education and Welfare, State of Alabama; Author of seven books and over one hundred articles on various aspects of rehabilitation: physical, neurological and psychiatric.

FOLSOM, JAMES C., M.D., F.A.P.A.: Diplomate of the American Board of Psychiatry and Neurology; Director, Rehabilitation Medicine Service, Department of Medicine and Surgery, Veterans Administration Central Office; Fellow, American College of Psychiatrists, American Psychiatric Association, American Geriatric Society; Member, Association of Medical Superintendents of Mental Hospitals, Editorial Board of STAFF Magazine, Alabama District Branch of American Psychiatric Association, Governing Council, Psychiatric Hospital Section, American Hospital Association; Member of the Board of Trustees of the Menninger Foundation, Topeka, Kansas; Chairman, Psychiatric Services Section, American Hospital Association. Formerly on the faculty of Menninger School of Psychiatry; Associate Clinical Professor of Psychiatry, Medical College, University of Alabama; Deputy Commissioner for Hospitals and Superintendent, Bryce Hospital, Alabama Department of Mental Health, Tuscaloosa, Alabama; Chief of Staff and Hospital Director, VA Hospital, Tuscaloosa, Alabama; Special Assistant to the Deputy Chief Medical Director, Department of Medicine and Surgery, VA Central Office, Washington, D.C.; appointed Consultant in Psychiatry, State Department of Mental Health; Chairman, 1971 State White House Conference on Aging (Alabama). Dr. Folsom has also distinguished himself as an editor and an active member and leader in numerous professional and civic organizations and is a recipient of a multitude of awards. He has published over thirty articles mostly dealing with "Attitude" and "Reality Orientation" therapies.

FREEMAN, HOWARD E., Ph.D.: Morse Professor of Urban Studies, Florence Heller Graduate School for Advanced Studies in Social Welfare, Brandeis University; Sociologist, Russell Sage Foundation, New York City; Consulting Editor, *Community Mental Health Journal;* Research Advisor, Institute of Nutrition of Central American and Panama of Pan American Health Organization, Guatemala City; Member of Mental Health Research Career Award Committee, N.I.M.H.; Member of Review Committee of the State Comprehensive Health Planning Program for Massachusetts; Research Consultant, National Institute of Nutrition, Bogota, Colombia; Member of Advisory Council on Manpower Utility in Mental Health Services, American Psychiatric Association; Research Consultant, National Center for Health Services Research and Development; Associate Editor, *Sociological Methods and Research,* Sage Publications, Inc. Among many previous research and teaching positions, Dr. Freeman was Research Associate in Sociology, Harvard University, School of Public Health; Lecturer in Sociology, City College of New York and Assistant Study Director, New York University; and consultant to many federal, state, and municipal agencies. He has published 120 books and articles, among them the classic "The Mental Patient Comes Home" (Freeman and Simmons).*

GLASSER LIFSON, BETTY A., B.A., M.S., C.S.W., A.C.S.W.: Coordinator, After Care Services, Region VI, Mass. Dept. of Mental Health; Member of Academy of Certified Social Workers, National Association of Social Workers, and many other national associations. Formerly Director, Social Rehabilitation Center, Rockland County Community Health Center, Pomona, N.Y.; Psychiatric Social Work Supervisor, Rockland State Hospital, Orangeburg, N.Y.; Director of Psychiatric Social Work, Department of Mental Health, Commonwealth of Massachusetts; Instructor of Psychiatry, Department of Psychiatry, (PSW) Tufts University School of Medicine; Associate in Psychiatric Social Work, Simmons College School of Social Work; Research Staff, Massachusetts Mental Health Center and Boston State Hospital. Author of a number of articles on mental health and Contributing Author of three books. Mrs. Lifson has been actively affiliated with numerous civic organizations.

KLEBANOFF, SEYMOUR, G., Ph.D.: Received the B.A. and M.S. Degrees in Psychology at Yale University and the Ph.D. in Clinical Psychology at Northwestern University. Following an internship at Worcester State Hospital, Mass., he served as Chief Psychologist at the Clarinda, Iowa, Institute of Mental Health, the Veterans Administration Hospital at Downey, Illinois, and the North Shore Hospital in Winnetka, Illinois. During World War II, he served as clinical psychologist in the Army Air Force. Since

*Dr. Freeman is currently director, Institute for Social Science Research, University of California, L.A.

1950, Dr. Klebanoff has been Chief of the Psychology Service at the Franklin Delano Roosevelt Veterans Administration Hospital in Montrose, New York and a member of the faculty of the Cornell University Medical College where he currently holds the rank of Clinical Associate Professor of Psychology in Psychiatry. He is a Fellow of the American Psychological Association and a Diplomate in clinical psychology of the American Board of Examiners in Professional Psychology. He has made an important contribution to the literature in the field of clinical psychology.

KLINE, NATHAN S., M.D., F.A.C.P., F.A.P.A.: Diplomate, American Board of Psychiatry and Neurology. (in Psychiatry) ; Associate Clinical Professor of Psychiatry, College of Physicians and Surgeons, Columbia University with many other international non-academic appointments; Director, Research Center, Rockland Psychiatric Center, Orangeburg, N. Y.; Director, Psychiatric Services, Bergen Pines County Hospital, Paramus, N. J. Recipient of twenty awards (including those of many foreign countries and two Albert Lasker Awards). Fellow, American Association for the Advancement of Science, and Fellow and member of numerous national and international societies, Dr. Kline has probably been personally involved in mental health programs of more foreign countries than any other psychiatrist. During his research career and as consultant in this field, Dr. Kline was Director of Research, Worcester State Hospital, and served on Committee on Research of the American Psychiatric Association. He has been a pioneer in psychopharmacological research. He is listed in "The 100 Most Important People in the World Today" (G. P. Putnam 1970) and is the author of more than 400 publications.

KUTNER, BERNARD, Ph.D.: Dean, Sargent College of Allied Health Professions of Boston University; Consultant, West Roxbury, Mass. Veterans Administration Hospital. A *cum laude* graduate of City College of New York with a medal in psychology Dr. Kutner received his doctorate in Social Psychology at Harvard University (Sigmund Livingston Fellow, Benjamin Cardozo Prize). He was on the faculty of Sarah Lawrence College, Brooklyn College, Cornell University Medical College (Director, Studies in Gerontology and Research Associate), Associate Professor, Department of Preventive and Environmental Medicine, Albert Einstein College of Medicine where he became Professor (Social Science) in the Department of Rehabilitation Medicine. He served on Mayor's Advisory Committee and on numerous other committees. Associate Editor, Journal of Health and Human Behavior. Former President, Division of Social Psychology, New York State Psychological Association, Dr. Kutner is a Fellow of a number of professional associations. His major field of interest has been psychosocial research including gerontology. He is the author of over seventy publications and numerous reviews and is listed in American Men of Science, The Social and Behavioral Sciences, and Who is Who in the East.

LEEDY, JACK J., M.D.: Diplomate of the American Board of Psychiatry and Neurology; Associate Attending Psychiatrist, The Brooklyn-Cumberland Medical Center; Director, Poetry Therapy Center, New York, N. Y.; Professor and Chairman, Department of Poetry Therapy, GROW, GROUP RELATIONS ONGOING WORKSHOPS, New York, N. Y.; Member of American Psychiatric Association; Founder and President, APT (Association for Poetry Therapy). Formerly Psychiatrist to the Bureau of Adult Hygiene, Department of Health, N. Y. City; Director, Mental Hygiene Clinic, Cumberland and Hospital, Brooklyn, N. Y.; Sr. Psychiatrist Mental Hygiene Clinic, Morrisania Hospital, Bronx, N. Y.; Neuropsychiatrist, Sydenham Hospital; and Psychiatrist, Mental Hygiene Clinic, V.A., N.Y.C., N. Y. Publications: Editor, *Poetry Therapy* and *Poetry The Healer* (Lippincott); Editor, *Compensation in Psychiatric Disability and Rehabilitation* (Charles C Thomas, Publisher).

MASSERMAN, JULES, H., M.D., F.A.P.A.: Professor of Neurology and Psychiatry and Co-Chairman of Psychiatry at Northwestern University. After graduating from Wayne University School of Medicine, he studied neurology at Stanford, psychobiology at Johns Hopkins, psychiatry at the University of Chicago, and completed formal training at the Chicago Psychoanalytic Institute. During these years his research studies, scientific writings and public services earned him the Phi Lambda Kappa National Award in Pathology, the Lasker Award "For outstanding contributions to the advancement of mental health through experimental investigations," several Gubernatorial and Presidential citations for state and national services, and many honorary lectureships here and abroad. Dr. Masserman is Vice President of the American Psychiatric Association. He has also been President of the Illinois Psychiatric Society, the American Society of Group Therapy and Psychodrama, the American Society of Biological Psychiatry and the American Academy of Psychoanalysis; and Chairman of the Illinois Psychiatric Research and Training Authority, Member of the Board of Trustees of various schools and training institutes, Councillor of the American Psychiatric Association, Fellow of the Center for Advanced Study in the Behavioral Sciences and Consultant in Psychiatry to the United Nations. President, International Association for Social Psychiatry. Dr. Masserman is the author of *Behavior and Neurosis, Principles of Dynamic Psychiatry, The Practice of Dynamic Psychiatry, The Biodynamic Roots of Human Behavior, Modern Therapy of Behavior Disorders* and other books; edits the annual volumes of *Science and Psychoanalysis* and *Current Psychiatric Therapies;* has published about 400 articles in physiology, neurology, psychiatry, history, sociology and philosophy, and has prepared thirty-three research and teaching films. We have learned from his friends that he also finds time for sailing his yawl, playing the viola, composing music, and learning the ever new from his patients, students and colleagues. His *Psychiatric Odyssey* is a fascinating autobiography.*

MENOLASCINO, FRANK J., M.D., F.A.P.A.: Diplomate, American Board of Psychiatry & Neurology in Psychiatry; Professor of Psychiatry and Pediatrics and Vice Chairman, Dept. of Psychiatry, University of Nebraska Medical Center; Senior Vice President, on Board of Directors, National Association for Retarded Citizens and Chairman, Research Advisory Committee; Clinical Director, Division of Preventive & Community Psych., Nebraska Psychiatric Institute; Advisory Board, Eastern Nebraska Community Office of

*Dr. Masserman was recently elected Secretary of the American Psychiatry Association.

Retardation; Editorial Boards: Exceptional Child Annual, Journal of Child Psychiatry and Human Development; Fellow American Academy for Cerebral Palsy; Fellow, American Orthopsychiatric Association, Research Education Committee; Member, American Association for the Advancement of Science; Member, American Association for Social Psychiatry, Division of the International; Member, American Association on Mental Deficiency (Chairman, Research Advisory Committee); Member, American Medical Writer's Association. Governor's Citizen's Committee on Mental Retardation. International Association for the Scientific Study of Mental Deficiency. Author of twelve books including "Psychiatric Aspects of Diagnosis and Treatment of Mental Retardation" and co-author of "Sensorimotor Training Project." Published twenty-four book chapters, forty articles and numerous book reviews.

MORITZ, TIMOTHY B., M.D.*: Diplomate of the American Board of Psychiatry and Neurology; Director of Community Mental Health Services for Rockland County; Director, Rockland County Community Mental Health Center, Pomona, New York; Clinical Assistant Professor of Psychiatry, Cornell University Medical College; Attending Psychiatrist, Chief of Department of Psychiatry and member of Executive Committee of Medical Staff, Summit Park Hospital, Pomona, N. Y., N.Y. State Rehabilitation Hospital, West Haverstraw, N. Y.; Assistant Attending Psychiatrist, Payne Whitney Clinic, Cornell University–New York Hospital Medical Center, Good Samaritan Hospital, Suffern, N. Y., Nyack Hospital, Nyack, N. Y.; Member, A.P.A.; Member, New York State Dept. of Mental Hygiene Task Force to review the Fleishman Commission Report, entitled "Children with Special Needs"; Member, Board of Directors, Rockland Community Action Council; Member, New York State Metropolitan Mental Health Directors Association (Vice Chairman); Member, American Association of Mental Health Administrators; Member, Rockland County Blue Ribbon Panel on Criminal Justice, (Chairman of Judiciary Subcommittee); Member, Phi Beta Kappa; Member, Alpha Omega Alpha (Medical Honorary Society) and many other organ-

*Note: Dr. Moritz has now been appointed Director of the Department of Mental Health and Mental Retardation for the state of Ohio.

izations. Honors: John Metcalfe Polk Prize for General Efficiency, Cornell University Medical College; Gainer Cup Award to Most Outstanding Fraternity Man, Ohio State University. Formerly, Unit Chief of Rockland State Hospital, Orangeburg, New York; Member, Board of Governors, Rockland County Health & Social Services Complex. Dr. Moritz has published a number of articles, mainly on drug abuse.

NAYLOR, HARRIET H., M.A.: Director of the Office of Volunteer Development,* Department of H.E.W. Formerly: Director of Educational Development for the National Center for Voluntary Action and field operations consultant; Director of Volunteer Services for the New York State Department of Mental Hygiene and Chairman of the Governor's Interdepartmental Committee on Volunteers; Training consultant with the National Board, YWCA, and a training adviser with the Girl Scouts; Past Vice President and Fellow of the American Association of Volunteer Coordinators and is a member of numerous organizations related to volunteer work. Member, Chairman Education Committee, Board, American Association of Volunteer Services Coordinators; American Society For Public Administration. Ms. Naylor is the author of several books and a number of articles related to volunteer work.

HYMAN PLEASURE, M.D., F.A.P.A.: Dr. Pleasure started his career with the N.Y. Department of Mental Hygiene in 1941, when he became supervising psychiatrist at Central Islip State Hospital where he remained through 1948. The following year, he became assistant director of Pilgrim State Hospital in charge of the Edgewood Division for Tuberculosis, leaving there in 1955 to become director of Middletown State Hospital, a post he held until his appointment as Deputy Commissioner for Community Services, 1966-1971. In 1971 he became Director of Rockland State Hospital and a Member of Rockland County Community Mental Health Board, positions he still holds. In addition, he has served as consultant at New Hampton State Training School, New Hampton, N. Y. and as medical director of the Department of Correction's Pilot Project for Young Offenders with Epilepsy. Dr. Pleasure re-

*Office of Human Development.

ceived both his bachelor and medical degrees at New York University where he was elected to Phi Beta Kappa. He interned at Cumberland Hospital, New York City Dept. of Hospitals, and served his residency at Dannemora State Hospital. He did post graduate work in neurology at Mt. Sinai Hospital and in psychiatry and neurology at New York State Psychiatric Institute. A diplomate of the American Boards of Psychiatry and Neurology and a fellow of the American Psychiatric Association, he has been certified as a mental hospital administrator by the American Psychiatric Association. His book, "A Pilot Project for Young Offenders with Epilepsy," was published under the auspices of the New York State Department of Correction and Interdepartmental Health and Hospital Council in 1964. He is the author of numerous articles in professional journals.

RACKOW, LEON L., M.D., F.A.C.P., F.A.P.A., F.A.M.A.: Diplomate of the American Board of Psychiatry and Neurology (in Psychiatry and Neurology) ; Certified as Mental Hospital Administrator; Clinical Professor of Psychiatry, New York Medical College. Until recently Director (and prior to that Chief of Staff) of V.A. Hospital, Montrose, N. Y. Dr. Rackow is currently Director, Transitional and Geriatric Services, Community Mental Health Board of Westchester County. He is a Fellow, American College of Psychiatrists. He is on Board of Directors, Westchester County Mental Health Assoc., Council for the Aging, Research and Study Group. Formerly: Member of A.P.A. Committee on Activities for Leisure Time; Programs Committee and Program Chairman for the Institute of Hospital and Community Psychiatry; Member of the Committee on Administrative Psychiatry and Chairman of its subcommittee for Planning and Revision; Program Committee, Joint Meetings of Association of Medical Superintendents of Mental Hospitals with Veterans Administration; Governing Council, Psychiatric Service Section, American Hospital Association; American College Forensec Psychiatry, Westchester County Medical Society and Section on P & N, Westchester Academy of Medicine; Assoc. Clin. Prof. of Psychiatry, Cornell University Medical College. Awards: Disabled American Veterans; AMVETS; American Podiatry Association; Veterans of Foreign Wars; Association Rehabilitation Directors; National Rehabilitation Award. He is the author of a number of articles on mental health.

SCHEFLEN, ALBERT E., M.D.: Diplomate of the American Board of Psychiatry and Neurology (in Psychiatry) ; Certified by the National Board of Medical Examiners and Philadelphia Psychoanalytic Institute; Professor of Psychiatry, Albert Einstein College of Medicine, Head of the Division of Human Communication at Bronx Psychiatric Center. Holds Research Positions at Bronx State Hospital and Jewish Family Service of New York. Member: A.A.A.S. General Systems Society; Bronx Psychiatric Soc., American Psychiatric Assoc.; Philadelphia Psychoanalytic Society; New York Academy of Sciences. Formerly, Temple Univ. Professor, Research Psychiatry; Director, Temple Univ. Residency & Research Training; Director of Psychiatric Research, Temple Univ.; Senior Scientist and Director of Research Training, Eastern Pennsylvania Psychiatric Institute; Fellow, Philadelphia Psychiatric Society; Honorary Fellow, Center for Advanced Study in the Behavioral Sciences. Member, Group Advancement Psychiatry; Member, Pennsylvania Psychiatric Soc. Author of sixty books and articles.

SILLER, JEROME, Ph.D.: Professor of Educational Psychology, Dept. of Educational Psychology, School of Education, NYU; Director of Training, Greenwich Institute for Psychoanalytic Studies; Director of Psychology Dept., Stuyvesant Polyclinic, N.Y.C.; Diplomate, American Board of Examiners in Professional Psychology (Clinical Psychology) ; Certified in Psychoanalysis, National Psychological Association for Psychoanalysis. Member: New York Society of Clinical Psychologists—Past President; New York State Psychological Association—Past President—Clinical Division; American Psychological Association—Member Executive Committee of Division 22 (Rehabilitation Psychology) and Fellow in three divisions; National Psychological Association for Psychoanalysis—Senior Member and Training Analyst. Honors: Ward Medal in Psychology and Psychological Honors, City College; Certificate of Honor, New York University. Formerly: Psi Chi, National Psychological Honor Society; Consultant, Social Rehabilitation Service, Dept. of H.E.W.; Consultant, Division of Vocational Rehabilitation, N.Y., N.Y. In addition to the above listed experiences, Dr. Siller had held adjunct professorships, lectureships, etc., at New York University, the City College of the City University of New York City, and Brooklyn College teaching a variety of psychological courses. He is the author of a number of publications.

TUCKMAN, ALAN J., M.D.: Associate Director, Rockland County Community Mental Health Center, Director, Division of Community Consultation Education and Outreach Programs, and Director, Rehabilitation Division. Instructor, Dept. of Psychiatry, Columbia University. Member: A.P.A.; A.M.A.; Rockland County Medical Society (Chairman Mental Health Committee). Formerly: Director, Home Care Service, Cumberland Hospital; Clinical Attending, Brooklyn Hospital; Staff, Internal Medicine, Pediatrics, New York Department of Health. Dr. Tuckman is the author of a number of papers on mental health.

WHANGER, ALAN D., M.D., DTM&H. (London): Diplomate of the American Board of Psychiatry and Neurology (in Psychiatry) and of the National Board of Medical Examiners; Assistant Professors of Psychiatry, Duke University School of Medicine, Durham, North Carolina; Director of Geropsychiatry Project, John Umstead Hospital, Butner, North Carolina; Scientific Association, Duke Center for Study of Aging; Chairman, Committee on Aging, of N.C. Neuropsychiatric Association. Lecturer in psychiatry, hypnosis, and geriatrics. Member, Governor's Advisory Committee for the Council on Aging; Member, Task Force on "Rehabilitative Care of the Mentally Ill Aged," Institute of Gerontology, University of Michigan. Honors: Capitol College Scholarship (academic award) ; Phi Eta Sigma, Scholastic fraternity; Phi Beta Kappa; Certificate of Merit of the American Academy of Dental Medicine. Member of A.P.A., American Geriatric, and a number of other medical societies. Author of a number of articles and presentations including exhibits and the production of a motion picture on the study of aging.

WINICK, WILLIAM, M.D., C.M.H.A., F.A.P.A.: Diplomate, American Board of Psychiatry and Neurology; Fellow, American Medical Association, American Psychiatric Association, American

Association for the Advancement of Science; Physician of the Year 1967; Chairman, Council of Directors, VA Medical District #1, Region 1; Hospital Director, Veterans Administration Hospital, Brockton, Massachusetts. Served in V.A. Hospitals: St. Cloud, Minn., Knoxville, Ia., Sheridan, Wyo., Augusta, Ga., Gulfport, Miss., Coatesville, Pa., and Brockton, Ma. Area Chief of Psychiatry and Neurology, Trenton, N.J. Clinical Associate at University of Pennsylvania and Women's Medical College, Philadelphia, Pa. Recipient of the Physicians Award by the President of the United States for an outstanding contribution to the welfare and employment of the Nation's handicapped men and women. Author of monograph Industry in the Hospital.

ZIMBERG, SHELDON, M.D.: Diplomate of American Board of Psychiatry & Neurology (Psychiatry) and Certified Mental Hospital Administrator; Project Director, Alcoholism Treatment Center, Hospital for Joint Diseases and Medical Center; Chairman, Task Force on Alcoholism and Drug Abuse of the New York County Branch of the American Psychiatric Association. Fellow, American Public Health Association. Member: American Psychiatric Association; A.M.A.; American Medical Society on Alcoholism; and others. Formerly: Lecturer in Psychiatry in Law and Psychiatry Seminar at Rutgers University Law School; Instructor in Psychiatry, Columbia University, College of Physicians & Surgeons; Chief, Division of Community Psychiatry, Harlem Hospital; Principal Investigator Research Project Comprehensive Approach to the Outpatient Treatment of Alcoholism; Director, Harlem Hospital, Center Alcoholism Unit; Deputy Director, Rockland County Community Mental Health Center; Associate Examiner, American Psychiatric Association Committee on Certification in Administrative Psychiatry; Chairman, Committee on Treatment of Alcoholism of the New York State Alcoholism Planning Task Force. Author of a number of publications on mental health, geriatrics and alcoholism.

AUTHOR'S BIOGRAPHY

JACK MEISLIN, M.D., F.A.C.P., F.A.P.A., F.A.A.P.M.&R.

BEING A DIPLOMATE of both the American Board of Psychiatry and Neurology (in Psychiatry) and the American Board of Physical Medicine and Rehabilitation (the only physician so certified for a decade and a half) is characteristic of Dr. Meislin's lifetime career of parallelism between Psychiatry and Rehabilitation Medicine. Assistant Clinical Professor, Department of Rehabilitation Medicine, Albert Einstein College of Medicine he was also Clinical Assistant Professor of Psychiatry, Cornell University Medical College and Special Lecturer, College of Physicians and Surgeons, Columbia University where he taught for 17 years psychiatric aspects of rehabilitation medicine. A Fellow of the American Psychiatric Association he was a member of committee on medical rehabilitation. As a Fellow of the Academy and member of the Congress of Physical Medicine and Rehabilitation he was chairman of committee on correlation of rehabilitation medicine and psychiatry. Consultant, Rehabilitation Medicine Service, V.A. Central Office, he also served as consultant to the V.A. psychiatry service as a member of committee on mental health and behavioral sciences. He was consultant, Social Rehabilitation Service, Department of H.E.W., Washington, D.C. For many years Chief of Physical Medicine and Rehabilitation Service at V.A. Hospital, Montrose, N.Y. where he pioneered a number of clinical and training programs, he became Chief of Staff of that hospital until he retired from V.A. to join the Rockland State Hospital where he served as deputy unit chief. Dr. Meislin is on the national medical advisory board of the American Association of Rehabilitation Therapists and Association of Medical Rehabilitation Directors and Coordinators. As Lt. Colonel in the U.S. Army Reserve Corps he was chief of physical medicine and chief of psychiatry services of his hospital unit. He is listed in "Who is Who in the East" and "American Men of Medicine."

FOREWORD

THE APPEARANCE OF *Rehabilitation Medicine and Psychiatry* fills a need for a comprehensive text. Doctor Jack Meislin shares with the reader over twenty years of experience in the practice of rehabilitation. He is a diplomate both of the American Board of Physical Medicine and Rehabilitation and of the American Board of Psychiatry and Neurology. The book also has chapters and special topics by a group of well-known experts.

Rehabilitation is the process by which the handicapped person is restored to the fullest physical, mental, social, vocational and economic usefulness of which the individual is capable. Rehabilitation in psychiatry is that part of treatment which seeks to maximize the patient's capacity for social adjustment and for living productively in the community. The individual should function in a social role in relation to family, work and community. An individual who has been psychologically oriented to accept the limitation of his disability is rehabilitated, according to Bernstein, when he has returned to productive work without fear or anxiety and with a sense of usefulness in his own eyes and in those of his associates. In my experience about one in every three patients released from a public mental hospital can return to his former job. The breakdown of all those released may be expressed in another way: 39 percent are good employment risks, 5 percent are poor risks, and 38.5 percent are too old to work.

Some factors I have found useful as guides to selection of patients for rehabilitation are choosing those with subacute or chronic mental illness who have residual symptoms, those with impairment of function due to drugs taken to control symptoms, those who lost job skills during prolonged confinement, those who were students or who never had a job and those with poor work history related to job satisfaction. Essential in every instance is the ability to cooperate and relate to others.

To make the transition from a mental hospital to home, the

patient must often give up a stable adjustment for an anxiety-evoking uncertain future. Job readiness involves an accepting attitude toward authority, intellectual and physical capacity, acceptable personal appearance, punctuality, capacity for concentration on the task at hand and the ability to take criticism and change behavior. Job skills call for proficiency in learning the required tasks and a production rate equal to that expected. These are not inconsiderable requirements for some.

After defining terms and identifying the goals of rehabilitation, the authors describe process and methodology. The applications are covered in sections on mental and geriatric patients and mentally retarded individuals and in various treatment systems, such as Veterans Administration (VA), Community Mental Health Center, and sheltered workshops. Also discussed are recreational therapies and the contributions of workers in various disciplines such as psychologists, social workers, rehabilitation counselors and volunteers. A variety of topics concludes the presentation, covering drugs, poetry, communication skill, bill of rights, work incentives and the psychosocial aspects of rehabilitation of the physically disabled.

In spite of the demonstrated success of the VA rehabilitation programs that developed after World War II, few psychiatrists and few other physicians today complete residency training with a clear understanding of how best to utilize resources for rehabilitation. This book is an attempt to develop that requisite understanding. Other factors have delayed development of rehabilitation in psychiatry: There are few referrals; those that are referred may not be able to hold a job; the time per case may be excessive in comparison with physical disabilities; and the end point of service that enables the case to be closed is not as sharp.

Resources to develop sheltered workshops, for the patient who cannot hold a full-time job for whatever reasons, have been lacking. The matter has been further complicated by the separation of funding sources at federal and state levels. There is ample evidence that these barriers can be overcome with great benefit for the individual patient who needs rehabilitation services.

This book hopefully will stimulate those already dedicated

workers in the field of rehabilitation to greater effort and encourage them to employ a more varied approach appropriate to patient need.

It is inevitable that rehabilitation services will expand as the social conscience seeks to improve the quality of life.

WALTER E. BARTON, M.D.

PREFACE

REHABILITATION MEDICINE and psychiatry are the only two medical specialties dedicated to the holistic approach to the disabled individual—preoccupied not only with the pathology of a single organ, but basically concerned with his total medical, emotional, social, educational, vocational and even avocational needs, with an ultimate objective of returning him to society, functioning at his fullest potential. Furthermore, each specialty is essential to the others in fulfilling its objective. Rehabilitation of the physically disabled cannot be accomplished without taking into consideration their emotional defense mechanisms related to their illnesses. On the other hand, psychiatry cannot accomplish its mission in most cases through a limited approach of psychotherapy and psychotropic drugs alone, without the assistance of comprehensive rehabilitation programs. And yet, it is quite revealing to learn how little psychiatrists and other mental health workers know about rehabilitation medicine and how insecure are physiatrists and rehabilitation therapists when confronted by psychological problems of their patients.

Therefore, it was my intent to introduce a comprehensive "textbook" which would familiarize each specialty with the function of the other, especially how to utilize each others' services for maximum benefit to the patient, with special emphasis on rehabilitation of the mentally ill. Furthermore, it has been my aspiration to produce—as nearly as possible—a source of reference in the field of psychiatric rehabilitation. The space and scope of this volume presented certain limitations in this area; however, the readers can be assured that no effort has been spared in obtaining the contributions of renowned (in some cases not only nationally but also internationally) specialists in the fields of psychiatry and rehabilitation medicine. I am very grateful to the contributors for their generous response.

A few of the chapters may not deal directly with techniques

of rehabilitation. However, it is my conviction that unless one is familiar with certain basic philosophies and modern trends in mental health, one cannot really appreciate the underlying processes involved and the challenges one must expect to meet in his client's return toward becoming a contributing member of our society. For the same reason a historical background of the various rehabilitation approaches to the emotionally disturbed was included.

I have observed the insecurities of the nonmedical staff and especially of rehabilitation therapists when dealing with the pharmacotherapeutic aspects of total rehabilitation. We therefore included a chapter on this subject not only to familiarize the reader with the basic psychotropic drugs and their effects but also to make him aware of the various side effects that are quite frequently observed during the treatment process. Furthermore, while innumerable volumes have been written on the use of language by the patient during therapy sessions, minimal attention has been paid to other aspects of conveying his feelings. We, therefore, considered it a valuable addition to the armamentarium of the rehabilitation process to include a chapter on nonverbal communication (body language) as well as a description of some of the cultural characteristics of the behavior of patients exhibiting patterns that may not be ordinarily familiar to us.

I would like to take this opportunity to express my deep gratitude to Doctor Walter Barton for his encouragement to Charles C Thomas, Publisher for their kind assistance and patience in publishing this volume and to the contributors for their efforts.

J.M.

INTRODUCTION

A LETTER FROM A PATIENT

I CANNOT THINK OF ANYTHING I have read or can say in print that would be as convincing as the following patient's letter to a director of a mental hospital in regard to the need and importance of rehabilitation activity programs in an institutional setting. This letter is printed *exactly* as it was written. The only exception is elimination of any actual names that may identify the institution. However, even this is hardly necessary, because regrettably the blanks could be easily filled in by the names of too numerous psychiatric hospitals where rehabilitation medicine is not given the high priority it deserves. And that is what this book is all about.

J.M.

December 20, 1972

Dear Doctor ———

I have been a patient at ——— Hospital, and I would like to write to you about what I think is a very serious problem for the patients there. The problem is *lack of activity* and, consequently, a terrible boredom for the patients. My object in writing is simply to bring this problem emphatically to your attention, even though you may be aware of it already. I desire to blame no one, just to present the case.

It may be thought that the wards are bustling bee-hives of activity, but I assure you this is not so. (Of course, I can only speak for certain of the wards I have been in, but undoubtedly it applies elsewhere also.) A visitor to our ward would meet a typical scene like this: several patients playing cards or chess, a number slumped into chairs watching TV, some sleeping in chairs, a few endlessly smoking cigarettes, and one or two asleep on the bathroom floor. The atmosphere is heavy with monotony, boredom, torpor. It seems that many patients have sunk into a heavy, vegetable state, which cannot entirely be attributed to their particular pathology. This state of torpor grows deeper with time, and the lack of exercise (another great lack). To avoid this lethargy I worked on several jobs, and walked several miles a day. Even then the boredom was hard to fight and compensate for. I was a patient for only six weeks; I pity those who have been there for months. To verify all of this, let one of your administrators live in a ward for one week. I believe that before the week was up he would cry for mercy. One man of about fifty put it to me this way, "You go crazy in your mind in this place." Poor English, but graphic in its truthfulness.

I could write on and on, Doctor, but I will be content with what I have said. I consider the lack of "things to do," as a problem of the first magnitude, as regards care of the patients. I also consider it a root cause of many other problems—smoking, lack of appetite, irritability and lethargy. If you will take this letter seriously, I will consider it very worthwhile writing.

Sincerely yours,

CONTENTS

Section IV
Socially Oriented Programs

Section V
Hospital Vocational Programs

Section VI
Behavior Modification Approach and Token Economy Programs

Section VII
The Geriatric Patient and the Brain Damaged

Section VIII
The Role of the Psychologist, Social Worker and Coordinator

Section IX
Role of Volunteers

Section X
State, Veterans Administration and Community Mental Health Programs

Section XI
Nonverbal Communication—Body Language

Section XII
The Rights of Psychiatric Patients

PART TWO
RESEARCH IN REHABILITATION OF THE MENTALLY ILL

PART THREE
ROLE OF PSYCHOPHARMOCOLOGY IN REHABILITATION

PART FOUR
THE MENTALLY RETARDED

REHABILITATION MEDICINE AND PSYCHIATRY

PART ONE

REHABILITATION OF THE MENTALLY ILL

Section I

SCOPE AND CONTRIBUTION OF REHABILITATION MEDICINE TO PSYCHIATRY

Chapter 1

DEFINITION AND SCOPE OF REHABILITATION MEDICINE

Jack Meislin

PHYSICAL MEDICINE AND REHABILITATION, formerly called "physical medicine" and also referred to as "physiatry," "physiatrics," and more recently "rehabilitation medicine," is a medical specialty which is not easy to define comprehensively and at the same time briefly. It is a field of medicine which utilizes primarily physical agents and physical, occupational, educational, recreational, and avocational activities in the prevention and diagnosis of disease and the *treatment of the individual with a disability* to prepare him for optimal adaptation in his community. The last phrase denotes the rehabilitation concept which implies an attempt to achieve an ideal goal of the best possible physical and mental function, maximum satisfaction of one's emotional needs, development of satisfactory social relationships and training in appropriate vocational or avocational pursuits, so that the disabled individual may become a fully contributing citizen of our society—a person with dignity. It is often a *reeducation in life.* The specialist in this field is called a *physiatrist.*

Although possibly the oldest specialty in application, physical medicine became formally recognized as a specialty by the American Boards only in 1947, and in 1949 it became known as "physical medicine and rehabilitation." Therefore, in following its evolution, we are actually tracing the history of utilization of its component parts which are many: light, heat and cold, water, electricity, sound (and magnetic energy), massage, manipulation, exercise, occupational and educational activities, art, music, drama, dance, sports and recreational facilities, *when any of these are used in a medical setting.*

Rehabilitation medicine and psychiatry are intimately related to each other; both are dedicated to the holistic approach to total rehabilitation and in this process each is essential to the other.[20,24] Furthermore, as Overholser expressed it more than two decades ago, "Psychiatry and physiatry have certain things in common: Both are new specialties, and both arose under conditions which occasionally savored of charlatanry, with the result that certain suspicions still linger in the minds of some segments of the public."[29]

Chapter 2

THE ROLE OF PHYSICAL MEDICINE AND REHABILITATION IN PSYCHIATRY: A HISTORICAL APPROACH

JACK MEISLIN

THE STUDY OF MAN'S ITINERARY through the ages is not merely of academic interest but is of practical importance in the evaluation of contemporary times. This knowledge may have a significant influence on our own destinies as well as the destinies of the generations to come. To quote Winston Churchill, "Without a sense of history, no man can truly understand the problems of our time," and "The longer you can look back, the further you can look forward."[31] Francis Bacon stated, "What is present depends much upon what is left behind."[2] Especially pertinent is the statement made centuries ago by the great physician and philosopher Maimonides in his "Prayer of Maimonides," an ethical guide to the medical profession, part of which reads as follows: "Today he (man) can discover his errors of yesterday and tomorrow he may obtain a new light on what he thinks himself sure of today."[31]

Indeed, while collecting data concerning the evolution of psychiatric practices which involve rehabilitation modalities and activities, one is most impressed by thc fact that many of the ideas and methods the medical profession is so proud of as modern and new have been explored and utilized not only hundreds of years ago but possibly even thousands. Some of the concepts and experiences of the ancients should be very humbling. Another disturbing realization has been that many of the unusual and *ridiculous* methods used in the past that are so apt to be referred to as *barbaric* and resulting from ignorance of the past ages, are not any more so than some of the procedures being utilized in this present decade of the "scientific" twentieth century. At least that is what the next generation is most likely to think. History of medicine and of the current approach to the mentally ill takes on a circular type of curve. History not only repeats itself but also forgets itself. Periods of retrogression follow periods of progression.

The author firmly believes that a historical review of medical practices is essential to the development of sound therapy not only in avoiding the pitfalls of the past but occasionally in reintroducing long-neglected useful practices. The revival of the lifesaving mouth-to-mouth resuscitation method (mentioned in the Bible) is a vivid illustration of the validity of this concept.

ARCHAIC AND PRIMITIVE MEDICINE

Primitive man has always blamed mental illness on the forces of nature (sun, moon, lightning, etc.), animals and objects which he deified: Mental disease occurred when gods took man's mind away. One of the oldest methods of permitting the evil spirit to escape was by trephining which was practiced even in the twentieth century by some Arab tribes in Algeria, having reached a high level of dexterity by the Inca civilization of Peru in the sixteenth century. Another means of inducing the evil spirit to depart was through massage. At first it was used in stroking the limbs in a centrifugal direction but later was applied centripetally. More recent examples of contemporary primitive medicine are the sandpainting ceremonies of the American Navaho Indians. These include art, physical therapy, psychotherapy, religion, magic, singing and drugs which are administered not only to the patient but to spectators as well.

Some of the oldest cultures leaving evidence of the practice of medicine were those of the Babylonians, Egyptians, Hindus and Chinese and, of course, the Greeks and the Romans. The Egyptians practiced laying on of hands in a manner similar to contemporary massage. They worshipped god Ra who represented the sun and light. Early Chinese physicians who had an aversion to shedding of blood used physical therapy, dry cupping, massage and gymnastics which were well developed. The first cold wet sheet packs were apparently applied by the Chinese centuries B.C. A physician prescribed for a woman "one hundred affusions of ice water, each followed by wrapping in a linen sheet."[15] In Babylo-Assyrian times many rituals centered about water, which was the sacred element of the gods. One of the means of driving the demon out and purifying the person was to pour water over his head.[27] Magic and incantations were used frequently, combined with physical administrations.

ANCIENT GREEK AND ROMAN MEDICINE

The earliest name in Greek medicine is that of Asclepius who lived in the thirteenth century B.C. Many temples of Asclepius offered treatment for various ills including mental illness. The temples provided games, plays, periodic festivals, recreation and amusements.[4] The first organized practice of medicine was developed in the early Greek culture. Hippocrates, who was born in 460 B.C. and died at the age of 85 according to some, and 109 according to others, attributed emotional disturbances to improper combinations of heat and humidity. To decrease excess humidity or increase heat, he advocated exercise which would control mental illness. He was the first to stress heredity and predisposition. Hippocrates was also aware of the psychosomatic approach. He defined love as a physical disease of cardiovascular origin characterized by such symptoms as flushing, rapid pulse, accelerated heart and anxiety. Hydrotherapy, presumably for relaxation of tensions was widely practiced in the Roman baths. There was even a variety of our present temperature-contrasting "Scotch douche" where the bathers in warm water were taken to the frigidarium where they were sprinkled with cold water.

Asclepiades, considered the father of psychiatry and geriatrics, lived more than 2,000 years ago and settled in Rome in 91 B.C. He was really advanced for his age: Although ancients recommended purging and darkness, he pleaded for light and well ventilated rooms for the mentally ill and never gave purgatives. He prescribed friction (massage), social activities, pleasant environment, occupational therapy to increase attention span and improve memory, music therapy to calm disturbed patients, as well as gentle rocking (hence possibly the expression "off one's rocker"). He opposed mechanical restraint.

In Rome spas enjoyed a great deal of popularity. The great Galen (130-200 A.D.), whose influence lasted until the eighteenth century, thought that climate had a great deal to do with psychological characteristics of people. He has been erroneously credited with the expression, "Employment is nature's physician."[18] He did say that exercise was nature's physician. He claimed that by delighting the mind, exercise can cure disease. He also advocated cupping. It is noteworthy that 1,600 years later Pinel blamed Galen's lack of interest in psychiatry for its retarded progress throughout the centuries.[1]

Another famous name in Roman medicine is that of Caelius Aurelianus of Sicca (Africa) who probably lived in the fifth century.[8] He recommended a careful regime for convalescents which included walks and reading, especially of books with incorrect passages to arouse interest in finding errors. He believed that neither conversation nor reading should be too exciting to cause mental strain and cautioned, "Theater performances should be arranged according to the humor of the patient, and later one can introduce lectures or disputations following the rules of rhetoric." Acquaintances should be present during these exercises and should follow with applause. Caelius spoke strongly against restraints. He understood the importance of proper interpersonal relationships and emphasized tactfulness in attendants in order to avoid antagonism. He also recommended light cheerful music for depressed patients and serious music for those with childish laughter. With the end of the Greco-Roman cultural influences, the earlier epoch of enlightened medicine and a reasonable approach to the mentally ill also terminated.

THE MIDDLE AGES

The period of the Middle Ages—from the Fall of the Roman Empire in 476 A.D. to the eleventh century—was considered the

Epoch of Retrogression in Europe. This was the era of witchcraft and demonology. Groups of "flagellants," obviously mentally disturbed persons, traveled through the European countries bearing crosses and candles and flogging themselves with heavy leather whips. Another form of getting rid of the devil was "dance mania" where people danced until exhausted (not unlike our present dance marathons).

Nevertheless, in North Africa and in Spain in the ninth century one sees the emergence of Arabian medicine. Rhazes (852-932), referred to as the "Arabian Galen," preoccupied himself with mental illness and localization of mental functions. He recommended chess as a cure for melancholia. Another famous name in Arabic medicine of the twelfth century was that of the Jewish philosopher Maimonides, physician to the caliph in Egypt. He advocated sunlight and defended a daily bath but warned the patient not to stay in it too long. He strongly recommended exercises, except those that lead to overexertion. He considered ball throwing and wrestling the best sports. It is noteworthy that he urged the elderly to participate in some sort of exercise. Although Maimonides ridiculed beliefs in witchcraft, sorcery, incantations, astrology, amulets and demons, saying there is no need for such foolishness, he nevertheless condoned their use if they helped to soothe a patient or prevent illness.

THE SEVENTEENTH CENTURY

In 1641 the oldest mental hospital in France, La Maison de Charenton outside of Paris, was founded. Here one finds frequent but odd utilization of hydrotherapy in the form of water dunking which was considered very helpful as a psychiatric remedy. Passive motion by means of a spinning stool was also described by Herman Boerhaave (1668-1738) as therapy for the mentally ill. This action went to an extreme because it was intended to produce unconsciousness in the patient, the rationale being that a reorganization of mental functioning would follow. Such dunking and twirling are not isolated instances in the history of psychiatric development; they became common practices in the eighteenth and nineteenth centuries.

THE EIGHTEENTH CENTURY

It was only natural that with the development of knowledge of the magic energy of electricity, it would be used extensively in the treatment of the mentally ill. In 1759 John Wesley reported on the large number of patients who benefited from this therapy. Several years later the Middlesex Hospital purchased an electrical machine and in 1793 a special "electrical dispensary" was organized in London. Within ten years most of the 3,000 treated patients were considered helped, and half of the treated were labeled cured.[33]

Earlier (in 1747) the same John Wesley, although not a physician, published a textbook called *Primitive Physick* recommending many hydrotherapeutic measures for various illnesses. For mania he had the following prescription: "Apply to the head cloths dipped in cold water, or pour cold water on the head out of a tea kettle, or let the patient eat nothing but apples for a month."[15] A melancholic patient, as she lay in bed, was treated by a douche of water accompanied by a volley of oaths![10]

During most of the eighteenth century the first principle in the treatment of lunatics was fear. An unsuspecting patient was sometimes induced to walk across a treacherous floor; it gave way and the patient fell into a "bath of surprise" remaining there half drowned and half frightened to death.[18] Such procedure was based on an ancient idea advocated by Thessalus of Tralles in the first century. The ancients called it *metasyncrisis* meaning a "thorough commotion" of the patient's fundamental constitution by some violent procedure after which a quiet atmosphere and administration of restoratives were expected to return the constitution to a normal state. This doctrine persisted for many centuries and has been used to interpret the effect of modern shock therapies.[2]

The great authority of that time, William Cullen (1710-1790), believed in occupational therapy: "I have been informed that some maniacs have been cured by being compelled to constant and even hard labor; and since forced attention to the conduct of any bodily exercise is a very certain means of diverting the mind from pursuing any train of thought, it is highly probable that such exercise may be useful in many cases of mania." In talking about hypochondriacs, Cullen said "there is nothing more pernicious to them than absolute idleness."[18] Johann Christian Reil (1759-1813), of the "Island of Reil" fame, made an important contribution to psychiatry by pleading for elimination of medieval treatment. However, Reil recommended frightening the patient "into his wits" as follows: "The reception of a lunatic should be amid the thunder of cannon; he should be introduced by night over a drawbridge, be laid hold of by Moors, thrust into a subterranean dungeon, and put into a bath with eels and other beasts."[2] These were classified as therapies under the euphemism of "therapies of noninjurious torture."

Nevertheless, the eighteenth-century psychiatry is to become known as the inception of the humanitarian approach to the mentally ill (the Enlightenment Era). At the end of this century one sees the development of what may be called a "psychiatric revolution."

THE NINETEENTH CENTURY

During the late eighteenth and early nineteenth century, one of the most enlightened psychiatrists of his time, honored as the father of American psychiatry—Benjamin Rush (1745-1817)—advocated intimidation in some cases and liberal use of bloodletting and emetics in others. He also used a specially constructed tight-fitting chair. The chair used for sedation was called—of all names—the "tranquilizer." A similar chair was used as an energizer for stimulation of movement—the "gyrator." In 1828 Burrows said in defense of gyration, "Any remedy that invites sleep acts more beneficially on the disturbed function of the brain than narcotics of any kind though producing that effect."

Nevertheless, the author must fully agree with Diethelm's statement: "It is unfair to speak, as is customary, of the barbaric treatment of mental patients in the nineteenth century. The physicians who proposed and used the swivel chair of Cox or the tranquilizer of Rush to produce nausea and resulting fatigue and sleep were probably as humanitarian as the psychiatrists today."[7]

Pinel and the Era of Moral Treatment

Although many before him practiced humane treatment of the mentally ill, Phillip Pinel (1745-1826), the Parisian who was born in the same year as Benjamin Rush, historically initiated the era of "moral treatment" in the year 1793 when his removal of chains from the patients of the Bicetre Asylum resounded all over the civilized world. He was not only a great humanitarian but also a great psychiatrist. From the point of view of rehabilitation medicine, however, his greatest contribution to psychiatry was his intensive treatment concept. Occupational and recreational therapy were included in addition to psychotherapy, and thus the role of reason was established. Pinel was given the honor by some of opening the era of modern psychiatry. Because of his intimate relationship with the insane, Pinel is considered as a pioneer psychotherapist with psychotic patients.

The spirit of moral treatment was captured by Charles Dickens during his American tour. In 1842 he reported on a visit to what is now the Boston State Hospital:

> Every patient in this asylum sits down to dinner with a knife and fork; and in the midst of them sits the gentleman (the superintendent). At every meal moral influence alone restrains the more violent among them from cutting the throats of the rest; but the effect of that influence is reduced to an absolute certainty and is found, even as a means of restraint, to say nothing of it as a means to cure, a hundred times more efficacious than all the straight-waistcoats, fetters and handcuffs that ignorance, prejudice and cruelty have manufactured since the creation of the world.[16]

No wonder that a wave of optimism swept over the mental hospitals in America from 1800 to 1850. The "cult of curability" was evident everywhere. Claims were made of 90 to 100 percent cure! However, soon this was followed by an era of disillusionment. The reasons for this setback are difficult to understand. The Civil War and the advent of rugged individualism were possibly to blame. Indifference to those who fell by the wayside, including the mentally ill, seemed to be a factor.

The nineteenth century saw the rise not only of modern psychiatry but also of physical medicine, especially hydrotherapy.

Oddly, the utilization of water in modern medicine was given the greatest impulse early in this century by an uneducated Silesian peasant, Vincent Priessnitz (1799-1851), whose success in the application of local and general cold earned him world-wide fame as the father of modern hydrotherapy. However, it was Professor Wilhelm Winternitz (1835-1917) of Vienna who, through research and writings, first established hydrotherapy on a sound scientific physiological basis. He was so enthusiastic about the effects of the cold wet sheet pack that he applied it to himself daily. Once after such application at night in his cold basement he apparently fell asleep and almost lost his life when the water froze and he had to be chopped out of the ice![5] In 1865 Professor Hebra of Berlin described the continuous flow bath which was later utilized as a sedative measure in mania and delirium. It is of historical significance that this treatment was used almost 100 years ago for extensive burns and decubiti of paralytic patients, a procedure highly favored again today.[38]

In the middle of this century one observes the formal development in France of what is now referred to as "industrial therapy" under the guidance of a pioneer in occupational therapy, Guillaume Ferrus (1784-1861), who worked with Pinel. Ferrus therapeutically assigned patients to farms, dairies and workshops. It is noteworthy that these activities developed more rapidly in the psychiatric hospitals in the United States than in his own country.

Large hospitals grew, with the result that little contact existed between physician and patient. Then, it was suggested that patients be placed in cottages or homes visited by supervisors (our present community residence or family care program). However, even several centuries before this, a much more extensive family care and occupational program was established at Gheel, Belgium.

PSYCHIATRIC REHABILITATION MEDICINE IN THE TWENTIETH CENTURY

Weir Mitchell's (1829-1914) "rest treatment" became popular in the latter part of the nineteenth century and extended into the twentieth century. Nevertheless, he also utilized many modalities of physical medicine. The twentieth century saw the advent of the gigantic static electricity generators. Static electricity sparks were used for the treatment of hysteria, a procedure very reminiscent of the "baquet" of Mesmer. Wagner-Jauregg's fever therapy for general paresis paved the way for extensive work on artificial fever by physical means such as the indoctotherm. Electropyrexia for general paresis and for gonorrhea was popular until the late 1940's when penicillin made everything else obsolete, although for a time a combination of penicillin and fever therapy was utilized. Fever therapy in a heat cabinet which raised the patient's temperature to 105° or higher was a procedure which caused not only the patient but also the physician to sweat. Deaths occurred occasionally. Hydrotherapy also flourished in the twentieth century as a treatment for the mentally ill. Simon Baruch, Professor of Hydrotherapy at the College of Physicians and Surgeons, Columbia University, and father of Bernard Baruch, whose support of the rehabilitation approach significantly influenced its development, wrote several books on hydrotherapy and also a text, *The Principles and Practice of Hydrotherapy,* printed in 1898. In 1920 he published a little volume entitled *An Epitome of Hydrotherapy for Physicians, Architects and Nurses.*[3] However, the only text in physical medicine devoted exclusively to psychiatric conditions appeared in 1932: *Hydrotherapy in Psychiatric Hospitals* was written by Rebekah Wright, a psychiatrist and hydrologist of the Massachusetts Department of Mental Health. This book, no longer popular, contains detailed prescriptions of water treatment for numerous psychiatric conditions. Hydrotherapy was a most potent sedative measure, available to psychiatrists for many years. Extensive utilization of continuous flow baths, referred to as "tubs," and cold wet sheet envelopment, known as "cold wet sheet packs" or simply "packs," had remained the basic therapeutic prescription for anxious and disturbed patients until the middle 1950's when the "reign of the packs and tubs" gave way to the current epoch of the tranquilizers.

Nevertheless, the specially constructed temperature-controlled continuous flow baths, which can rarely be seen now, were quite effective in sedating the anxious and restless patients. The cold wet sheet packs are still used successfully in a few psychiatric hospitals in instances where neurotropic drugs fail to achieve their tranquilizing effect in severely disturbed patients. It was not unusual to find the "tub and pack room" the quietest place in a building for acutely disturbed patients, even though the most difficult patients were being treated there at the time. This bears witness to the efficacy of the treatment. Furthermore, some patients actually requested this therapy, feeling that it met their emotional needs. The rationale of the application of cold wet sheet envelopment has never had the benefit of reliable research. Ultraviolet radiation had also been suggested in the treatment of mental illness. In 1925 Francis Humphris of London wrote this about ultraviolet light: "Ultraviolet radiation will naturally suggest itself in many mental conditions—melancholia, for instance. . . . By ultraviolet radiation of the whole body its phosphorus content is raised." He then quoted an article in *Lancet* describing the drop of phosphorus ratio in such mental conditions as *dementia praecox* and "maniac depressive insanity," concluding, "It may be that this would give us a key to a treatment for some forms of insanity."[13] Unfortunately, this key did not fit.

The psychobiological concepts of Adolf Meyer (1866-1950) should be of special interest to those in the field of psychiatric rehabilitation medicine. Meyer's approach is a holistic one which is concerned with all aspects of the individual's adaptation in life—preoccupation with the patient, his disease and his social and occupational adjustment. He considered occupation as a matter of prescription and felt that a patient could say in his physical activity what he could not express in a formal interview. Although one would hardly associate psychoanalysis with physical medicine, it is of interest that as a practicing neurologist, Freud extensively utilized electrotherapy in the treatment of neuroses. Furthermore, he stressed that "Work is the greatest tie to reality."

The Era of the "Total Push"

A milestone in activity therapy took place in the late 1930's when Abraham Meyerson of the Boston State Hospital introduced the "Total Push" program,[28] advocated primarily for the chronic hospitalized schizophrenic. He felt that prolonged hospitalization produced a condition of "prison stupor." Meyerson characterized schizophrenia as a retreat from social contact into delusion and described the hospitalized schizophrenic patient as one who lives in a motivational vacuum where such stimuli as rewards and punishments are no longer operative and disappear from his life. Lack of exercise, sunshine and work constitutes another type of vacuum—a physiologic vacuum.

Physical therapy was an important part of the Total Push program: "The value of showers, douches, massage and rubdowns, because they give a start to the patient's energies, and second, because of their general tonic effect on the organism, has been demonstrated by our experience. Therefore, there should be the utilization of these measures in a routine, steady fashion, day by day." Ultraviolet irradiation was recommended. Exercise and games were essential ingredients of the program: "If the patient will not actively exercise at first, passive motions carried on by a physical trainer break down this resistance very readily." Throwing of a bean bag to women or of a medicine ball to men was described as effective in getting the cooperation of the patient. Formal exercises were considered of great value. Praise, blame, rewards and punishments (by taking away the rewards), proper grooming and diet were part of the total push. (These were the precursors of behavioral therapy and token economy.) Chess and checkers were utilized extensively in an armamentarium of games, and patients were taught music, dancing and craftsmanship and were trained in occupational therapy.

Although the Total Push program originated in a state hospital, the usual state hospital activity therapy programs have lagged behind those of the VA hospitals. However, some state hospitals later developed significant rehabilitation programs. At the Boston State Hospital, research in psychiatric rehabilitation was given strong impetus by Walter Barton, a pioneer in rehabilitation of the mentally ill, and by Milton Greenblatt, who later succeeded him as superintendent of that hospital. In general, however, while such research is on the increase, innumerable areas in rehabilitation of the mentally ill are still awaiting scientific investigation. In recent years research grants offered by the Social and Rehabilitation Service of the U.S. Department of Health, Education and Welfare (HEW) and by other federal agencies have significantly stimulated research activities in the field of psychosocial and vocational rehabilitation. While the designation, Total Push, is awkward, its basic concept remains the nucleus of current comprehensive rehabilitation programs.

Chapter 3

REHABILITATION MEDICINE IN CONTEMPORARY PSYCHIATRY

Jack Meislin

A revolutionary change took place in the role of physical medicine and rehabilitation in psychiatric hospitals after World War II. Although similar programs were in existence at the Institute of Living in Hartford and at the Menninger's facilities at Topeka, most of the comprehensive departments of physical medicine were established in VA psychiatric hospitals.[23] At the inception of these programs, some psychiatrists were given intensive courses in physical medicine and were designated as "Chiefs of Physical Medicine and Rehabilitation Services." These comprehensive services included expanded physical therapy (and hydrotherapy) and occupational therapy sections. However, other disciplines became integral components of these departments. Corrective therapy directed by physical education specialists, manual arts therapy supervised by industrial arts graduates and educational therapy taught by qualified teachers were added to the physiatric armamentarium.[26] Industrial therapy gained professional acceptance and was supervised usually by a manual arts therapist, with former nursing personnel having direct contact with patients in various hospital maintenance activities. In these sophisticated programs, a patient could be trained in acetylene torch welding, receive a high school equivalent diploma or work as a telephone switchboard operator. Some VA psychiatric hospitals also offered training to blind mental patients and those with hearing and speech problems. At a later date recreational therapy joined the others, within the physical medicine and rehabilitation service. A nonmedical assistant, a coordinator, was assigned to the chief of the rehabilitation medicine service, not only to relieve him of nonmedical and administrative duties, but also to act as a general rehabilitation specialist. These valuable associates were usually drawn from the ranks of one of the sections and were familiar with all aspects of the department.[25] Modified Jacobson's progressive relaxation techniques[14] were at times, but not often enough, practiced with tense neurotic or even psychotic patients. In one such program relaxation exercises were combined with readings from Longfellow's *Hiawatha,* recited by the hospital librarian. The patients usually reacted by falling asleep; however, it was never determined whether the soporific effect was due to the relaxation exercises or the monotonous readings. A unique program involving relaxation techniques, developed by Paul Roland (then a corrective therapist at the Chillicothe VA Hospital), was described in detail by John E. Davis, himself a pioneer in psychiatric recreation.[6] Psychodrama has also been used successfully in many hospitals. Recently, poetry and dance therapy joined music as popular activities.

Medical rehabilitation boards were instituted to provide comprehensive evaluations of patients with unique and difficult rehabilitation problems and to act as screening boards for programs requiring special responsibilities on the part of the patients, such as the "Member-Employee Program." The compensatory factors in this program consisted not only of monetary remuneration but also of such status symbols for members as having their meals in the staff dining room and possessing door keys. These medical rehabilitation boards were comprised of significant figures involved in the treatment of the patient: the treating psychiatrist, the nurse, clinical and counseling psychologists, the social worker, the rehabilitation therapist and the patient's work supervisor. At times members of the community, such as the patient's potential employer or a member of a community vocational agency, were also present at the meetings. The chief of the physical medicine and rehabilitation service was the chairman of the board, and the coordinator of that service was designated as the secretary. In addition, selected department chiefs and, at times, the chief of staff acted as consultants at the board meetings.

All above-mentioned programs (with the exception of hydrotherapy) have been retained as still very useful elements of modern rehabilitation efforts.

THE ERA OF THE TRANQUILIZERS

In the mid-Fifties tranquilizers (also referred to as psychoactive, psychotropic, antipsychotic, ataractic and neuroleptic drugs) were introduced into the armamentarium in the treatment of the mentally ill. The impact of the tranquilizing drugs influenced the scope and organization of the physical medicine and rehabilitation services in psychiatric hospitals. As already mentioned, gradually the intensive around-the-clock hydrotherapy treatments (the so-called "packs and tubs") diminished in scope. There is now hardly a psychiatric hospital that still maintains continuous flow baths, and the rare administration of the cold wet sheet treatments (packs) has been relegated to the nursing service. Very few hospitals still utilize the stimulating scotch douche (preceded by exposure to heat in thermal cabinets) and sedative needle showers, as well as general ultraviolet treatments at times administered to groups by means of a lighthouse-type apparatus.

With the advent of psychotropic drugs, one can see considerable expansion of the open-door and open-gate policies of allowing many of the hospitalized psychiatric patients to leave their wards and hospital. However, this was an outcome not only of the tranquilizing drugs, but also of a different approach to the mentally ill. The new objective of hospital psychiatry was no longer to cure the patient of his psychosis but to render him functional regardless of residual symptoms as long as these did not substantially interfere with his subjective life or his relationship with others. One also sees the establishment of such transitional programs as day hospitals where patients living in the community come to the hospital to continue their rehabilitation programs during the day. On the other hand, in the night hospital program the hospitalized patient would work or train in the community during the day and return to the hospital at night until such time as it became plausible for him to work and live in the community. Numerous new industrially oriented programs became an essential part of psychiatric rehabilitation. An important trend towards smaller psychiatric hospitals led to the establishment of the now well-known *unit system*. Under the unit system, in large psychiatric hospitals "acute intensive" (or reception) and "continued treatment" services, were broken up into several smaller units functioning as if they were independent hospitals in themselves. Each unit was supervised by a unit chief who was directly responsible to the chief of staff or clinical director. Each unit admitted and discharged its own patients, providing them with the desired continuity of treatment. Most units operate on the basis of geographical distribution of their clients.

REHABILITATION MEDICINE IN UNITIZED PSYCHIATRIC HOSPITALS

The emergence of formalized physiatric services in psychiatric hospitals after World War II was the first step in the continuous growth of these services since then. A one-physician service soon became a unit staffed by two or even three physiatrists and psychiatrists, and a once purely consultation department of physical medicine and rehabilitation acquired bed sections for psychiatric rehabilitation as well as for rehabilitation of patients with physical disabilities. For instance, at the Franklin Delano Roosevelt VA Hospital at Montrose, New York, the Physical Medicine and Rehabilitation Service included a specialized Unit Bed Service on a par with other psychiatric units. The philosophy behind the establishment of such a unit suggests that, while the concept of a unit system in a large psychiatric hospital maintains continuity of care in the same familiar milieu, *for selected patients* there is a need for a transitional sociovocational program which would be less protective and would simulate the competitive atmosphere of the stresses and realities of community life.[19] A separate halfway house on hospital grounds with its individual rooms and minimum of supervision offers opportunities for self-sufficiency. A part of the rehabilitation unit consists of a "pre-community residence" section supervised by a social worker where long-term patients were reeducated in the graces of community living in a homelike atmosphere which includes a dining room and a kitchenette. A patient rehabilitation employment program functions under the direct supervision of a counseling psychologist. Various compensatory monetary incentive programs where patients are paid either on a contractual basis or for services rendered in hospital maintenance are utilized in the unit which is closely integrated with the physical medicine and rehabilitation service under the overall supervision of the chief of that service. Patients from the rehabilitation unit also attended community adult education classes in the local high school. Group vocational counseling sessions were held in the evenings, so as not to interfere with daily intensive vocational rehabilitation programs. An active patient council was effective in the self-governing functions of the unit. However, this rehabilitation program was not limited to the hospital itself. Rehabilitation therapists and volunteers representing various disciplines carried their programs (in coordination with the social work service) into the foster homes and multiple residence establishments in the community, as well as to nursing homes where former hospital patients resided. Sponsors of foster homes and directors of nursing homes are given instruction in suitable occupational and recreational programs. Furthermore, this type of rehabilitation medicine department provided professional training in psychiatric rehabilitation for physiatrists from all over the United States and for therapists. A pilot residency training program in physical medicine and rehabilitation was established in this psychiatric hospital with emphasis on psychosocioeconomic aspects of rehabilitation and the significance of therapist-patient relationships.[21] Education of the community with the objective of obtaining an understanding of patients' problems and of achieving their acceptance as potential contributing citizens took place not only through liaison men, such as vocational rehabilitation specialists, but also by meetings at the hospital to which representatives of various industries and vocational agencies were invited for discussions and demonstration of the preparatory programs in which the patients were engaged. These inroads from the hospital into the community represent the direction of emphasis of psychiatric rehabilitation. In the community one sees rapid growth and expansion of rehabilitation services for psychiatric patients in halfway houses and sheltered workshops, as represented by such pioneer institutions as the Fountain House and Altro Sheltered Workshop in New York City. The growth of community psychiatry with the development of community centers opened new vistas and challenging opportunities for rehabilitation medicine.

Rehabilitation: Maximum Opportunity for Optimum Function.

REFERENCES

1. Ackerknecht, E.: *A Short History of Psychiatry*. New York, Hafner, 1959.
2. Altshule, M.D.: *Roots of Modern Psychiatry*. New York, Grune, 1957.
3. Baruch, S.: *An Epitome of Hydrotherapy*. Philadelphia, Saunders, 1920.
4. Bender, G.: *A History of Medicine in Pictures*. Detroit, Parke-Davis, 1961.
5. Castiglioni, A.: *History of Medicine*. New York, Knopf, 1947.
6. Davis, J.: *Recovery from Schizophrenia*. Springfield, Thomas, 1957.
7. Diethelm, O.: An historical view of somatic treatment in psychiatry. *Am J Psychiatry, 95*:1165-1179, 1939.
8. Drabkin, I.: *Caelius Aurelianus: On Acute Diseases; and, On Chronic Diseases*. Chicago, U of Chicago Pr, 1950.
9. Fenichel, O.: *The Psychoanalytic Theory of Neurosis*. New York, Norton, 1945.
10. Garrison, F.: *Introduction to the History of Medicine*, 4th ed. Philadelphia, Saunders, 1929.
11. Guthrie, D.: *A History of Medicine*. Philadelphia, Lippincott, 1946.
12. Harris, R., and Meislin, J.: Motivational Significance of Achievement Exercises. *VA Department of Medicine and Surgery Information Bulletin of the Psychiatry and Neurology Division*, IB 10-40, April 1953.
13. Humphris, F.: *Artificial Sunlight and its Therapeutic Use*. London, Oxford U Pr, 1925.
14. Jacobson, E.: *Progressive Relaxation*. Chicago, U. of Chicago Pr, 1938.
15. Kellogg, J.: *Rational Hydrotherapy*. Battle Creek, Modern Medicine Publishing Company, 1923.
16. Lebensohn, Z.: American psychiatry – retrospect and prospect. *Med Ann DC, 31*:379-392, July 1962.
17. Lewis, N.: *A Short History of Psychiatric Achievement*. New York, Norton, 1941.
18. Licht, S.: *Occupational Therapy Source Book*. Baltimore, Williams & Wilkins, 1948.
19. Meislin, J.: A Comprehensive Approach to the Rehabilitation of the

Mentally Ill. *Excerpta Medica International Congress Series* no. 150, 2428-2430, 1966 (Proceedings of the IV World Congress of Psychiatry, Madrid, 1966).

20. ———: Physical medicine and psychiatry: Editorial. *Arch Phys Med, 32:* 733-734, 1951.
21. ———: Psychiatric aspects of physical medicine and rehabilitation: Therapist-patient relationship. *Arch Phys Med Rehabil, 36:*25-31, 1955.
22. ———: The psychiatric sheltered workshop in rehabilitation of the mentally ill. *Arch Phys Med Rehabil, 35:*224-227, 1954.
23. ———: Rehabilitation of the Mentally Ill. In Pattison, H.: *The Handicapped and their Rehabilitation.* Springfield, Thomas, 1957.
24. ———: The role of physical medicine and rehabilitation in psychiatric hospitals: Editorial. *Arch Phys Med Rehabil, 46:*451-452, 1965.
25. ———: Role of the physical medicine and rehabilitation coordinator in psychiatric hospitals. *J Phys Ment Rehabil, 4:*25-29, 1951.
26. Meislin, J., and Phillips Adler, E.: Educational therapy. In Dunton, W., and Licht, S.: *Occupational Therapy.* Springfield, Thomas, 1956.
27. Mettler, C.: *History of Medicine.* New York, Blakiston, 1947.
28. Meyerson, A.: Theory and principles of the "total push" method in the treatment of chronic schizophrenia. *Am J Psychiatry, 95:*1197-1204, 1939.
29. Overholser, Winfred: Physical medicine and psychiatry, some interrelationships. *JAMA, 138:*1221-1222, December 25, 1948.
30. Peffer, P.: Money A rehabilitation incentive for mental patients. *Am J Psychiatry, 110:*84-92, 1953.
31. Rogers, F.: *A Syllabus of Medical History.* Boston, Little, 1962.
32. Rush, B.: *Medical Inquiries and Observations Upon the Diseases of the Mind.* Philadelphia, Kimber & Richardson, 1812.
33. Schneck, A.B.: *A History of Psychiatry.* Springfield, Thomas, 1960.
34. Schullian, D., and Schoen, M.: *Music and Medicine.* New York, Schuman, 1948.
35. Sigerist, H. E.: *A History of Medicine.* New York, Oxford U Pr, 1951.
36. Slovenko, R., and Knight, J.: *Motivations in Play, Games and Sports.* Springfield, Thomas, 1967.
37. Winnick, W.: *Industry in the Hospital.* Springfield, Thomas, 1967.
38. Wright, R.: *Hydrotherapy in Psychiatric Hospitals.* Boston, Tudor Press, 1940.
39. Zilboorg, G.: *A History of Medical Psychology.* New York, Norton, 1941.

Section II

BASIC CONCEPTS IN REHABILITATION OF PSYCHIATRIC PATIENTS

Chapter 4

REHABILITATION OF THE MENTALLY ILL – A HOLISTIC APPROACH*

JACK MEISLIN

HOW DOES REHABILITATION OF THE MENTALLY ILL DIFFER FROM THAT OF THE PHYSICALLY DISABLED?

MODERN CONCEPT of a physician's responsibilities designates him as "the therapist of a person, no longer merely the therapist of a disease."[9] Because of this idea of treating an individual with a disease rather than the disease itself, strictly speaking, one should not attempt a classification of the ill as "psychiatric" or "physical." Actually, behavior of a person is a somatic manifestation. In a living person one cannot divorce the soma from the psyche. Whatever influences the body also affects the mind–and vice versa–and the impulse is reflected throughout the organism (the Gestalt theory). One *can* speak, however, about individuals with *predominantly* physical or mental symptoms. Nevertheless, there is a practical distinction between the rehabilitation of an individual with major somatic problems and one with a severe emotional disturbance. In physical illness or bodily injury the patient's personality is, as a rule, unchanged, his mental faculties are preserved, and he can usually return to his previous social milieu. At times it is necessary for this patient to change his vocational objective because of the physical limitations.

*For this presentation we have drawn from material (revised and augmented) in our chapter in Pattison's *The Handicapped and Their Rehabilitation* (Springfield, Charles C Thomas, Publishers, 1957) and from a presentation "The Need for an Intermediary Institution," an abstract of which was published in *Hospital & Community Psychiatry* (March 1969).

The effects of mental illness are much more uprooting in terms of return to one's previous life patterns. In the psychoses there may be a total change in the personality of the individual. This makes it frequently impossible for him not only to go back to his old job but even to resume his previous social relationships. In a sense, rehabilitation of the mentally ill is more of a "total rehabilitation" where a patient has to be frequently reeducated in the general way of life as if he were undergoing a rebirth from childhood, to which he may have actually regressed emotionally.

The present concept of management of hospitalized psychiatric patients is not always to expect a complete cure, which may be improbable, but to discharge certain patients into the community as "social recoveries."[7] This means that the psychiatric patient is considered to have achieved maximum benefit from hospitalization when he is able to make even a limited adjustment in the community more or less regardless of remaining symptomatology, unless such symptoms significantly affect the welfare of the patient himself or that of his family or community. The fact that the patient may even be hallucinating or remaining subject to delusions is not, *per se,* a contraindication to his return to the community as long as he does not react to those false perceptions or ideas so as to threaten the life-style of other individuals or severely disturb his own peace of mind. In the author's opinion, it is this change of philosophy that has played a special role in emptying mental hospitals during the last two decades. Of course, the introduction of psychotropic drugs made an important contribution to the flow of patients into the community.

The rehabilitation of the psychiatric patient presents a special problem: how to prepare the mentally ill patient to be able to function in the community socially and vocationally in spite of any residual symptoms. Therefore, part of the rehabilitation process is not only to reduce or eliminate the psychopathology but also to reeducate the individual in social and vocational skills to enable him to face situations that he will encounter in his community.

REHABILITATION OBJECTIVES

As so aptly expressed by Jay Hoffman:

> It (rehabilitation) refers, of course, to a process and to a series of

> techniques. . . . But it is also a philosophy — an attitude — a state of mind — a mode of approach to illness. It involves a continuing emphasis on the patient's assets and a realistic minimizing of his liabilities. It considers that the best hospital in the world is not as good for the patient as a modest home and job in the community. It believes that we dare to be satisfied with less than full cure if it does not seem reasonably possible that we can achieve such with the resources available to us. It aims for the best possible functional restitution in the patient.[2]

To obtain the best rehabilitation results, one must set before himself in advance the specific goals or objectives that he strives to achieve with each individual patient. These depend upon the limitations set by the patient's particular condition and his personality potentialities. However, what is usually not taken into consideration is that rehabilitation is a *dynamic process* and not a static situation. This means that the therapeutic approach must vary constantly with the changes and progress of the patient's condition. Therefore, the Immediate Therapeutic Approach (I.T.A.) depends upon the existing current condition of the patient (c). Expressed mathematically, the management of a patient at a given moment may be considered as a "function" of his condition:

$$\text{I.T.A.} = f(c).$$

WHAT CAN REHABILITATION MEDICINE DO FOR THE MENTALLY ILL?

The author found it useful to go about this problem by following an outline of the objectives of medical care *in general.* These principles apply equally to management of the psychiatric patient.

General Objectives of Medical Care

1. Prevention (or prevention of recidivism).
2. Diagnosis or evaluation.
   a. For a proper therapeutic program.
   b. For prognosis (degree of injury, change of vocation, manner of living, insurance purposes, etc.).
3. Treatment.
   a. *Symptomatic* method.
   b. *Definitive therapy,* the aims of which are the eradication

of the etiological factors. In this category also is *specific* treatment, which has been proven decidedly effective for certain conditions (such as penicillin for lues).

c. Prevention of complications.
d. *Sustaining*—to prevent aggravation of existing pathology.

4. Rehabilitation.
   a. For optimal *institutional* adaptation, or in a *sheltered environment.*
   b. For optimal adaptation *in the community* as a contributing citizen—with dignity, *resettlement* (a propitious terms used for rehabilitation in the British literature).

The question which immediately begs an answer is, *Does rehabilitation medicine have a specific treatment for any of the mental conditions?* Basically the answer is *no.* There is nothing in the armamentarium of the physiatrist which can, in itself, be considered specific in the cure of a given mental disease. This is not to imply that this field of specialty cannot provide, at times, a therapeutic situation which plays a predominant role in the psychotherapeutic effect upon the patient's basic emotional problem. On the contrary, there are many cases on record where the patient treated in a section of this service exhibited dramatic improvement and even recovery, credited to a combination of a certain physiatric treatment and a favorable therapist-patient relationship.

In terms of prevention of mental illness *per se,* rehabilitation medicine can play only a secondary, general role of utilizing certain "tonic" measures, such as a system of exercises, which assist in maintenance of good health. As a general rule a healthy individual is less prone to develop mental illness. For instance, serious physical diseases are responsible for many depressive reactions seen in psychiatric practice. However, it can play an important part in prevention of recidivism by properly preparing the patient socially and vocationally to enable him to maintain himself in the community.

A definite although indirect contribution can be made towards the diagnosis or evaluation of the patient's illness. In certain cases electrodiagnosis may help establish the condition as hysteria vs. a paralysis due to a nerve lesion. However, in the majority of cases the assistance in evaluation of the patient's condition is given to the psychiatrist via reports or through progress notes describing in detail the patient's behavior, attitude and verbalization in the clinic.

As far as treatment is concerned, as mentioned above, rehabilitation medicine cannot boast of any specific definitive measures of its own which have been, by themselves, consistently effective against a certain illness. The primary contribution is mostly symptomatic. However, through its various therapies, rehabilitation medicine may make the patient more accessible to such definitive therapy as group or individual psychotherapy (the specific tool of psychiatry). Various physical modalities (such as special exercises) can be potent means of controlling disturbed behavior in patients.

A number of hospitalized psychiatric patients will probably never leave the hospital. Left alone, many of these patients would undoubtedly regress emotionally to the point where they would be dependent on others for most of the activities of daily living. Even though in some cases no significant improvement can be expected, a *sustaining program* of physical and social activities can at least keep these patients from a retrograde course. This type of approach to the chronic patient should be reassuring to those therapists who become discouraged when these patients do not show any noticeable progress.

Rehabilitation emphasizes, of course, social and especially vocational programs. Here occupational therapy, manual arts therapy (or MAT administered by medically oriented graduates in industrial arts), educational therapy (E.T. offered by qualified teacher-therapists) and hospital industry activities help prepare the individual patient for satisfactory community living, whether this be completely independent or in a sheltered environment.[3]

The Team Concept in the Rehabilitation of the Mentally Ill

The rehabilitation process of the psychiatric patient is of such complexity and consists of so many factors to which he is exposed in the hospital milieu, that no one discipline or method by itself can assume the total responsibility for his management, if optimal results are to be achieved. A comprehensive rehabilitation program can be compared to a symphony orchestra. If one were to listen to a single instrument individually the tones produced would be meaningless and ineffective in most cases. It is only in the total harmonious, well integrated and properly conducted efforts of all the necessary instruments that the really beautiful and meaningful harmony of the musical theme is created. On the other hand, occasionally, and at an appropriate time, a single musical instrument is selected to play a solo. Similarly it is in a well integrated and properly directed team approach that the rehabilitation of the patient is best accomplished. At times selected methods or disciplines may play the predominant role in helping the patient find his proper place in society. Also, the emphasis on a particular type of therapeutic approach may be different at the beginning of an individual's illness than during the period of convalescence when the major responsibility changes from one group of the therapeutic team to another.

The Twofold Function of a Rehabilitation Service in a Psychiatric Hospital

Although rehabilitation of a psychiatric patient is not limited to the contribution of a single hospital department, a well established physicial medicine and rehabilitation service is particularly well equipped to offer the patient the type of training or preparation which will facilitate his adjustment in the community. However, the rehabilitation department does not limit its service to resocialization and vocational rehabilitation of the patient. It also concerns itself with many of the diagnostic and therapeutic aspects, symptomatic and definitive, of general patient care. One must not forget or minimize the fact that with very few exceptions, such as the rare incidence of rheumatoid arthritis in schizophrenics, the mentally ill are just as prone to develop various physical (and particularly neurological) diseases and injuries which require medical attention regardless of the superimposed mental condition. Physical medicine can be of great assistance in problems of electrodiagnosis, evaluation of the peripheral vascular conditions, tests of muscular strength and function and many others. By the utilization of such physical agents as heat, cold, massage, exercise, mechanical apparatus and occupational therapy, many patients with symptomatic conditions have been relieved from pain or discomfort, and in a number of cases these physical agents have been of assistance in rendering the patient physically functional.[4]

The Rehabilitation Therapist's Double Tool

In addition to his specific tool of technical knowledge of a skill in a specialized field, every rehabilitation therapist has another common tool and that is the "therapist-patient relationship."[5] This tool of skill in interpersonal relationships cannot be overemphasized regardless of the type of medical care. Even in dealing with so-called "physical disabilities," this relationship is extremely important in supplementing one's technical knowledge in the treatment of a patient as an individual. When dealing with psychiatric patients it becomes preponderantly so. In fact, as has been suggested by Karl Menninger, a proper relationship with the patient may, in certain cases, be of even greater importance than the actual material therapy itself.* At times knowledge of proper attitudes may significantly alter the therapeutic effects. This brings up another important aspect of rehabilitation therapy in the mentally ill.

The Specificity of a Rehabilitation Prescription for Mental Conditions

One of the important problems in the treatment of the mentally ill is the ability to meet the patient's emotional needs. Ideally those activities and therapies which meet the basic personality wants of the patient would be most effective. However, there are so many variable factors and situations involved that proper prescription of attitude or selection of activity becomes an extremely complicated challenge. The first and probably the most important task is how to understand and evaluate the patient's basic personality problems. Secondly, even though theoretically a certain type of activity presumably suits a given emotional need, the patient does not always react favorably to such a program. Furthermore, at times it is extremely difficult, if not impossible, to create a therapeutic situation which would be specific enough to satisfy a selected psychological demand.

An attempt has been made to classify activities according to

*The activity serves as an important catalyst. (J.M.)

personality traits and needs. In the author's experience, this has not always been successful. Even though he feels that there are certain types of behavior problems, like extreme aggressivity, which would be helped by hostility-releasing devices, this general procedure has definite limitations. It seems that a general well-established relationship between the therapist and the patient will succeed in some instances regardless of the type of modality or even, possibly the type of specific approach attempted by the therapist. Perhaps this is so because the natural sincerity and dedication of the therapist may be of much greater import to the suspicious patient than an organized attempt by the former to produce a desired effect within the patient.

Nevertheless, there are many emotional needs and behavior problems which may be helped to a greater degree by the selection of specific activities. The hostility and excessive aggressiveness of many disturbed patients can be sublimated by the use of such activities as sports, heavy loom work and moderately strenuous laboring assignments. On the other hand, the "hypokinetic" patient would require gradual progressive socializing activities. Destructive tendencies can be managed in occupational therapy, for instance, by requesting the patient to take things apart. At times patients with guilt feelings and related depression can be helped by assignment to so-called expiatory or propitiatory menial activities which would satisfy the need to atone for real or imaginary "sins." Paranoid patients may benefit by being able to express their ideas of persecution and grandeur through the inoffensive legitimacy of such creative literary works as satires. The obsessive-compulsive individual should be given assignments which do not require exactitude. Those with needs to excel require projects which are easily within their capabilities. These are some of the modalities of a more or less specific nature which have been suggested as suitable therapeutic prescriptions for specific emotional needs. There is no aspect of the rehabilitation of the psychiatric patient which needs more elucidation through research data, and where such information would be more appreciated and welcome, than the problem of specific activities to meet the individual needs of the psychiatric patients.

Specific *attitudes** of the therapist-patient relationship also require much more intensive investigation. For instance, if possible, it may be desirable to assign a patient with needs for masculine identification to a male therapist with positive personality traits. Patients suffering from character and behavior disorders have to be treated with a kind but firm approach which will discourage the patient's tendencies towards manipulation of environment. On the other hand, during the acute stage of illness, many patients are extremely fearful, requiring much reassurance and a definite permissive attitude. In this connection, a general rule-of-thumb policy of maximum assistance to the patient during his acute phase of illness has been followed. This attitude is progressively modified with the patient's improvement. He is gradually weaned from dependence upon the therapist and trained to be as self-sufficient as possible. During the later stages of the patient's convalescence, the attitude of the therapist should be completely objective, indicating to the patient that he (the patient) has achieved a stage of maturity where it is no longer necessary or proper for him to depend upon others for unwarranted assistance. In fact, one can go even further and present the patient with stressful situations which would test his ability to cope with the usual pressures of everyday community life. One cannot overemphasize the need for a changing, dynamic prescription appropriate to the state of the patient's health during the process of rehabilitation. Of course, it is unrealistic to be changing the patient's prescription of attitudes and therapies on a daily or even weekly basis; however, it is desirable to do so several times during his period of hospitalization: first, when he emerges from the acute disturbed phase where symptomatic treatment was primarily indicated, and secondly, when the effect of definitive therapy brings the patient to the transitional stage. This transitional phase evolves, approximately, when it is felt by the medical staff that the patient has reached a stage of health when it is timely to plan his early return to the community. After the first or *tactical* phase of the patient's therapeutic management and the transitional phase during which a thorough reevaluation of the patient's condition and objectives should be made, the third general phase of

*Explored by James C. Folsom a contributor to this volume.

his rehabilitation may be considered as *strategic.* During this stage the emphasis is placed upon activities that would facilitate his future social and vocational readaptation to community life. The patient should be personally involved in decisions regarding his rehabilitation plans, which should be initiated upon his admission to the hospital.

THE REHABILITATION ITINERARY

The Tactical Phase of Psychiatric Rehabilitation

The following discussion takes the patient from the moment he first enters the hospital, usually in a disturbed emotional state, until such time as he is ready to reenter the community. The acute phase usually represents a period shortly after onset of an acute episode of mental illness. Much of the disturbed behavior of the patient, his aggressivity and assaultiveness, can be interpreted as a reaction to fear. It is necessary to take immediate steps to prevent any aggravation of his condition which may even result in a fatal outcome, such as what may occur in extreme irreversible catatonic excitement. At this time symptomatic treatment is urgently needed. Psychotherapy, nursing care and drugs are utilized to sedate the patient. An attitude of reassurance to the patient that he need not fear bodily injury is imperative. Some of the facilities of the physical medicine and rehabilitation service can be most helpful in this symptomatic approach. Although the use of hydrotherapeutic measures, because of the effectiveness of tranquilizing drugs and other psychiatric procedures, has been limited to selected cases, they may prove to be very potent and useful methods of sedation. In the case of the hyperactive disturbed patient, cold wet sheet packs, although rarely used now, can be, in the author's opinion, at times effective in relaxing a patient where other means have failed and where physical restraint is used instead* The symptomatic measures mentioned above have also lost their popularity partly because they are passive therapies while the modern trend emphasizes a predominantly active program of participation by the

*An article describing the reactivation of cold wet sheet packs appeared in *Psychiatric News,* a publication of the American Psychiatric Association. The title was "Hydrotherapy Said Helpful with Patients as Drug Substitute" (September 20, 1972).

patient. Such treatment can be provided by therapeutic pools and in the corrective therapy section where the patient is given an opportunity to release his aggressiveness, hostility, destructive tendencies and assaultiveness. The following example illustrates this premise:

Case of T.P.

Analysis of this young patient's dynamics pointed towards extreme hostility against his father, a well-known athlete, matched only by the threat to his own ego as a weakling. This patient was prescribed corrective therapy with the specific objective of achieving superior skill on the punching bag. Such activity not only offered him a means of release of aggressions but also served to increase the young man's own self-esteem.

During the acute and semiacute stages of the diesase, many anxious and tense patients can be helped by relaxation techniques such as those suggested by Jacobson in his work on progressive relaxation. Occupational therapy can offer a great deal to the patient in the early stages of his psychiatric illness. The clinical situation offers an excellent opportunity for establishing a proper therapist-patient relationship. Numerous activities lend themselves a variety of needs. Finger painting is still at times a suitable method of expression for the patient, and this activity can also serve as a diagnostic procedure.

The Intermediate, Transitional or Reevaluation Phase

Although three principal stages of the hospitalized psychiatric patient's rehabilitation have been designated, there is, of course, no clear-cut division between them. However, when the patient's condition is improved sufficiently so that his ward psychiatrist and the team begin to visualize the probability of the patient's return to the community in the near future and when they feel that the time has come to make definite plans for that future, this is the transition or intermediate phase during which a thorough reevaluation of objectives is indicated. It requires a team approach consisting of such key figures as the ward psychiatrist, the nursing staff, social worker, psychologist, vocational counselor, representatives of the rehabilitation service and others such as members of the clergy, dieticians and volunteers. At this meeting are discussed the patient's physical and mental condition, motivation, capabilities, social and vocational inclinations, assets, potentialities and economic needs. A problem-oriented analysis can be helpful in a holistic rehabilitation approach. Furthermore, the question arises whether the patient is able to return to live with his family, if he has one, or whether other plans are necessary. It may be desirable to place the patient in a family care or adult home program, or a halfway house, if available, even though he has relatives of his own. From the vocational point of view, return to the previous type of work may not be feasible either for psychiatric reasons or possibly as a result of physical complications. At times the patient's previous occupation may have served as a contributing or aggravating factor of his illness. It is, therefore, necessary to reevaluate the patient's potentialities in another type of vocational choice. Conclusions drawn from aptitude tests and counseling interviews, especially supplemented by information as to how the patient functions in prescribed on-the-job activities, will help the rehabilitation team to plan his vocational future. When the selection of a vocational skill is made, the patient is placed in a situation in the hospital where he can benefit from exposure to a vocational experience.

The Convalescing Phase

During this phase, when the patient is in close temporal proximity of the community, the need for definitive therapy requires less emphasis in contrast to social and prevocational preparedness, which begins to play a predominant role in the rehabilitation of the hospitalized mentally ill patient.

Frequent sessions with the social worker and the vocational counselor become part of the preparedness program. Once the vocational objective has been established, the patient is placed either in manual arts therapy, educational therapy or in industrial activities and is assigned to an activity where he can practice the skill that he expects to utilize as a wage earner in the community. The importance is, however, on the establishment of good work habits and proper industrial interpersonal relationships. An individual may be a master craftsman, but if he is unable to relate positively to his fellow workers or to his supervisors, he is inadequate as a wage earner. He could not maintain himself on a job for any length of time. Therefore, it is one of the rehabilitation objectives to primarily prepare the patient for such interpersonal relationships as are required in the community industry. He must be prepared to take direction and criticism from his supervisors without undue emotional reaction. Just as the psychotherapist's attempts to develop a proper relationship with the patient may be considered an effort of *engagement* in therapy, a similar problem arises when *disengagement* from the therapeutic relationship becomes necessary. Often this poses a more serious conflict than the original situation. The process has to be accomplished with minimal emotional trauma to the patient. In general, "hospitalitis" is a real entity because of the fear of loss of secondary gains.

Case of W.T.

This middle-aged patient was hospitalized because of a psychotic depression. During his acute illness, he was able to make a good adjustment in occupational therapy where he exhibited an inclination for woodworking. When his condition improved, the patient was transferred to manual arts therapy where he excelled in cabinet work. Even though Mr. T. had recovered from his acute illness and was making an excellent hospital adjustment, any mention of his return to the community evoked a severe anxiety reaction. The patient was presented before the medical rehabilitation board. He was asked to state three wishes. The patient promptly replied "To remain here, to remain here and to remain here!"

Nevertheless, it was felt that an intensive approach by a social worker was called for, with the hope of motivating him to make an attempt to resettle in the community. After a number of sessions of very tactful contacts and an opportunity for a carpentry job, the patient volunteered to go out on a trial visit. His adjustment outside the hospital has been very successful ever since he left its walls years ago.

In the convalescing stage there is a difference in the actual performance requirements of the patient's vocational assignment from his previous activity prescription. It now becomes important to stress the significance of a satisfactory outcome of his efforts. The patient is expected to exert a great deal of care and accuracy in his work. Another factor which is frequently disregarded in work assignments of psychiatric patients is speed. During his prevocational training the patient is placed into a situation simulating, as much as possible, actual community working conditions; and while the production factor must never play a role during the definitive treatment assignments, it now becomes a necessary part of the rehabilitation program. The number of hours that the patient spends in his prevocational activities should be increased so as to come as close as possible to the eight-hour workday. This principle applies even more so to vocational preparedness programs in the community, especially in view of emphasis on brief hospitalizations.

Special Rehabilitation Measures to Bridge the Gap Between Hospital and Community Adjustment

As the author has indicated elsewhere,[6] one of the reasons for such a large number of readmissions to mental hospitals is lack of vocational preparedness to meet the demands of community industry. This, of course, is only one of the factors causing recidivism. The other reasons for readmissions are reactivation of the mental condition and unsatisfactory social environment. There is, however, so much interaction among all three of these that it is frequently impossible to distinguish between cause and effect. The main problem seems to be how to narrow the gap between the protective environment of the hospital and the hostile competitive society. An outstanding contribution towards the rehabilitation of the mentally ill has been Peffer's introduction of the "Member-Employee Program" whereby selected patients are placed on employee status with limited salaries as a preparatory step toward community employment.[8] Other arrangements which have been helpful in bridging the sociovocational gap between the hospital and the community are the "night hospital" programs. Here, until a more permanent arrangement can be made, the patient is able to work or study in the community during the day while he is still making his temporary home in the hospital.

INTERMEDIARY FACILITIES FOR THE MENTALLY ILL

With the open-door and open-gate policy, there has been a continuous exodus into the community of a number of patients, many of whom had been previously considered as career hospital residents.* This has developed into a sort of contest among various psychiatric hospitals to outdo each other in discarge rate statistics. These statistics, however, can be not only quite misleading, but even paradoxical: Ironically, the magic discharge number which every hospital is trying to increase sometimes also encompasses those in the category of "discharged by death!" On the other hand, quite significantly, this discharge rate also includes many patients who have been repeatedly discharged and readmitted. The open gates of mental hospitals have become revolving gates. In fact, it has been said not so jokingly, "A good alcoholic is worth a dozen discharges a year." The annual readmission rate is still more than 40 percent, and almost two thirds of the patients return to the hospital within a period of four years. What is being done and should be done to facilitate the rehabilitation itinerary of the mentally ill from patient status to full community citizenship?

Basic Factors in Rehabilitation of the Mental Patient

In order to prepare the mental patient for optimal adaptation in his community (the definition of rehabilitation), one must first attempt to modify the biological process of the patient's mental illness *per se*. Secondly, one need develop satisfactory social relationships so that he can get along with his fellow human beings. And thirdly, one must consider his need for vocational preparedness so that he can become more or less self-sufficient economically as a full-fledged contributing citizen of our society—an individual with dignity. These three elements are, of course, intimately interrelated (Fig. 5-1).

Transitional Programs

A psychiatric hospital with a strong rehabilitation orientation provides the elements of these basic needs. It also offers a number

*Some of the emptied buildings can be converted into apartments for certain long-term patients and their dedicated spouses or mothers (or fathers).

BASIC FACTORS IN THE......
TOTAL REHABILITATION of
PSYCHIATRIC PATIENTS...

HOSPITAL◆◆◆◆◆COMMUNITY

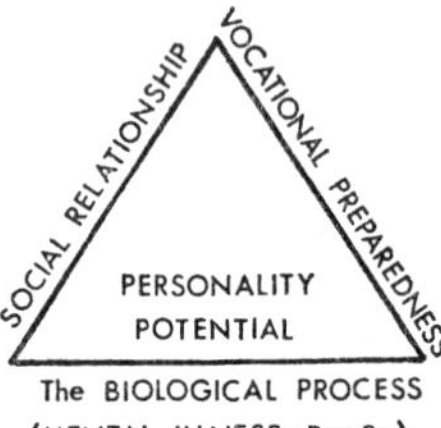

* ACCEPTANCE for LIVING.
* EDUCATION (TRAINING).
* EMPLOYMENT.

Figure 5-1. Basic factors in the total rehabilitation of psychiatric patients.

of community-oriented programs. Many of these already described have been in existence for some time; others have been developed within recent years. The recreational boat rides, camping trips and restaurant and theatre parties are just a few of the methods utilized in familiarizing our patients with community living. Group shopping tours for patients who have been hospitalized for a long period of time offer them an opportunity to make their own purchases in regular stores, in some instances for the first time in twenty or thirty years. The highly expanded community residence or foster home programs date back hundreds of years to Gheel, Belgium. However, the walls of hospital isolationism have been penetrated by having physicians, nurses, psychologists, rehabilitation therapists and volunteers venturing into these homes and working with the patients alongside the social workers. Nevertheless, much follow-up effort is still necessary by vocational counselors to eliminate the "rocking chair brigades" in the adult homes, many of these chairs being occupied by the able-bodied. (They must be the followers of Asclepiades who recommended music and gentle rocking about 2,000 years ago as therapy for mentally ill.)

Need for Intermediary Institutions

In spite of all efforts of preparing hospitalized patients psychologically and sociovocationally for post-hospital community adjustment, there is still a large number of patients who cling to the security of intramural existence. They *can* be brought closer to the community. On the other side of the coin, the alarming number of patients who are being hospitalized or rehospitalized can be reduced. It is noteworthy that in the majority of cases this apparent need for rehospitalization is not due primarily to serious psychopathology but is frequently a result of various degrees of sociovocational maladjustment. While hospitals are doing a great deal in preparatory rehabilitation work, the author certainly agrees with Albert Glass that, "The most difficult phase of treatment comes when a patient leaves the hospital." (This may explain why some of the "best" hospital programs are doomed to failure, unless they are followed up and carried over into the community). Many of our patients in the community are not functioning at their highest potential. Mental hygiene clinics have been of great help in sustaining the patients with emotional problems; however, their scope is quite limited. Halfway houses are not, as a rule, rehabilitation oriented. Therapeutic centers, such as the Horizon House in Philadelphia and the Fountain House in New York City, have made a significant contribution to the management of the mental patient's post-hospital adjustment. But, these are still scattered institutions. In general, however, wherever there are social rehabilitation services in community mental health programs, they lack the urgently needed residential facilities. In order to achieve and maintain the highest-level function of our psychiatric patients in an open society, there is a dire need for intermediary facilities or centers with adequate residential facilities as crossroads toward the fulfillment of this objective. Both VA and state hospitals—the two largest groups of psychiatric organizations in the United States—should join their efforts to those of mental health community establishments in creating such intermediary facilities on a regional basis.

ORGANIZATION OF INTERMEDIARY CENTERS OR COMPLEXES

The objective of the regional intermediary institutions—to be designated as centers or complexes—is to offer rehabilitation oriented residential facilities containing various therapeutic, social and vocational services as well as work-for-pay opportunities to facilitate a transition into the community for many convalescing hospitalized psychiatric patients, where other available methods have not succeeded or are of secondary benefits. On the other hand, these centers would also offer treatment programs to meet a broad spectrum of the needs of the community's mentally ill population with the goal of maintaining them as functional members of society. Thus the centers would act as two-way screening devices. Unlike the usual mental hospitals, they should be located in or near populated areas and within easy access of facilities essential to fulfill the social, vocational, educational, spiritual and recreational needs of the patients as citizens of the community. It is important to include facilities for temporary or even prolonged residence for patients not suffering from an acute major psychiatric condition requiring services in a traditional psychiatric hospital. These facilities, although especially urgently needed for younger persons, would also offer the family of a psychiatric client (here, usually the elderly) an opportunity for his temporary care while they go on vacation or attend to other needs. This will serve as a significant motivating factor for the relatives to take the hospitalized patients into their homes.

An important aspect of the organizational design of these centers is for them to be intimately related to the psychiatric hospitals in the area. Key staff members of these hospitals would also provide part-time services to the centers to afford continuity of treatment. This will facilitate the transition of many of our insecure hospitalized patients into community living, the project acting as a "psychological decompression chamber," in assisting the dependent patient to assume the role of a community citizen. The centers would maintain various therapeutic, occupational and recreational day, evening and weekend programs. They would also sponsor social clubs. In fact, some of the hospital services may have to be duplicated at these centers with the advantage of keeping the patient outside the traditional hospital walls. The basic premise is that only severely ill patients requiring care not available elsewhere should be in a hospital. As obvious as this concept may appear in reference to patients with general medical conditions, these criteria are by no means being applied to psychiatric patients. Thus, society has been persistently supporting a *double standard of medical care* in regard to hospitalization of psychiatric vs. nonpsychiatric patients. This has led to the creation of veritable "ghettos" composed of individuals in mental institutions whose membership qualification is merely inability to maintain themselves *independently* in our society.

Some temporary limited emergency services should be available around the clock. Such services may play an important role in avoiding first admissions to a mental hospital with the advantage of the patient escaping possible "hospitalitis" and the stigma of a record of having been a mental hospital patient. The services should also include home visits by psychiatric teams. Furthermore, a most needed step in the rehabilitation of the hospitalized mental patient to dignified community citizenship is the availability of adequate selective work opportunities and of transitional and sheltered workshops–medically supervised places of remunerative employment where the disabled individual living in the community can hold a job in accordance with his physical and emotional resources.[6] These workshops should be a component of the intermediary complexes, although they need not be physically within the architectural structure of the center. The economy of the intermediary institution vs. the prohibitive costs of hospitalization would contribute to the support of some of these programs.

Public Education

A public education department is an essential element of the functional design of the intermediary complexes and should be operating in close liaison with chambers of commerce and various industrial institutions of the area. In order to rehabilitate our psychiatric patients, it would be of little benefit to prepare them biologically (psychologically), socially and vocationally, unless these patients are also accepted by our community for training or education and employment.

John Blasko, in his "A Bill of Rights for Patients"[1] raised some vital issues pertaining to civil rights of a special segment of our population. He feels that the patient has fundamental human rights based on certain needs, among them the opportunity to work in a job appropriate to his skills and to receive adequate training, placement and supervision. The industrial community owes *all* our disabled this opportunity (with federal or state assistance, if necessary, in such forms as subsidies or tax modifications). A certain percentage of productive activities of the national industries should be allotted to the disabled on a selective basis according to their capability to produce. In a *New York Times* column, "Life for Handicapped," describing a village for the disabled in the Netherlands, Howard Rusk concluded with the following: "In the United States, where we have by far the most comprehensive rehabilitation services of any country in the world, the greatest unmet need is for sheltered facilities where the severely handicapped can live and work in dignity." That is particularly true for the mentally ill.

REFERENCES

1. Blasco, J. J.: A bill of rights for patients. *Staff, 3*:1-2, March-April 1966.
2. Hoffman, J. L.: An overview of existing programs of rehabilitation. National Rehabilitation Association Conference, May 27, 1956.
3. Meislin, J.: The function of a physical medicine and rehabilitation service in a VA psychiatric hospital. Veterans Administration, *Department of Medicine and Surgery Information Bulletin,* Physical Medicine and Rehabilitation Service IB10-*52*:7-12, January 1954.
4. ———: Management of somatic complications in psychiatric patients. *JAMA, 165*:1107-1110, November 2, 1957.
5. ———: Psychiatric aspects of physical medicine and rehabilitation: Therapist-patient relationship. *Arch Phys Med Rehabil, 36*:25-31, 1955.
6. ———: The psychiatric sheltered workshop in rehabilitation of the mentally ill. *Arch Phys Med Rehabil, 35*:224-227, 1954.
7. Ozarin, L. D.: Moral treatment and the mental hospital. *Am J Psychiatry, 111*:371-378, 1954.
8. Peffer, P. A.: Money: A rehabilitation incentive for mental patients. *Am J Psychiatry, 110*:84, 1953.
9. Rennie, T. A.: Relation of psychiatry to internal medicine. *Bull Johns Hopkins Hosp, 65*:265, 1939.

Chapter 5

THE THERAPEUTIC TRIAD

JULES H. MASSERMAN

HISTORICAL APPROACHES TO THE ESSENTIALS OF THERAPY

PHYSICAL THERAPIES: Since paleolithic times, man has tried to mitigate his fears of his inimical universe through his sciences and technologies. In two of the most important of these—medicine and surgery—he has sought to find means to cure his ills and restore his skills by empiric medicaments ranging from herbs and minerals to the first specific use of quinine for malaria in 1820, and various procedures from the ancient binding of fractures to the modern embedding of plastic hearts. Psychiatry, as a branch of medicine, has always employed pharmacologic, surgical and other modes of relieving man's material fears and their somatic reflections and, fortunately, is once again intensely developing this important rubric of therapy.

SOCIAL: Scientific and technical advances, however, have historically proved inadequate for man's quest for security, inasmuch as

1. Expanding knowledge revealed mysteries and challenges beyond man's puny powers, however much he learned and applied; and
2. Each man realized that the tools his neighbors developed could be as destructive or as lethal as his own.

Therefore, man learned to seek ever more inclusive human allegiances, ranging from parental and familial ties through the clan, tribe, city and state to their present limits in highly uncertain international pacts. Within all of these aggregations, specially selected men were given specific trusts and tasks toward enhancing group securities: soldiers for protection (which of course included external conquest); kings and constables for internal government; and medicine men who, as protophysicians, treated illness, and as psychiatrists, corrected deviations from locally accepted norms of conduct—physical and community functions that, fortunately, are being reintegrated into modern psychiatry.

MYSTICAL: But these uneven and sometimes inchoate strivings toward social organization, even when combined with man's pyramiding technical knowledge and skills, have never yet been enough to allay a third and even broader concern, since no consensus of human scientists, however learned, has ever been able to control the heavens, secure the future or even remotely approach the nature or meaning of life or the inadmissible concept of nonexistence. Man has therefore always erected transcendent cosmic systems, presumably within his kin and operated by supernatural beings whom he could conveniently control either directly or through designated mediators here on earth. These again were priests and medicine men who, in their temples and sanatoria, were thus wishfully charged with this third task: not only to minister to the physical and social needs of men, but also to influence in their favor the mystical goals and gods of the universe. It would obviously require too large a volume to cite in detail this three-fold treatment of the triple trepidations of man throughout history, but perhaps a brief recall of how, with both conscious and intuitive skill, each aspect of the therapeutic trinity was in turn invoked during one enlightened period—for example, in the Asklepiad Sanatoria of ancient Greece—may serve to illustrate the general theses. In essence, the method employed in these classically effective mental health centers (named after the son of Apollo—the handsome, incorruptible god of music, mind and medicine—and thereby the very image of every psychiatrist) mitigated man's Ur-anxieties as follows:*

First, by Restoring Physical Well-being: After the patient had left his contentious home and travelled to one of the Sanatoria in the Salubrious environs of Cos, Memphis or Knidos, he was welcomed not

*Adapted from J.H. Masserman: "Man's Eternal Anxieties and Compensatory Illusions," *Illinois Medical Journal, 12:*1-16 (1965).

by a clerk or social worker but by no less a parent-surrogate than the Head Priest or Priestess, who then further cheered and reassured him by conducting him past piles of discarded crutches and bronze plaques bearing testimonials from grateful ex-patients. Immediate attention was then concentrated on restoring the patient's physical well-being through rest in pleasant surroundings, nourishing and appetizing diets, relaxing baths and massages, and the carefully measured administration of nepenthics — drugs that resembled modern ataractics in that they apparently tranquilized both the patient and the doctor. Indeed, the Greek word *therapeien* itself meant service, just as later the Latin *curare,* to care for, gave rise to our term cure. (Ur-need I)

Second, by Recultivating Human Relationships: In accordance with this objective, equal effort was expended in counteracting the patient's Ur-anxiety of social isolation as follows:

Confidence in the Physician: Then as now, the patient was encouraged to relate to his therapist:

First, as a kindly and protective parental figure who provided a source of security and comfort.

Second, as a learned and experienced teacher, whose counsels for more restrained and balanced, and therefore healthier and happier, modes of life could be followed on rational and practical grounds (e.g. as in the various Stoic schools).

Third, as a more personal mentor uniquely interested in the supplicant's complaints (present illness) and willing to explore their relationship to the patient's past experiences (psychiatric history), their meanings and values (symbolisms) and acquired patterns of goal-directed action (operational analysis), in order that the verbal understandings so derived would lead to more satisfying, lasting and useful adaptations (operational insight). Socrates required his students to work through their own verbal perplexities, and Plato understood the unconscious significance of dreams and symbols. Aristophanes, in his delightful comedy, *The Clouds,* pictured the distraught Strepsiades lying on a couch and trying to acquire understanding through fantasy and free association; less passively, Soranus records the cure of a case of hysteria in a virginal bride by a form of direct action that would shock Masters and Johnson.

Fourth, the patient-physician relationship (transference) led to an avid acceptance of the efficacy of the physician's quasi-scientific, quasi-mystical remedies, some of which were physically painful and thereby covertly punitive for, and expiative of, former social and religious transgressions. Among these were not only a vast variety of unpleasant purgings, bleedings, coolings, roasting and broilings, but even more direct physical and surgical interferences with cerebral function, such as the Egyptian practice of trephining the skull and incising the cortex or, as described by Pliny the Elder, subjecting the patient to convulsive therapy by discharging electric eels through the head. We read of Hippocrates' condemnations of the ignorance and superstition inherent in many of these "false remedies" but this alone proves how widely practiced, then as now, they must have been.

But the patient's social rehabilitation was not left to such partial and intermediate transactions with the physician alone; concurrently, his essential group relationships and skills were recultivated through the following modalities:

The Use of Music, which provided esthetic expression and encouraged group belongingness through feelings of conjoint rhythm and harmony.

Calisthenics and Dancing, which afforded similar possibilities of reorientative interaction and communion.

Competitive Athletics, not only for the joy of healthy action but for public recognition through nondestructive competition and reward.

Dramatics: Here the poetic psychiatrist (and there can be no other) may well ask: What writings better explore or epitomize basic human relationships than the plays of Euripides, Sophocles or Aristophanes? And what productions can offer the patient, either as witness or participant, more varied identifications, vivid experiences or vicarious solutions of his own interpersonal problems? The Greeks cherished and utilized these tragedies and comedies for their deep human empathy and ageless significance, endlessly varied their themes and were personally involved as actors, chorus or affectively moved audience — and thus explored in essence the basic interactions utilized in modern psychodrama or other forms of group therapy.

Social Rehabilitation: This offered a transition between a passive dependence on the sanatorium to an eventual recognition of the advantage of a return to the community and service for the common good.

Finally, the Greeks in their wisdom also recognized the third human Ur-necessity of a *Belief in Some Inscrutable but Transcendent Order* — and, parenthetically, demanded that Socrates pay the ultimate penalty for threatening man's trust in the existence of immortal celestial beings. To capitalize on this ultimate faith, the Asklepiad Sanatoria, like many hospitals today, were built and operated by some religious cult, which added the following powerful factors to therapy:

1. a "divinely revealed" doctrine in which all believers could feel an exclusively self-elevating bond of fellowship,
2. a reassuring ritual which, through its origin in human needs and through millennia of empiric refinement, included such exquisitely gratifying proceduers as

a. the symbolic eating and drinking of the parent-god's body in the forms of mystically potentiating food and wine (as exemplified in the ancient worship of Melitta and Mithra).

b. the temple hymns, sung and played in the simple, repetitive, hypnotic cadences of a mother's lullaby–and often resulting in "temple sleep" (two thousand years later, Mesmer was to discover "animal magnetism" and, through Charcot and Janet, mislead Freud; and Bernheim was to warn, "It is a wise hypnotist that knows who is hypnotizing whom." Such escapist trances were then varied with food, drink and Dionysian sexual indulgencies to be triply, enjoyed, since they also honored one's permissive and accommodating gods.

c. the "anointing" or "laying on of hands" to cure an injured bodily part–a direct reminiscence of the soothing parental stroking of an injured child, which has ever since been exemplified in the healing powers of the king's Touch, exploited in the seventeenth century by Greatrakes the Stroaker, and is still sought by the emotionally immature and physically deprived who are avid of massage and chiropractic.

d. the ethereal, elevating *Emphasis on the Spiritual* — a concept as fundamental to life as is the neonate's first breath or *spiritus.* Every human is variously *in*spired, acquires an *esprit de corps,* becomes *dis*pirited, and finally *ex*pires so that his immutable *spirit* can begin life anew. And here, too, the physician-priest functions in knowing the spiritual world or purveying professed contrition and remorse to the spirits of our fathers, and in requiring only a gratifying small penance with which to avoid the horrors of eternal punishment. Meanwhile, the temple then and now furnishes a divinely protected sanctuary from earthly stresses and problems, much as Lourdes is a haven of comfort and healing today.

e. Finally, the priest also mediated the supreme promise of all religions or, for that matter, of all scientific systems: the conquest, through life eternal, of man's most grim and implacable enemy, death itself.

These then, were the ancient — and are the eternal — practices that embody what physicians have intuitively known for centuries: that although no man can ever be certain of his health, friends or philosophy, the illusions of security in each of these spheres are essential to his welfare; and that all methods of medical-psychiatric therapy are effective only insofar as they restore physical well-being, foster more amicable interpersonal relationships, and help the patient amend his beliefs so as to render them more generally acceptable and useful.

THE COMPARATIVE APPROACH TO THE ESSENTIALS OF THERAPY

To supplement this historical survey, it would require another shelf of books to review the current and equally illuminating anthopologic, ethnic and transcultural studies of Gillin, Margolin, Lambo, Kiev and Leighton, Ziferstein and the author's own comparisons of Soviet techniques to those of other sociopsychiatrists with sufficient breadth of interest and objectivity to investigate the therapeutic practices of other societies. So also, it would take an integrative genius to demonstrate that all of these fall into the familiar rubrics of physical, social and metaphysical readaptation. However, even if one does not go so far afield, perhaps a more parochial reexamination of the various therapeutic practices in our own culture, from colonic lavage to Christian Science, may demonstrate a similar triune basis. This, of course, requires an unusual willingness to concede that cherished concepts and cults are comparable—a challenge that few are willing to accept. Nevertheless, playing the role of pre-henbane Socrates in a peripatetic dialogue with psychiatric residents and analytic trainees, the author has sometimes put forth some outrageous postulate such as, "Resolved, that electroshock therapy (EST) and psychoanalysis are essentially more alike than different in their basic therapeutic actions and effects." In the past, though not so often recently, this usually evoked a storm of protest that they were incomparably different, in that EST was "physical," "enforced," "impersonal," "stereotyped," "rigidly conducted," "suppressive," "antimnemonic," "intellectually impairing," etc. whereas, in contrast, psychoanalysis was "psychologic," "voluntary," "exquisitely interpersonal," "flexible," "evocative," "restorative of memory," and "designed to develop to the full the patient's cognitive and adaptive capacities" through "insight."

At this juncture, the author occasionally pointed out that the last assertion directly begged the question since, in the historical and comparative contexts of the subject, insight itself could be defined only as that temporarily ecstatic state in which patient and therapist had once shared or were now sharing mutual illusions as to the cause and cure of the former's difficulties. With this additional goad, some of the author's residents began to explore subtler dimensions of therapeutically operative symmetry between electroshock and analysis and came up with the following disconcerting similarities:

PHYSICAL PARAMETERS: Both methods offer an escape from the mundane stresses of external reality to a sensorially isolated crib or couch provided and protected by a parental surrogate for about the same total number of recumbent hours in hospital or office.

Both methods serve to disorganize current patterns of deviant behavior: EST by cerebral diaschisis, analysis by semantic and symbolic interpositions between concept and reaction.

INTERPERSONAL PARAMETERS: In both methods, the patient selects (whether voluntarily or by equivalent social pressure) *the method of therapy and the therapist* he regards as most suitable for his needs.

In both methods, the therapist sympathetically accepts the patient as more or less helpless and ill, is convinced of the special validity of his own therapeutic theories and the efficacy of his techniques and, thus, rounds out an operationally effective *folie a deux.*

In both methods, there are more or less overt, but inevitable, physical, economic, social and other punishments for the persistence of abnormal conduct: more incarceration, exclusion of visitors, postshock headache and other adverse sanctions in EST; or more time, expense and patronizingly disillusioning interpretations in analysis. Conversely, there are desirable reacceptances and rewards for progress toward more comforming behavior (the "patient compliance" of Ehrenwald) : the expanding privileges, therapists' approval, renewed familial hegemony and finally, membership in Recovery, Inc. after "successful" EST; and after analysis—at least until recently—acceptance in the sophisticated elite of the "thoroughly analyzed" at cocktail parties or, in the case of Institute trainees, admission to the local psychoanalytic society.

Mystical: Finally, in both cases patient and therapist join in an essentially worshipful belief that either Cerletti or Freud respectively brought divine salvation to spiritually ailing mortals, to be attained through prescribed rituals of suffering, expiation, enlightenment and the reacquisition of grace. Any agnostic who, at national meetings, has attended the section on electroconvulsive therapy or, at a discreetly noncommunicative distance, has been to a seminar of psychoanalytic theory and therapy, will unmistakably have experienced the devotional aura as well as the scientific import of both proceedings.

Similar operational parallels can, of course, be constructed between vitamin therapy and nondirective counseling or between *dauerschlaff* and psychodrama. Such comparisons should, of course, never obscure the specific attributes and special potentials of each method, but outside the bounds of reductional sophistry, objective analysis may help clarify the universal factors of therapy being considered here *viz.* to help the patient realize that his formerly cherished modes of conduct in the three spheres of physical, social and philosophic adaptation are no longer either necessary or profitable; and to learn, by exploration and personal experience, that new ones will prove more personally pleasurable, socially advantageous and existentially compatible.

EXPERIMENTAL VALIDATIONS OF THE ESSENTIALS OF THERAPY

This leads to the final heuristic resource: the experimental approach to the study of "normal" behavior and the treatment of its deviations. In the words of Adolf Meyer, every friend and patient can be studied as a ready-made "experiment of nature," but for more adequate controls and precise analysis, animal research is necessary. The author has elsewhere rather extensively reviewed the rationale, ethologic evidence and experimental studies under this rubric; here, it is feasible only to summarize in outline form the premises tested and the methods of inducing and reversing aberrant behavior that emerged from such studies. The four biodynamic principles which evolved are these:

Biodynamic Hypotheses

1. *Motivation:* The behavior of all organisms is actuated by physiologic needs and, therefore, varies with their intensity, duration and balance.

2. *Perception and Response:* Organisms conceive of, and interact with, their milieu not in terms of an absolute external reality, but in accordance with their individual genetic capacities, rates of maturation and unique experiences.

3. *Range of Normal Adaptation:* In higher organisms, these factors make possible many techniques of adaptation, which in turn render the organisms capable of meeting stress and frustration and maintaining an adequate level of satisfaction by (a) employing new methods of coping with difficulties when the old prove ineffective or (b) by modifying the goals or substituting new ones when the old become unattainable.

4. *Neurotigenesis:* However, when physical inadequacies, environmental stresses or motivational-adaptational conflicts exceed the organism's innate or acquired capacities, internal tension (anxiety) mounts, neurophysiologic (psychosomatic) dysfunctions occur, and the organism develops overgeneralized patterns of avoidance (phobias); ritualized behavior (obsessions and compulsions); regressive, hyperactive, aggressive or other deviant social transactions; or bizarrely dereistic (hallucinatory, delusional) responses corresponding to those in human neuroses and psychoses.

EXPERIMENTAL NEUROSES: As indicated in the fourth principle, marked and persistent deviations of behavior were induced by stressing individual animals between mutually incompatible or traumatically unpredictable patterns of survival, e.g. requiring a monkey to secure food, after a conditional signal, from a box which might *unexpectedly* contain a toy snake—an object as symbolically dangerous to the monkey as a live one, harmless or not. In this connection, the author further amended Freudian doctrine by demonstrating that fear in the sense of dread of injury need not be involved at all; i.e. equally serious and lasting neurotigenic effects could be induced by facing the animal with difficult choices among mutually exclusive satisfactions—situations that parallel the disruptive effects of prolonged indecisions in human affairs. Either form of conflict or uncertainty produced physiologic and mimetic manifestations of anxiety, spreading inhibitions, generalizing phobias, stereotyped rituals, psychosomatic dysfunctions, impaired social interactions and other persistent regressions and deviations of conduct.

Constitutional Influences: Animals closest to man showed symptoms most nearly resembling those in human neuroses and psychoses, but in each case the neurotic syndrome depended less on the nature of the conflict (which could be held constant) than on the constitutional predisposition of the animal. For example, under similar stresses spider monkeys reverted to infantile dependencies or catatonic immobility, and cebus developed various psychosomatic disturbances including functional paralysis; whereas vervets became diffusely aggressive, persisted in bizarre sexual patterns or preferred hallucinatory satisfactions such as chewing and swallowing purely imaginary meals while avoiding real food to the point of self-starvation.

Methods of Therapy: Since the author induced experimental neuroses in animals not only to study their causes and variations, but primarily to search for the principles of therapy, this portion of the work was assigned the most time and effort. After the trial of scores of procedures, only nine general methods, significantly parallel to those used with human patients, proved to be most effective in ameliorating neurotic or psychotic symptoms. Again in summary, these techniques could be marshalled under physical, social and—if the term is used in a broadly operational sense—"mystical" subheads as follows:

Physical Methods

1. The satisfaction of one or more of the biologic needs that induce the impasse, such as hunger or thirst as opposed to sex, or exploratory drives vs. fear of injury—conflicts that often induce corresponding difficulties of adaptation in humans.

2. Removal from the laboratory to a less stressful environment: e.g., a better home, job or climate—or even an occasional vacation from the cumulative strains of daily life.

3. The provision of opportunities to reutilize critically in-

hibited skills; as a parallel example, inducing a crashed, unhurt, but temporarily phobic fighter pilot to fly another plane immediately, and thus dispel his mounting anxiety over his loss of previous mastery over his milieu, by rapid technical rehabilitation.

4. The administration of various drugs that gave the animal temporary relief by blunting perceptions and dampening excessively intense or prolonged aversive responses. Significantly some neurotic animals which experienced such effects from the ingestion of alcohol sought out the drug if made available and became avid alcoholic addicts.

5. The use of electroshock or other methods of producing sufficient cerebral anoxia and diaschisis to disrupt undesirable patterns of behavior, provided they were more vulnerable than those more deeply established and ingrained.

6. The employment of surgical or electrocoagulative techniques to produce neurologic lesions and similar disorganizations of aberrant behavior.

Social Methods

1. The resolution of the motivational conflict by directed guidance kept within the organism's readaptive potentials ("ego strength") as may be attempted clinically in so-called "behavior therapy" for obsessive-phobic neuroses.

2. Association with an accepting group of well-adapted ("normal") organisms, as in sending a problem child to a good school, i.e. where children behave in the manner desired.

3. The retraining of the animal by carefully individualized guidance, the experimenter acting as a personal therapist who helps the subject reexplore early experiential conflicts and dispel their neurotigenic effects; as in psychoanalysis, helping the patient recall early traumatic events and reevaluate their residues in the here and now by corrective emotional experiences vis-a-vis the therapist and elsewhere in a physically, socially and philosophically reevaluated world.

Mystical Connotations

If this term is extended to its full meaning of behavior based on faith in the unprovable, then a dog's unreasoning confidence in its master's magical prowess and devotion to its interests may also be extended to therapeutic techniques 1 and 3 as described under "Social Methods" above.

CLINICAL SUMMARY

If, then, all of the historical, comparative and experimental data here indicated were to be integrated and interpreted, three essential principles of therapy could be clinically formulated as follows:

First, one must discard the cold armor of "professional dignity" and accept each patient not as a diagnostic challenge or a recipient of "specific therapy for the organic pathology" (a repulsive solecism) —nor, least of all, as only another research case— but as a *troubled human being seeking comfort and guidance* as well as relief from physical suffering. These broader requirements should be met in the psychiatric aspects of general medical therapy as follows:

> Regardless of whether the patient's complaints are considered as primarily organic or functional, bodily discomfort and dysfunction are to be relieved by every medical and surgical means available including, when indicated, carefully prescribed sedatives and hypnotics temporarily useful in dulling painful memories and relieving apprehension and quieting agitation. In the author's research studies and clinical experience, he has found that the barbiturates, bromides, aldehydes and other well-tested drugs, when wisely used, are often preferable to many of the widely promoted but dubious ataractics and tranquilizers; however, in nearly all medical and surgical specialties it is recognized that such surcease, often of questionable pharmacolgic origin, is merely the first stage of therapy. As soon as the patient's tensions and anxieties have abated sufficiently to make him more accessible and cooperative, one must strive to revive his initiative, restore his lost skills and encourage him to regain the confidence and self-respect that can come only from useful accomplishment.
>
> But since no man is an "island unto himself," the wise physician, whatever his specialty, has a broader task: to recognize that his patient may be deeply concerned about sexual, maritial, occupational and other problems that may also seriously affect his physical and social well-being. This involves an exploration, varying in depth and duration but always discerning and tactful, of the attitudes and values the patient derived from his past experiences; of his present goals and tribulations; of his effective (normal), socially ineffective (neurotic)

or bizarrely unrealistic (psychotic) conduct; of the ways in which these patterns relieve or exacerbate his current difficulties and whether they are accessible to available methods of medicopsychiatric therapy. It is customary at this point for the psychiatrist to warn his colleagues in other fields off his supposedly esoteric preserves; instead, it has been the author's gratifying experience that in most cases any intelligent, sensitive physician can, in the time available, conduct the essential psychotherapy required. In essence, this will consist of using gentle reasoning, personal guidance and progressive social explorations to help the patient correct his past misconceptions and prejudices, abandon infantile or childlike patterns of behavior that have long since lost their effectiveness, revise his goals and values and adopt a more realistic, productive and permanently rewarding (mature) style of life. In this skillfully directed reeducation (good psychotherapy, despite a recent fad to the contrary, is about as nondirective as good surgery), the enlightened cooperation of his family, friends, employer or others may, with the patient's consent, be secured and utilized fully. By such means the patient's second Ur-defense will be strengthened by renewed communal solidarity and security — a *sine qua non* of dyadic and group therapy.

Lastly, to mitigate his existential Ur-anxiety, the patient's religious, philosophic or other convictions, instead of being deprecated or undermined, should be respected and strengthened insofar as they furnish him with what everyone requires: a belief in life's purpose, meaning and value. In this fundamental sense, medicine, being a humanitarian science, can never be in conflict with philosophy or religion — since all three seem to be designed by a beneficent providence to preserve, cheer and comfort man — and thereby constitute a trinity to be respected by any physician deeply concerned with man's health and sanity.

Indeed, with respect to these latter terms, it is of historic-philologic significance that the term *sanatos* implied to the ancients the indissolubility of physical and mental functions *(mens sanis in corpora sano);* so also, our more modern word "health" can be traced to the Anglo-Saxon *hal* or *hol,* from which are derived not only physical *haleness* and *healing,* but the greeting, *"Hail, friend!"* and the concepts of *wholeness* and *holiness.* Once again Greeks, Romans and Gauls have bequeathed to us, in the rich heritage of a syncretic language in which reality and illusion merge, their recognition of the indissoluble trinity of physical, social and philosophic components of health and sanity.

REFERENCES

1. Masserman, Jules H.: *Behavior and Neurosis.* New York, Hafner, 1964.
2. ———: *Biodynamic Roots of Human Behavior.* Springfield, Thomas, 1968.
3. ———: *Culture, Law and Psychiatry.* New York, Nunellen, 1973.
4. ———: *Handbook of Psychiatric Therapies.* New York, Science, 1973.
5. ———: *Practice of Dynamic Psychiatry.* Philadelphia, Saunders, 1955.
6. ———: *Principles of Dynamic Psychiatry,* 2nd ed. Philadelphia, Saunders, 1961.
7. ———: *Progress in Psychotherapy,* vols. 1-5. New York, Grune, 1957-1962.
8. ———: *A Psychiatric Odyssey.* New York, Science, 1971.
9. ———: *Science and Psychoanalysis,* vols. 1-21. New York, Grune, 1958-1973.
10. ———: *Theories and Therapies of Dynamic Psychiatry.* New York, Science, 1973.
11. ———: *Youth, A Transcultural Approach.* New York, Grune, 1968.
12. Masserman, Jules H., and Salzman, Leon: *Modern Concepts of Psychoanalysis.* New York, Philos Lib, 1962.
13. Masserman, Jules H., and Schwab, John: *Man for Humanity.* Springfield, Thomas, 1972.
14. Masserman, Jules H.: Theory and Therapy in Dynamic Psychiatry. New York. Jason Aronson, 1974.

Section III

REHABILITATION OF HOSPITALIZED PATIENTS

Chapter 6

THE ART AND SCIENCE OF REHABILITATION

Leon L. Rackow

A rehabilitation program in a psychiatric hospital means the conscious management of daily life through creating, supporting, developing and restoring an appropriate life-style for the patient in the direction of personal, vocational and social autonomy. The intent is to return the patient to society, a society which is highly complex with a multiplicity of choices and resulting conflicts. The program must enable the patient to meet these circumstances, adjust to them and remain in the society to which he returns. One must provide opportunities to learn and experience coping behavior techniques that can translate to social and vocational living and to develop degrees of competence commensurate with the patient's remaining assets. The consumer of these services—the patient—requires more attention and has new expectations and needs, to help him face the complex tasks inherent in contemporary society.

As psychiatric problems are increasingly treated in general hospitals, in community mental hygiene clinics and on an ambulatory basis, the prescription of social and vocational rehabilitation for patients will become increasingly important. For rehabilitation therapy to hold its own with other psychiatric treatments and for it to return patients to social living and remunerative work, a definitive system of prescription and evaluation of results which can be quantified are required. In addition, as pay-for-work programs become universal in large psychiatric hospitals, a system for their justification and support will be required for reporting to the funding agencies. The emergence of new treatment concepts in psychiatric hospitals, notably the multidisciplinary team approach, raises the question of how to realign the rehabilitation medicine service (RMS) in accordance with current thinking and practices in psychiatric rehabilitation.

The author presents a social and vocational rehabilitation program which can be definitely prescribed and assessed for results. The group and professional identities of the different therapists are retained while a broad-spectrum therapeutic approach is developed for the individual patient. Rehabilitation modalities are reorganized into three functional lines of prescription—physical, social-behavioral and vocational—with the therapy assignments within each line indicated in a rough rank-order of complexity and skill. Each of the seven disciplines within the rehabilitation medicine service represented professional skills and a body of knowledge. Optimal functional utilization of this knowledge and skill is best achieved by respecting the professional identity of each discipline. See Table 6-I.

The professional identity of existing rehabilitation medicine staff is retained even though personnel would have functional assignments in more than one program. How the functional approach applies in a similar manner to the delivery of services to patients may be briefly described at this point. These functional lines of treatment in physical rehabilitation are

A. Physical Therapy	Diagnostic testing and measurement
	Physical and hydrotherapy
	Prosthetic, orthotic and assistant appliances
	Surgical, orthopedic, cardiac, pulmonary, medical rehabilitation
B. Corrective Therapy	Therapeutic exercise
	Geriatric physical sustaining activities
	Functional restoration

Prescription of therapy can be made to three major programs

and sections within each one, depending on individual needs. The therapists, while retaining their professional and group identity, will function in and across each line of treatment. The prescription process will be a discrete one by the physican and a rehabilitation board. For each patient there will be developed a therapy plan in one or all of the three functional lines, defined for that individual patient's need. Periodic reevaluation by this same treating and review board will assess progress in each therapeutic approach used. Changes of prescription within and across each line can thus be determined as soon as needed and then reported to the primary psychiatrist. In this schema it is possible to prescribe for patients in a definitive way within each line among the therapists of different skills, and across all three programs. A schizophrenic patient might be in the physical rehabilitation program for physical therapy for an old fracture and for language retraining for a psychologically determined speech impairment; in the social-behavioral program for music, sports and adult education; and in the industrial rehabilitation program for work experience in a sustaining monetary incentive program and for high school equivalency courses. This would have a patient in all three functional programs receiving attention from therapists from several of our traditional rehabilitation medicine sections. A definitive rehabilitation prescription is made for the patients in treatment, and it is tied in with the activities of other treating services and with other treatment programs:

1. The physical restoration program includes a physical rehabilitation ward with reality testing and operant conditioning wards, nursing home care units, community nursing homes, home care programs and foster homes which are specially selected for veterans whose psychiatric illness is complicated by a physical condition.

2. The social-behavioral program coordinates with a psychiatric rehabilitation ward, an attitude therapy section and various sheltered living situations such as foster homes, family homes, independent living, cooperative living situ-

TABLE 6-I
REHABILITATION MEDICINE SERVICE

		Designation of Rehabilitation Units			
	Physical Rehabilitation Unit		*Social (Behavioral) Rehabilitation Unit*		*Industrial Rehabilitation Unit*
PT:	Diagnostic testing and measurement Physical and hydrotherapy Prosthetic, orthotic and assistant appliances Surgical, orthopedic, cardiac, pulmonary, medical rehabilitation	*OT:*	Activities of daily living (social) Arts and Crafts Hobby clubs	*OT:*	Testing and evaluation: vocational aptitude and skills, work tolerance; work habits, interests Prevocational exploration, training and work experience
CT:	Therapeutic exercise Geriatric physical sustaining activities Functional restoration Driver Educ. (Practice)	*REC:*	Resocialization therapy Interpersonal relationships Music, art therapy and recreation Leisure time activities In-and out-hospital social events Recreational swimming In-and out-hospital social clubs Psychosocial centers	*ET:*	Preparation for employment (end-of-course tests, high school equavalency college credits, vocational and industrial testing). Educational preparation and training for higher education, business, clerical occupations, etc. Programmed learning Reading improvement
REC:	Physical reconditioning Sports Therapeutic swimming	*CT:*	Sports — participant and spectator Physical fitness	*IT:*	Testing through simulated work activities Group and individual work assignments
ET:	Communication skills for blind, aphasic, etc., speech therapy, language restraining Mobility and dexterity skills, retraining for	*ET:*	Language improvement and retraining Adult education Current events and reality orientation (geriatric) Halfway houses on grounds	*MAT:*	Industrial rehabilitation counseling Work-for-Pay Programs

	blind and aphasic Driver Educ. (Theory)	a. In-hospital industrial rehabilitation programs Motivational (RITE) Sustaining (PRICE) Transitional (PREP)
OT:	Activities of daily living (physical) Community care and adjustment	b. Community Employment (night hospital) supervised independent c. In-hospital employment (day hospital) Consultation services Community Adjustment

ations with other patients, specially created social structures, quarterway and halfway houses, etc.

3. The industrial rehabilitation program encompasses observed full-time employment in the hospital or in industry, outpatient care, mental hygiene clinics, home bound industry, sheltered workshops, sheltered industrial work jobs and community incentive programs, etc.

The professional identity of the therapists is maintained in their traditional roles in occupational therapy, educational therapy, etc., even though they would have functional assignments in all three programs as generalists. The rehabilitation service is headed by either a psychiatrist with rehabilitation interest or a physiatrist with psychiatric interest. This chief of the rehabilitation medicine service could be a "working chief" who heads either the physical or social-behavioral line. In keeping with medical manpower, skill shortages and accumulating experience in comprehensive clinics, the individual with the most appropriate skills, training and interest is designated to head each of the three line programs, under the overall supervision of the physician chief of service. The physical rehabilitation program could be headed by a physiatrist, an orthopedist, a surgeon or a general physician. The social-behavioral program should preferably be headed by a psychiatrist, but consideration could be given to a clinical psychologist, psychiatric social worker, psychiatric nurse, etc. The vocational rehabilitation program would best be headed by an occupational psychiatrist, an occupational physiatrist, a counseling or industrial psychologist, a vocational rehabilitation specialist, an RMS coordinator or a therapist who had graduate training in psychiatric rehabilitation, etc. These skilled staff members from the different disciplines outside of rehabilitation medicine might well be assigned to rehabilitation medicine service and not be located in psychology, social work service, nursing, etc.

The descriptions of each of the programs, which have been organized to accomplish the objective of consolidating the various RMS sections along functional lines to achieve improved patient-and-program-oriented services, follow.

1. Rehabilitation medicine is composed of personnel from physical therapy (PT), corrective therapy (CT), recreational therapy (RT) and occupational therapy (OT), with the principal focus on the physical aspects of treatment.

For the most part patients treated in the physical rehabilitation unit are drawn from the medical and surgical services, neurological service, RMS bed service, PMI* wards and the nursing home unit. Patients from psychiatric services who require treatment for a specific short-term physical condition remain the responsibility of the programs rendering major RMS treatment, i.e. social rehabilitation and industrial rehabilitation.

Likewise, patients from the physical rehabilitation unit who participate in activities of the other units will continue under the supervision of the RMS unit having major treatment concern.

The physical rehabilitation unit is under the medical direction of a physiatrist who, together with representatives from PT, CT and OT will constitute the unit planning team. The line structure will permit more effective utilization of the skills of all personnel, prevent duplication of essentially similar treatment, provide direction for the efforts of all concerned personnel at every stage of treatment and make possible more frequent patient evaluation through the medium of team conferences, thus providing a continuum for the attainment of short- and long-range rehabilitation goals.

Significant features of this unit will include intensive treatment for patients from the outpatient service and visits to community homes housing psychiatric patients with physical conditions.

2. The social-behavioral rehabilitation unit draws its manpower from recreational, corrective, occupational and educational therapy. The basic program offered is directed primarily toward meeting the treatment needs of the psychiatric patient for motivational awakening, interest and psychomotor stimulation, reawakening of intellectual faculties, socializing experiences, reactivation of reality situations, a sustaining form of activity and in general an evaluation of potential for in-hospital and com-

---

*Psychiatric medically infirm. (Editor)

munity adjustment. In this patient population are the long-term hospitalized, the acutely ill patient and very often the newly-admitted patient who requires a period of observation before a definite staff disposition can be made.

Functioning under the direction of its chief, the planning team in this line will develop a graduated, balanced program of activities, and an integrated approach designed to meet the treatment objectives recommended by the building treatment team, where rehabilitation service orientation is provided by the active participation of a rehabilitation specialist.

The social-behavioral rehabilitation unit structure is sufficiently flexible to enable patients to participate either in large or small group activities or in an appropriate combination of both. The patient can easily be moved from one form of activity to another depending upon his evaluation by his therapy team within this unit. (There will be special emphasis on utilization of the nursing assistant in charge of small groups by assigning him a role in the activity program under the supervision of RMS therapists.)

Active collaboration with social work service in the pre-community-residence program, and in the foster home and community residence programs, is maintained both in and out of the hospital. Patients residing in the community will be followed to insure maximum utilization of community resources available to them.

3. The industrial rehabilitation unit is composed principally of rehabilitation personnel from manual arts and industrial, occupational and educational therapy; and a vocational rehabilitation specialist. Included within the scope of this unit are those occupational therapy personnel who conduct general exploratory shops to evaluate aptitudes and skills of patients to determine their readiness for upgraded work-simulated activities in the more vocationally oriented therapies, with work tolerance, work habits and prevocational exploration and testing.

The basic concept of an industrial rehabilitation unit is to provide a continuum of activity that ranges from exploratory industrial experiences within the various therapies to more advanced and intensive retraining in new or previously acquired skills, and beyond that into hospital work assignments, transitional work-for-pay programs and sheltered and regular community employment. To achieve this continuum, personnel in the industrial rehabilitation unit furnish practical aptitude evaluations in work-simulated activities and in actual work experiences, both in small group situations and in individual assignments. There is augmentation of the physical tolerance of patients for specific work assignments from an initial period of four hours daily to a maximum up to a full eight hours.

Progressive occupational reality testing is accomplished through the medium of work-for-pay, both government appropriated and contractual community-based employment. The services of a vocational rehabilitation specialist are utilized to operate the in-hospital work-for-pay programs and the community work-for-pay assignments for predischarge patients. Collaboration with psychology services in the selective placement of suitable patients in community employment provides a vocational continuum assuring a sustained vocational adjustment. The vocational rehabilitation specialist is also responsible for the establishment of work-for-pay programs in community residences, wherever feasible. (Rewarded Industrial Therapy Employment (RITE) and Patient's Rehabilitation Employment Program (PREP) are additional work-for-pay programs, government sponsored, of a transitional nature that are an outcome of a successful adjustment to hospital work assignment.)

Overall responsibility for the industrial rehabilitation line is that of the designated chief who will be directly involved in implementing the specific assignments of patients in the industrial rehabilitation unit, in accordance with the general objectives established by the building treatment team, on which there is again RMS orientation through the rehabilitation specialist who is a member of the psychiatric treatment team. Acting in concert with the section chiefs of the RMS therapies in the unit, the RMS coordinator meets with the industrial rehabilitation planning team to review the general objectives set forth by the building treatment team for each patient and to determine his industrial rehabilitation program. At periodic intervals there will be patient evaluation meetings of all personnel concerned, including other allied health personnel as required to assess the progress of each patient and to develop alternative plans or progressive advancement of the patient along the continuum.

Communication with the building treatment team will be maintained throughout the assignment of the patient by the RMS coordinator, apprising the team of any significant changes through the rehabilitation specialist (liaison therapist) or through RMS progress reports.

In order to achieve the major objective of integrating more closely the three RMS units with overall hospital treatment and to insure increased participation in the treatment team, the RMS operations are aligned with the existing hospital structure. Table 6-II, entitled "Flow of Referral and Progress Report," illustrates graphically the interrelationships between the hospital treatment team and the three RMS units. The table highlights the role of the rehabilitation specialist, the RMS liaison representative on the treatment team, who is the link between RMS and the treatment team. Also highlighted are the three RMS planning teams, which parallel the building treatment teams insofar as patient treatment in RMS is concerned.

A significant aspect of the restructured RMS is the built-in-provision for greater mobility and progression of patients within RMS as well as the improvement of communication and record keeping pertaining to patient treatment. In the past, paperwork had been a major obstacle to mobility of the patient. Now only an initial consultation request is needed throughout the assignment; no additional requests or referrals from the ward are required. Major and minor changes in treatment are accomplished through periodic reevaluations and, whenever indicated, through permitting patients to move from one section to another within the functional units or from one unit to another upon reevaluation.

Another advantage of the restructured RMS method of operations is the concept of priorities as applied to the evaluation process by each of the three RMS rehabilitation units. The highest

TABLE 6-II

PM&RS PILOT STUDY
FLOW OF REFERRAL & PROGRESS REPORT

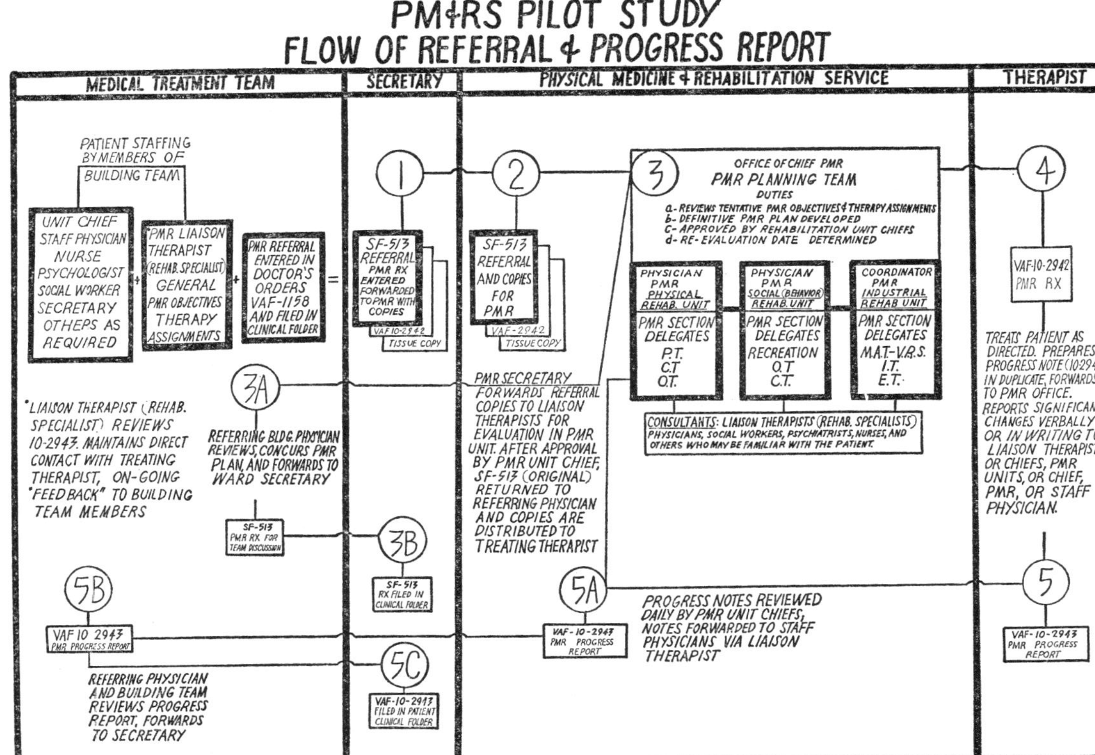

priority is given to the newly admitted patients whose tentative RMS assignment is reviewed within ten days. Next in order are those patients who have completed their objective or those for whom a staff disposition is imminent. Then come those for whom a change in therapy is considered desirable at the request of either the therapy section or the rehabilitation specialist (liaison therapist), based on decisions of the building treatment team. The lowest priority is assigned to those patients whose therapy objective is of a sustaining or maintaining nature. This class of patients will receive periodic reevaluations based on a recent progress report.

The scheduled planning team meetings within each unit facilitate communication among treating therapists on a wider scale than has heretofore been the practice, since more systematic evaluations of patients take place on a regular basis. Opportunities are provided for therapists to participate on the planning teams, especially when treatment problems and planning common to the therapies in each unit are encountered in the evaluation process.

In communicating the progress of patients in the rehabilitation service, the narrative format has too often not been sufficiently informative because not all therapists are equally skilled in writing, and in addition, preparing the narrative represents a time-consuming task. Narrative reports are often impressionistic and, depending as they do on the insight of the writer, frequently do not present a clear picture of the patient, making interpretation difficult. In this procedure the author will continue to utilize the narrative format, but will offer optional overprinted forms, which are more structured and objective, and less time-consuming to prepare.

Verbal communication between rehabilitation and other hospital personnel involved in the treatment of patients has been reinforced by the addition of the rehabilitation specialist who, through his attendance at team and staff meetings, is able to transmit significant changes to all concerned. This does not preclude direct verbal communication by treating therapists with staff physicians and other members of the building treatment team whenever timely transmission of ideas is required. As in the past, therapists will continue to report significant treatment data verbally to rehabilitation physicians and functional line chiefs, and they in turn will maintain direct personal communication with staff physicians.

The scheduled planning team meetings within each line unit will facilitate communication among treatment therapists on a wider scale than has heretofore been practical, since more systematic evaluations of patients will take place on a regular basis. Opportunities will be provided for therapists to participate on the planning teams, especially when treatment problems and planning common to the therapies in each unit are encountered in the evaluation process.

A restructured RMS invariably leads to a redefinition of the roles of several categories of personnel. The coordinator, the rehabilitation specialists and the section chiefs were identified for immediate consideration to meet this objective. A new position, the rehabilitation specialist's, was established as seen from the Table 6-I and from the detailed description of functions.

The expanded role of the coordinator in the pilot study is in recognition of the professional leadership assumed by incumbents of this position in many psychiatric hospitals in implementing such innovations as work-for-pay programs. The expertise developed by coordinators in vocationally oriented RMS programs provided the basis for the delegation of the coordinator in the pilot study to head the industrial rehabilitation unit, equating his new role to associate and/or assistant status with the physiatrist.

The newly-created position, rehabilitation specialist, is an expanded version of an older adaptation of RMS to the team concept in psychiatric hospitals. The RMS member was initially designated a liaison representative, but with limited responsibilities in relation to patient treatment. The new concept of the RMS member is that of a team consultant on all matters pertaining to RMS treatment of the psychiatric patient.

In addition to expanded responsibilities as rehabilitation specialists, section chiefs play a major role in each of the planning teams, and they may be called upon to substitute for the unit heads on occasion or to act regularly as assistants with cross-sectional authority.

After almost three years of exploratory operation of a rehabilitation medicine service under the kind of functional restructuring herein described, the author presents a reliable appraisal of the program.

The consolidation of the various rehabilitation medicine service sections along functional lines has resulted in improved patient-and-program-oriented services when compared to the baseline of operations prior to restructuring. There was also considerable improvement in intraservice and interservice communication in relation to patient treatment. Operational obstacles have been eliminated to expedite the inflow of referrals to the rehabilitation medicine service and the outflow of progress reports. Closer integration with overall hospital treatment has been established through the augmentation of liaison representation by therapists serving with each multidisciplinary team in the major psychiatric services and in the numerous smaller special programs in the hospital. The planning teams in the three functional units conducted more in-depth initial evaluations of medical rehabilitation and subsequent reevaluations of patients than had hitherto been possible, resulting in greater flexibility of services and in increased mobility of patients, both laterally among the units as well as vertically within each unit.

The initial impression that personnel in the rehabilitation medicine service can demonstrate dynamic capacities to successfully assume new treatment roles paralleling those of other members of the multidisciplinary team has been confirmed. Therapists and supervisors serving as liaison representatives regularly attend building staff and ward team meetings, as well as the planning team meetings held almost daily within each of the functional units in the rehabilitation medicine service. In addition, these specially selected personnel engage in in-depth interviewing of patients seen in the various staff and team meetings in order to recommend treatment objectives and therapy assignments in the rehabilitation medicine service that are in conformance with data and goals developed within their multidisciplinary team. Some of our liaison representatives have truly emerged as qualified rehabilitation specialists in rehabilitation medicine service activities, assuming the role of generalists by virtue of their enhanced professional capabilities.

The chiefs of the three functional units have likewise demonstrated similar dynamic qualities to exclude any need to seek out professional leadership from among other mental health disciplines to perform the required functions. In this connection, the expanded role of the coordinator of the rehabilitation medicine service as head of one of the three major units (industrial) has been justified by his performance as a member of the multidisciplinary team on a comparable level with other nonphysician service chiefs.

With the rapidly changing scene in society, in psychiatry and in hospitals and with the development of concepts of the "right to treatment," rehabilitation psychiatry must move forward. One must examine what skills and insights can be offered. Therapists must expand their scope beyond the traditional boundaries of their particular specialty. This is not to deny their skills but to explore how better to utilize them to provide needed services to the consumers—the patients. Since the length of stay in psychiatric hospitals becomes increasingly shorter, one must deliver services expeditiously and efficiently, providing for carry-over into the community. One must explore increasingly what patients need; what deficit they have; what assets, skills and potential they retain; and how their remaining assets can best be utilized for their treatment. One must regularly explore the consumers' desires, needs and responses and make the delivery of care and treatment an art and a science.

Section IV

SOCIALLY ORIENTED PROGRAMS

Chapter 7

RECREATIONAL THERAPY

John Eisele Davis, Sr.

Introduction

In the historical evolution of medicine from "sorcery to science," various forms of treatment have emerged as both physical and psychological modalities. In this process, selective physical activities have been refined and, in many cases, elevated to the status of therapy utilized by professional practitioners. As an acceptable part of this social process, recreation has attained the professional status of an ancillary therapy and the designation, "recreational therapist," has become a part of both social and medical literature.

Recreational therapists are now working in the nation's neuropsychiatric hospitals and rehabilitation centers providing a distinctive professional service to the psychotic and the neurotic individual, changing the image of treatment from the medieval concept of punishment and custodial care to the social ideal of today stressing active treatment and rehabilitation. It is in this galaxy of humane and vibrant treatment that the modern recreational therapist functions.

Psychologists, social service personnel, corrective therapists, manual art therapists, educational therapists, vocational counselors and others in the growing armamentarium of rehabilitation will find this concept and practice of recreational therapy of practical importance to their specializations. The refinement of techniques with increased clinical experience and better public understanding is developing these potentials into more sophisticated therapeutic tools. For the researcher particularly, play becomes a language useful not only in more effective treatment but in diagnosis and prognosis as well.

RECREATIONAL THERAPY

The Therapeutic Potential of Recreation

It is necessary to explore the phenomena of play as recreation and to delve into its basic structure and its psychological elements to understand its appeal to the individual in need of its services and to the medical educator attempting to disseminate its values. The therapist must understand and appreciate the unlimited variations of recreation as a vehicle of therapy. Some are the following:

1. Play is above all natural, and therefore allows the individual to express his own personality without the inhibitions which frequently distort behavior in the mentally sick.
2. Play is free and expressive. There is sheer physical abandon in play activity, not present in other types of active behavior.
3. Play is extraverting, serving to free the patient from himself into the interests and activities of others.
4. Play is modifiable, its many forms and graduations providing activity suited to the capacity and interests of many types.
5. Play may be competitive, awakening and expressive of aggressive traits.
6. Play may be cooperative, developing team organization and group feeling.
7. Play may be redirective, pointing the patient's interest toward more social behavior.
8. Play may be sublimatory giving outlet to blocked impulses, urges or desires, leading to a more acceptable level of behavior.
9. Play is interpretive, unfolding the patient's nature and showing his attitude toward himself, his environment and life generally.
10. Play may be progressive, enabling the patient to attain higher steps of social and physical advancement.
11. Play is integrative, enabling the patient to focus his attention and to organize his motor and mental field into a constructive pattern.

12. Play is inherently satisfying, attracting many patients (who are unable to do other things), into pleasurable and constructive activity.

From the foregoing, it is evident that the various types and gradations of play offer a distinctive and unique medium for a determination of the personality traits and treatment of the patient. The infectious nature of the play activity has the inherent quality of attractiveness. The patient becomes more labile under the influence of play participation and is more likely to give effective cooperation. These various aspects of play call attention to the fact that recreation is simply a highly motivated and significant part of life itself, and therefore, its development and modification for therapy is restricted only by the depth and width of the concepts employed. Recreation may be thought of as an art, a science, a discipline or simply as a point of view. One may stress the mechanics of the activity, the aim and the mental attitudes. Such a synthetic view encompasses the most helpful concept of its use as therapy.[1]

General Aims of Recreational Therapy

In order to project realistic aims of recreation as therapy, one must determine just what it is, its nature and structure. For this purpose, recreational therapy may be defined as "the medical employment of free play (formal and informal) including art (verbal and nonverbal) activities."

Recreational therapy, if it is to become an integral part of activity therapy in modern treatment, must fit into the objectives of physical medicine rehabilitation which provides diagnostic techniques and appropriate specialized therapy to

1. contribute to more prompt recovery and shorter hospital stays for patients with acute medical or surgical problems,
2. assist the long-term or handicapped patient to adjust to the demands of an appropriate posthospital economic and social environment in order to reduce the possibility of readmission and
3. help the patient whose discharge is improbable to achieve a measure of independence within the hospital which will reflect savings in the cost of his hospitalization.

Specifically, physical medicine rehabilitation therapy is directed so as to

1. restore function to the maximum level of which the patient is capable,
2. qualitatively and quantitatively evaluate the degree of impairment and the extent of residual capacity for social and economic activities involved in the medical rehabilitation objectives determined appropriate for him and
3. furnish practical and effective motivation for rehabilitation.

In line with psychoanalytic concepts, more specific therapeutic aims have been developed in the employment of recreational activities:

A. For relief of guilt feelings, repetitive activities and a general attitude of firmness upon the part of the therapist are employed. Various exercises are modified so as to make them monotonous or boring including such diverse activities as exercise on the rowing machine, cleaning bowling balls, dusting stall bars and cleaning the floors of the exercise clinic. The patient may be placed in the play situation so as to minimize the ego satisfaction one would normally gain as a result of skill performance. An "underdog" relationship may be established so as to allow the patient to drain off some of his excessive need for the emotional relief of guilt feelings.

B. For socially acceptable creative accomplishment, the patient should be placed in an activity situation which will provide success. He should have an opportunity to succeed through the discharge of his ability without extreme effort and should be given recognition and praise for his accomplishment. The therapist should be careful not to expose the patient to an overly competitive situation in which he might become humiliated. In addition to the manipulation of the patient into various positions on the various sports teams so as to build up his feelings for success, such other activities as keeping athletic records, scoring, umpiring and teaching others to play are indicated as a means of giving the patient socially creative accomplishments.

C. For acceptable expression of aggression, recreation becomes a most important adjuvant in treating the hostility of the psychotic and psychoneurotic patient. It is commonplace to note the hostile individual working off his aggression against people by hitting the punching bag. There are many ways in which active recreation may be of distinctive value in this relationship, through more or less direct activity such as hitting a ball or more indirectly in such gross activities as swimming. In various types of hitting games, the patient may identify the object with persons in his fantasy. Such games as handball, paddleball and water polo are particularly effective for these specific therapeutic aims. By lifting weights many patients are able to develop a gradual and systematic discharge of their hostility in a more constructive pattern of therapy. The role of the therapist is two-fold here: (a) to encourage direct verbal expressions of conscious hostility and (b) to encourage suppression of hostility. The play experience therefore should be structured so as to allow the patient to "blow off steam," to verbalize his thoughts without censorship.[1]

Classification of Activities

Activities can be classified as (A) informal play, (B) calisthenics and other formal activities, (C) art forms and (D) creative play

The psychotic and psychoneurotic patients are able to accommodate themselves to one or more of a myriad of spontaneous activities from simple to complex. The activities can range from elemental phylogenetic forms such as swimming to the highly complex gradations of baseball, tennis and golf in which precise trainable skills are developed. It should be pointed out in this connection that the nonorganic types such as the schizophrenic have no impairment of their motor sphere and can perform the most intricate athletic skills once they become interested and motivated, while the organic types characterized by the *dementia paralytica* category can perform only simple and uncomplicated physical movements such as throwing a ball. In neurological cases illustrated by the *encephalitis lethargica* group, one is confronted by a syndrome of slowed, retarded movement, and compensating elements of accurate performance are retained. For these individuals such sport activities as billiards and pool are indicated. These patients are easily motivated and enjoy such activities that challenge their sense of accuracy.

The recreational therapist, to be effective in dealing with psychiatric types, must be able to understand the motivational-psychological elements entering into each individual case. As he gains increasing clinical experience, he will be impressed with the problems of enlisting the various disease categories into purposeful activities. In general, he will find that the schizophrenic group must be directed away from their fantasy and daydreams. They are farther divorced from reality than the manic depressive group, for example. In working successfully with them it will be necessary to explore the early life history of the individual to seek preformed play patterns. For example, if the schizophrenic patient has played baseball in his youth, it may be possible to reactivate his performance in this activity or at least some part of it, such as throwing and catching a baseball. On the other hand, the *dementia paralytica* patient, an organic type, is easily inducted into play activities since he frequently has grandoise ideas and life presents itself as a happy experience. His disordered judgment will prompt him to attempt activities far beyond his skill capability. He enjoys play and the therapist should modify the activities to meet his lowered skill adaptation level.

FORMAL ACTIVITIES: Calisthenics, graded in complexity and tempo to meet the distinctive interest and motor levels of the psychotic and psychoneurotic patient, is recognized as a valuable adjunct to the overall armamentarium of therapy. Calisthenics, carefully graded, would be adapted to provide an opportunity for patient leadership and would be planned beyond the areas of physical exercise as a psychotherapeutic activity involving group discussion and social interplay. A program of group calisthenics must become more than formally directed exercise if it is to attain a valid therapeutic status. Socializing elements in which the therapist encourages patient leadership, group interplay and verbal discussion provide an ideal repertoire to be utilized by the therapist. The informal potentials of calisthenics should be developed.

The disinterested lethargic patient may present a characteristic problem shown in a slowing up of the tempo of the exercise and a gradual restriction of the range of movement. Modification of the exercise to include touching certain points of the body, such as the knees and the feet, may help to promote a fuller range of movement. The therapist should, however, understand that the problem is psychogenic except in the organic cases and should seek means to attract the patients attention by the provision of more interesting experiences. He should look for preformed play patterns and, in general, should explore the distinctive needs of the patient rather than the purely recreational aims. He should delve deeply into the modern therapeutic philosophy of play as a cooperative, as well as competitive, experience in renewed attempts to create a more effective social milieu.

ART FORMS: Art, one of the newer forms of therapy, provides an important element in medical recreation. As a fundamental viewpoint, it should be noted that art involves the creative expression, by the individual of a slice of life itself in relationship to his total way of living and is not merely a revelation of psychic material. Art may be used as a portrayal of an interest in the objective world, in the coordination of the seeing eye and the recreating hand, while at the same time providing a picture of the personality of the artist. This multidimensional aspect has made art attractive to the psychotic individual. In this regard, one must realize that the recreational therapist works with two forms of expression, the objective and the subjective. The patient confronts his material surroundings and tests their reality at the objective level. He expresses his emotional feeling, his fantasies and delusional ideas at the so-called subjective level. In the literature, painting is recognized as a valuable art form. Haun informs us:

> Under the medically oriented guidance of a competent instructor, the fine arts (painting especially) have three potentially significant values to the psychiatric patient:
>
> 1. They afford an important vehicle for a reaction in which material at almost any level of consciousness can be externalized. Since the limiting factors consist only of the artistic conventions accepted by the patient, the results are usually remarkable both for their frankness and/or their relevance to the problem.
>
> 2. They enforce the use of as much of the total personality as the

patient is able to mobilize and, for this reason, exert a greater integrating force than the noncreative occupations. As the result of total personality involvement, the created object becomes identified with the patient and the field is prepared for an important extension of his self-critical faculty into the world of reality.

3. The process of creation enforces a manipulation of tangible objects and, in this respect, is oriented toward reality and away from intrapsychic phenomenon. The products of creation which are invariably intended as nonverbal communications at times represent the first break in the crushing loneliness of the psychotic, the first human bridge from illness to social health.[3]

CREATIVE PLAY: The highest form of recreation is exemplified in creative play which unveils not only the physical, but also the spiritual, world and reveals the soul of the individual, his innermost nature. To understand the psychological impact of creative play as a milieu of recreational therapy, it must be realized that the mental patient is ever seeking overt ways to express his unique personality as he tries to change the world around him to conform to his bizarre life-style. These artistic expressions at times provide an acceptable, nonverbal communication to the outside world. Adolph Meyer expressed his therapy potential as follows: "A patient can tell in his activity what he cannot tell in the formal interview."[4] This basic statement provides a fundamental differentiation between the verbal and nonverbal levels of communication. The psychotic patient reveals his ideas, feelings and desires in his physical activities, especially in the spontaneity of free play. His verbal communication is most frequently confused and in some cases incoherent. For the regressed psychotic patient, play may well become the most effective language. For example, definite traits of aggression, submission and even hostility are shown in his play activities.

Understanding the modifiability of play structure, its gradations, tempo and color, the therapist is able to give the psychotic patient a broad and deep panorama of zeastful activities in which his hopes, discouragements, triumphs and defeats are given ample opportunity for expression. The artistic complement of recreation is best illustrated by the dance, an activity of the highest allure to the psychotic patient. The gyrations of the dance, the movement of the body in tune with physiological and phylogenetic energies and motivations, the changing environment and the rhythm and tempo of music combine to create an ideal milieu for expressive therapy. Group, companion or individual dance forms merge disordered antisocial patterns into a social and socializing relationship of special significance in the evolution of the dance as a valuable therapeutic medium.

Research

Stein, Sieka, Goldstein and Johns[2] describe an innovative research project in recreational therapy involving psychiatric patients in a hospital setting. Many of the principles of behavioral analysis are applied.

About fourteen months ago, after organization of a behavioral rehabilitation ward for medical and psychiatric patients, it became apparent that without recreational rehabilitation many patients were unable to successfully adjust to community life. They would return to alcoholic behavior or severely limited activity eventuating in physical and emotional deterioration, even though vocational remediation may have been accomplished. Moreover, many of the physically and emotionally handicapped veterans treated had no viable recreational repertoires, and on further examination remarkable deficits were found in their histories indicating a failure of supportive leisure time behaviors and activities.

In response to these and corollary findings, the recreation and ward staffs conceived a developmental recreation program employing many of the general principles of applied behavior analysis. The involvement of the recreation service directly on the unit was enthusiastic even though the program was somewhat revolutionary and had no precedent in the literature.

The principles of behavioral measurement and reinforcement were applied to recreational development in three consecutive stages or phases: Initially, a volunteer "behavior manager" trained in applied behavior analysis and recreation is assigned to selected patients and assists them in an analysis of their total recreational repertoire. Phase One is an *exploratory* stage in which the patient counts and records daily the number of new activities he investigates and attempts in and out of the hospital. He maintains a behavior chart on the rate of his activity in this phase and in the succeeding phases. Phase Two consists of measuring and charting a more limited number of recreational activities which are *sampled* and engaged in more intensively; again these may be hospital- or community-based. In the third and final phase, the managers assist patients in measuring gains in *proficiency* in the activities on which the patient elects to concentrate the highest proportion of his time.

Managers consistently reinforce their patients for gains in each phase through positive verbal and social feedback contingent on data collection. The author finds that the patients accelerate their rates of recreational behavior as a function of this reinforcement. As increasing proficiency is gained the manager is phased out, since the patients' ability to perform is itself reinforcing; thus, the manager's praise is eventually replaced by the rewarding aspects of the activity. It is also apparent that increases in social contact are closely associated with increasing recreational pursuits. Thus, healthy socialization is an additional outcome which is similarly charted and reinforced.[2]

Perspective for the Future

Recreation has become a part of the way of life in America and, as an essential, is destined to grow at the fast pace of the country's social and economic development. Recreation is a slice of life itself, and its myriad forms and gradations are reflected in both local and universal play patterns. Similarities of play structures in the various cultures are explained as the result of man's biologic inheritance while variations are produced by social and environmental forces.

To gain a realistic perspective of recreational therapy in the future one must understand the following:

1. New forms of play will evolve with the changes of industrialized living and the dynamic psychosocial philosophy which is permeating the modern community, and these new forms create innovative activities with definite therapy potential.

2. The physical techniques of play will be modified further and refined to meet the medical requirements of this new professional discipline.

3. The therapeutic aims of recreation will be directed primarily to the social needs of the community rather than to the indiscriminate demands of the crowd.

4. Play will be explored as "the language of the patient," though he may be able to communicate with the doctor, nurse, therapist and his fellows.

5. For the regressed, negativistic, nonverbal patient, play will be examined as the potentially preferable vehicle for effective communication.

6. New observational methods pertaining to psychologically oriented techniques of spontaneous play and formal activities will enable the therapist to gather valuable behavioral data of special significance and assistance to the doctor and the psychologist in the determination of treatment, diagnosis and prognosis.

7. The present stress in training in recreational techniques will shift to an examination and study of the psychodynamic potential of spontaneous play and also of the formal activities such as calisthenics which complete the exercise repertoire.

8. Leaders in the growing areas of recreational therapy will pay increasing attention to its public image and will project this relatively new discipline to the community as an effective arm of the comprehensive medical practice and rehabilitation regimens which are restoring the disabled and elevating the quality of life.

REFERENCES

1. Davis, John Eisele: *Clinical Applications of Recreational Therapy*. Springfield, Thomas, 1952, pp. 9-11, 64-67.
2. Goldstein, Mark Kane, Johns, Jerry, Sieka, Frank L., and Stein, Gerald: Personal communication. February 7, 1974.
3. Haun, P.: *Psychopathological Art*. Paris, France, International Congress of Psychiatry, 1950. Monograph prepared by the Veterans Administration.
4. Personal communication.

Chapter 8

POETRY THERAPY: AN ADDED DIMENSION IN REHABILITATION

Jack J. Leedy

A well chosen anthology is a complete dispensary of medicine for the more common mental disorders and may be used as much for prevention as cure.

Robert Graves

Possessed of intuitive wisdom, the Greeks recognized the healing power of poetry. They worshipped Apollo, the personification of the sun and the father of Aesculapius, as a dual god of medicine and poetry.

Poems, like dreams, are another road to the unconscious. We live in prose and dream in poetry.

Poetry therapy is the use of poetry as an added dimension in treatment. The principles and techniques of poetry therapy are now used in individual and group psychotherapy, and in poetry therapy groups as part of social rehabilitation programs. Poems are written during sessions by the patients about symptoms, fantasies, dreams, daydreams, conflicts or relationships with relatives, friends or associates. Catharsis, or the release of deep feelings through the writing, reading or discussing of the poems, is therapeutic. The patients also bring poems written by others to their sessions, as these poems remind them of their own symptoms or conflicts. The therapist will also choose verses useful in therapy, however fine or poor they may appear to critics old or new. Some of them may be of the most inferior, some of the most superior, orders of poetry: For poetry therapy, the standard is not whether the work is good or great poetry, but whether it will help heal the ill.

A great pioneer in the use of poetry in general medicine and internal medicine is Doctor Paul F. Whitaker of Kinston, North Carolina. Doctor Whitaker has served as President of the Medical Society of the State of North Carolina, Vice-president of the American College of Physicians, President of the Seaboard Medical Association and President of the Medical Foundation of North Carolina. The book *More Than Medicine*[2] compiled and edited with his wife, Ruth N. Whitaker, tell of Doctor Whitaker's experiences in the use of poetry as treatment in medical practice and contains many of the poems he has written for the past fifty years.

Setting a world precedent in 1968, Doctor Whitaker presented lectures in poetry therapy as part of his course in human ecology to the medical students at the University of North Carolina School of Medicine at Chapel Hill. His poem, "Personal Satisfactions," sums up his philosophy:

If I can through kind and thoughtful action
Bring to another peace and satisfaction;
If I can by sympathy and understanding
Guide another to a safe and happy landing;
If I can by words of kindness spoken
Ease the pain of a spirit broken;
If I can help fulfill the longing
And bring a soul from night to morning;
If I can aid in solving even one frustration
And guide another to a happy consummation;
Then I bring myself a happy inner glow
As real as sunlight on the drifted snow.

The Uses of Poetry

INSOMNIA: Rather than immediately prescribing a sedative to relieve insomnia, the physician should try to encourage his patients to read one or more of the following poems several times before bedtime, and to give these poems a fair chance to work (there have been no deaths reported from an over-dosage of poetry):

"Hymn to the Night"	Henry Wadsworth Longfellow
"A Ballad of Dreamland"	Algernon Charles Swinburne
"To Sleep"	William Wordsworth
"Night"	Paul F. Whitaker
"Oft, in the Stilly Night"	Thomas Moore
"The Things That Cause of Quiety Life"	Henry Howard, Earl of Surrey
"A Good Night"	Francis Quarles
"To Sleep"	John Keats
"Now the Day is Over" (hymn)	
"Care-charming Sleep"	
"Thou Easer of All Woes"	John Fletcher

There are spelling weaving poems that are also worth trying: "La Belle Dame Sans Merci" by John Keats, "Annabel Lee" by Edgar Allan Poe, "Tintern Abbey" by William Wordsworth. Using poems to induce sleep is similar to the use of sedatives. Some patients respond to one and not to another. Most effective in the author's patients' experiences has been "A Ballad of Dreamland." Though the patients may require a sedative, these poems will help relax them and thereby encourage them to sleep.

ANXIETY: Rather than rushing to prescribe a tranquilizer for nervousness, the physician should first consider suggesting one or more of the following poems to his patients:

"Anxiety"	Paul F. Whitaker
"I'm Nobody"	Emily Dickinson
"The Road Not Taken"	Robert Frost
"Time, You Old Gypsy Man"	Ralph Hodgson
"Ode On A Grecian Urn"	John Keats
"The Day Is Done"	Henry Wadsworth Longfellow
"I Celebrate Myself"	Walt Whitman
"She Dwelt Among The Untrodden Ways"	William Wordsworth
"The Lake Isle of Innisfree"	William Butler Yeats

In the labor room, the husband or boyfriend is encouraged to read these poems to his beloved. Hospitalized patients, particularly those who are about to be operated upon, are encouraged to write poems about their fears, fantasies and anxieties. Patients will be able to write important things in poetry that they are unable to say face-to-face to the doctor or nurse. As a result of releasing powerful feelings in their poetry, the patients require fewer preoperative tranquilizers and sedatives. These same principles may be used postoperatively.

Through his poetry the patient entices the interest of his therapist. In effect, the patient says: "Here are my sorrows and my joys and my fears. It pleases me to share them with you."

The late Doctor Smiley Blanton told of the power of poetry to help his patients when they felt anxious, overwhelmed, frustrated, defeated, angry or bereaved. He used poetry with his patients as an ancillary therapy to buoy their flagging spirits through the use of direct encouragement, hopeful examples and exhortation, and he urged his patients to memorize poems to carry them through times of crisis.

In 1928 the late Eli Greifer, a poet and pharmacist, began a campaign to show that a poem's didactic message, its quite explicit moral, has a specific healing power in itself and can help relieve anxiety. He founded the Messagists Club and the Remedy Rhyme Gallery in Greenwich Village, New York City, As a volunteer he organized a poetry group in 1959 at Cumberland Hospital, Brooklyn, New York. His ideas have spread to hospitals, nursing homes, rehabilitation centers and organizations such as the State Island Aid for Retarded Children, Inc., where poetry groups have become a part of the total treatment plan. He is a marvelous exemplar of the volunteer who, under guidance of the physician, can be of crucial help to patients.

Depression and Suicide: In addition to prescribing antidepressant medications, the therapist should encourage his patients to write of their hostilities and guilts which usually precipitate depression.

When choosing poems for his patients, the therapist should suggest poems that are close in feeling to the mood or mental tempo of the patients. This is the important isoprinciple of poetry therapy. Depressed patients are helped by poems sad and gloomy in tone, yet having stanzas that reflect hope and optimism, especially toward their conclusion. By reading, studying, memorizing, reciting or creating this kind of poem, or interpreting the poem in spontaneous body movements, depressed patients come to feel that they are not alone in their depressions, that others are also depressed, that others have been depressed and have recovered from their depressions and that no disgrace attaches to victims of extreme alterations of mood. For them, crying precipitated by a poem is often therapeutically helpful; the poem becomes symbolically an understanding person with whom they can share their despair.

The therapist should avoid poems that offer no hope or that might increase guilt feelings or that encourage and glorify suicide. Poems that encourage silence and discourage vocalization, particularly feelings of hostility, are contraindicated.

For a few days to several weeks before a suicidal attempt, there are prodromal clues or indirect hints of unconscious intentions that may be detected in the patients' poems. These patients want to be rescued and want their deaths prevented. The patient's internal debate in the Supreme Court of the mind often results in a five to four decision for death; five factors make life intolerable, and four encourage the patient to go on living. The physician should try to convert this one vote from death to life by counteracting the patient's feeling of hopelessness. One way is for the therapist and the patient to write a poem together. Not concerned with spelling, rhythm or rhyme, the patient first writes a line, and then the doctor writes a line. This alternating procedure continues until the poem is complete, and neither has anything further to add. Often this technique relieves tensions and establishes communication. The patient's ego defenses are reinforced, and his feelings of hope, love and trust are renewed. He wants to live.

Many suicidal patients want to contribute a lung or a kidney for a transplant operation. Reports show that if suicidal patients donate a pint of blood, often their suicidal trends are alleviated. If these patients are encouraged to write a poem and donate it to the doctor, the poem symbolically represents an organ or a pint of blood and is thereby helpful therapeutically. Writing a poem is like converting blood into ink.

In the book, *Poetry Therapy*,[1] which the author edited, there is a list of poems suitable for use in poetry therapy. For depressed patients, poems like the following are suggested:

"Today"	Thomas Carlyle
"Light Shining Out of Darkness"	William Cowper
"The Chambered Nautilus"	Oliver Wendell Holmes
"The Day Is Done"	Henry Wadsworth Longfellow
"On His Blindness"	John Milton
"Ode To The West Wind"	Percy Bysshe Shelley
"The Celestial Surgeon"	Robert Louis Stevenson
"In No Strange Land"	Francis Thompson
Psalm 23: "The Lord Is My Shepherd" *(Dominus regit me)*	
"The Eternal Goodness"	John Greenleaf Whittier
"Tears"	Paul F. Whitaker

Drug Addiction and Alcoholism: Poetry therapy is now being used in detoxification centers such as the Bernstein Institute and in the Odyssey[3] and Samaritan Houses in New York. The poems of Kahlil Gibran as found in *The Prophet* are helpful to addicts. Is it not worthwhile trying to convert drug addicts to poetry addicts? How wonderful it would be to progress from heroin to Herrick, Henley, Holmes, Hopkins, Hughes, Homer, Heywood, Hogg, Hardy, Herbert, Holderlin, von Hoffmannsthal and Hilda Doolittle.

The most difficult patients are drug addicts, and now the doctor has a new ally, the metaphors of the poet, which may be more meaningful than technical scientific language with all its precision and clarity. To establish one meaningful relationship with a drug addict through a poem, where two minds may meet for however brief a period, is a thing not to be dismissed lightly. And who is to say that poetry does not release the energy for this first outreach to a more meaningful way of life?

Many may have to travel the lesser known highways in order to arrive where they are. Poetry is one of these highways—one that has not been too heavily traveled yet. It may be that for some it will provide a safer, more meaningful journey, because of them the signposts are written in langauge he can read and understand.

If children must get high on something, they should be encouraged to get high on poetry. Surely the poems of William

Blake, Lewis Carroll, Countee Cullen, Emily Dickinson, Bob Dylan, Robert Frost, Langston Hughes, Ben Jonson, John Keats, Paul F. Whitaker, Stephen Spender, Wallace Stevens, Robert Louis Stevenson, Arthur Lerner, Dylan Thomas, Robert Burns, Walt Whitman, William Shakespeare and William Butler Yeats are able to give children bigger kicks than heroin, LSD, marijuana or glue.

The poems of the parents of children and adolescents in treatment are of special interest. At times there are clues in these poems that reveal that the parent on an unconscious level actually wants his or her child to become an addict. At this point the therapist could try counseling and guidance with the parent. If these measures fail to resolve the parental conflicts, psychotherapy would be indicated.

Physicians have a new tool, poetry therapy, in the total treatment plan for alcoholics. Doctor Ruth Fox, former medical director of the National Council on Alcoholism and past president of the American Medical Society on Alcoholism, now uses the principles and techniques of poetry therapy with her alcoholic patients.

PSYCHOSOMATIC (PSYCHOPHYSIOLOGICAL) DISORDERS: Peptic ulcers and other psychosomatic disorders may be interpreted in part as poems struggling to be born. This is to imply that these patients have emotional conflicts that are precipitating and perpetuating factors of their psychosomatic disorders, and that these conflicts can be defused and sometimes resolved with the use of poetry as an added dimension in the total treatment plan. Unique here is the process whereby poetry therapy contributes to the liberation of the patients' imprisoned or frozen creativity. As the patients write, talk and react to their own poetry, the material produced serves as a therapeutic tool, which, when added to the traditional therapeutic measures, enables the patients to accelerate their healing.

The poem may touch off a series of psychic events that contribute to the patient's feeling of well-being in a way similar to what is experienced after having been involved in a creative act. In the creative process, the magnet of unconscious interest scans the storehouse of memories and their associated affects, attracting the image experiences related to the conscious theme. The organizing ego so molds and shapes these into a communicable form that other egos that perceive reality in a somewhat similar fashion can sense the poet's ideation and affective messages. Thus, it is the world of reality that provides the standard datum that serves as the common medium enabling the patient's unconscious to receive stimuli from the poet's unconscious. The patient has shared in a process of recreation. Perception has been expanded, doubts and uncertainty reduced, feelings validated and guidelines underscored. For a brief period the patient has felt a human feeling that was his very own. For a while he was "with it," in and of the world of human feeling. He has established a beachhead on the shore of a troubled sea and now has the hope of being able to fan out in many directions.

Psychosomatic diseases often start as defense against the intrusion by outside schedules upon biologic patterns. In attempting to control the unpleasant routine, the counterroutine begins to control the young protestor. Most mothers know by instinct that rhythmic movements soothe and relax the baby. Doctor Jules Masserman explains this dependency on rhythm as one of the magic "Ur-defenses" of man, the miraculous transformation of chaos into pleasurable order. The outside beat is incorporated into a personal beat and order of time. The rhyme and rhythm of poetry often have a much more compelling force than the actual meaning of the words. Through rhythm, old phylogenetic memories are aroused, and rhythm helps us memorize what formerly seemed chaotic.

Rhythm, in short, is life itself. The tune is the mind. In the rhythm and repetition of themes in poetry, emotional abreaction takes place.

REFERENCES

1. Leedy, Jack J. (Ed.): *Poetry Therapy*. Philadelphia, Lippincott, 1969.
2. Whitaker, Paul F. and Ruth N.: *More Than Medicine*. New York, Carlton, 1969.
3. Leedy, Jack J. (Ed.): *Poetry The Healer*. Philadelphia, Lippincott, 1973.

Section V

HOSPITAL VOCATIONAL PROGRAMS

Chapter 9

INCENTIVE THERAPIES

William Winick

HISTORY OF INCENTIVE PROGRAMS IN EUROPE AND AMERICA

Work as a treatment modality for mental illness has a history dating back to antiquity. The literature indicates it was used by early physicians such as Hippocrates and Galen. Early pioneers in hospital psychiatry wrote of its ameliorating and beneficial effects. Among the advocates of this form of treatment were Pinel, Tuke, Rush, Kirkbride and Bryant.

For years patients carried out many work assignments in hospitals and performed very well, oftentimes with expertise equal to that of a paid employee.

In the early 1920's Holland developed sheltered workshops where the patients were paid. After World War II, a number of sheltered workshops for the disabled, including care of the mentally ill, were established. They provide a job for everyone capable of working. Under various laws the government subsidizes the handicapped worker under what is known as the Social Employment Scheme or under Poor Law provisions. The Dutch are convinced that investment in their mental defectives and chronic schizophrenics has paid off handsomely.[2]

In The Hague Doctor N. Speyers has a unique system whereby he controls all admissions to a 200-bed hospital for a population of 600,000. Every mentally ill patient is screened by Doctor Speyers' office, and if at all possible, the patient is placed in a sheltered workshop and on any other indicated therapy, as well as in a living arrangement in the community that will meet his needs. Every attempt is made to prevent hospitalization. By these means Doctor Speyers prevents admissions to the hospital and maintains the patient in the community. Hospitalization is provided only when the patient is too ill to use any of the available resources.

It has been noted that the Dutch have demonstrated through their rehabilitation program that it is possible to raise the productive capacity of the handicapped. The other far-reaching accomplishment that has been demonstrated is that hospitalization can be averted, or the period of hospitalization can be shortened, if there is a community-based program for patients.

In Germany Doctor Herman Simon at Guetersloh pioneered a paid work program in 1927. His work was based on the conviction that inactivity and frequent exposure to the spectacle of degraded behavior are mentally and socially demoralizing. He made every effort to offer all of his patients productive work. His writings reveal him to be a warm humanitarian who believed in discipline and development of sound work habits, with an appeal to the patient's basic responsibility to his community.

In France Doctor Paul Sevadon has been the leader of paid work programs. He has developed two hospitals: one outside Paris and the other near Versailles. He has very well staffed hospitals with personnel who have a great deal of enthusiasm and conviction for his programs of social and occupational therapy. Patients receive pay for the work they do for the hospital community. The hospital is organized along democratic lines and patients are encouraged to be involved and active participants. Doctor Sevadon feels that mentally ill patients regress and that work at various levels of complexity helps them to a more mature personality integration. This theory has not been proved; however, some observers are impressed with the stimulating environment and high morale, which are important ingredients of the therapeutic community.[4]

In Russia patients are seriously occupied in meaningful work. They produce materials for practical use, such as fountain pens, buttons, hammocks, gymnasium equipment, fabrics and furniture. The Soviet Union considers work the most meaningful and significant of human activities. The Soviet psychiatrists place less emphasis on particular capacities than they do on the individual's response to a total situation in which his capacities, interests and motivation all play a part. Their work therapy is not a "make work" program—no aimless tinkering, no feeble attempts at ceramics, finger painting, etc. They have a practical, realistic approach to patients and have high standards of proficiency.[29]

The Scandinavian countries, Switzerland and the British Isles have work therapy programs. In England there are probably the most sophisticated and the best developed work therapy programs. They have been imaginative and are known for their rehabilitation of the chronically mentally ill. They have had long experience with such programs, and after World War II these gradually expanded. Programs consist of a wide array of sheltered workshops in and out of hospitals, making and selling products, subcontracting and operating small businesses for a profit. They also provide a variety of sheltered living arrangements such as their hostels, foster family care, hotels within the community and discharge cottages on the hospital grounds.

Some of England's better known hospitals having industrial therapy are Banstead Hospital (Sutton), Netherne Hospital (Coulsden South, Surrey), Cheadle Royal Hospital (Cheadle, Cheshire), Mapperly Hospital (Nottingham) and the Glenside Hospital (Bristol).[2]

Although the British were pioneers in industrial therapy even prior to World War II, it was after war that they began to put much more emphasis on this program. A survey made by the late H. B. Kidd, D.P.M., consultant psychiatrist to Towers Hospital (Leicester) shows that seventy-eight of ninety hospitals treating psychiatric patients now have "industrial therapy."[9]

Maxwell Jones, who developed the therapeutic community concept, had an important influence on the expansion of work therapies for mental patients in England. He stressed that what matters most is the patient's ability to interact with other people in a satisfactory way and to accept authority. He emphasized social rehabilitation as most important if the patient is to obtain employment and adjust to it.[15]

Paid work (or industrial therapy programs, as they are known in England) has had a difficult time being accepted across the Atlantic Ocean in the United States. Although there were isolated programs established over the years, it was not until the advent of psychotropic drugs in the early 1950's that more and more chronic patients were responding to these drugs and becoming capable of working and returning to the community. Some sheltered workshops began to recognize this problem and started in a limited way to accept these patients. The Altro Workshop, which was primarily involved in rehabilitating tuberculosis patients, is one of the pioneers in this area. Under Bertram Black, its staff began accepting and working with the mentally ill. The Goodwill Industries and the Jewish Vocational Services have also played an important role in the development of sheltered workshops in this country.

There were very few in-hospital paid programs. In the late 1950's and 1960's a few programs began emerging, such as at Central Islip State Hospital (Long Island, New York, Metropolitan Hospital (Waltham, Massachusetts) and the VA Hospitals (Bedford, Massachusetts; Brockton, Massachusetts; and Palo Alto, California). VA psychiatric hospitals have always placed a great deal of emphasis on the work role in treatment programs for their patients. It, therefore, has been a natural evolutionary process for these hospitals to have a high level of interest in work as a treatment modality. The agency itself is charged by law with the responsibility of providing vocational education and rehabilitation.

The sheltered workshop movement in the community is a growing one. More of them are providing placements for former mental patients as well as for mental retardates. The approach now is to take care of the multihandicapped. There is no question that workshops will continue to grow and will play a very important part in the maintenance of these people who need such help and support.[1,3,13,14,30,31]

A growing emphasis is being placed on community psychiatry, short periods of hospitalization and early placement in the community. This has been an outgrowth of the studies made by the Joint Commission on Mental Illness and Health, as well as the Community Mental Health Acts of the 1960's. There is also a growing emphasis on community rehabilitation and incentive work programs being utilized in halfway houses, comprehensive health centers and mental hygiene clinics. There is also a growing movement for more sheltered living arrangements in combination with work placements and business arrangements as pioneered by Fairweather, et al.[7] at the Menlo Park Division of the VA Hospital, Palo Alto, California.[8]

The roles of union and management are changing toward greater acceptance of the mentally ill as employees. Industry in some instances provides on-the-job training and transitional work experiences. Industrial managers are very receptive to rehiring their employees who have required psychiatric treatment. There are specific programs which are geared to orienting the business community to the need for work for the former mental patient. Rehabilitation specialists and placement personnel play an important role in supporting these ex-patients who are placed in industry, and they act as a liaison between the treatment team and the industry or individual who has hired them.[17]

Two of the prime examples of unions working closely with manufacturers on this problem are those of the Amalgamated Clothing Workers of America and the New York Clothing Manufacturers. They have taken an enlightened approach and work closely with the industries they are associated with the help and assist members who have an emotional disorder which interfers with their work adjustment.[18]

THERAPEUTIC EFFECTS AND MEANING OF WORK

Why are there proponents of work as therapy, pursuing it zealously and promoting its use? Anyone who has worked with chronically mentally ill patients recognizes that motivating patients to work and providing useful, meaningful work for a large number of patients are difficult. Traditional therapies, such as occupational therapies and hospital assignments in the laundry, in the greenhouse and on the wards performing housekeeping chores, and other such assignments without pay, did not in the main do much for patients' morale, nor did they bring much meaning to the patients.

Peffer, in his use of the member-employee program in VA hospitals, assigned patients responsibilities and provided opportunities for decision-making as well as paying them for their work, which had a wholesome effect on them. He made the point that money was a "powerful motivator" and that patients are much more responsive to paid assignments.[24]

Those who have experience with incentive programs see marked changes in the behavior of the patients in contrast to transitional programs where patients function in a very routine, oftentimes sleepy fashion.

In reviewing studies of large samples of patients, such as the Oakland (California) Bureau of Social Work and the VA Psychiatric Evaluation Project Studies, it becomes clear that traditional treatment programs are unsuccessful in returning the majority of patients to the community as self-supporting members. The large-scale studies of Freeman and Simmons[8] and of Gurel[11] have shown that the common practice of expecting a patient to find and to hold regular employment on his own after hospitalization is unrealistic.

A study at the Brockton (Mass.) VA Hospital indicates that much employment of the mentally ill simply reflects the common practice of automatically withholding the opportunity for an institutionalized patient to work while hospitalized.[28]

Simmons points out that many hospital programs have ill prepared the mental patient for the world of work or for community living, thus leading to relapses and rehospitalization. The importance of work and its ability to prevent personality disorganized seems to be ignored in the treatment process.[25]

Since work is important to all of us and necessary, it is incumbent upon treatment centers to provide training and experience for mental patients to reenter the community and be able to be employed. The paid work program offers this opportunity. The reason this is so is that it can make realistic demands on the patient, and he must accept these if he is to remain on the program. He must adhere to rules of promptness, observe quality and quantity standards and learn to relate to fellow employees and supervisors. He must put up with noise and dirt, observe coffee break schedules and no smoking rules and learn to become a reliable, proficient employee. This kind of experience is the nearest to a real work situation that can be provided a patient. It is an excellent mechanism for providing this experience and also is a means whereby the patient's abilities and readiness for outside employment can be evaluated. This kind of information makes placement of a patient in industry much easier.

Work has other meanings for the patient in terms of teaching him skills and good work habits. He also learns how to socialize. He feels less lonely and isolated, becoming a part of a group. He avoids boredom and receives satisfactions from the respect and acceptance of his fellow workers. He changes his self-concept from that of a patient to that of a worker, which is extremely important especially as he prepares to enter the community. This kind of a transitional program makes it much easier for him to adjust. The work he does has meaning for him, as he is being paid for it. He is the recipient of a positive reinforcement, his paycheck. He gains more control over his environment by virtue of the fact that he has money and can do things that he wishes to do for himself. Time has meaning because he is being paid for it. The patient does not evade his assignments because he knows that absenteeism means loss of money[24]

Work is meaningful to people in different ways, according to Freud, depending upon the experiences the individual has had with parental figures or siblings during the first five or six years. The individual is conditioned to authority and to attitudes during this period. He carries over these attitudes to the work situation.

Neo-Freudians like Erickson do not agree *in toto,* feeling that the latency period, when the adolescent first begins to think about work, to separate from the family and to look to achievement awards, is a very important period for the individual in his attitudes toward work and its meaning for him. There is a need for the individual to have good working models with which to identify. It does appear that this is borne out by studies and reports on the underprivileged and those who work with them in sheltered workshops or on-the-job training.[12]

Man validates himself through his work. His role in society is the occupation he follows. People know him by the work he does. Society categorizes him and people identify him by his vocation. They also have certain expectations of him when his type of work is known. There are prestigious and nonprestigious jobs. That is not to say, however, that one job is more rewarding or satisfying to the individual than another. It is important that all work be respected, for each and every working member of our society is making a contribution to it. Work and involvement of people in it are necessary for a stable society and for their mental health. The great depression of the 1930's and the recent recession highlighted once again the importance of work to man and to his emotional needs.

In general the analysts recognize that work is important and look upon it as a means of gratifying the instincts. Freud made an important point that work was a means of binding man to reality and to the human community.

Menninger regards work as a sublimation of the aggressive instincts. Hendricks theorizes the existence of a third instinct which is to master the environment through work. Lanton writes about work as being motivated by the instinct of self-preservation. Weil says that work placates the superego and acts as a safety valve in our intrapsychic life. Obendorf interestingly showed the close relationship that there is between work and play, as well as how they are the means for relieving tension and gaining pleasure in both instances.

Neff rightly points out that the analysts have not taken into account the role that social and cultural factors play in work. He thinks that the psychologists have done a better job of explaining work because they have had to respond to demands made on them by industry and education. In their work and studies they have specialized in "the detection, measurement and description of individual differences in occupational behavior." He feels that these are more practical and down-to-earth procedures. The psychologists stress that environment plays as much a part as the psychological needs of the person in his work behavior and choices. They also have a high level of interest in human personality development and its relation to work as well as work choices.[22]

TYPES OF INCENTIVE PROGRAMS

There are a variety of ways of providing paid work programs and incentive therapies within and outside the hospital. A description of a few programs, of which there is a wide variety of modifications being used in different inpatient and outpatient settings throughout the country, follows.

Incentive and Work Therapy Programs Within the Hospital

The Token Economy or Behavioral Modification Program was introduced by Allyn and Azrin for treatment of the chronic schizophrenic. It was introduced to modify behavior of patients who were difficult to motivate and who also had behavior problems. The program consists of the patient's participating in social, self-care and work programs for which he is rewarded or reinforced with tokens.

With these tokens the patient can purchase certain rewards, such as watching TV, attending recreational activities, receiving off-station privileges or having access to certain kinds of sleeping quarters, and other like arrangements which can be classified as luxuries relating to the routine treatment and care procedures.

In order to motivate patients and alter certain undesirable target behaviors, a consistent approach should be taken by all of the personnel in the treatment setting. This is a great advantage in coping with patients who are poorly motivated or have disruptive behavior.

There are a variety of techniques that are well documented in the literature. Controlled studies showed that tokens given to reward desirable behavior increased its frequency. Removal, or random administration, of tokens led to a decrease in the frequency of target behavior.

Behavioral modification and operational conditioning are being applied more and more in the more progressive sheltered workshops. This has been a necessity since many sheltered workshops are accepting patients with behavioral and motivational problems.[19]

These techniques are based on the experimental work of Skinner. There are two basic premises: (1) All behavior is essentially learned, and therefore, it is assumed it can be unlearned; (2) rewards will increase a certain behavior, and negative reinforcers will diminish a given behavior. (This is based on the age-old theme of reward and punishment, as well as the Freudian pleasure-pain principle.)

The Compensated Therapy Program is designed to provide patients with an hourly wage that varies from thirty to sixty cents per hour while they are assigned to a work therapy program. It is primarily for patients who are functioning at a higher level than those on the token economy program. Some of them are on full or partial privileges or are still under supervision of a nursing assistant and are assigned to a group who performs hospital work.

Others in this program may be assigned to a shop that manufactures or fabricates articles to be sold and, from the profits, may receive a daily salary averaging from fifty cents to a dollar a day.

The patient can be assigned to a variety of placements under the supervision of an employee, with a goal of developing good work habits and providing him with an opportunity to learn the skills entailed in the assignment. Some of these jobs involve gardening, landscaping, greenhouse work, housekeeping, messenger service, laundry, dietetic or labor assignments, assignments to the garage, or carpentry, plumbing and electrical shops.

For many years mental patients have worked on therapeutic assignments without remuneration. In some instances they worked so well that hospitals were reluctant to discharge them.

With the advent of compensated therapy programs patients are better motivated in their assignments and, hopefully, can be discharged earlier. Many states now have laws which require that patients be paid, with the idea not only to motivate patients through financial reward, but also to eliminate peonage. Enlightened patients know of their right to treatment and are unwilling to be assigned to work programs without remuneration. In a study made in 1968 there were twenty-six states paying patients for their labor. There has been significant progress in this area, affirming the importance of money in motivating patients in work therapies.[21,24]

The Member-Employee Program consists of chronic mental patients whose psychoses have gone into partial remission and who are discharged and employed by the hospital. They received as remuneration one-third the salary of the average position. They are under supervision, live in unsupervised quarters and have the same rights as any other employee to come and go as they please after working hours. If indicated, they still participate in treatment programs, which are a means of preparing the patient for employment in the community. There is the opportunity to restore old skills and to learn new ones, providing a bridge, as it were, back into the community.

The following are some of the positions filled by member-employees: dental technician, clerk-typist, finance clerk, custodian, kitchen helper, baker, butcher, carpenter's helper, machinist's helper, locksmith's helper, occupational therapy aide, nursing assistant and storekeeper.

Sheltered Workshops Within the Hospital: Many mental hospitals now have some type of sheltered workshop. It is a growing trend. There are different types of arrangements for sponsoring or developing them. Some are initiated by private, nonprofit corporations, others by local mental health associations, whereas most of them have been the direct repsonsibility of a state or veterans' hospital.

The basic approach to the sheltered workshop is that it is a treatment unit that simulates work in industry as closely as possible. The shop must adhere to safety standards. It has work rules that the patient must abide by if he is to continue to be assigned to the shop, and he must meet the production demands. These shops provide opportunities for patients to work on the most modern machinery supplied on a loan basis by the contracting industry. (This is the procedure used at the Brockton, Massachusetts VA Hospital in the CHIRP Program—Community-Hospital-Industry Rehabilitation Program. The patients are conditioned to good work habits and they have an opportunity to demonstrate to themselves their ability to adapt to a realistic work opportunity. It is an ideal test situation for personnel to assist patients in developing skills and proper attitudes toward fellow employees and supervisors and to prepare them for placement in the community.

Patients average six hours a day, working at the minimum hourly wage, unless they are on piecework. They may be assigned by the psychiatric team, a therapist in occupational and manual arts and educational therapy, a vocational psychologist, or at their own request if the psychiatric team concurs. All diagnostic categories can use this form of therapy. An age limit is not placed on the patients because some in their seventies derive as much benefit as the younger, "employable" patients.

The following criteria are used in the CHIRP workshop in assigning a patient:

1. The patient shows no acute behavior disturbance.
2. The patient does not indicate homicidal, suicidal or antisocial behavior at the time of assignment. There is evidence of good impulse control.
3. The patient has privileges and does not abuse them.
4. The patient reacts well in interviews.

5. The patient is capable of maintaining attention and concentrating on a task.
6. The patient has capacity for following instructions.
7. The patient has made good response to hospital treatment.
8. The patient makes a good adjustment on occupational and manual arts and on educational or industrial therapy assignments.
9. The patient needs retraining before he is employable.
10. The patient need not have a good prehospital history; it is desirable but not essential.
11. The patient needs funds.[30]

Some shops fabricate and sell articles for their support. Others use subcontracting from industry, which is by far the most popular hospital sheltered workshop. Some examples of such subcontracts are grinding and soldering jewelry; salvaging copper wire coils; gauging metal parts; collating and assembling printed material; cutting addressograph plates; operating an addressograph; collating catalogues; general clerical work; burnishing and repairing dents in copper items; welding; packaging; separating mixed metal items; sorting out defective or plastic parts; building palettes and wooden tote boxes; operating a kick-press; compression moulding; surface grinding of metal parts; blanking out metal parts on a lathe; grinding numerals on aluminum shoe-lasts; painting miniature soldiers; decorating jewelry; inspecting, polishing and packaging stainless steel ware; packing electric toothbrushes; assembling and packing encyclopedias; cutting and assembling plastic gutters; assembling car radio chassis; inspecting and testing electronic components; working on camera subassemblies; putting springs in radio knobs; packaging labels; salvaging parts from outmoded computers; and filling ink bottles.[30]

Work Therapy Programs Outside the Hospital

Sheltered Workshops Sponsored by Agencies Involved in Providing Noncompetitive Terminal Employment for Marginal Employees Capable of Meeting Demands of Competitive Employment. Such marginal employees are still productive, can live outside the hospital, but still need the support of a protective work environment. Very few of these patients are capable of leaving this setting.

Transitional Sheltered Workshops such as those sponsored by the Goodwill Industries and the Chicago Jewish Vocational Services are more sophisticated and demanding. They simulate realistic and competitive work. The client is provided prevocational evaluation, vocational evaluation, personal and social adjustment, work experiences, development of proper work habits, actual job sampling, vocational training and job placement in the community.

Industrial Workshops are owned by businesses that specifically hire primarily the handicapped individual if he can compete and produce.

The Night Hospital allows the patient to be employed during the day and return to the hospital at night for further treatment if he still needs the security of the hospital. This approach can be used for the individual or for groups of from five to ten who leave work in an industry. At the Brockton VA Hospital the author has had success with groups of moderately ill patients working under the supervision of a nursing assistant in an industrial setting. Some patients who have been hospitalized for a long period of time need the support of a group in order to leave the hospital and work in an industrial setting.

Federal Selected Placement: The federal government has taken an enlightened approach toward providing jobs for the mentally restored. They have a 700-hour appointing authority—a trial appointment by which mentally restored persons can demonstrate their ability to perform a given job. Satisfactory performance for 700 hours can be used as a basis for Schedule A appointment with prior approval by the U.S. Civil Service Commission. This is an excellent method for a patient to establish a successful work record and makes it easier for him to obtain a job within or outside of the government.[26,27]

Sheltered Living—Working Arrangements

The Business Commune or the Lodge Program, as introduced by Farnsworth, et al. at the Palo Alto VA Hospital, whereby patients are prepared in the treatment setting to move out into the community as a group. They provide their own living accommodations and support themselves by establishing a business. They use peer solutions to their problems of maintaining themselves. In the meantime they receive support and security from each other while living in a family setting away from the hospital.[5]

This is a self-governing approach, and through their responsibilities and involvement their life is much more rewarding. They develop pride in their ownership of a successful business. Fairweather points out that "pride cannot develop with autonomy unless meaningful work as society defines it is also available to members, so that the responsibilities implied by autonomy are meaningful."[7] It is important for society to establish social status and roles for former mental patients and marginal people if they are to function effectively in that society and be accepted by it. The Lodge approach does this.[7]

There is a growing number of *halfway houses* since the 1960's. Some of the better known are Fountain House, New York; Council House, Pittsburgh; Horizon House, Philadelphia; Thresholds, Chicago; Portals House, Los Angeles; and Hill House, Cleveland. They have developed out of a need of mental patients discharged to the community, but still needing a great deal of support and help in developing social skills and obtaining work in order to adjust to a life of new responsibilities. The number of people requiring this kind of assistance has increased rapidly because of the emphasis on early discharge and the use of the psychotropic drugs. Many more patients are also being treated in the community in general medical hospital psychiatric units where rehabilitation measures are not stressed.

The halfway house emphasizes social skills and work, with eventual job placement. Most of them provide transitional employment with their own setting in the form of custodial, maintenance, dietitic and clerical jobs. They also have facilities for temporary living in. Imaginative and unique ideas have been used to orient, train and assist the patient in developing the skills he needs for everyday living and obtaining employment. Some of the agencies go to great lengths to obtain employment for their clients. They have arranged for individual and group placements, as well as devising sliding wage scales where the agency may pay the entire wage or share payment with an employer, depending on the productivity of the client, some have leased gas stations and arranged work crews to rehabilitate abandoned housing. Arrangements have been made with county governments, agencies, and private industry to provide transitional and permanent employment. Some agencies have their own sheltered workshops and rehabilitation counselors to assist with placement and to support both the client and the employer.[10,16,26]

GENERAL COMMENTS ABOUT WORK THERAPY AND ITS FUTURE

In all of the incentive programs it must be emphasized that the degree of illness that the patient has does not mean that he cannot work. The potential for patients' ability to work is often overlooked. There are no good psychological testing instruments to predict performance; however, they may give hints and useful information about patients' abilities. Mentally ill patients who appear to be quite ill often perform very well and react with proper social amenities because they are receiving proper cues in the working situation. Emphasis should be placed on the assets rather than the liabilities of the patients. One should use what is well about them. One of the last functions lost by mental patients is their ability to work.[23]

Everyone has a right to employment, even if mentally ill. Many patients can return to their communities, but it is very important for them to be engaged in some form of employment and be productive for their own self-esteem and for maintenance of their mental health to whatever degree they have attained. Many patients can live in communities if they receive proper supportive services. This has been demonstrated by pilot projects.

Patients must have access to incentive programs if they are to be able to remain in the community and, more importantly, to be accepted. A worker who earns is much more acceptable than a non-worker living on welfare. With the advent of community psychiatry and the interest of providing people with an alternative to spending their lives in mental hospitals, many more kinds of work opportunities must be provided. One can hope for a cure for the mentally ill, but at the level of development of the "art" of psychiatry at this point in time, one must think in terms of what he is capable of doing.

Incentive programs are only a part of the broad spectrum of programs for helping the mentally ill, but they should be used more and should play a more important role. The European countries are much further advanced in this respect than the United States, because of enlightened legislation. Our local, state, and federal governments will need to be more supportive and will need to provide the leadership and funds for these programs. Much work remains to be done by everyone in this area of rehabilitation if the demands of a growing number of people within and outside mental hospitals are to be met.[18,20]

REFERENCES

1. Bellak, L., Black, B. J., et al.: Rehabilitation of the mentally ill through controlled transitional employment. *Am J Orthopsychiatry, 26*(2): 285, 1956.
2. Black, B. J.: *Industrial Therapy for the Mentally Ill — Observations on Development in Western Europe and Significance for Programs in U.S.* Bronx, Altro Work Shops, 1966.
3. Black, B. J.: The protected workshop in the rehabilitation of the mentally ill. *Psychiatr Q Suppl, 33*(1):107, 1959.
4. Carstairs, G. M., Clark, D. H., and O'Connor, N.: Occupational treatment of chronic psychotics. *Lancet, 2*:1025-1030, 1955.
5. Daggett, S. R.: The Lodge Program. *Rehabil Rec, 12*(6):31-34, 1971.
6. Fairweather, G. W.: *Social Psychology in Treating Mental Illness, An Experimental Approach.* New York, Wiley, 1964.
7. Fairweather, G. W., Sanders, D. H., et al.: *Community Life for the Mentally Ill: An Alternative to Institutional Care.* Chicago, Aldine, 1969.
8. Freeman, H., and Simmons, O.: *The Mental Patient Comes Home.* New York, Wiley, 1963.
9. *Frontiers of Hospital Psychiatry, 3*:7, 1966.
10. Glascote, R. M., Cumming, E., et al.: *Rehabilitating the Mentally Ill in the Community.* Washington, Joint Information Service, 1971.
11. Gurel, L.: Patterns of Mental Patient Posthospital Adjustment. *Intramural Report 65-1.* Washington, Program Evaluation Staff, VA Hospital, 1965.
12. Havighurse, R.: Youth in Exploration and Man Emergent, In Borow, H. (Ed.): *Man in a World of Work.* Boston, HM, 1964.
13. Hubbs, R.: The sheltered workshop in psychiatric rehabilitation. *Am J Orthopsychiatry, 34*(1):76-79, 1964.
14. Industrial Symposium: Industrial Therapy of the Mentally Ill and Mentally Retarded. Boston, September 29 to 30, 1966. In conjunction with the Eighteenth Mental Hospital Institute. Private transcript of pro-

ceedings on file at the Medical Library, VA Hospital, Brockton, Maine.
15. Jones, M.: Social rehabilitation with emphasis on work therapy as a form of group therapy. *Br J Med Psychol, 33*:67, 1960.
16. Lamb, H. R. and assoc.: *Rehabilitation in Community Mental Health,* San Francisco, Jossey-Bass, 1971.
17. Margolin, R.: Bridging the gap with the member-employee program. *J Assoc Phys Ment Rehabil, 13*:20-21, 1959.
18. May, P. R. A.: Work rehabilitation in the United States. *Occup Ment Health, 1*:13, 1971.
19. Meyer, V., Chesser, E. S.: *Behavior Therapy in Clinical Psychiatry.* Baltimore, Penguin, 1970.
20. Morris, G. H. (Ed.): *The Mentally Ill and the Right to Treatment.* Springfield, Thomas, 1970.
21. National Association of State Mental Health Program Directors: *Study #26: Rate of Pay for Patient Labor.* Washington, D.C. 1969.
22. Neff, W. S.: *Work and Human Behavior.* Chicago, Aldine, 1968.
23. Olshansky, S.: Some assumptions challenged. *Community Ment Health J, 4*:153-157, 1968.
24. Peffer, P.: Money: A rehabilitation incentive for mental patients. *Am J Psychiatr, 110*:84-92, 1953.
25. Simmons, O.: *Work and Mental Illness.* New York, Wiley, 1965.
26. Street, D. R.: *The Place of Work Therapy in the Treatment of the Mentally Ill: Psychiatric Studies and Projects,* vol 2. Washington, American Psychiatric Association, 1964, p. 12.
27. U.S. Civil Service Commission: *Handbook of Selective Placement in Federal Service Employment.* Washington, D.C., June 1969.
28. Walker, R., and Winick, W.: New patients can do meaningful work. *Hosp Community Psychiatry, 18*(7):210-212, 1967.
29. Wayne, G. J.: Work in the Soviet Union. *Ment Hosp, 12*:21-23, 1961.
30. Winick, W.: *Industry in the Hospital.* Springfield, Thomas, 1967.
31. Winick, W., and Walsh, F. X.: Community, Hospital, Industrial Rehabilitation Program. *Mental Hosp, 15*:147-150, 1964.

Section VI

BEHAVIOR MODIFICATION APPROACH AND TOKEN ECONOMY PROGRAMS

Chapter 10

TOWARD A NEW HOSPITAL PSYCHIATRY

Teodoro Ayllon

"The times they are a changin'," as the song goes, but the concept of treatment in the mental hospital has remained virtually unchanged through the last twenty years. The notable exception is the introduction of psychopharmaceuticals around 1956, which has had a dramatic effect upon the population of mental institutions. According to (USPHS) figures the number of resident patients in state mental hospitals was reduced from 550,000 in 1956 to 400,000 in 1968. This means that in a period of twelve years, approximately 12,000 patients left the hospital every year. What can be loosely termed as the "therapies" (psychotherapy, group therapy, milieu therapy, occupational therapy, etc.) have been practiced to some extent for more than thirty years. Psychopharmaceuticals have been very helpful to the therapist in that they have reduced the number of patients to be treated, and have made those in hospitals more amenable to treatment. That these therapies are still highly valuable there is no doubt, but speaking generally, they are conducted only by highly trained and costly personnel such as psychologists, psychiatrists and social workers. Although occasionally one now hears about nurses conducting the same efforts, this is often done as a last recourse and almost apologetically. However, because of budgetary crises, many state hospitals are virtually functioning with a skeleton crew of mental health professionals, and the end is not in sight. It is clear that unless there is an immediate reappraisal of the objectives of the state mental hospital, there will be virtually no one but attendants to care for the patients.

One might ask what a hospital superintendent can do. The answer, it seems, is for him to learn about new developments in behavior modification. The development of procedures of behavior modification has rested upon the work of those who practically live with the patients—the attendants and nurses. These are the key personnel, essentially the therapists of tomorrow—the only persons who make the difference in the life of the patient while he remains in the mental hospital. It was with the assistance of attendants and nurses that a series of experiments was conducted to determine the relative effectiveness of behavioral procedures in a mental hospital setting.[1,3-9] It is important to describe some of the highlights of this research and then discuss the implications of these findings for the operation of the hospital of tomorrow.

Initially, there was a concern with patients' symptoms because they were specific, observable and, therefore, measurable. One interesting example of a peculiar symptom was that of a female patient who had displayed obsessive-compulsive behavior for nine years. She was regarded as hopeless since she had gone through individual therapy and group therapy—"the works"—without any apparent benefit. It is commonly known that these therapies are based largely on the ability of the patient to communicate verbally. This particular patient, however, refused to talk and, therefore, she was regarded as unsuitable for further psychotherapy. Designing a behavioral treatment which would not be limited by the ability of the patient to speak with anyone[1] was then attempted.

The most prominent feature of the patient's illness was hoarding towels. She collected towels daily from the forty patients on the ward and kept them in her small room. The staff went daily to the patient and asked very politely for the towels that belonged to the rest of the patients. But she simply refused to give up her towels. Obviously, this represented a logistical problem to the ward staff. How were they going to give baths to forty patients when one patient kept thirty towels for herself? And so, there was some need for more drastic measures, like somebody going to her room and taking all the towels away from her. This is a very common approach which is often the only thing that can be done when dealing with the real practical problems on the ward. The usual interpretation attached to such symptoms is that they reflect a deep need for love. Hoarding towels is thus regarded as just a symptom of this need. This analysis may be very useful as a way of conceptualizing a problem, but it certainly was not very helpful to the attendants or the nurses since they still had to figure out what to do about the towels.

First, they attempted a quantification of the symptom—hoarding towels. They began by weighing them, but found counting easier. This approach illustrates the importance of directly measuring the behavior or behaviors that are to be treated. Measuring the symptom minimizes guessing and provides a sensitive check on the effectiveness of the treatment procedures. Indeed, the first procedure was to discontinue the old method of telling the patient not to collect towels or taking them away from her. Instead, attendants were instructed to give towels to the patient. Now, without going into the fine points about data that is available on the use of satiation as a way to reduce behavior, suffice it to say that the staff were interested in extending this finding to an applied therapeutic situation. This procedure required that the attendants give the patient an average of seven towels a day. At first the patient was very happy to receive the towels and for the first time in twelve years she coherently indicated her pleasure and welcomed the attendants with words like, "Oh, you found my towels, that's wonderful, thank you, nurse, thank you." Although the patient was delighted with this new state of affairs, the staff was getting impatient about finding a solution to the problem of hoarding the towels. So after a few days a decision was made to go for broke and the average number of towels given daily was increased to sixty. She seemed rather puzzled at the new change as reflected in such comments as "It takes me all day to put my things away now, you know. . . . I don't think I need so many towels, maybe I have enough now." She continued keeping the towels neatly in her hoom, however, on her bed, her bureau and her chair. But the towels kept on coming since the staff wanted the patient to decide to get rid of them, not just to complain about them. Verbal behavior was not enough; the attendants wanted action. That was the idea behind giving the patient more and more towels.

At this point, it seems that the efforts of keeping about 700 towels in order were a little too much for her. Handling 700 towels became a full-time job. The patient began complaining that she could not stay up the whole night folding towels and placing them on the dresser and the bureau and so on. Of course the attendant, very understandingly, answered "Well, you know you do the best you can and we'll just try to give you what you need." The important thing to remember at this point is that the patient was not being coerced either to keep or give up the towels. But the patient became less efficient in arranging the towels and was even irritated by their presence as was evidenced by her throwing a couple of towels at the nurse after four weeks of treatment. She then found out that nobody picked the towels up and nobody brought them in again, so she tried another two or three towels and put them outside her room, and again they did not come back. It took only a few days for her to dispose of towels literally by the hundreds until she was left with only one towel. So there is a moral to this story: "Happiness is having your own towel."

One of the most conspicuous aspects of mental illness is the rather bizarre content of conversation displayed by a mentally ill person. In an effort to explore the influence of social interaction on the frequency of bizarre talk, a patient whose verbal behavior was sufficiently stereotyped as to permit standard recording by the nurses was selected.[7] The patient basically had two classes of verbal behavior: One dealt with Queen Elizabeth and other members of the British Royal Family, and the other class excluded any such references. These two categories were first identified and then taught to nurses, who in turn recorded the patient's conversation in terms of the categories. Each nurse had to meet a quota of contacts with the patient daily. This ensured a constant number of opportunities for the patient to react verbally to the nurse. What, of course, could not be kept constant was the frequency of patient-nurse contacts when these were initiated by the patient and not by the nurse. Prior to this attempt at quantifying the content of her conversation, she had been reported to make utterances solely concerned with the royal house and her part in it. In practice, it was found that the probability of one subject rather than another being produced in her conversation with nurses was fifty to fifty. With this bit of information, the staff wondered what would happen if nurses listened to and appeared concerned each time the patient touched upon her rather colorful topic, but appeared disinterested and busy whenever she omitted any references to the royal family. The findings were rather thought-provoking. It turned out that the reassurance and attention given to the patient when she displayed psychotic verbal behavior increased the frequency of such language to twice its original level. At this point a procedure suggested itself: The staff wondered what would happen if the reassurance were to be discontinued when she engaged in her bizarre talk. Therefore, all psychotic content was selectively ignored, and any instances of "healthy" talk were followed by smiles and concern from nurses. (Until this point, it was not possible to predict what actually might happen by so doing.) The results were startling. It was found that when the nurses ignored the bizarre talk, it quickly decreased. On the other hand, the "healthy" talk increased from 50 to 80 percent of her verbal output when the nurses' attention followed it and stabilized at a level greater than 30 percent of the original.

Oftentimes the nurses' social attention can seem to be necessary for the physical survival of the patient. This was the case with one patient who continuously had been fed by the nurses in various manners. She had been spoon-fed, tube-fed, and on extreme occasions, intravenously fed. Her refusal to eat unassisted, it had been assumed, was an integral part of her psychosis. This treatment had been going on for fourteen years. Then the nurses' assistance was withdrawn entirely, and within four days the patient, by then ravenous, ran to the dining room and proceeded to eat on her own.[2]

These and other behavioral applications[6] seemed to suggest that the major source of reinforcement for many of the behaviors displayed on the ward was traceable to the particular feedback given to the patient by those working there. The notion that consequences attendant to behavior played a major role in the probability of occurrence of that behavior was, of course, not new. What seemed new was that the social reaction of nurses to patients appeared to have a specific influence on the maintenance of many ward behavior problems.[7]

It should be made clear that to generalize these findings to other behaviors in the mental hospital, it was necessary to demonstrate that attention and concern shown by nurses to patients are always reinforcing events. In practice, it was found that many patients reacted to the attention of the nurses as they would to an aversive event, and at best some reacted with total indifference. Nor was this experience confined to the use of the nurses' attention as a reinforcer. In a series of attempts to isolate some reinforcer of wide applicability, a variety of consumable items such as peanuts, cigarettes, M&M's,® cookies, ice cream and so on were used. The outcome of such attempts was rather discouraging: Each, and sometimes several, items were effective as reinforcers, but typically they required a preselection of the individuals who seemed to be particularly affected by such events. Lindsley,[10] in his pioneering work with psychotic patients, had also found many of these potential reinforcers to be just that—potential. This represented a severe limitation in working with the chronic schizophrenic patient, in view of the objective which was to isolate or develop a reinforcer of wide applicability.

Nor was the selection of a reinforcer the only problem. Indeed, the selection of behavior represented as much of a problem. Up to this point, most behaviors had been dealt with primarily because of the ease in measuring them. Repeated attempts at objectively measuring behavior in a free field environment involved serious methodological problems. About this time the author went to Anna State Hospital to work with Nathan Azrin, devising time-sample behavioral recordings and analyzing the data so derived, until it became painfully clear that time-sample measures were simply impractical with respect to most types of behavioral applications. With hard work to devise standardized behavioral measures, the indiscriminate character of our behavioral recording became more apparent. All types of behaviors were measured, without distinguishing their functional characteristics in the environment. Gradually, the author began thinking in terms of behaviors which were functional in the ward environment. Parallel with this development, it became evident that it was not sufficient to identify behaviors which were functional, but that they should also have relevance to other environments. For some patients, this meant that they should learn behaviors which were functional to life in the hospital, while for others it meant that the behaviors should have relevance to living outside the hospital.

But what are the functional behaviors typically observed in mental hospitals? Except for behaviors such as eating, dressing and other self-care activities, patients have little opportunity to engage in a functional relationship with the environment in which they live. In thinking about the possible useful behaviors that patients might engage in, it was obvious that the dimensions of useful behavior were not known. To get an idea of such dimensions, it was interesting to speculate what would happen if the performance of the attendants was evaluated in those terms. Would that give a better idea of what the dimensions of useful behaviors were? The employees were observed working on jobs such as serving meals, washing dishes, cleaning, mopping and general housekeeping duties. In addition, they picked up the dirty linen, counted the pieces, wrote the number of the appropriate slip and then took the bundle of clothes to a collection place for pickup service by the laundry people. The attendants also made beds, gave baths, conducted patients outside the ward, ran errands and performed sundry other duties which occupied most of their eight hours of shift work. These were useful behaviors, undoubtedly necessary for the functioning of the ward. But the problem in defining similar behaviors for the patient still existed. The attendant's functional behavior was known, but it was not understood what this meant in terms of the patients. In effect, after thinking it over, the author wondered if much of the work of the attendants would be regarded as the target behavior for patients to learn. An additional requirement for selecting a behavior was that it should lead to an enduring change in the environment when it occurred. A specific example of such behavior would be washing dishes immediately following a meal. The physical change in the environment that results from this behavior is the cleanliness of the dishes. Other examples that leave an enduring change in the environment are mopping the floors, serving meals, doing clerical work such as typing, filing, etc. Each of these behaviors fulfills, as well, the initial requirement that a response be useful and necessary. At least, the target behavior also had relevance to the functioning of the patient either in the hospital or in the community. To the extent that such performances as the ones described above have components that touch upon other work activities outside the hospital, they were regarded as particularly helpful to work with. Still, the one problem not dealt with was how to accomplish the measurement of the behavior. It is obviously impossible to observe each patient every moment of the day and night in order to record when and whether the patient was mopping the floors, setting the table or folding the laundry. By arranging the environment so that the response selected could only take place at a designated time and place, the author finally made contact with the underlying features of previous measurement.

So, for example, the mop was available only at a specified time of the day and for a specific duration. This same requirement was imposed on other behaviors. In this manner, the attendants could easily identify the behavior since it was usually restricted to a time and place.

Now that there was an identifiable, functional behavior which could be easily recorded by the attendants, the author returned to the original problem which was to find some type of reinforcing stimulus of general applicability. This objective seemed rather futile in view of the fact that the hallmark of chronic schizophrenic patients is the apparent absence of effective reinforcers for them. To avoid *a priori* definitions about what might constitute an effective reinforcer for this type of patient, the author decided to rely on direct observation of patients' behavior. Close scrutiny of them indicated that they showed a wide range of behaviors, but more significant was the frequency with which they did some things instead of others. For example, some continuously asked to leave the ward; others chose to remain isolated in their rooms and rarely participated in any ward activity. Still others attended social functions every time they were offered. For example, some had a 100 percent church attendance, and others had a similarly high record of attendance at movies. A few consistently requested to speak to the doctor, social worker or psychologist. Premack[11] has expressed a general principle that of any two behaviors the one that has a high probability of occurrence can be used to reinforce the low-probability one. Following this principle, the author proposed to interest the patient in engaging in low-probability or "useful" behaviors at a scheduled time. In this manner the patient's high-probability behavior would operate as a reinforcer to increase the frequency of behaviors rarely displayed. In fact, work, leisure and comforts were being defined in the context of the patient's environment.

The following illustration may help to clarify the application of the Premack principle. A patient who had a perfect attendance record at church was informed that the pass to allow her to go to church was available for making her bed. Since making her bed was a low-probability behavior, the staff wanted to strengthen it by making the access to church follow it. The patient, with a little grumbling, made her bed, requested her pass and went to church. The problem encountered, however, was that it was often impractical to offer the reinforcer without causing numerous interruptions of the patient's ongoing behavior. It was the impracticality of such a procedure that finally led the author to use a conditioned reinforcer to bridge the delay between the occurrence of the response and the availability of the reinforcing stimulus. Specially made tokens that were not obtainable outside the ward environment were used. The tokens could later be exchanged for the reinforcing stimulus selected by the patient. When the appropriate behavior was displayed, the attendant reinforced the patient with tokens. A methodological advantage provided by the use of tokens was that they minimized the subjective aspects of the patient-attendant interaction at the time of reinforcement delivery. In addition, the token allowed the development of a standardized procedure for the delivery of the reinforcement and its exchange.

To determine the effectiveness of these behavioral procedures in maintaining the desired behaviors, a series of experiments were undertaken. The experimental design consisted of carefully measuring the desired behaviors for a period of time during which they were followed by reinforcement. The next stage of the design required that the reinforcement procedure be discontinued in some manner. The third stage of the experimental design required that the reinforcement procedure be reinstated. Careful measurements of the behavior throughout these three periods made it possible to evaluate the role of the reinforcement procedure in maintaining the desired behaviors.

One of the first experiments was designed to answer the following question: What determines the choice or selection of jobs? Intangible factors associated with job satisfaction were often offered as explanations for the patients' specific job selection. It was found that after familiarizing themselves with several jobs, the patients tended to prefer some over others. The experimenters wondered what would happen if token reinforcement were made available only for those jobs least preferred by the patient. Would the patients continue working at their preferred jobs because of the intrinsic factors involved in the jobs themselves? Would they perhaps quit working altogether as a natural reaction against someone manipulating their environment? The results showed neither of these outcomes. The patients continued working, but the job they selected was the one which was least preferred, but for which tokens were available. The previously preferred jobs which paid no tokens were not selected. When token reinforcement was reinstated for the preferred jobs, the patients resumed full-time work on them. The jobs selected for study in this experiment were full-time jobs which resembled those performed by normal individuals in the hospital. This made it possible to evaluate the strength of uncontrolled subjective likes and dislikes vs. the reinforcement procedure in selecting a job.

These results indicated that the patients would shift their

selection of jobs depending on which job resulted in token reinforcement. The question to be asked next was, "Was work *per se* reinforcing enough to be continued without any payoff?" The experimenters knew that one job was preferred over another because of the payment, but they did not know just how reinforcing the job, in and of itself, might be.

Because the attendants paid the patients for working, the patient-attendant interaction was an additional factor which had to be considered in a design which would test the reinforcing properties of work. If the experimenters had simply quit paying tokens at the end of the job, they would have automatically terminated this relationship and could not have determined whether the tokens or the interaction was responsible for the changes in work patterns. The solution was to design an experiment in which the patient-attendant interaction continued.

This time, however, the attendants, instead of waiting for the completion of the desired performance to reinforce the patient, anticipated the patient and gave each one his usual number of tokens at the beginning of the day before his job was to be performed. The results showed that the performance of the full-time jobs by the patients decreased to zero when the token reinforcement was given independently of the performance. On the very first day when the reinforcement procedure was reinstated so that the patient was given the tokens following the completion of the job, there was an immediate return to the high level of performance.

At this point, the experimenters wondered if these results were perhaps an artifact of the type of patients involved in full-time work. The question was what would hapen if the same procedure were to be used with more disturbed patients, that is, with those who worked as little as fifteen minutes and perhaps only as long as three hours? This time all forty-four patients on the ward were included. Although the jobs varied in complexity from sweeping the floors to running an automatic dishwasher and operating a movie projector, the results were similar to those obtained with the full-time jobs. When the token reinforcement was delivered independent of the performance, the number of hours at work decreased to nearly zero. When the token reinforcement was reinstated for completion of the desired performance, the number of hours at work returned to its original level.

The investigators then decided to see if they could simulate quantitatively the effects of the major characteristics of the typical ward environment, one in which token reinforcement was absent and where the privileges and other desirable items were available freely and generally independent of the patient's performance. Would the high level of performance still be maintained? The results obtained when the token reinforcement was discontinued indicate that the freely available privileges do not help to maintain the high level of performance. Quite the contrary, during this period patients in general lost interest in their work, that is, they worked fewer hours. In fact, their work decreased to less than one fourth of its original level. These results offer a very good estimate of the probable level of performance in a typical ward: The patient's level of productivity, in a sense, is underestimated, and he is likely to be working at one fourth of his potential.

Since, up to this point, one feature of the experimental manipulations was the all-or-none use of the reinforcement procedure, the experimenters asked themselves what might be the effect of relative amounts of reinforcement on the desired behaviors? To study this situation, they designed an experiment where the patient was given experience with two different jobs. The completion of each job was rewarded by two different amounts of reinforcement, one larger than the other. Given that both resulted in tokens, which job would the patient select? As it turned out, the patients selected the job which resulted in the larger amount of reinforcement. When the magnitude of payoff was reversed so that the job which initially paid least came to pay the most, then the patients switched to that job. These results indicated then that the presence or absence of reinforcement was not the only determinant of the high level of performance, but that the relative amount available for the job was also important.

In summary, the reinforcement program was effective in

maintaining the performance because tokens were given for the desired performances. When the tokens were no longer given, then those performances decreased. When the token delivery was changed from one job to another, the performance of the job for which tokens were not available decreased immediately to nearly zero. The mere act of giving tokens did not maintain the high level of performance as is seen in the experiment where tokens were given before the completion of the job. The payment had to be contingent upon job completion. These results demonstrate that the reinforcement procedure used was so effective that the influence of other factors was relatively minimal when reinforcement was absent. Further, these results indicate that this motivational system would be extremely potent for a wide range of psychiatric problems. First of all, the population of patients included mental retardates, schizophrenics, paranoids, organic psychotics, manic depressives and so on. Such a wide range of diagnostic classifications might have revealed some differential effect on the type of psychiatric diagnosis. Yet, the results show that patients from all of these classifications had a higher level of performance under the reinforcement procedure. While the number of years of hospitalization ranged from one to thirty-seven years, this factor did not affect the patient's performance either. Neither age, which ranged from twenty-four to seventy-four, nor level of education, seemed to be a significant factor either, for the reinforcement program was effective with young and old and with patients whose education ranged from primary school to college.

What can a program like this mean for the hospital of tomorrow? This program was designed to facilitate the patient's rehabilitation by making him a responsible, functioning, human being. Because it has been found to be effective in maintaining both short and simple performances, and long complex ones, this program could be employed to enable patients to become responsible for the functioning of their hospital environment. Instead of allowing the patient to regress, to become dependent, or what is worse, to eventually vegetate, this procedure could maintain the patient operating at maximal level as he would have to upon return to the outside world. The hospital, then, would not be a place in which one would be encouraged to escape, a place in which all comforts would come automatically. In a motivating therapeutic environment such as the author is suggesting, the patients themselves would cook, serve meals and do all housekeeping chores. They could also go beyond these simple tasks to the servicing of other needs of the institution such as painting walls, repairing furniture, doing the hospital laundry and sealing the storm windows.

Eventually, the hospital could establish vocational training in such areas as mechanics, machine operation, cosmetology and food preparation. Courses could also be offered in high school and college so that patients might, if they chose, pursue an academic education. This training could then assist the patient in making the necessary adjustment to the outside world. The motivational level in occupational behaviors would be maintained by the opportunities for reinforcement, which would include such social activities as dances, movies, church, picnics and shopping trips to town, and other environmental advantages like a private bedroom or a preferred bedspread. Similarly, psychotherapy, either private or group, could be made available contingent upon some appropriate and useful behavior. Thus, the choice of patients for therapy would not be the exclusive prerogative of the administration or of the psychiatrists, as it is presently. These procedures would make psychotherapy available to all for the small price of behaving as responsible adults. There would never have to be any "giving up" on patients.

A fresh approach to mental hospitals is long overdue. These institutions, by their very nature, possess powerful sources of reinforcement which can be harnessed for the motivation of the patients within their walls. It is here that the behavioral methodology can help in conceptualizing not only the relevance of the goals of the hospital but also the relative effectiveness of methods used to generate and maintain behavior in this environment. Indeed, hospitals need no longer be anachronistic human warehouses, but centers for reeducation and rehabilitation. The major objective of the hospital of tomorrow should be to generate in the patients a desire to rejoin the human family by way of acquiring skills with which to maintain themselves after their release.

REFERENCES

1. Ayllon, T.: Intensive treatment of psychotic behavior by stimulus satiation and food reinforcement. *J Behav Res Ther, 1*:53-61, 1963.
2. Ayllon, T.: Paper read at American Psychological Association. Chicago, September 1960.
3. Ayllon, T., and Azrin, N. H.: The measurement and reinforcement of behavior of psychotics. *J Exp Anal Behav, 8*:357-383, 1965.
4. Ayllon, T., and Azrin, N. H.: Reinforcer sampling: A technique for increasing the behavior of mental patients. *J Appl Behav Anal, 1*:13-20, 1968.
5. Ayllon, T., and Azrin, N. H.: *The Token Economy: A Motivational System for Therapy and Rehabilitation.* New York, Appleton, 1968.
6. Ayllon, T., and Haughton, E.: Control of the behavior of schizophrenic patients by food. *J Exp Anal Behav, 5*:343-352, 1962.
7. Ayllon, T., and Haughton, E.: Modification of symptomatic verbal behavior of mental patients. *J Behav Res Ther, 2*:87-97, 1964.
8. Ayllon, T., Haughton, E., and Hughes, H.: Interpretation of symptoms: fact or fiction? *J Behav Res Ther, 3*:1-7, 1965.
9. Ayllon, T., and Michael, J.: The psychiatric nurse as a behavioral engineer. *J Exp Anal Behav, 2*:323-334, 1959.
10. Lindsley, O. R.: Operant conditioning methods applied to research in chronic schizophrenia. *Psychiatr Res Rep, 5*:118-139, 1956.
11. Premack, D.: Toward empirical behavior laws: I. Positive reinforcement. *Psychol Rev, 66*:219-233, 1959.

Section VII

THE GERIATRIC PATIENT AND THE BRAIN DAMAGED

Chapter 11

REHABILITATION AND THE MENTALLY DISABLED GERIATRIC PATIENT

ALAN D. WHANGER AND EWALD W. BUSSE

The Elderly and Their Problems

OLD AGE IN OUR SOCIETY is a condition to which many aspire, but which few want. One of the main reasons that many have negative feelings toward the latter phase of the life cycle is that it is commonly associated with mental and physical deterioration. Some of these negative stereotypes are reflected in the answers to a simple question put to many hundreds of professional and lay persons as to what percentage of all Americans over age sixty-five they think are in some type of institution. The average guess is nearly 50 percent! Fortunately the correct answer is about 4 percent, but still that is about a million older Americans who are in care-giving institutions. Of course, this does not reflect the actual incidence or severity of disability. Some studies have indicated up to a 30 percent prevalence of diagnosable psychiatric disorders among the general older population, with about 15 percent probably being significantly disabled. In longitudinal studies among community living volunteers conducted at the Duke University Center for the Study of Aging and Human Development, only about 40 percent of the subjects were free of some psychological problems.[13] The incidence of new psychiatric disease is about 100 times as great among those over age sixty-five as among those under age fifteen. It is too easy to lump all of the 20 million older Americans into a group, with the resulting stereotypes and prejudices that befall any minority group. It is more valid to think of those from age sixty-five to seventy-four as elderly, and those over seventy-five as aged, as this latter group has a much higher prevalence of significant disorders. Among all those over age sixty-five, however, chronic physical disorders are present in about 79 percent, with 45 percent having some disability, 6 percent being confined to their living quarters, and 2 percent being restricted to their beds.[9] The exact coincidence of mental and physical disease and its relation to disability is not known nationally, but surveys have recently been conducted at the Duke University Older Americans Resources and Services Project in Durham County. Among those living in the community, 13 percent were considered to have a significant disability (from moderate to total) from mental diseases, 25 percent were limited by physical diseases, and 21 percent were disabled to carrying out the usual activities of daily living (ADL). A similar survey was conducted among all of the institutions (retirement homes, boarding homes, nursing homes and mental hospitals) caring for the elderly, showing an institutionalization rate of about 5 percent. Of those in boarding type facilities, 62 percent were impaired mentally, 32 percent physically and 83 percent in areas of ADL. Those in nursing type facilities showed an 80 percent impairment mentally, 93 percent physically and 100 percent in areas of ADL.[48]

The author's studies tend to confirm earlier ones by Goldfarb[24] and Stotsky,[45] showing the enormous prevalence of mental disease in nursing home facilities and the strong correlations between mental and physical conditions. Multiple and often interrelated pathologies are characteristic of the older patient.

While it is obvious that there is a large reservoir of mental and physical disability in the community, much of the rehabilitation efforts will go to those in various institutions. In this chapter, various aspects of the complex relationship between rehabilitation medicine, psychiatry and the older patient will be considered.

Modification of Goals of Rehabilitaton of the Elderly

Working with chronic older patients has been one of the least attractive areas of medicine. One generally likes to restore function and cure disease, and failure to do this may threaten professional self-esteem. One likes grateful patients, and old people often complain. One likes to save lives, but old patients confront the professional with the mortality of man. Medical personnel tend to work in areas of familiarity, and until quite recently there has been only a small body of knowledge about aging and few enthusiastic teachers. Ours is a youth- and production-centered society, and the elderly are often deemed of little social worth. Good care requires money, and society has been singularly ineffective in providing adequate funding and structures for treating the elderly. Freud (in his younger days) declared that old people are no longer educable, and many have perpetuated that myth by their disinterest and therapeutic nihilism. In successful psychotherapy with the elderly, modifications of techniques and goals are needed, as indicated by Pfeiffer and Busse.[38] In the same way, modification of techniques and goals of rehabilitation must be made in light of the problems, pathology and possibilities of each elderly person. The idea of rehabilitation being the restoration of the handicapped person to the fullest total usefulness of which he is capable defines the task for some of the elderly, but this demands too much of others. Another useful concept is that of Rudd and Margolin[43,44] of "maintenance therapy," which attempts to retard deterioration in patients who are chronically ill by arresting or slowing the process, even if temporarily. For other elderly persons a legitimate goal is to use various methods in a supportive way to relieve the suffering and loneliness of someone who is inexorably deteriorating. One can render a disservice to the older patient either by doing too little or too much.

Physical Factors Causing and Complicating Psychiatric Disorders

In assessing any psychiatric disorder of an older person, a thorough medical workup should be part of the diagnostic procedure. In many cases, the first sign of a physical disorder will be an alteration in the mental status. Common problems manifested in this way are mild cardiac decompensations, urinary tract infections, fecal impaction and toxicity from various drugs. Wolff[55] observes that the elderly with digestive disturbances, especially peptic ulcer, tend to be moody and irritable and that those with diabetes are often emotionally unstable. Vitamin deficiencies and nutritional problems can contribute to mental malfunction,[50] and such states are fairly common in this age group. Cerebral vascular insufficiency, ranging from minimal memory impairment to massive stroke, may produce problems varying from marked alterations in body image to depression and apathy.[54] Loss of sensory input is extremely common, with diminution of hearing, vision, smell, taste and pain. Our society generally tends to discourage physical contact and touching, especially of older men.

Bower[6] and others consider some of the symptoms of the elderly who already have impairment from neural damage, to be secondary to sensory deprivations. Perhaps related are observations of the diminution of the vibratory sense in the elderly, which is roughly proportional to the degree of organic brain syndrome.[51] A distinct correlation between hearing loss and paranoid ideation has been noted.[49] Kreitler and Kreitler[28] observed that physically inactive older people developed distortion of their body image as being broader and heavier than reality, which led to further physical restriction, clumsiness and increased fear of physical activity. They also felt that this physical inactivity inhibited the discharge of "free floating tension," with resultant restlessness, sleep disturbances and internalized self-destructive aggression. Chronic illness in itself may produce a variety of emotional complications.[11] Frustration can lead to excessive anger, abnormal dependency or depression. In his multiple attempts to regain physical and psychological equilibrium, the elderly patient may experience intense helplessness, despair, guilt and anxiety. Physical inactivity and bed rest are regressive psychologically; and an older person may lose the ability to walk, with possible loss of continence, after two or three weeks of bed rest for whatever cause.

Environmental Factors Influencing Geropsychiatric Illnesses

Environmental factors frequently complicate mental illness. The process of institutionalization and depersonalization, as described by Goffman[23] and others, which frequently accompanies a move by an emotionally disturbed person into a large facility, can be especially devastating to older persons whose adaptive capacities are marginal anyway. The foreboding surroundings, the "sick role" expected of him, the loss of his social structure and familiar environment, the lack of meaningful activity and the loss of hope all may lead to depression, regression and increased morbidity and mortality.

LEARNING AND PERFORMANCE CAPACITIES IN THE ELDERLY AFFECTING REHABILITATION

As cited previously, Freud once reinforced the old adage that "you can't teach an old dog new tricks." People are not dogs, however, and in recent years several factors relevant to learning and performance in the elderly have been discovered. These obviously are important to those working to rehabilitate older patients. Eisdorfer and others have found that poor test results of the aged may be attributed as much to factors that inhibit learning and the ability to offer appropriate responses as to any actual decrease in the person's capacity to learn.[19]

Insufficient time to respond leads the elderly to make errors of omission, in which they simply will not make any response, rather than risk a wrong answer. Slowing the pace of a task increases the performance rate. Learning is inhibited by excessive anxiety and stress. Studies at Duke University Center for the Study of Aging have shown that older people not only became more distressed and aroused in a learning situation, as compared to the young, but that this level of arousal peaks about fifteen minutes *after* the learning task is over and persists for some time. Obviously this heightened arousal and anxiety could well make learning more difficult, causing a vicious cycle of increasing stress relative to task complexity.[46] On the other hand, afferent impulses received repetitiously in an unchanging, monotonous environment will be literally tuned out by the brain receptors.[52]

Motivation is obviously a major factor in learning and performing, and the values of an older person may vary markedly from those of the therapist. Learning may not have had a high cultural priority for many elderly, and they need tasks that are meaningful to them. It may be of help to let the older person define his own incentives, as suggested by Filer and O'Connell.[20] The elderly do not like being treated like children and will resist tasks that seem infantile or foolish to them. Activities may have meaning to the extent that they either are related to lifelong interests or provide financial reward so that they can be considered as legitimate work.[39] This helps to maintain feelings of productive capacity and enhances both social- and self-esteem.

Studies have shown that most of the elderly with major organic or functional psychoses have significant deficits in current learning ability, which produce significantly deficient behavior in novel situations. In light of this fact, Lindsley suggests the design of "prosthetic environments" which would help compensate for specific behavioral deficits by making them less debilitating.[32] Discriminative stimuli are environmental events which signal when a response is appropriate and when it should not be made. The sensitivity of the elderly to these stimuli can be enhanced by several means, e.g. prosthetic amplifiers such as hearing aids, eyeglasses, large print signs, vivid colors, multiple sense displays and expanded auditory and visual input; and such as slowed speech in which the voice is normal in tone and volume, but the words are spread out. Lindsley also suggests "response force amplifiers" so that the weak and disabled can still function by using such devices as electronic door openers, voice amplifiers, push button telephones and rate switches which would make electrical equipment safer to use. Various feedback mechanisms could help in training movements and responses. Various reinforcers need to be found to immediately and effectively reward appropriate behavior and responses. There is still much to be learned. However, it may well be that mechanisms which would help the disabled elderly to communicate better with "normal" people and to produce in some way for society, would enable them to become much more positively reinforcing to normal individuals and, hence, to suffer much less neglect.

MODIFICATIONS OF REHABILITATION APPROACHES IN THE GEROPSYCHIATRIC PATIENT

Much of the content of the rest of the chapters in this book will have relevance to rehabilitation in the older mentally disabled patient. Herein, modifications of these various techniques to make them more applicable to the aged will be discussed.

Physical Therapy and Exercise

In view of the enormous incidence of associated or coincidental physical impairment in the elderly mentally ill, the various physical therapies can play a crucial role in the maintenance or rehabilitation of the patient. Strokes and fractured hips occur frequently and require obvious therapy to restore strength and use. Waugh mentions several goals which help enhance function and hence decrease excessive dependency.[47] Among these goals are the maintenance of muscle and cardiac tone to prevent debility and enhance endurance; the stabilization of vasomotor tone, the lack of which probably contributes to the pathologically low blood pressures seen in many of the elderly mentally ill; the enhancement of nutrition and body metabolism to help prevent such deforming and inhibiting problems as osteoporosis, decubiti and contractures; and provision for another valuable patient-therapist relationship. Waugh uses general conditioning classes, followed by individual treatments, both graded and determined by the medical condition of the patient. Regular bodily exercise in the elderly involves release of kinesthetic stmuli which in turn provide emotional satisfaction. Kreitler notes that this breaks the vicious circle caused by distortions of body image due to prolonged inactivity, and reestablishes a feeling of security.[28] Evaluation of physical potential and gait training are important, and where a podiatrist is lacking, the physical therapist may be able to help with some of the common foot problems such as calluses, corns and overgrown toenails that hobble many of the elderly. Many of the pain problems of the elderly, as well as withdrawal, malaise and weakness, may be ameliorated by heat, massage or hydrotherapy. The main limiting factors are the diminished tolerances, due mainly to impairments of sensation and circulation.[3] The individual treatment sessions will need to be shortened and the total number increased. Wolff mentions the use of scotch douches and friction with cold water to stimulate generally weak and fatigued elderly patients, and warm baths and three-quarter packs to calm agitation and restlessness[55]; but as far as it is known, these are rarely used now. Milbank describes a therapeutic pool program for mentally ill geriatric patients.[36] The human touch and close attention of the therapist is probably of as much importance as the particular treatment modality.

Occupational Therapies

The occupational therapies cover a wide variety of activities. Wolk, et al.[57] and Wolff[56] set out the following as general goals in the aged: encouragement of group activities and socialization, improvement of the physical status, enhancement of self-esteem and confidence, development of socially acceptable means of expressing aggressive drives, and retardation of further isolation and regression. These may include the more traditional sorts of arts and crafts, adapted to the elderly, such as those described by Gould and Gould,[26] Merrill[35] or Fish.[21] Men are more likely to prefer such activities as woodworking, leather work and gardening, while women are more likely to engage in sewing, weaving and making clothes and quilts.

Milieu Therapy and the Therapeutic Community

Within recent years there have been major shifts from the idea of custodial care for the elderly psychiatric patient to comprehensive programs designed for maximal rehabilitation. Many have developed innovative and therapeutic treatment programs in recent years for the impaired elderly, such as Cosin,[15] Riemer,[41] Blanton,[5] Davidoff,[16] Lewandowski,[30] Davis,[17] Albers,[2] Lehrman,[29] Nathanson[37] and Berger and Berger[4]; but they have probably been most fully developed in the United States by the group at the University of Michigan under Donahue[18] and Gottesman.[25]

The basic premise is that the traditional facilities for elderly psychiatric patients expect them to play the passive, dependent, sick role, which leads to further regression. The therapeutic milieu prepares the patient to return to the community by offering him the social roles of normal society and helping him to learn to be a worker, citizen, consumer and friend within the protective environment of the hospital. The program includes workshops where contract work progressively varied for the person's abilities is carried out for pay. The wards are made more homelike with the patients wearing their own street clothes. Men and women are housed on the same wards, and the patients operate ward stores and functions. All of the patients participate in ward planning, and the staff functions as a democratic team. All treatments offer the patient a structured series of meaningful demands, with jobs broken down into their simplest components for the confused and regressed and made progressively more complex as the person's ability improves.[27]

Recreation Therapy

Recreation for the older person with mental disorders is too often provided by a television set and an occasional bus ride. The older person obviously needs times of diversion, relaxation and pleasure, but recreation should be directed to the preservation or restoration of creative functions, as these have often atrophied in the aged. Especially in the elderly, there is overlap between the various traditional therapeutic modalities. Such recreational activities as walks, dancing, rhythmical exercises, gardening, bowling or fishing provide valuable exercise. The more sedentary recreational activities such as sewing, weaving, woodwork, painting, pottery, cooking and games often seem strikingly like occupational therapy. Perhaps this points up the desirability of broadly trained and versatile rehabilitation therapists working with the aged. Some useful books have been written, such as those by Williams,[53] Merrill[35] or Lucas.[33]

Other valuable services provided by the recreation therapist are the ongoing evaluation of the progress and capacities of the geropsychiatric patient and the provision for adaptive programs of therapy.

Music Therapy

Especially among the elderly mental patients, music can be a valuable tool in rehabilitation. Boxberger and Cotter[7] reported that music therapy in the aged had the following results: improvement in personal appearance, a decrease in aggressiveness and incontinence, more appropriate behavior, a reduction in response to hallucinations and a decrease in undesirable patient noise. Movement to music and rhythm bands are helpful in expressing feelings, in socializing and in getting some exercise as well. Religious songs and hymns seem to be especially significant to the elderly, and some very demented patients may participate enthusiastically with some surprisingly remembered verses. This almost automatic type of vocalization can be used as a basis for restoration of spontaneous speech as described by Bright in her helpful book which includes sections on music in psychotherapy with the aged.[8]

Habit Training

Deterioration of personal hygiene, especially toilet habits, is very common among the elderly mentally disabled. Certainly, incontinence can be caused by many factors such as neurologic disease, urinary infection, disorientation and general senile deterioration; but it can also be an expression of hostile rejection because of feelings of not being given enough attention or care as noted by Macmillan and Shaw.[34] Many elderly people have only a brief time between the awareness of the need to void and the act. Hence, having toilets close by, marked with bright colors and a silhouette on the door may help the person to get to the toilet in time. Taking some incontinent patients to the toilet every two hours during the day and every three hours at night may help to restore patterns of continence, or at least to reduce the regressive state of soiled clothes.

Reality Orientation

A helpful technique of working with confused elderly patients has been developed by Folsom,[22] which he calls "reality orientation." One phase of this is a daily thirty-minute class of about six confused patients with an instructor (often an attendant) who in a calm, friendly way goes over, with each one, basic personal and current information such as his name, the place, the date, the weather, the menu and upcoming events. Much of this material is on a large board, and the instructor immediately verbally rewards correct responses with a "very good." As the person improves, more complex materials are added, such as time telling, reading and object manipulation. The second phase is the continual reality orientation that goes on in the whole environment where there are scattered bulletin boards with orienting information. The whole staff continually reinforces this by telling the patients who they are and what events are taking place. A number of quite organic elderly patients who are simply unable to retain the information, but who remember where to find the reality orientation board to get the facts, have been noticed. This seems to have a calming effect on some disturbed elderly patients who are frightened by their confusion.

Sensory Training

Methods of working with extremely organic or regressed elderly patients have been described by Bower[6] and Richman.[40] They feel that part of the confusion is secondary to sensory deprivation and cerebral "disuse atrophy." The method of sensory training uses a small group, with each person getting attention. Each sense receptor is stimulated individually, and the patient gets group feedback and consensual validations. The goal is to increase sensitivity and discrimination of feelings. The following modalities are used: kinesthetic and proprioceptive awareness of movements and of positions of body parts, tactile discrimination of textures and body contact, olfactory identification of odors, auditory attention to sounds and visual control of eye movements and fixation of attention, such as looking at oneself in a mirror. The sessions are ended by social and cognitive stimulations, such as singing songs and playing rhythm instruments. It is felt that patients who are too disabled to participate in any other complex activity can take part in this type of sensory training.

ENVIRONMENTAL FACTORS AFFECTING REHABILITATION IN THE ELDERLY

Many of the surroundings in which the elderly mentally disabled find themselves are designed more for economy, security or the convenience of the staff than for the well-being of the patient. The following are suggestions that would enhance self-esteem, social interaction and motivation and bring about more effective functioning. Some patients do better on open wards, while many prefer private or semiprivate rooms. Having a choice available allows the patient to have a say in his locale. Dining facilities with small tables and home-style meals help social interaction. Sitting areas should be subdivided so as to provide social groupings, rather than simply having chairs around the walls. Stairs or even a threshold step in a shower stall may present formidable barriers to an older patient with a paralysis or tremor. Handrails and safety devices in the toilets and showers may enable the person to carry out hygienic functions with a satisfying degree of independence. The elderly have increased difficulty distinguishing colors, and dull colors do tend to produce dreary, depressed feelings. The therapeutic use of bright contrasting wall paints, door colors and floor tiles to stimulate and activate the confused and partially blind has been reported by Agate.[1] Some think that the elderly need peace and quiet and, hence, maintain a funeral silence in the environment. This deprives the older patient of vital orienting background noises and reduces the ability to hear in some, as pointed out by Busse.[10] It is important that temperature be maintained between 68°F and 83°F, since many geropsychiatric patients have their already impaired temperature-regulating mechanisms further compromised by psychotropic drugs and inactivity, so that hypothermia, dehydration or hyperpyrexias can easily occur. Adequate lighting is important with the elderly, as dimness tends to lead to disorientation and depressed feelings. Bright light also is needed to help distinguish color and detail and to assist in lipreading and word distinction.

PSYCHIATRIC FACTORS IN REHABILITATION OF THE ELDERLY

The older person may react to illness in a variety of ways, some of which interfere with rehabilitation. As Clow[14] points out, some react to relatively minor physical illness with worry, bitterness, avoidance of any kind of activity and withdrawal from contacts. This may well represent a "masked depression," and the person may be settling on a passive suicide by refusing any treatment. Some of the elderly are fiercely independent and deny illness a great deal to avoid getting into situations where they will need to rely on others for help. Others will find illness a good excuse to indulge in previously frustrated dependency strivings and will thus resist rehabilitation efforts actively or passively. Many elderly people use hypochondriacal complaints to voice unrecognized wishes or problems; hence, rehabilitation efforts directed at the complaints will often fail until the basic strivings are met.[12] Many elderly people (and not a few of their physicians) will assume that many problems, both physical and mental, are just part of old age and hence will have little motivation to seek out assistance or to persist with it. Iatrogenic problems are very common in the elderly, one of the most common being adverse drug reactions. These produce a variety of psychiatric disorders, as well as physical effects, such as muscular rigidity and assorted dyskinesias and tremors. Discharge from a treatment facility may be delayed because the therapists have failed to be active enough in rehabilitation or because the family resists the discharge of the older patient. The author agrees with Risdorfer's[42] observations that early rehabilitation of the elderly is virtually mandatory, since discharge gets progressively more difficult if the patient is not out of an institution within about three months. The family and community tend to close off behind the patient unless special efforts are made to keep these lines of communication open.

The problem of inadequate treatment and rehabilitation among the elderly psychiatric patient has been pointed out by Linden,[31] who notes that static immobility, unimaginative nursing routines and failure to comprehend the ordinary human needs of nonpsychotic oldsters mean anguish, disease, premature demise, unproductive stagnation, deterioration and misery for the older persons thus deprived. Some of the elderly, however, who have been in a rehabilitation program, will be reluctant to leave it because that environment is so much better than the one they anticipate outside, and they will deny health and readiness to leave. Be that as it may, it is necessary to pursue the rehabilitation of the mentally disabled geriatric patient with flexibility, determination and humaneness. Indeed, it is increasingly important to train others in these types of rehabilitation in order to continue these efforts wherever the older person might be, so that the gains that he makes can be nurtured and sustained and his life can continue to be as meaningful and pleasant as possible.

Summary

The older mentally disabled people have a particular risk because of the multiplicity of their problems, the pessimism or nihilism of most therapists toward the elderly, the low priority put on their rehabilitation by our society and the lack of coordination of efforts. It is essential to recognize that the elderly do have problems which make it necessary to modify goals of rehabilitation for them. There are both physical and environmental factors which contribute to and complicate psychiatric disorders in the aged, and the learning and performance capacities of the geropsychiatric patient affect his rehabilitation. Various modifications of rehabilitation approaches are dealt with in terms of physical therapy and exercise, occupational therapy, milieu therapy and therapeutic communities, recreation therapy, music therapy, habit training, reality orientation and sensory training. Both environmental and psychiatric elements which facilitate or hamper rehabilitation are dealt with. Early and effective rehabilitation efforts with the mentally disabled geriatric patient will pay off with a return of a reasonable level of function in many and with a happier and fuller life for those whose disease can only be ameliorated.

REFERENCES

1. Agate, J.: *The Practice of Geriatrics,* 2nd. ed. Springfield, Thomas, 1970, pp. 357-384.
2. Albers, D. A., Howard, G. W., and Pasewark, R. W.: The geriatric profile index: A system for identifying, managing and planning for geriatric patients in state hospitals. *J Am Geriatr Soc, 17*(11):1108-1112, 1969.
3. Andrews, G. R., and Ofner, F.: The limitations of reflex heating therapy in the elderly. *J Am Geriatr Soc, 20*(2):84-87, February 1972.

4. Berger, M. M., and Berger, L. F.: An innovative program for a private psychogeriatric day center. *J Am Geriatr Soc, 19*(4):332-336, 1971.
5. Blanton, J. L.: Essentials for rehabilitation in the aged. *J Am Geriatr Soc, 2*:174-178, 1954.
6. Bower, H. M.: Sensory stimulation and the treatment of senile dementia. *Med J Aust, 1*:1113-1119, January-June 1967.
7. Boxberger, R., and Cotter, V. W.: Music therapy for geriatric patients. In Gaston, E. T. (Ed.): *Music in Therapy*. New York, Macmillan, 1968, pp. 269-290.
8. Bright, R.: *Music in Geriatric Care*. Sydney, Australia, Angus and Robertson, 1972.
9. Busse, E. W.: The geriatric patient and the nursing home. *NC Med J, 33*:218-222, 1972.
10. Busse, E. W.: Problems affecting psychiatric care of the aging. *Geriatrics, 15*:673-680, 1960.
11. Busse, E. W.: Some emotional complications of chronic disease. *Gerontologist, 2*:153-156, 1962.
12. Busse, E. W.: The treatment of hypochondriasis. *Tri-State Medical Journal, 2*:7-12, 1954.
13. Busse, E. W., Dovenmuehle, R. H., and Brown, R. G.: Psychoneurotic reactions of the aged. *Geriatrics, 15*:97-105, 1960.
14. Clow, H. E.: Psychiatric factors in the rehabilitation of the aging. *Ment Hyg, 34*:592-599, 1950.
15. Cosin, L. Z.: A statistical analysis of geriatric rehabilitation. *J Gerontol, 7*:570-578, 1952.
16. Davidoff, E.: Psychiatric aspects of geriatric rehabilitation. *NY State J Med, 55*:2200-2201, August 1955.
17. Davis, J. E.: Evaluation and planning for the elderly psychiatric patient. *Geriatrics, 18*:238-246, 1963.
18. Donahue, W., Hunter, W. W., Coons, D., and Maurice, H.: Rehabilitation of geriatric patients in county hospitals. *Geriatrics, 15*:263-274, April 1960.
19. Eisdorfer, D.: New dimension and a tentative theory. *Gerontologist, 7*:14-18, 1967.
20. Filer, R. N., and O'Connell, D. D.: Motivation of aging persons. *J Gerontol, 19*:15-22, 1964.
21. Fish, U. H.: *Activities Program for Senior Citizens*. West Nyack, Parker Pub, 1971.
22. Folsom, J. C.: Reality orientation for the elderly mental patient. *J Geriatr Psychiatry, 1*:291-307, 1968.
23. Goffman, E.: *Asylums*. Chicago, Aldine, 1961.
24. Goldfarb, A. I.: Prevalence of psychiatric disorders in metropolitan old age and nursing homes. *J Am Geriatr Soc, 10*:77-84, 1962.
25. Gottesman, L. E.: Organizing rehabilitation services for the elderly. *Gerontologist, 10*:287-293, 1970.

26. Gould, E., and Gould, L.: *Crafts for the Elderly*. Springfield, Thomas, 1971.
27. Gralewicz, A., Hill, B., and Mackinson, M.: Restoration therapy: An approach to group therapy for the chronically ill. *Am J Occup Ther, 22*:294-299, 1968.
28. Kreitler, H., and Kreitler, S.: Movement and aging: A psychological approach. *Medicine and Sport, Vol. 4: Physical Activity and Aging.* Basel/New York, Karger, 1970, pp. 302-306.
29. Lehrman, N. S., and Friedman, J. H.: A treatment-focused geriatric program in a state mental hospital. *J Am Geriatr Soc, 17*(11):1092-1096, 1969.
30. Lewandowski, T.: Evaluation of patients in a geriatric rehabilitation unit of a state mental hospital: Use of a rating scale system. *J Am Geriatr Soc, 10*:526-531, 1962.
31. Linden, M. E.: The new philosophy of care for the aged. In Leeds, M., and Shore, H. (Eds.): *Geriatric Institutional Management*. New York, Putnam, 1964.
32. Lindsley, O. R.: Geriatric behavioral prosthetics. In Kastenbaum, R. (Ed.): *New Thoughts on Old Age*. New York, Springer Pub, 1964.
33. Lucas, C.: *Recreation in Gerontology*. Springfield, Thomas, 1964.
34. Macmillan, D., and Shaw, P.: Senile breakdown in standards of personal and environmental cleanliness. *Br Med J, 2*:1032-1037, 1966.
35. Merrill, I.: *Activities for the Aged and Infirm*. Springfield, Thomas, 1967.
36. Milbank, F. L.: A therapeutic pool program for mentally ill geriatric patients. *J Assoc Phys Ment Rehabil, 19*:52-54, 1965.
37. Nathanson, B. F., and Reingold, J.: A workshop for mentally impaired aged. *Gerontologist, 9*:293-295, 1969.
38. Pfeiffer, E., and Busse, E. W.: Mental disorders in later life — affective disorders; paranoid, neurotic and situational reactions. In Busse, E. W., and Pfeiffer, E. (Eds.): *Mental Illness in Later Life*. Washington, D.C., American Psychiatric Association, 1973.
39. Pincus, A.: New findings on learning in old age: Implications for occupational therapy. *Am J Occup Ther, 22*:300-303, 1968.
40. Richman, L.: Sensory training for geriatric patients. *Am J Occup Ther, 23*:254-257, 1969.
41. Riemer, D.: Rehabilitation program for chronically ill elderly patients in a neuropsychiatric hospital. *Arch Phys Med Rehabil, 35*:754-759, 1954.
42. Risdorfer, E. N.: Review of results in a geriatric intensive treatment unit: Some prospects. *J Am Geriatr Soc, 18*:47-55, 1970.
43. Rudd, J. L., and Margolin, R. J.: Basic concepts in the rehabilitation of hospitalized aging patients. *J Am Geriatr Soc, 8*:531-536, 1960.
44. Rudd, J. L., and Margolin, R. J. (Eds.): *Maintenance Therapy for the Geriatric Patient*. Springfield, Thomas, 1968.

45. Stotsky, B. A., and Frye, S.: Comparison of psychiatric and nonpsychiatric patients in nursing homes. *J Am Geriatr Soc, 15*:355-363, 1967.
46. Troyer, W., Eisorfer, C., Wilkie, F., and Bogdonoff, M.: Free fatty responses in the aged individual during performance of learning tasks. *J Gerontol, 21*:415-419, 1966.
47. Waugh, J. W.: Objectives of physical medicine and rehabilitation in a chronic disease and geriatrics facility. *J Am Geriatr Soc, 10*:522-525, 1962.
48. Whanger, A. D.: Classification of the institutionalized elderly. A paper presented at the twenty-sixth annual meeting of the Gerontological Society, November 1973. In preparation for publication.
49. Whanger, A. D.: Paranoid syndromes of the senium. In Eisdorfer, C., and Fann, W. E. (Eds.): *Psychopharmacology and Aging.* New York, Plenum Pub, 1973, pp. 203-211.
50. Whanger, A. D.: Vitamins and vigor at 65 plus. *Postgrad Med, 53*:167-172, 1973.
51. Whanger, A. D., and Wang, H. S.: Clinical correlates of the vibratory sense in elderly psychiatric patients. *J Gerontol, 29*:39-45, 1974.
52. Wheeler, P. C., and Wolcott, L. E.: Three vital considerations in geriatric rehabilitation. *J Am Geriatr Soc, 18*(4):303-309, 1970.
53. Williams, A. M.: *Recreation in the Senior Years.* Compiled for the National Recreation Association. New York, Associated Press, 1962.
54. Wolcott, L. E., and Wheeler, P. C.: Rehabilitation and the aged. In Chinn, A. B. (Ed.): *Working With Older People. Vol. IV: Clinical Aspects of Aging.*, Washington, D.C., U.S. Dept. of HEW, Public Health Service publ. no. 1458, 1971.
55. Wolff, K.: *The Emotional Rehabilitation of the Geriatric Patient.* Springfield, Thomas, 1970.
56. Wolff, K.: Rehabilitating geriatric patients. *Hosp Community Psychiatry, 22*:8-11, January 1971.
57. Wolk, R. L.: Seiden, R. B., and Wolverton, B.: Unique influences and goals of an occupational therapy program in a home for the aged. *J Am Geriatr Soc, 13*:989-997, 1965.

Chapter 12

REALITY ORIENTATION: A TECHNIQUE TO REHABILITATE ELDERLY AND BRAIN-DAMAGED PATIENTS WITH A MODERATE TO SEVERE DEGREE OF DISORIENTATION

James C. Folsom

At the May 1966 annual meeting of the American Psychiatric Association, the author read a paper titled, "Reality Orientation for the Elderly Mental Patient." The introductory paragraph stated:

> Of all the men and women who have reached the age of sixty-five since the dawn of mankind, 25 percent are alive today. Life expectancy at birth in 1900 was 47.3 years; in 1939 it was 69.7 – an increase of more than twenty-two years. Today's figures are even higher – clearly the trend is for an even longer life. The aged population is expected to more than double in the forty years between 1960 and 2000. Due to this increasing lifespan, one of the most critical problems facing the mental health field is the large number of geriatric mental patients.

Many elderly individuals who are not mental cases show a significant degree of confusion. This leads to serious problems in their management, not only in organized homes for the aging, but also in their own homes. Frequently a minor manifestation of confusion leads to the individual having his decision-making ability taken away from him and dependency forced on him—both factors compounding the damage.

Beginning in 1959 at the Veterans Hospital in Topeka, Kansas and recognizing the increasing significance of the problem of geriatric mental patients, a pilot study in the rehabilitation of these patients was undertaken. A rehabilitation bed service for geriatric mental patients was established. The focus of this pilot study was to use the full treatment potential of all employees on a fifty-bed unit. This program was described by Esther Lucille Brown:*

> A revaluation of care of the unit for elderly patients indicated that physical needs were being well met, but emotional needs of individual patients required concentrated attention. Since nursing assistants are with the patients far more than anyone else, the question was one of how they could be motivated and helped to assume the responsibility that extended well beyond the daily physical care of their charges.
>
> The nursing supervisor suggested to the nursing assistants that they might like to learn more about the total patient-care program for this group of senile, if not psychotic, men. Hence, they were given time to visit the physical and corrective therapy units where they could find out about the objectives of treatment of those two services. The nursing supervisor met with them regularly to provide opportunity for discussion of what they had learned, as well as discussion of their own skills and interests.
>
> At about this time a questionnaire was designed to survey quickly the different skills and interests of each nurse and nursing assistant. The completed questionnaires were viewed as a prospective aid not only in assigning the most interested personnel to the various activities on and off the unit, but in stimulating initiative among the ward staff in wanting to organize patient groups.
>
> The focus of the meetings led by the nursing supervisor then became one of encouraging the nursing assistants to plan, develop and expand patient activities in their own way, but in close relationship with their charges. The objective of these activities was described to the nursing assistants as "helping the patient to share group experiences." Attention was also focused upon encouraging the nursing assistants to see and think about the patients as individuals.
>
> At the request of the nursing supervisor, her meetings with the nursing assistants were replaced by those of a rehabilitation team, whose purpose was to demonstrate the importance of the nursing assistant as a member of the treatment group and to overcome his re-

*This description has been prepared from the unpublished paper "An Aide-centered Activity Program for Elderly Patients" and from a brief visit this author made to the program. The authors of the paper are James Folsom, Jacob Gier and Llewellyn White, two of the physicians and the nursing supervisor referred to in the text.

luctance to talk and to share in the planning of activities. All the members of a complete rehabilitation team, as constituted in the Winter VA Hospital, attended the meetings whenever they could. They included the chief psychiatrist of the geriatrics section, the internist for the section, the chief of the Physical Medicine and Rehabilitation Service — who is a psychiatrist — the nurses and nursing assistants of the unit, a social worker, occupational therapist, corrective therapist, physical therapist, librarian, recreational leader and volunteer worker.

The nursing assistants were asked to suggest activities they would like to start with patients — such as ceramics, yard work or singing. They then received initial assistance in planning from the appropriate adjunctive therapists and began working with small groups of patients under the supervision of these therapists. If they exhibited sufficient interest and ability, they were shortly encouraged to use their own initiative in creating activity programs. As a result, patients who had spent much of their time sitting idly in a dayroom or pacing the floor agressively because of inadequate numbers of occupational and recreational therapists were introduced to a variety of group undertakings on the unit, out-of-doors or in the hospital shops.

The meetings of the rehabilitation team were also used to emphasize the potential value of every staff-patient relationship. Furthermore, they provided a place where nursing assistants were invited to bring their problems with individual patients. Among these senile men, irritability, agitation, hyperactivity, noisiness or even assaultiveness were not uncommon and created difficult management situations. Through group discussion, ways could often be found for reducing a patient's tension, thus making things more comfortable for him, the other men and the nursing assistants. The very opportunity to express frustration and anxiety in a sympathetic group tended, moreover, to reduce stress among the nursing assistants.

In the opinion of the physicians and the nursing supervisor, the principal value of this program lay in its recognition of the importance of the nursing assistant as a member of a total treatment group, in its according him status through the meetings of the rehabilitation team and in his then assuming his place in the overall planning of patient activities.

The Topeka VA program was considered successful in halting and sometimes reversing the progress of confusion and the development of further dependency in the patients. A pilot study based on the same concepts was tried a year later at the Mental Health Institute (a 1000-bed state hospital) in Mt. Pleasant, Iowa. At the time the project was started, a review of the previous three years' experience showed that only 3 percent of the geriatric patients had improved enough to return to prehospital adjustment.

The focus of this program, as in Topeka, was to utilize available personnel to the fullest extent. The author also planned to emphasize various techniques of attitude therapy. To optimize the results of the program, certain ground rules were considered essential. To be admitted to this new pilot study geriatric ward, patients had to be (1) over sixty-five; (2) able to walk; (3) new in the program; (4) mentally ill (the degree of illness, such as total disorientation, incontinence of urine and feces, smearing of excreta, etc., was no bar to admission to the program).

Within six months the staff had established guidelines and had developed techniques for helping the confused elderly patient reorient himself to reality. The case study of an 89-year-old patient illustrates some of these techniques in action. The following was taken from his hospital record:

> This 89-year-old, widowed, white male entered for the first time on February 11, 1962. He was brought by the deputy sheriff. He was brought on an ambulance cart. His wrists were in steel cuffs. He was so tightly bound that the steel was cutting into one of his wrists. He could not be aroused, being heavily sedated. It was stated that he had been quite upset for about three weeks. He had been receiving Librium®, Thorazine® and chloral hydrate. He had attacked nursing home personnel and other patients prior to being brought here. He had been wandering around the county in a confused state.
>
> At Intake Staff, when asked how he was getting along, he replied, "Fair." He continued by saying, "I guess I'm OK. I've not been very good here lately. It seems like they put my stuff away. Some fellow told me they put it away over in that shed. I guess I'm doing pretty well." When asked where he was, he paused for a long time and replied, "I'm pretty well . . . I'm . . . let's see . . . oh . . . it's . . . When asked when he was born he replied, "I don't remember."

What could possibly be done for this 89-year-old man who was so disoriented and disturbed? The following material shows how treatment was initiated in the geriatric ward:

> An attendant from the admitting ward escorted Mr. Smith to the geriatric ward and introduced him to the attendant, Mrs. Johnson. Mrs. Johnson did not force herself on him; she recognized that he was

not sure of himself. She knew that one of his chief complaints had been that all of his belongings had been stolen from him and had been put in a "shed out there." Mrs. Johnson had discussed Mr. Smith's admission with several other staff members before his arrival. They decided that the proper approach was to stay with him as much as possible and to remind him constantly that his belongings were safe. They planned careful orientation to the ward setting.

Mrs. Johnson's first overture was to take Mr. Smith into the clothing storage room and show him the cubicle which held his clothing. He was surprised. Mrs. Johnson explained that all of his things would be gathered together and placed there. He would be able to check on them as frequently as he desired.

The next step in the orientation program was to show Mr. Smith his own bed. Mrs. Johnson told him that the bed with the blue bedspread was his, and that the chair next to it was his, and that he should try to help keep these things straight and keep his bed made when he was not using it.

Mrs. Johnson next showed Mr. Smith the bathroom. He responded immediately to this. He had been extremely untidy on the admission ward. Indeed, he had been so untidy that the physician on the admission ward thought that he should not be sent to the active geriatric treatment ward, but should go to the "untidy" ward in the geriatric building. The staff of the active geriatric treatment ward disagreed because Mr. Smith met all their requirements for admission, and they agreed to accept him in spite of his untidiness. When shown the bathroom, he immediately asked, "May I use it?" He went in, closed the door, used the toilet and came out after having buttoned his clothes, washed his hands, etc.

Mrs. Johnson then took the patient to the dayroom. She explained to him that he did not need to try to remember all the people's names, but that he should remember each time to tell other ward members who he was.

Mrs. Johnson held Mr. Smith's arm lightly while introducing him in order to give him some confidence and to see that he went with her.

After Mr. Smith was introduced to all the ward personnel as well as the patients, she took him to one of the work tables. Another nursing assistant was helping the other patients with ceramics. No effort was made to force Mr. Smith to participate. He was given time to "get his bearings" before any active participation was expected.

Within a few minutes, the second nursing assistant had moved in and was talking with Mr. Smith and being supportive, while Mrs. Johnson stayed at the table to keep him from feeling isolated.

This careful orientation to the ward was considered to be of utmost importance. A baseline of acceptance, concern and expectation of participation in one's own recovery was established. A feeling of calmness, consistency and security was communicated to the patient. He could now give up some of his feelings of loneliness, worthlessness, apathy, confusion and disorientation. The staff was trying to help him give up his illness.

Each patient was carefully considered to find areas of "wellness." When we found such an area, we tried to expand its boundaries. We felt that it was of utmost importance to keep the ward environment as calm as possible, and we tried to reinforce the staff's valiant efforts to remain calm in the face of any disturbance, thereby encouraging the patients to do likewise.

At first some of the patients seemed to know nothing, not even their own name. With such patients, the staff made repeated efforts throughout the day and night to call the patient's attention to his own name and help him to relearn who he was. We made no effort to hide from the patient the fact that he was in a mental hospital. Indeed, we encouraged the patient to accept the fact that he was in a mental hospital and that we, the treatment team, held out hope for his eventual return to his own community living.

As the employees on the geriatric treatment ward became better acquainted and learned to function as a team, guidelines were established. Reality orientation as used here implies a specific set of ideas to be followed. They are

1. a calm environment;
2. a set routine;
3. clear responses to patients' questions, and the same types of questions should be asked of the patient;
4. talking clearly to the patient, not necessarily loudly;
5. clear directions to patients; if need be, guidance for them to and from their destinations;
6. reminding them of the date, time, etc.;
7. not letting them stay confused by allowing them to ramble in their speech, actions, etc.;
8. firmness when necessary; and
9. sincerity.

These guidelines were formally stated early in 1962. Approximately two years later, the chief nurse at the Mental Health Institute, Mt. Pleasant, Iowa, Beverly A. Benfer,[1] added two more points: "Make requests of patients in calm manner, implying patient will comply," and "consistency."*

Every effort was made to maintain as much continuity as possible. For example, the patients were not moved from the ward area for their meals. The dayroom served as living room, activity center, occupational therapy clinic and dining room. When the patients saw the tables being prepared for meals and the occupational therapy equipment being removed to make way for the food carts, they knew that it was time to get ready for meals. In this way the patients were given the responsibility for making some decisions on their own. They would go and clean up for meals without having to be reminded that it was time to do so.

Routines were established early. Patients who could not remember their own names were greeted on awakening by name. The individual awakening them would also give his own name. Patients were told repeatedly that they did not have to try to remember the names of other patients or employees but that they should be willing to give their own name when asked. Every effort was made to answer the patient's questions as honestly and as simply as possible. Personnel spoke to the patients in short sentences, reminding themselves constantly that they should not shout at the patients. It was observed early in this treatment program that many people seemed to think that all elderly patients were deaf. It was soon found that if one spoke distinctly and slowly that the elderly patients could understand quite well. Many of them, even though hard of hearing, could read lips fairly well.

Patients who had difficulty with time orientation were given small calendars. A game was made of marking off the days. Some patients, after a few days or weeks of being reminded to mark their calendars, would come with a great deal of pride to the office to show the nursing staff that they had already marked their calendars and to remind the nurse that it was time for her to mark the calendar on the office wall.

---

*Kramer and Johnston[3] elaborate on these same eleven points.

When patients would begin to ramble in conversation or to talk unrealistically, they would be directed back to reality-oriented endeavors. If they began to show erratic behavior, such as purposeless movements; picking at their clothes; buttoning and unbuttoning their clothes; and tearing clothing, furniture, or curtains; they were given purposeful things to do.

When necessary, the staff would be firm with the patients to show them that they were going to help them control behavior which was disturbing not only to other people, but often to the patient himself. Through all of this the personnel maintained an air of sincerity, holding out to the patient hope that he could improve his behavior and return to his prehospital life.

In all contacts with the family, personnel planned frequent visits by the family to the hospital. The staff always reminded them that every effort was directed toward helping the patient to return to his prehospital adjustment at the earliest possible time. In addition to reminding the families that they were expected to visit, staff would assist the patient in writing letters.

During the first six months of this pilot study, "Reality Orientation for the Elderly Mental Patient," 49 percent of the patients admitted improved sufficiently to return to their prehospital adjustment. The figures for the entire year of the pilot study showed 57 percent of the patients returned to their prehospital adjustment. Following the completion of the one-year pilot study, this program was expanded to the wards containing the other several hundred geriatric patients then residing at the institute.

In 1965 a program of reality orientation for the elderly mental patient was begun at the VA Hospital in Tuscaloosa, Alabama. The philosophies and techniques of the program in Tuscaloosa were described by the author in a speech to a group of rehabilitation therapists as follows:

> We believe consistency of approach is the key to the rehabilitation of the confused patient. Each person who comes in contact with the patient must understand his treatment objective, know and use the same type of approach when working with the patient. To achieve this consistency of treatment, we have found the team approach to be the most effective means of communication both for the staff and for the patient. Attitude therapy is basic to all our treatment programs

at Tuscaloosa, and the treatment of geriatric or psychiatric medically infirm patients is no exception. When a patient is admitted to a unit, an attitude is prescribed for him by the treatment team. The "active friendliness" attitude is usually prescribed for the geriatric patient. This is an ego-building attitude which helps the patient feel that he is worth something after all, that someone cares, that life has not passed him by. Other attitudes may be prescribed by the team depending on the behavior the patient is exhibiting. If the patient is found to be confused, he will be placed on twenty-four-hour reality orientation and may be placed in one of the basic or advanced classes. The determination for placement is based on psychological testing, social history and behavior observed on the unit.

Orientation to reality is taken at its most basic meaning. If the patient does not know his own name, he is first taught his own name. If he does not know where he is and where he is from, these facts are taught next. Then he is taught such things as the day, week, month, year, his age, etc.

Placement on the reality orientation program is done by prescription of the ward physician after the entire treatment team has reviewed the case at a treatment planning conference. The degree of disorientation is not too significant. Particularly is this true concerning newly admitted cases. We have seen patients enter the hospital not even aware of their own names, and yet after a reality orientation program on the ward, we have found them quite capable of reorientation to reality. Our experience has been that some patients may continue to exhibit confusion and lack of orientation for a period of many weeks, and only then begin to show some evidence of being able to learn material again and to recall. Once the patient is able to grasp any bit of information, such as his own name, the name of his spouse, his address, his birthday, etc., then he begins to recall and to be able to use ever increasing amounts of material previously known.

The reorientation to reality goes on around the clock in that the patient is constantly reminded of who he is, where he is, why he is there and what we are expecting of him. In addition to this around-the-clock orientation, we have specific classes in reorientation. These are divided into two parts — a basic class which meets one half-hour one time each day, five days a week, and an advanced class which also meets once a day — Monday through Friday. Continuity is maintained through class adherence to scheduling and also to seeing that the same personnel are assigned to these classes as consistently as possible.

The following is a case study of a patient who was treated in the author's reality orientation program:

Mr. Farmer was a 77-year-old veteran who had been employed

at the hospital for many years as a nursing assistant. After retirement, he had two heart attacks and a number of small strokes. With each illness he was hospitalized in a general hospital; then he was sent home dependent on his family for twenty-four-hour care. After the last stroke had left him paralyzed on the left side, the family, financially and physically exhausted, had him admitted to the VA hospital.

Mr. Farmer was brought to the hospital admission on an ambulance stretcher. His wife and daughters were reluctant to bring him to the VA.

When Mr. Farmer, arrived on the unit, the daughter—who is a registered nurse by profession—gave the nurse a copy of the care plan they had been using for her father. She told the nurse that her father was to be up in a wheelchair four times a day on a sheepskin, to prevent pressure ulcers. He was to be fed, as he was unable to feed himself. Also, his teeth did not fit well, so the food should be soft. He had to have an enema every other day. Since he had an indwelling catheter, it was necessary to irrigate the catheter regularly. He made frequent demands, and they attempted to do whatever he wanted since he was very confused much of the time.

On arriving on the geriatric ward, the nursing assistant began reality orientation by telling Mr. Farmer where he was, who he was and what was expected of him. He also introduced Mr. Farmer to other staff members.

At the daily nursing team conference session, each staff member shared his knowledge of Mr. Farmer. They discussed the information given to them by his wife and daughter. The nursing team found Mr. Farmer very confused and disoriented, indeed. They decided to place him on 24-hour reality orientation and to encourage him to do all he could for himself.

Physical therapy was begun on the ward with follow-up by the nursing staff. Soon Mr. Farmer was able to be up in the wheelchair most of the day. The staff was careful to show him his bedside locker, the location of the dayroom, the bathroom and the dining room. Mr. Farmer was fed for a few meals; then his tray was placed before him, and he was told he could go ahead. He took his spoon and, shaking all the way, lifted food to his mouth. Even though he spilled a good deal, he was pleased to be able to feed himself. The staff encouraged him to continue. In a very few days he was able to feed himself without assistance.

Soon after admission a treatment planning conference was conducted for each patient. Mr. Farmer was interviewed by the team leader. Each person had had some previous contact with the patient and was able to relate to him in a personal way.

After due consideration, the team decided to schedule Mr. Farmer for the basic reality orientation classes daily in addition to twenty-four-hour reality orientation. The corrective therapist recommended that Mr. Farmer be sent to his clinic daily to learn to walk again. All personnel were to treat Mr. Farmer with the attitude of active friendliness. His catheter had been removed, and enemas were not needed. He had already begun the habit training program to reestablish natural bowel and bladder patterns. He was to be encouraged to do as much for himself as possible.

The patient's family become a part of the total treatment program from the day of admission. A staff nurse explained to Mr. Farmer's wife and daughter the treatment plan for Mr. Farmer. She showed the family how the reality board is used to help the confused patients become oriented again. The family was encouraged not to agree with the patient's confused statements, but to help him by being consistent with reality orientation.

Mr. Farmer started attending the reality orientation classes a few days after admission. These classes are kept small so that each man gets individual attention.

On Mr. Farmer's third day in the corrective therapy clinic, he was already making progress on the parallel bars. He was later able to walk to reality orientation classes with the aid of his cane.

His confusion became only sporadic. He knew who he was, where he was, the date and the instructor's name. After a few days, he could read the reality board, tell the time and identify common objects.

Activities play a very important part in the rehabilitation process. Mr. Bowles, occupational therapist, helped Mr. Farmer learn a simple activity which was calculated to restore fine movements in his hands and to build his confidence in himself. With confusion often comes a very short attention span. As the patient becomes more oriented, he is able to concentrate for longer periods of time on more complicated activities.

Discharge planning is begun on admission and continues until the patient is reestablished at home. The social worker emphasized to the family the use of reality orientation techniques. She stressed the importance of allowing the patient to be as independent as possible when he went home. His family was so skeptical of being able to take him home that a series of conferences with the family were required before they were convinced that he would not need total nursing care. They had to believe that he could recover and take care of his own needs if he was to continue to make progress at home.

Two months after admission, Mr. Farmer was ready to go home. Because the family felt so insecure, he was given a twenty-nine-day leave instead of a discharge. The staff assured the family of full support and encouraged them to call at any time they needed help. He got along so well he was discharged from this leave with outpatient follow-up.

One year later Mr. Farmer returned to the outpatient clinic for a routine check-up. He no longer used a cane, but walked wherever he wanted to go. He visited the unit and the reality orientation classroom. He had only praise for the care he received. He said he did not remember coming to the hospital, but he felt like he was in a dream and suddenly began to wake up. He said it was for him "a return to life."

Our experience suggests that a reality orientation program has potential in preventive medicine. The confused, elderly person will benefit more if oriented when the first signs of confusion are noted. The program should begin in the hospital following a stroke, when postoperative confusion is seen or when confusion develops at home following a major loss or change. It is the author's firm belief that if such a program for the confused elderly individual is initiated and followed consistently in the community, many will be able to function and need never be admitted to a psychiatric institution.

The following factors are important in dealing with the problems of the aging:

1. Refuse to believe in hopelessness — combat the usual brain washing that occurs when an elderly person has a stroke, exhibits confusion, forgetfulness, etc., i.e. hold out constantly the expectation of better performance in the future.
2. Accept each person for his own worth.
3. Believe that senility is caused — or to say it another way, senile behavior is shaped — then becomes habitual and beyond the individual's control; however, since it is understandable and has a cause, then it can be reversed.
4. Let the personnel, nonprofessionals as well as professionals, see the pleasures of helping a confused, untidy, senile old person become oriented so as to be capable of self-determination in his own affairs.
5. Help oneself and one's fellow employees learn to defend the position that senility is not an absolute and that it can be reversed.

Rehabilitation therapists play an extremely important role in all aspects of the care and treatment of the aging individual. It is of utmost importance that they work closely with other members of the multidisciplinary treatment team—the physicians, nurses, psychologists, dietitians and social workers; and most important of all, they must communicate and cooperate with those staff members who are with the patient the most—the nursing assistants.

REFERENCES

1. Benfer, B. A.: Geriatric-psychiatric nursing. *Bull Inst Gerontol, Suppl 12,* 10, 1963.
2. Brown, E. L.: Improving staff motivation and competence in the general hospital, part two. In *Newer Dimensions of Patient Care.* New York. Russell Sage, 1962.
3. Kramer, C. H., and Johnston, G. F.: Correcting confusion in the brain-damaged. *Geriatric Nurs, 1*(1):23-25, 1965.

Section VIII

THE ROLE OF THE PSYCHOLOGIST, SOCIAL WORKER AND COORDINATOR

Chapter 13

PSYCHOLOGICAL SERVICES IN THE REHABILITATION OF HOSPITALIZED PSYCHIATRIC PATIENTS

SEYMOUR G. KLEBANOFF

THE PRESENTATION OF PSYCHOLOGICAL SERVICES in the psychiatric hospital setting may be accomplished through varied and diverse organizational structures. It is possible to delineate the traditional triadic functions of clinical psychology which include psychodiagnostic assessment, psychotherapy or behavior modification and research; and to add to these a group of more unique, more recently evolved and less conventional modalities of psychological services. An alternate or perhaps additional approach would be a presentation of the manner in which numerous options or specialties within the field of psychology have acquired significant roles in the overall rehabilitation of hospitalized psychiatric patients. In this respect, one must consider the contribution to rehabilitation not only of such specialties as clinical and counseling psychology, but also of social psychology, experimental psychology, physiological psychology, neuropsychology and personnel psychology. A most striking evolution of the scope of role development compares with the historically significant contributions of those who paved the way circa 1930. And yet, the roots of present-day delivery of psychological services in the psychiatric hospital are so clearly traceable to the pioneer contributions and concepts of such persons as Wells at Boston Psychopathic Hospital, Shakow at Worcester State Hospital, Wechsler at Bellevue Hospital and Wittman at Elgin State Hospital. The current emergence of the diverse and complex range of psychological functions in psychiatric rehabilitation seems intimately related to the efforts of those who earlier demonstrated that psychodiagnostic testing along with research in such assessment could play a very meaningful part in the evaluation of rehabilitation goals.

In hospitals or institutions for behavioral deviation, the assessment function of the psychologist was the precursor of subsequent role development. As assessment test techniques developed and as less structured qualitative test methods were designed, the institutional "psychometrist" deferred to the developing professional role of the hospital clinical psychologist. The earliest assessment technique included evaluation of intellectual functioning of a global kind, followed by the development of specialized test methods to assess components of overall intelligence. With the development of tests of memory functioning, judgment, abstract or conceptual thinking, personality content and structure and even specialized tests for the evaluation of organic brain impairment, the psychologist was thus prepared to make a significant contribution to rehabilitation. Further, as vocational interest and aptitude assessment methods were developed, the armamentarium of the psychologist was now relatively complete.

And so the assessment function through test methods emerged as the earliest role of the hospital psychologist in psychiatric rehabilitation. Since the global concept of rehabilitation has many component segments such as vocational rehabilitation, social rehabilitation and psychiatric rehabilitation, the role of the psychologist assumes broad dimensions. The psychologist would be expected to assess vocational aptitude, interest and potential through the use of a wide range of reliable and valid test methods. Such evaluative findings are significant when adequately communicated to the multidisciplinary mental health team, with special reference to educational and rehabilitation therapists who should be prepared to initiate in-hospital training to achieve the vocational rehabilitation goals. Simultaneous with the in-hospital vocational training, the hospital psychologist should be conducting group guidance sessions, group counseling programs and individual counseling with patients. Issues such as motivation, the impact of the world of work, job tolerance and the existing job market in the community must be thoroughly discussed in the preparation of the patient.

The vocational rehabilitation of more chronic psychiatric patients with lengthy periods of continuous hospitalization becomes more complex. Many patients in this category have achieved the psychiatric and social levels of rehabilitation necessary to live and work in the community, but have become so dependently institutionalized that they manifest acute panic and even exacerbation of symptoms at the prospect of leaving the hospital. In such cases, transitional vocational and social rehabilitation programs are vitally necessary, and the hospital psychologist has numerous contributions to present in such programs.

Thorough psychodiagnostic clinical evaluation of the psychiatric status of the patient is a primary requirement. The psychiatric status of the patient must be compatible with realistic posthospital planning. The contribution of the hospital psychologist in the area of group psychotherapy may become significant in achieving the required level of social rehabilitation for return to the community and the world of work. In certain instances a more intensive individual psychotherapeutic approach by the psychologist may be indicated to prepare chronic patients for transitional work-therapy programs. It is, however, critical that communication among all disciplines of the mental health team be meaningful and consistent since successful total rehabilitation of the psychiatric patient requires a multidisciplinary process of activity and involvement.

Once the patient is prepared to enter a transitional rehabilitation program, the role of the psychologist continues to be extremely active and meaningful. By means of psychodiagnostic and vocational test assessment along with the counseling and psychotherapeutic function, the psychologist would be expected to recommend those transitional programs for which the patient is prepared, with special reference to the specific occupational or educational goals to be developed. It has been our experience that monetary-incentive work-therapy programs are the most effective because of the realistic nature of the motivation. Thus, at the earliest level of vocational rehabilitation, patients might be assigned to a contract clinic within the hospital wherein they are remunerated on a piecework basis while their capacity for full-time work tolerance is evaluated. Another approach would involve an individual industrial therapy assignment within the hospital; and when the patient can tolerate full-time work, he receives an hourly wage. During these activities, the psychologist continues to provide continuous vocational counseling and guidance along with psychotherapy when indicated. As a result, a global and dynamic rehabilitation process emerges.

As the rehabilitation process moves forward, patients are expected to move toward more complex and realistic work-therapy activities. Many patients are now prepared to enter a halfway house program with a night-hospital transitional program. In such cases, the patients hold fulltime jobs in the community setting and return to the security of the hospital in the evening. In the case of younger patients, the community activity might be a vocational training school or a college curriculum and return to the hospital in the evening. It has been the experience at the Franklin Delano Roosevelt VA Hospital that patients who have been continuously hospitalized for several years encounter extreme difficulty in making the adjustments to working and living in the community simultaneously. Readmission to the hospital seems markedly reduced when the patient takes these critical rehabilitation steps one at a time. Thus, the emphasis is initially placed upon first attaining a successful work experience in the competitive community environment while continuing to live at the hospital. The final step in the vocational rehabilitation process of chronic patients occurs when the patient begins living in the community. In the VA Roosevelt Hospital program, it is the responsibility of the hospital psychologist to effect the community vocational placement of the patient, but always in very close collaboration with rehabilitation therapists. Finally, the follow-up process by the psychologist in the work setting and by the social worker in the home setting is crucial to long-term rehabilitation success.

The author has been delineating the role of the hospital psychologist in the very vital aspect of the vocational rehabilitation of the patient. However, satisfactory community living and working requires an adequate level of social and psychiatric rehabilitation which must be carried on simultaneously with the vocational rehabilitation sequence. The hospital psychologist should be involved in numerous activities related to enhancing socialization and symptomatic improvement. Group psychotherapy or counseling has proven to be a most valuable approach in this respect. In recent years, psychologists have turned to behavior therapy or behavior modification techniques of various kinds with considerable success in a relatively brief treatment regimen. In the VA Roosevelt Hospital setting, an inpatient behavior therapy unit is utilized with token economy and other reinforcement methodologies in symptom removal and improved socialization. In addition, there is a centralized behavior modification clinic conducted by a psychologist utilizing biofeedback techniques to desensitize troublesome acute symptoms which impede the total rehabilitation process. Another modality which appears to enhance social rehabilitation is family group therapy which is frequently administered by the hospital psychologist. An additional approach to psychiatric rehabilitation is the use of self-confrontation therapy through videotape methods wherein the patient has an opportunity to view and become disenchanted with certain problematic behavioral symptoms and ultimately to reject such behaviors.

The role of the social psychologist in the psychiatric hospital setting must not be minimized in the total rehabilitation process. Such therapeutic concepts as the "therapeutic community" or "milieu therapy" are increasing in frequency, and it becomes notably crucial that the hospital psychologist be thoroughly aware of the pragmatic utilization of the constructs of social psychology. Social psychologists, sociologists and cultural anthropologists are assuming increasing roles in the psychiatric hospital multidisciplinary approach to rehabilitation. The development of self-reliance and independence is enhanced by self-government and other patient self-regulating methods. Social interaction groups conducted by nursing assistants, undergraduate college students or volunteers, with the psychologist playing a consultant role, have proven most effective in the social rehabilitation of hospitalized patients.

Finally, a strong current trend is observed which involves the concept of the "hospital psychologist"—a generalist in the practice of applied psychology. To provide the full range of psychological services in the rehabilitation of hospitalized psychiatric patients, one notes the gradual emergence of a professional psychologist trained in the specialties of clinical, counseling, social, experimental and physiological psychologies and neuropsychology. Such is the ubiquity required of the hospital psychologist engaged in the total rehabilitation of psychiatric patients.

Chapter 14

THE ROLE OF THE PSYCHIATRIC SOCIAL WORKER*

BETTY ANN GLASSER LIFSON

THE DEVELOPMENT OF PSYCHIATRIC SOCIAL WORK AND SOCIAL PSYCHIATRY

The Common Base of Social Work Practice

FROM THE BEGINNING OF PROFESSIONAL social work in settlement houses and charity organization societies of late nineteenth-century America, social workers have been actively concerned with helping the poor, the sick and the disabled to live, work in and adjust to the community. Early social work methods focused on the idealistic, yet realistic, goal of the elimination of poverty and disease through social legislative action, institutional reform and socioeconomic aid to individuals or families, the latter method gradually evolving from charity work, friendly visiting and social treatment, into the highly conceptual and creative theory of social casework as first expounded by Mary Richmond and her colleagues.[19,22]

Social Work and Mental Illness

In their day-to-day dealings with the problems of the poor, social caseworkers continually found themselves faced with situations created and complicated by mental illness. Through experience, they were learning the social significance of mental disease

*This paper could not have been written without the instruction, guidance and personal recollections of Maida H. Solomon, the standard-bearer and steadfast champion of psychiatric social work since its inception in 1913, in the Social Service Department of the Boston Psychopathic Hospital.

and were becoming aware that emotional disturbance frequently was at the core of a client's inability to use concrete help. Organized social interest in mental disease appeared as early as 1874 when a paper on "The Duty of the States Toward the Insane Poor" was presented at the National Conference of Social Work, soon followed by a section in that organization on "Feeblemindedness and Insanity," which became, in 1917, the Mental Hygiene Section of the National Conference of Social Work.[6]

Social Work and Hospital Psychiatry

Social Workers as Aftercare Agents

At the same time that social caseworkers were becoming interested in learning more about mental disease in relation to social maladjustment, hospital psychiatrists were beginning to turn their attention to the social situations of patients ready for discharge. As far back as 1894, the American Neurological Association expressed interest in the social readjustment of former mental hospital patients by establishing a Committee on Aftercare of the Insane. In 1906, Louisa Lee Schuyler, a social worker, made an investigation of the aftercare societies in England, and with the backing of the New York State Charities Aid Association, proposed a plan to the New York State Commission on Lunacy for the initiation of similar societies in this country. This proposal resulted in the formation of a subcommittee on Aftercare of the Insane to study, plan and develop a program for patients discharged from New York state hospitals. In that same year, the New York State Charities Aid Association employed a graduate of the New York School of Philanthropy (now the Columbia University School of Social Work) to be the first Aftercare agent in the United States. In 1911, due to persistent efforts of the State Charities Aid Association, the first aftercare worker to be paid by state funds in this country was appointed by the New York State Commission on Lunacy and assigned to Manhattan State Hospital.

By 1914, social workers had been appointed as aftercare agents in Massachusetts, New Jersey, Pennsylvania and Illinois to follow up patients discharged from state hospitals. By this time in New York State, there were aftercare workers employed in eleven state hospitals and social workers placed in fourteen outpatient departments maintained by state hospitals, as well as the twenty clinics for nervous and mental disorders in New York City.

Social Work in General Hospitals

Around this same period, 1907 to 1914, social services were being established in psychopathic wards and neurological clinics of a few general hospitals in New York and Massachusetts. In Boston's Massachusetts General Hospital, social workers were being assigned to the neurological clinic to carry out treatment plans under the direction of neurologists, physicians and psychiatrists, for patients diagnosed as suffering from psychoneurosis and psychosomatic illnesses. In 1912, Doctor Adolf Meyer became the first director of the Phipps Outpatient Clinic at John Hopkins Hospital, Baltimore, Maryland and in 1913, he appointed the first social worker in a psychiatric outpatient clinic of a general hospital.

Psychiatric Social Work Becomes a Speciality

In this same year, 1913, in the newly opened Boston Psychopathic Hospital, a social service was organized to assist Doctor E. E. Southard and his associates in the study and treatment of mental diseases. It was in this social service department, under the direction of Miss Mary C. Jarrett, that the functions of social work with mental patients were first outlined, as well as the first use of the name, "psychiatric social work," for the practice of social work in relation to psychiatry, and the first program of special training for psychiatric social workers. Specific duties of the psychiatric social worker were taking the social history of new patients as an aid to the doctor in diagnosis, as well as in discovering and dealing with social problems; seeing that the family of the patient understood the physician's directions; acting as a liaison agent between the physicians and social workers in the community; attending clinics for case demonstrations; taking part in discussions; and writing reports of the physician's findings to social agencies to be supplemented by oral reports and consultations.[23]

The Origins of Vocational Rehabilitation

Employment of neurotic or psychotic individuals, difficulties encountered in holding positions, problems of placement and adjustment to work were considered major concerns of the psychiatric social workers at the Boston Psychopathic Hospital, thus early identifying social workers with the vocational rehabilitation of the mentally ill. In 1919 at the National Conference of Social Work, Mary Jarrett, by defining the treatment function of social work as the "restoration of the capacity for normal living or provision for the greatest possible comfort,"[13] also provided the first definition of mental health rehabilitation.

Psychiatric Social Work in Federal Hospitals

When the United States entered World War I in the spring of 1917, psychiatric social work was well established as a new area of social work, and its leaders were involved in planning social services for mentally disabled veterans in Army and Navy hospitals and in establishing additional training facilities for the psychiatric social workers who would be needed to staff these services. In 1919 under the auspices of the U.S. Public Health Service, the American Red Cross undertook to organize in federal hospitals social services similar to those in state mental hospitals, and fifteen graduates of the first year (1918) of training at the Smith College School for Social Work were placed in charge of psychiatric social work in VA hospitals. By 1920, there were social service departments in forty-two federal hospitals designated for the care of former servicemen and servicewomen with service-connected mental disabilities. The Red Cross carried full responsibility for the social work program until 1926 when the U.S. Veterans' Bureau (now the VA) established a social work section as part of its medical service and began taking over the social service program in the Veterans' hospitals. At that time, Civil Service requirements were drawn up, and the functions of psychiatric social work in VA hospitals were first outlined.

The Development of Social Psychiatry

The growing use of social workers to collaborate with physicians in the treatment of psychiatric illness during the second decade of the twentieth century initiated some medical concepts and treatment patterns in hospital psychiatry that were to lie fallow during the period between the two World Wars and to be reactivated after World War II in the practice of community psychiatry.

In this decade of 1910 to 1920, the traditional medical history gave way to a comprehensive life story of the patient, as hospital psychiatrists began to discover that the study of all aspects of their patient's daily life was pertinent to diagnosis and treatment; and their social work assistants were beginning to include knowledge of classification of mental disease and the interrelationship of physical disease and mental breakdown in their investigations of the patient's home, work and social circumstances. Concurrently, as psychiatrists began to learn more about the lacks and the difficulties in their patient's childhood and home life, the concept of hospital treatment including social service information, guidance and support to significant others in the patient's social milieu became established. In the context of exchanges with the social worker, as the psychiatrist treating the patient's emotional ills became more aware of the current family relationships, discharge planning began to include social work preparation for the patient's return to a favorable community climate, as well as the extension of social work service after the patient's discharge and outside of the office, hospital or clinic, to facilitate community adjustment and to prevent relapse.

By 1920, in various sections of the country, in state hospitals, psychopathic hospitals, general hospitals, federal hospitals and outpatient clinics for mental and nervous disorders connected with these hospitals, the two new fields in medicine and social work—dynamic psychiatry and psychiatric social work—were joining forces in a psychosocial method of practice that has come to be known as social psychiatry—the body of knowledge and theory on which the methods and techniques of community psychiatry are based.

THE DEVELOPMENT OF THE PSYCHIATRIC TREATMENT TEAM

In the early 1920's, a new dimension was added to the horizon of the young fields of dynamic psychiatry and psychiatric social work by the child guidance movement and, particularly, by the organization of child guidance demonstration clinics, established throughout the country by the Commonwealth Fund after studies of psychotic, neurotic and delinquent World War I soldiers revealed signs of disturbances in childhood.

Two years of careful planning by leaders in the fields of psychiatry, psychology and social work produced a child guidance program model that contained the seeds of some of the most enduring policies in modern mental health treatment structure. The concepts of the multi-disciplinary team approach, consultation and education of community caretakers, along with individual treatment of the child and funds for child guidance staff training that were built into the model, not only were widely copied in other fields, but also had a significant bearing on the direction of the growing profession of social work in general and on social work education and the fledgling field of psychiatric social work in particular. The most important concept, in terms of its impact on psychiatric social work, has been the psychiatric treatment team.

The child guidance clinic treatment team, composed of a psychiatrist, a psychologist and a social worker, jointly responsible for a diagnostic workup and treatment plan for each child, placed the psychiatric social worker for the first time in the position of an important member of a clinic team, as a representative of a professional field expected to make its own contribution. In this context, one of the chief responsibilities of the social worker was the study and analysis of the social situation of the child in his relationship with his family, school associates, playmates and community groups, including a history of the child starting at birth, usually obtained in an interview with the mother. Gradually the social worker of the team took on the role of "intake" worker, the person who made the first contact with the parents, set up the admission procedure or referred the parents and their child to a more appropriate facility. As case histories accumulated, it also became apparent that the attitudes and emotional problems of the parents were usually the cause of the disturbed behavior of the child and that the study and treatment of children must also involve study and treatment of the parents.

Within the environment of the child guidance clinic movement, the distinction between the psychiatrists who deal with emotional problems of the patient and the social worker who confines treatment to changing of attitudes and environment began to break down; and the psychiatric social worker began to share treatment cases, oftentimes taking responsibility for working with the parents, particularly with mothers, while the psychiatrist worked with the child.

As the work load of the guidance clinics increased, the functions of the treatment team began to overlap; and the close relationships of the team members enabled the social worker's clinical and research techniques to become enriched by association with psychiatrists and clinical psychologists and, in turn, enabled these disciplines to become more knowledgeable about social work skills and techniques as well as to encourage able social workers to take an increasing share in treatment, research and community education and consultation.[24]

THE EXTENSION OF PSYCHIATRIC SOCIAL WORK INTO OTHER FIELDS

During the decade of the 1920's, fostered by the growing interest in mental hygiene, the influence of psychiatric social work was spreading out beyond hospital social psychiatry and the clinic psychiatric treatment team into related fields of health, education and welfare. In some of these areas, the psychiatric social worker remained in a working relationship with psychiatrists whose services were also in demand by such agencies as courts, schools and child welfare agencies. In some, however, social workers found new positions in which they were designated as psychiatric specialists, consultants or coordinators, by virtue of their past experience in a psychiatric setting. Some examples of newly created positions that extended psychiatric social work, perhaps too soon and too thinly and certainly, to the deprivation of the patients in state hospitals, far beyond the psychiatric hospital and outpatient settings, are as follows.

THE MENTAL HYGIENE ASSOCIATION: The National Committee for Mental Hygiene appointed a psychiatric social worker as educational consultant in 1924, and by 1932 there were sixteen psychiatric social workers employed in mental hygiene societies as community organizers and mental health educators, responsible for community surveys and public relations, and for planning mental health education programs, conferences and seminars. After the 1940's, these positions were held for the most part by social work specialists in group work or community organization, as executive directors of mental health associations.

PUBLIC HEALTH NURSING: During the middle 1920's and early 1930's, psychiatric social workers, as consultants or educators, were employed by the large public health nursing organizations in the country to give courses in mental hygiene, hold regular informal group discussions with the district staffs and case consultations with nurses who brought in some of their most difficult problems for discussion. Social work consultants often accompanied nurses on home visits to acquaint the social worker with the types of problems the nurses were handling. Psychiatric social workers have continued to consult with public health and visiting nurse associations in the present, as more and more psychiatric nurses qualify as mental hygiene educators in their own field, and as public health and visiting nurse associations take over responsibility for care of mental patients in the community if the assignment is clear and consultation is available.[1]

FAMILY AGENCIES: In the 1920's and 1930's, knowledge of psychiatric and mental hygiene was steadily permeating the whole family casework field. At first special positions for psychiatric social work consultants were created by large family agencies such as the New York Charity Organization Society and the United Charities of Chicago. The trend, however, was developing whereby psychiatric social workers were entering the family welfare field as staff members to work directly with clients presenting problems relating to mental disease or serious emotional maladjustment. This trend was accelerated by the shifting of the function of helping those in financial need from the family welfare agencies to the federal public agencies and special relief agencies newly established during the depression years. The increasing demand for psychiatric social workers in family agencies contributed, in large measure, along with the child guidance movement, to the serious depletion of trained and experienced psychiatric social workers from state hospital staffs.

PUBLIC WELFARE: The advent of the New Deal in the wake of the Depression of the 1930's, brought on the greatest ground swell of social legislation and programs in our country's history. Although social work leaders contributed to the drafting of the legislation and many left positions in hospitals and clinics to aid in the advisory, administrative and training programs in various public welfare, social security and other government agencies, after the height of the depression few psychiatric social workers remained in public welfare. Some of the surface reasons were the relatively few psychiatric social workers in the country at the time; small enrollments in schools of social work during the depression years; increasing demand for psychiatric social workers in child guidance, mental hygiene clinics and family welfare agencies; and the preference of psychiatric social workers for positions in agencies that emphasized treatment and clinical practice. It is the writer's belief, however, that psychiatric social workers have been deterred from entering the public welfare field or from staying in it for a long term because chronic overloading of clients and paperwork, critical shortages of resources and structural constraints in this field, or any other, render workers helpless and unable to use their professional training and experience to help the client.[27]

PSYCHIATRIC SOCIAL WORK AND PSYCHOTHERAPY

Since the 1930's, teachers of casework classes at schools of social work and field work supervisors, influenced by the teachings and writings of prestigious psychiatric social workers, such as Gordon Hamilton, Annette Garrett and Florence Day, have incorporated Fruedian principles and derivatives of psychoanalytic techniques into the essential casework process. In 1930, Virginia Robinson's book, *A Changing Psychology in Social Casework,*[20] presented a concept of social casework as individual therapy through a treatment relationship that stimulated widespread interest in the use of a relationship as the chief dynamic in social work treatment and in the role of the social worker as a therapist. During this period of identification with psychoanalysis, in many of the large family welfare agencies in Eastern cities, social workers were attending seminars given by outstanding European disciples of Freud; were being analyzed themselves; and, borrowing from their analysts, were introducing such techniques as the fifty-minute office appointment hour and "passive listening" into casework, leaving them little time to attend to the social needs of their clients. In some casework agencies, while consultation with psychiatrists was sometimes available, responsibility for direct treatment of clients' personality disturbances, independent of psychiatry, was being added to casework practice.[12,17]

During the later 1930's and 1940's, the number of referrals—from understaffed, overloaded state hospital aftercare programs, psychiatric clinics with long waiting lists, as well as public welfare agencies—of clients with severe ego disturbances to family casework agencies increased significantly and to the point of serious concern among leading medical and social work practitioners. In one of the many articles written on the subject, a psychiatrist consultant and a psychiatric social work supervisor in Boston's VA Mental Hygiene Clinic acknowledged that "in critical times and especially in war, professional standards may have to be relaxed temporarily in order to deal with the greatest number of people for the greatest good." They go on to state, however, that "the problem remains whether workers in social agencies should become involved in intense therapeutic relationships with their clients" and to conclude that "the competence of the psychiatric social worker to deal with psychological conflicts may be developed through experience and training under the guidance of qualified psychiatrists."[16]

From this point of view, widely held in psychiatric circles during this period, the emphasis was not so much on psychiatric social workers (and other disciplines) providing intensive treatment or psychotherapy, given that there never are enough psychiatrists to meet the need, as on providing treatment based on adequate training and on-the-job supervision as needed (by seniors of the same discipline) under the direction of psychiatrists with or without psychiatric consultation. Gradually, as more treatment modalities became available, the title of psychotherapist came to be applied to those professionals qualified for practice in any form of therapy.

PSYCHIATRIC SOCIAL WORK AND COMMUNITY PSYCHIATRY

The Influence of the War Years

World War II marked the beginning of a growing interest in psychiatry and mental hospitals among America's lay populations and a turning back to the social psychiatry concepts of the early part of the century among the professional populations. For the first time in our country's history, mental illness, as experienced by our nation's military forces, was being spotlighted in newspapers and magazines as an acute reaction to overwhelming environmental stresses that could be reversed with or without brief hospitalization. Conscientious objectors, serving their military tour of duty as hospital attendants, were telling the news media about deplorable conditions on the back wards of mental hospitals and about the hapless poor, homeless and elderly who lived there. Professionals returning from military service to civilian positions brought with them innovative methods of dealing with the return of huge numbers of psychiatric casualties to action as quickly as possible and began to apply these methods—such as brief psychotherapy, group therapy and on-the-spot intervention—to patients referred to psychiatric clinics, as well as to some patients being admitted to mental hospitals.

In the wake of massive federal legislative planning and action on behalf of the returning veteran, several bills were passed by

Congress that were to have far-reaching effects on the rehabilitation of the mentally ill and disabled as well as on the growth of psychiatric social work and the expansion of its role in community psychiatry. One of these was the Vocational Rehabilitation Act as rewritten in 1943, mainly to initiate a comprehensive vocational and social rehabilitation program for both physically and mentally disabled veterans (Public Law 16). The act's most important provision, however, from the point of view of mental health was the extension, under Public Law 116, of rehabilitation services not only to physically disabled civilians but, for the first time, to the mentally disabled as well.[18]

Psychiatric Social Work and VA Rehabilitation Programs

Expanded and newly built VA hospitals and mental hygiene clinics all over the United States, well equipped and well staffed, took the lead in initiating social and vocational rehabilitation programs and clinical research projects, as well as in continuing experimentation with front-line treatment modalities. Hundreds of psychiatric social workers went to work during and after the war years on psychiatric wards and outpatient clinics of VA hospitals. Of these, many were involved in developing the basic philosophy, concepts and techniques of mental health rehabilitation and, as pioneering rehabilitation specialists, participated in planning and implementing programs experimenting with community living and vocational placement for World War II veterans, as well as for chronic patients in the VA hospitals' psychiatric wards.[21]

Psychiatric Social Work and Group Therapy

During this period too, particularly in VA facilities, psychiatric social workers were beginning to experiment with techniques of group therapy, based on their experience in war zones, as a new method of treatment for the mentally ill. The main focus of group therapy as originally practiced by psychiatric social workers in VA hospitals was in preparing large numbers of hospitalized veterans for discharge and for community living. In some state mental hospitals, as well as VA hospitals, social workers were helping nursing staff organize scheduled daily activity groups for the purpose of helping patients learn how to become self-reliant and resourceful before moving out into the community.[3] At this time too, families were being seen by social workers in life education groups for the purpose of helping relatives of patients about to be discharged to understand and learn how to cope with residuals of mental illness and mental disability. In various psychiatric settings, social workers were sitting in as recorders in psychotherapy groups led by psychiatrists and psychologists and then were becoming coleaders or group leaders of the same group in the absence or departure of the leader or in a newly formed group. The seeds of group therapy sown during the war years, mainly by military clinical psychologists, took firm root during the 1950's and 1960's as an interdisciplinary treatment modality, so that many psychiatric social workers now specialize in group work practice, and all social work clinicians use group therapy along with individual casework (and many other practice modalities) to meet various different client treatment goals.[25]

The National Mental Health Act

Public awareness of new brief methods of treatment of mental illness and of the acute need for mental health professionals in depleted state hospital staffs paved the way for the passage of the National Mental Health Act of 1946, which provided funds for training, research and community services concerned with mental health (and from which, in 1949, emerged the National Institute of Mental Health). The existence of federal grants-in-aid under this act enabled states in which there were no state hospital outpatient clinics (almost half of the United States) to begin planning for outpatient psychiatric services in addition to institutional care.[28]

It was stipulated in the grants that these outpatient services must have as a basic component a psychiatric social work (PSW) staff well qualified to conduct pertinent operations of the clinic or service beginning from early administrative organization, extending through direct services to the patient and including a portion of the responsibility for community interpretation.

The Development of Federal Stipends for Expanding PSW Training

To help fill the need for personnel in these newly established out-patient psychiatric services, as well as in many other new community services and programs, the provisions of the Mental Health Act encouraged schools of social work to apply for assistance in training additional workers and to institute third-year programs for experienced psychiatric social workers. Based on the prospect of such assistance, plans were proposed to increase total enrollment from approximately 400 students specializing in psychiatric social work in the years 1946 to 1947 to 1200 by the year 1949, with approximately thirty additional students in advanced training for a doctorate degree in social work practice, administration and research.

The concept of providing stipends was of lasting significance in the recruitment of a heterogenous student body and in allowing experienced workers to become qualified for teaching and administrative positions. However, the addition of 600 graduates a year, most of whom were women, who before the arrival of women's liberation were equally apt to marry and retire as to seek employment, was not sufficient to meet the countrywide demand for workers, particularly intensified by the new community services and programs being sponsored during these years first by the National Mental Health Act, and after 1949, by the National Institute of Mental Health (NIMH).

Psychiatric Social Work and The Changing Mental Hospital

The Influence of Psychopharmacology

In the 1950's, the development of psychotropic drugs that could be used to deactivate psychotic symptomatology and tranqualize agitated patients was eagerly seized upon by hospital administrators as a possible solution to the dilemma of the ever increasing numbers of chronic patients living out their lives in back wards of every state hospital in the country.

Chemotherapy, adding its impact to that of the new treatment approaches transplanted from military to civilian settings, was the key that opened hospital gates, unlocked ward doors, let visitors and volunteers in and facilitated the possibility of rehabilitation and community placement for thousands of mental hospital inmates. In these early years of the first changes in hospital patient treatment from custodial to therapeutic care, psychiatric social workers planned and participated in pilot studies funded by private research foundations, drug companies and the newly emerging National Institute of Mental Health. Studies of milieu therapy, socioenvironmental aspects of patient treatment, partial hospitalization, emergency services and home-visiting teams, were, in certain pockets of the country, changing the social organization of mental hospital wards in a dramatic and irreversible way that never happened, for example, in correctional institutions. Reconstitution or rehabilitation rather than cure became an important new concept in the treatment of chronic patients.[9,10,11]

Encouraged by the results of these pilot studies, Congress, in 1956, authorized funds for special Mental Health Project grants to support the development of improved methods of care, treatment and rehabilitation of the mentally ill and also passed a record appropriation which almost doubled the NIMH budget for 1957 and enabled significant expansion of the overall program. Funds for NIMH and the special Mental Health Projects Program continued to be appropriated in larger amounts each year during the Kennedy-Johnson era of mental health advocacy and the War on Poverty.[4]

Psychiatric Social Work and the Mental Health Manpower Crisis

New treatment approaches for acutely ill patients, new after-care programs for discharged patients and the new ethic of therapeutic care for long-term hospital patients—all demanding additional social work time—caught psychiatric social workers, and large state hospital social service departments especially, in a severe manpower squeeze. As the 1960's progressed, enactment of unprecedented federal legislation for the care of the mentally ill in the community, including provisions in the Medicare law aimed at rehabilitation programs for geriatric populations in mental hospitals; authorization for public welfare agencies to provide, under Medicare and Medicaid, monthly sustenance checks for elderly and disabled patients discharged from mental hospitals; and work-training programs under the Economic Opportunity Act for indigenous workers, students and paraprofessionals in mental hospital and mental health programs, further exacerbated the problem of the widening gap between the demand for and the supply of psychiatric social workers.

Concerned about the deleterious effects of manpower shortages on the quality and the quantity of delivery of services, psychiatric social workers and the social work profession as a whole became immersed in a search for remedial measures. The National Association of Social Workers undertook a long-term study of the question of effective utilization of social work manpower in mental hospitals and aftercare programs.[2] As the hospital social workers involved in this study began, for the first time, to sort out the social service functions that could be performed by persons of differential levels of training and experience, it became clear that many time-consuming concrete services for patients and their families, largely neglected by the harassed professional, could be better carried out by nonprofessional social service teams under the guidance and supervision of a psychiatric social worker. From this sorting out of functions came a series of career ladders whereby members of a social service team could, by education, training and experience, move up into the professional field. It signalled the beginning of experimental use of volunteers and employment of various categories of nonprofessionals in social service departments in psychiatric settings, and in fact set a whole new direction in psychiatric social work practice which, until the manpower crisis of the 1960's, had been committed to employing only professional social workers to perform all social work functions in psychiatric services.

Psychiatric Social Work and the Dismantling of the Large State Hospital

In the decade of 1957 to 1967, Vocational Rehabilitation Administration grants, NIMH grants and pharmaceutical grants for rehabilitation projects and projects demonstrating new community care approaches, designed mainly by enterprising psychologists with psychiatrists as principal investigators, were being awarded in impressive numbers to research-minded mental hospitals throughout the country. The bulk of the efforts toward closing back wards of state hospitals during this period were conducted as research and demonstration projects funded by the Vocational Rehabilitation Administration through major rehabilitation legislation (Public Law 83-565) enacted during the Eisenhower administration.[26] Grant funds were used mainly to employ a research team and an adequate ward staff and to establish vocational rehabilitation services in the hospital.

The Expansion of the Psychiatric Treatment Team

Within the structured research designs of these three- to five-year demonstration and research projects, the processes involved in the mammoth task—complicated by three decades of neglect—of moving chronic patients, many of whom had lived in the hospital for over twenty years, into the community, were carefully worked out by the research team and followed through by an ever expanding treatment team. Psychiatrists prescribed medication and closely followed its course; nurses attended to patients' physical needs; ward staff plus occupational, recreational, music, art and dance therapists were engaged by the research team in organizing activity groups enabling patients to learn or relearn ordinary social skills and to develop special skills; token economy methods of behavior modification were charted by psychologists; work therapy was provided by vocational rehabilitation counselors, based on evaluative testing; and community placement was the province of the social worker based on a thorough assessment of the patient's past environment as well as current functioning and resources. Representatives of community agencies, volunteers and students rounded out a treatment team that often numbered more than twenty persons, each involved in some aspect of treatment planning for one patient's reentry into family and community life. Through this total team approach to the multidimensional problems of the hospitalized poor, in which psychiatric social workers were the primary advocates and coordinators, team participants learned to respect and value the professional contributions of a multidisciplinary staff and the unique contributions of gifted paraprofessionals who in turn were learning to voice their opinions and doubts without apology or trepidation during team meetings.

Volunteers

Volunteers, particularly college student volunteers[8]; mature case aides[7]; in some hospitals, VISTA volunteers[15]; and, to a lesser extent, graduate students of all disciplines—medicine, nursing, social work, psychology, pastoral counseling, law, education, etc.—played a very special part in motivating chronic patients to try community living and in helping them through the difficult transition from hospital to community. In planned programs where one or two hours were devoted weekly to receiving orientation, direction and guidance, and three or four hours to patient contact, volunteers were able to befriend one or a few particular patients at a time in a way not possible for professionals. The mental health volunteer movement, in which psychiatric social work played a large role, spread from college campuses in the late 1950's to all segments of the community and reached its peak as a vital force in the dismantling of the large state hospital some ten years later.

Aftermath

The literature of 1957 to 1967 was replete with reports of demonstration and research studies of successful community integration of former long-term mental hospital patients. After demonstration projects were over, however, and the research staff dispersed, community placements became more and more routinely carried out even to the extent of some hospital administrations issuing a mimeographed order to ward psychiatrists that so many chronic patients should be discharged each month in order to maintain a steadily decreasing hospital census. Haphazard discharges by untrained and unsupervised hospital personnel and lack of hospital budget allocations for professional staffing of aftercare programs played a large role in the phenomenon of the 1960's known as the "revolving door" whereby the census of chronic patients would drop 500 to 1,000 a year, but admissions would soar due to large numbers of readmissions of recently discharged patients as well as new admissions, and led to the "closed-door" policy in recent years of refusing admission to chronic recidivists.

PSYCHIATRIC SOCIAL WORK AND COMMUNITY MENTAL HEALTH

Psychiatric Social Work and the Community Mental Health Clinic

One of the recommendations of the historic "Final Report of the Joint Commission on Mental Illness and Health," delivered to Congress in 1961, was, "A national mental health program should set as an objective one full-staffed, full-time mental health clinic available to each 50,000 of the population."[14]

In the existing community mental health clinics of the 1960's, whether serving children only, or both children and adults, operating as outpatient departments of general or mental hospitals or as independent agencies sponsored by mental health associations, it was a known but rarely articulated fact that due to extreme shortages of psychiatrists and psychologists, part-time and full-time psychiatric social workers, all working overtime, carried the bulk of day-to-day treatment. In many clinics senior psychiatric social workers were delegated a large share of community consultation, as well as the responsibility for in-service training for less experienced colleagues and graduate students. They also wrote letters and prepared statistics, reports and grant proposals often signed by the psychiatrist-director. Most of them in these hectic years of mental health expansion were dividing their time between the clinic, medical school faculties and private practice and consultation. These senior psychiatric social workers, too, were beginning to enter the field of private practice with relatives of psychiatrists' private patients as clients. In all of the clinics, the medical model prevailed to the extent that the focus was on patient treatment, and on the medical responsibility of the director for treatment, medical records and matters of policy and administration, although education, consultation, research and some preventive programming did exist.

Psychiatric Social Work and the Community Mental Health Center

In 1963, when a cooperative Congress passed the Community Mental Health Centers Act, authorizing federal grants for planning networks of comprehensive health services that would insure continuity of care for the populations residing in the towns and cities of the catchment areas, many knowledgeable social work clinicians collaborated with psychiatrists and psychologists in applying for these grants. This initial legislation was followed by appropriations for federal cost-sharing for construction of mental health (and mental retardation) centers and in 1965 by a sharing formula for grants to assist in staffing the community mental health centers. Between 1964 and 1970, over 300 community health centers were funded by the NIMH.[5]

Many existing mental health clinics, as well as existing day-hospitals, inpatient units and emergency services, formed the nucleus of essential services of newly organized mental health centers, bringing along their staffs and their medical model of operation. The mandate encompassed in the Community Mental Health Centers Act, however, was equal responsibility between consumers and staff for the mental health of the entire population of the catchment area. It will be many years before long established agencies, with their invested boards, set goals, philosophies and policies, which have been brought under the umbrella of the community mental health center as contract agencies, will be able to integrate with each other; with new services; with state, general and VA hospital systems; and with the NIMH goals for community mental health centers. Nonetheless, movement toward networks of geographically separated but coordinated health and welfare services is under way. At the same time there is a distinct movement toward diversified citizen participation in mental health, beyond the volunteerism of the 1950's and 1960's, as board members of community mental health centers or of contract agencies with a voice in budget allocations and agency policies, as consumer advocates and, particularly, as employees. New staff positions have been created, and job descriptions written, with flexible educational, experience and training requirements for a wide variety of citizens participating on mental health center teams as workers, aides, caseworkers and homemakers. Many of these indigenous workers of all ages and all ethnic, cultural and economic backgrounds, as they began to acquire experience, went on to community colleges and universities, and some to graduate schools of social work to become part of the new breed of psychiatric social workers who are political activists, client advocates and institutional change agents as well as clinicians. Within the climate of the comprehensive mental health center that functions as the nucleus for the mental health services of the community it serves, the practice of modern-day psychiatric social work has seemingly found its element and has effectively flourished.

Psychiatric Social Work in the Present

During the Nixon administration, however, the era of federal governmental investment in mental health expansion, research and training came to an end. Cutbacks in community agency federal funding, federal research grants and presidential confiscations of grants-in-aid and Office of Economic Opportunity (OEO) funds in the early 1970's caused hospital and mental health center budgets to be cut, staff positions "frozen" (vacated positions left vacant) and new programs and new staff positions abandoned. In addition to the drying up of funding sources, the burgeoning of undergraduate social welfare majors and community college human services curricula, civil service career ladders and new careers in mental health, all sanctioned by the social work profession, led program directors to employ holders of a B.A. and graduates of two-year colleges as social workers; and in drug and alcoholism programs, former drug abusers and problem drinkers were employed in positions that formerly would have required professional qualifications. For the first time in the history of psychiatric social work, new graduates of schools of social work found it difficult to get a job or to get exactly what they wanted in the way of clinical experience and supervision. The impact of politics on the profession of social work has been brought home forcefully by the election and reelection of a president so reactionary in his views toward social services for the poor and the disabled that the extent of the damages done to the fabric of human services in this country is not yet known. A tendency of some state governments to follow the presidential attitude towards psychiatry and its allied professions is to be watched and deplored. By this same token, however, in the 1970's politically sophisticated psychiatric social work clinicians have formed a National Federation of Societies for Clinical Social Work, an organization composed of state societies for clinical social work, one of whose main aims is to promote licensing laws in every state that will provide standards and safeguards for social workers in private practice, and provisions in these licensing laws that will include licensed psychiatric social workers as independent providers of service in any national health insurance plan enacted into law by Congress. Also, in this decade, experienced and highly skilled psychiatric social workers, many of whom have doctoral degrees in social welfare, administration, clinical social work and community mental health, are beginning to compete for the first time with equally well-qualified psychiatrists and psychologists for directorships of mental health programs and administrative positions in mental health centers.

As the 20th century draws to a close, the writer looks forward to the coming of age of mental health professionals, each one so secure in his professional identity that together they can lead a psychiatric treatment team composed of representatives of all population strata, including psychiatric patients and their families, beyond community mental health into a new era of the "therapeutic society."

REFERENCES

1. Anderson, M., Manning, M. J., and Glasser, B. A.: Nursing and social work roles in the cooperative home care and treatment of the mentally ill. *Nurs Outlook,* February 1963.
2. Barker, L., and Briggs, T.: *Differential Use of Social Work Manpower.* New York, NASW, 1968.

3. Bellsmith, B., and Edward, J.: The role of a social group worker at Central Islip State Hospital. *JPSW, 17*:139-145, 1948.
4. Brand, J. L.: The United States: A historical perspective. In Williams, R., and Ozarin, L. (Eds.): *Community Mental Health, an International Perspective*. San Francisco, Jossey-Bass, 1968, pp. 18-43.
5. Brown, B. S.: *Mental Health and Social Change*. Austin, Hogg Foundation for Mental Health, 1968.
6. French, L. M.: *Psychiatric Social Work** New York, The Commonwealth Fund, Oxford U Pr, 1940.
7. Gelineau, V., and Evans, A. S.: Volunteer case aides rehabilitate chronic patients. *Hosp Community Psychiatry, 21*:91, March 1970.
8. Greenblatt, M., and Kantor, D.: Student volunteers and the manpower shortage. *AJP, 118:* March 1962.
9. Greenblatt, M., Levinson, D. J., and Williams, R. H.: *The Patient and the Mental Hospitals.* Glencoe, Free Pr, 1957.
10. Greenblatt, M., York, R. H., and Brown, E. L.: *From Custodial to Therapeutic Care in Mental Hospitals.* New York, Russell Sage, 1955.
11. Greenblatt, M., Moore, R. F., Albert, R. S., and Solomon, M. H.: *The Prevention of Hospitalization, Treatment Without Admission for Psychiatric Patients.* New York, Grune, 1963.
12. Hamilton, G.: A theory of personality: Freud's contribution to social work. In Parad, H. J. (Ed.): *Ego Psychology and Dynamic Casework.* New York, Family Serv, 1958.
13. Jarrett, M. C.: The psychiatric thread running through all social casework. *Proceedings of the National Conference of Social Work,* 1919, p.p. 587-593.
14. The Joint Committee on Mental Illness and Health: *Action for Mental Health: Final Report.* New York, Basic, 1961.
15. Lifson, B. A., Martin, J., and Solomon, M. H.: *VISTA: A Story of Innovation at Boston State Hospital.* Monograph in preparation.
16. Michaels, J. J., and Gay, E.: Psychiatric casework and its relationship to psychiatry. *JPSW, 27*:123-128, 1948.
17. Neuman, F.: The preparation of the caseworker for psychotherapy. *The Caseworker in Psychotherapy.* New York, Jewish Board of Guardians, 1946.
18. Obermann, C. E.: *A History of Vocational Rehabilitation in America. Minneapolis,* T. S. Denison & Co., Inc., 1965, p. 45.
19. Richmond, M. E.: *Social Diagnosis.* New York, Russel Sage, 1917.
20. Robinson, V. R.: *A Changing Psychology in Social Casework.* Chapel Hill, U of NC Pr, 1930.
21. Rudd, J., and Margolin, R. S.: *Selected Readings in Rehabilitation: Re-*

*This book was used as a source of reference until 1936 in regard to dates and historic firsts in psychiatric social work.

habilitation Medicine, Volume II. Medford, Psychiatric R.M.D., Inc., 1969.

22. Siporin, M.: Social treatment: A new old helping method. *Social Work, 15*:13-25, 1970.
23. Southard, E. E., and Jarrett, M. C.: *The Kingdom of Evils.* New York, Macmillan, 1922.
24. Stevenson, G. S., and Smith, G.: *Child Guidance Clinics: A Quarter Century of Development.* New York, The Commonwealth Fund, Oxford U Pr, 1934.
25. Stream, H. S.: Choosing among practice modalities. *Clinical Social Work Journal, 2*:3, 1974.
26. Switzer, M. E.: The expanding program of the vocational rehabilitation administration. *Hosp Community Psychiatry, 17*:81, March 1966.
27. Wasserman, H.: Early careers of professional social workers in a public child welfare agency. *Social Work, 15*:93-101, 1970.
28. Wittman, M.: Some objectives in training for psychiatric social work. *JPSW, 17*:129-132, 1948.

Chapter 15

THE ROLE OF THE MEDICAL REHABILITATION COORDINATOR IN PSYCHIATRIC HOSPITALS

VINCENT T. CIRCHIO*

THE POSITION OF MEDICAL REHABILITATION COORDINATOR† in VA hospitals dates back to the close of World War II, when comprehensive rehabilitation programs were established for psychiatric patients. In addition to the already available disciplines of physical therapy and occupational therapy, several newer therapies, namely, corrective therapy, educational therapy and manual arts therapy, were introduced in VA psychiatric hospitals. These newer therapies, first used successfully in the armed forces during World War II, helped broaden the concept of psychiatric rehabilitation to encompass to a greater degree the needs of the "whole" patient. To put this concept into practice, all five therapies were joined to form one service designated "Physical Medicine Rehabilitation," headed by a psychiatrist and including a professional associate, the executive assistant. The latter had earlier supervised educational therapy and manual arts therapy initially under the title, "Chief, Medical Rehabilitation," and later under a new title, "Chief, Education and Retraining."

---

*The author acknowledges the encouragement of Doctor Leon L. Rackow, Director, and Doctor Stefan J. Cenkner, Chief, Rehabilitation Medicine, Franklin D. Roosevelt VA Hospital, Montrose, New York.

†Medical rehabilitation coordinators are indebted to Mr. Joseph H. Van Schoick, former special assistant in rehabilitation medicine at VA Central Office, Washington, D.C., for his significant contributions to the development of their professional role.

Today the rehabilitation medicine service in many psychiatric hospitals may also include blind rehabilitation, speech and audiology, music therapy, a bed service for rehabilitation medicine, as well as a vocational rehabilitation specialist for monetary incentive therapy. In some hospitals, rehabilitation medicine has developed close ties with such specialized treatment programs as half-way houses, day care centers, night-hospitals, drug and alcoholic addiction wards, nursing home care units, pre-community residence wards and mental hygiene clinics.

Concurrent with the growth and development of rehabilitation services in VA psychiatric hospitals, there was parallel movement in the same direction as well as the introduction of similar specialities in rehabilitation centers, community agencies and hospitals. In many such facilities, management of paramedical specialties became the responsibility of nonmedical rehabilitation specialists, while medical practices were directed by qualified physicians.

The February 1973 membership directory of the Association of Medical Rehabilitation Directors and Coordinators lists a wide variety of titles for the nonmedical rehabilitation specialist, such as director, administrator, executive director, rehabilitation director, supervisor or rehabilitation therapies, activities director, rehabilitation counselor and director of environment therapy, to mention the most commonly used titles equivalent to medical rehabilitation coordinator in VA.

The association, founded in 1953 and chartered in 1955 in the state of California, is an educational and professional organization established to foster the concept of total rehabilitation of all disabled persons through unified and coordinated methods and to provide a means for professional growth and advancement for all trained personnel in the field of medical rehabilitation. The association has established a program of certification designed to provide the medical profession and the public with the highest competency and ethics in the administration of rehabilitation medicine.

In a brochure entitled "Requirements and Standards for Rehabilitation Directors and Coordinators," the association cites twelve paramedical specialties which are employed in the rehabilitation program directed by its membership: physical therapy, occupational therapy, corrective therapy, manual arts therapy, educational therapy, vocational counseling, social service, speech therapy, recreation therapy, rehabilitation counseling, music therapy and industrial therapy. These twelve disciplines are indicative of the diverse professional fields and the variety of individual interests that represent the total team effort in rehabilitation.

Brent[1] viewed multidisciplinary involvement as contributing to the difficulty in formulating a clear definition of rehabilitation, with specialists in each field describing rehabilitation as the end product of their special methods or techniques. The variations in concept, according to Brent, exist because the various specialists tend to define rehabilitation in terms of those values and contributions specific to their own disciplines. Taking a somewhat similar view, Hamilton,[2] in discussing in-hospital rehabilitation programs, notes that "attempts to define the various roles of the professional personnel concerned frequently run into difficulty over matters of the rigidity of professional points of view, rivalries and, most important, the tyranny of terminology. . . .Differing points of view, differing backgrounds and differing emphases have not only made a rich contribution to the development of in-hospital rehabilitation, they have also been a source of confusion in the discussion of the programs."

Brent further observed that "competent leadership and well-organized system of coordination are essential" in order to prevent incoordination of the various specialties involved in rehabilitation. According to Hamilton, "The more highly we develop teamwork among the specializations available to rehabilitation, the more necessary this coordinative service becomes." To achieve practical coordinated application of individual specialized skill, Brent recognized that "the coordinator of the various rehabilitation specialties requires multidisciplinary knowledge and experience as well as special administrative skills to develop a harmonious, cooperating team."

The rehabilitation picture by 1973 with respect to multidisciplinary teamwork was not so grim as that painted by Hamilton in 1950. The problems of incoordination of the rehabilitation specialties noted by Brent in 1956 had all but disappeared in the intervening years with the general recognition of rehabilitation coordination as a professional activity for someone skilled in human relations, in the setting of a psychiatric hospital.

As the nonmedical leader of a harmonious and cooperating rehabilitation team and as a professional co-worker of the physician, the coordinator has become the true generalist, free from the bias of any one specialty, including the one in which he received his basic orientation and training. In the course of his experience, he has learned to demonstrate an equal concern for all paramedical disciplines, avoiding identification with one or more specific therapies in order to attain the high degree of cooperation of all specialists, which is an essential feature of a well-integrated rehabilitation program. Of all the paramedical specialists, the coordinator has become the most familiar with the objectives, special techniques, rationale and terminology of all the paramedical specialties that are components of rehabilitation medicine, as well as those in the independent services within the hospital and the community.

Thus far, the focus has been on the coordinator and the paramedical specialties in rehabilitation medicine. Of equal importance is the relationship between the coordinator and the physician. The pioneer study of the role of the medical rehabilitation coordinator in psychiatric hospitals by Meislin,[4] published in 1951, remains the basic reference on the early status of the position.

Based on his experience in VA psychiatric hospitals as chief, rehabilitation medicine, Meislin concluded that the importance of having a coordinator in a large, active psychiatric hospital cannot be overestimated. Meislin felt it to be imperative that "physicians be free to exercise their medical skills without being overwhelmed by administrative and personnel matters which exist in proportion to the size of the program." In dealing with the relationship between physician and coordinator, Meislin considered it to be "more in the nature of a 'partnership' where both have the same goal in mind; the physician takes care of all medical matters, while the nonmedical 'partner' manages the administrative matters." Meislin was not alone in taking this restricted view of the functions of the coordinator: It was the prevailing concept among many other physicians and management officials at the time.

It is interesting to compare Meislin's earlier dichotomy (medical matters and administrative problems) of partnership in explaining the contributions of the coordinator with his (Meislin's) 1964 memorandum to the author, who had then completed five years of service as coordinator under Meislin. The pertinent paragraphs of this memorandum follow:

> As rehabilitation specialist, the coordinator exercises his professional therapeutic capacities in reviewing the rehabilitation objectives of many problem cases and readmitted patients. He interviews these patients and presents his recommendations for rehabilitation and even suggests specific therapies for evaluation and final prescription by the chief, Rehabilitation Medicine Service (RMS). Because of the high degree of training, experience, as well as knowledge of the hospital policies, and especially a deep understanding of the rehabilitation philosophy and therapeutic principles of the chief, RMS, it is rare that any major changes have to be made in the coordinator's recommendations when the final prescription is written and signed by the chief, RMS or any other psychiatrist on our service.
>
> When the prescription is finalized, the RMS coordinator discusses the rehabilitation objectives of the given patient with the concerned chiefs of RMS sections, indicating to them various useful approaches toward achievement of optimum results. Because of the coordinator's training, experience and familiarity with all aspects of rehabilitation, and because of his knowledge of the function and objectives of each section, he is in an excellent position to coordinate therapeutic rehabilitation activities and to suggest specific measures whereby the various sections would be working harmoniously towards the same goal. The coordinator also frequently suggests to the chief, RMS, changes in therapeutic activities and schedules of individual patients.

This is indeed a different kind of partnership from the one envisioned by Meislin in 1951, when he wrote, "The coordinator's assignment will be restricted to matters not requiring medical judgment." The position of coordinator had, by 1964, evolved into something more like full collaboration in many facets of the treatment program requiring psychiatric judgment; and in addition, the coordinator enjoyed full participation in his relationship as an intermediary between therapist and physician on strictly psychiatric matters. This enhancement of the functions of the coordinator was not a fortuitous circumstance limited to one psychiatric hospital and to the experience of one physician and his coordinator.

It is apparent in this instance, as in many others that developed in the VA and elsewhere, that the scope of the nonmedical expert in rehabilitation had been foreseen by Metcalf[5] as early as 1953, when he found three major functions of the coordinator that might be of greatest value to the physician, the third one of which is quoted because of its relevance to psychiatric situations:

> The third point is concerned with psychiatric illness. While the same difference between physician and lay rehabilitation expert exists here as in the more tangible physical disabilities, the distinction is somewhat more nebulous when, in fact the executive (rehabilitation coordinator) has a degree of psychological insight. In this situation the psychiatrist may delegate somewhat more responsibility to his lay assistant than the physician who treats physical disability can ever delegate to his nonmedical assistant.

To translate the trend in psychiatric rehabilitation seen by Metcalf into a feasible working relationship, it was essential that the physician had the willingness to train the coordinator, who also had to demonstrate willingness and aptitude to learn. That these preconditions did not prevail everywhere is apparent; but where they did, one can recognize that the growth and development of the position of coordinator was in accord with the principle of "man-on-the-job," which will now be examined in greater detail.

Meislin understood the burden placed on the physician in coping with the overwhelming variety of medical and administrative problems in a large psychiatric hospital when he stated, "The efficiency of such a program may depend not so much on the physician himself, but upon the individual designated to assist the physiatrist in the administration of nonmedical matters."

Someone on the rehabilitation team had to be found to assume a key role in addition to the physician: someone to assume continuing responsibility for the outcome of services performed by each discipline as related to the total needs of the patient, someone capable of making discriminating use of the diversified rehabilitation resources in the hospital and community, someone with specific experience and training to assure that the policies of the hospital and the physician in charge are put into practice.

To illustrate more concretely how the man-on-the-job concept is implemented in an actual work situation, reference is made to

Knudson,[3] former chief, rehabilitation medicine, VA Central Office, who reported on a commentary submitted to him by a physician on the performance of his coordinator. The highlights of the commentary from Knudson are quoted here in abbreviation form, showing how the physician perceives the role of the coordinator:

> (1) His observations and guidance on rehabilitation matters have been instrumental in insuring the fullest physical, social, mental and economical return possible of our disabled patients. . . .(2) As coordinator between the respective sections, he is responsible for evaluating and determining the patient's response to rehabilitation techniques for the purpose of insuring adequate treatment and the total team approach. . . .(3) He reads and studies every source that becomes available on rehabilitation from both the administrative and medical aspect. . . .Not only does he stay abreast of the wider aspects of rehabilitation, but by constantly orienting the various therapists, the entire service profits by learning new methods, techniques and procedures. . . .(4) He, therefore, possesses an excellent background of knowledge. This enables him to make decisions or establish courses of action which are unusually worthy. . . .(5) Perhaps one of the principal contributions he has made is the superior manner in which he can instruct, orientate, inform and/or convince our personnel. . . .Each and every employee in the service turns to him for a completely unbiased and unprejudiced opinion. . . .(7) He is frequently called upon to give orientation lectures to other hospitals and civilian agencies which cover not only the overall aspect of rehabilitation but also the specific therapies utilized in the individual sections. . . .(8) His judgment, interpretations and recommendations are of an unusually high caliber. This applies equally well to all such matters as personnel, budgets, equipment, schedules, workload, morale and the rehabilitation of the seriously disabled patients.

How therapists perceive the role of the coordinator may be exemplified by the following unsolicited thoughts received by the author from a therapist who saw the coordinator primarily as a manager of men and as an administrator:

> What is a rehabilitation director and coordinator? He is a leader of men – dynamic, resourceful, imaginative. He often acts like a sergeant who must drive his men to achieve the objective. He is impatient with those who move too slowly toward the goal line. When apathy and inertia paralyze the staff, he must carry the ball alone against all opposition. He serves management faithfully but still retains his primary loyalty to rehabilitation medicine. He is rarely ac-

> corded recognition and praise when due; more often he is called to task when deficiencies are noted. He is master of a thousand details, but not too overpowered by their weight to lose sight of the goals and purposes of rehabilitation medicine. When operations appear to be hopelessly bogged down in an administrative tangle, he can be relied on to bring order and progress. He always seeks the simpler and more efficient way of doing things so that limited resources of manpower, space, equipment and materials can be better utilized in accomplishing the mission of rehabilitation medicine. Again I ask: What is a rehabilitation director and coordinator? All that I have written and much more that words cannot describe.

This tribute to the coordinator as viewed from the ranks of the ancillary therapist is indeed comforting, even though there is an obvious idealization of the role of the coordinator, with many of the virtues and none of the weaknesses cited.

New scope and dimensions have recently been added to the professional responsibilities of the coordinator in a number of large VA psychiatric hospitals, where the rehabilitation medicine service has been restructured functionally into two or three major programs, with the coordinator designated to direct one of these programs, while continuing to perform his previous functions for the entire service. Depending on local considerations in those hospitals where restructuring has occurred, the coordinator has been designated to head either the social-behavioral, or the industrial (vocationally oriented) program, or possibly a combination of both functional programs.

In assuming direction of the industrial rehabilitation program, for example, the coordinator accrues the following broad responsibilities:

1. the planning, development and implementation of a comprehensive vocationally oriented program;
2. control over rehabilitation medicine service manpower involved in three disciplines: educational therapy, manual arts therapy and industrial therapy, comprising the functional industrial program;
3. maintenance of liaison and the establishment of professional working relationships with all psychiatric services, psychology and social work service; and

4. liaison responsibilities and working relationships exercised in connection with community-based contractors for work-for-pay activities, sheltered workshops in the community and all state and local agencies involved in employment.

It should be emphasized that the functional restructuring of the rehabilitation medicine service is still essentially in a pilot or demonstration stage of development, awaiting further evaluation of its effectiveness, and has not been adopted as a pattern of VA-wide application. Nevertheless, it represents a significant extension of the coordinator in a key leadership role in the vocationally oriented area of psychiatric rehabilitation. The thrust of this development, together with the implementation of new multidisciplinary approaches in mental health care now under way in VA psychiatric hospitals, point to the future utilization of the coordinator as the specialist in the industrial aspects of rehabilitation medicine.

Other major responsibilities of the coordinator not heretofore considered in detail include his functions as a rehabilitation specialist, personnel and fiscal manager, public relations officer and management official.

Function as a Rehabilitation Specialist

He develops with therapists the significance of the rehabilitation medicine objective in relation to the overall psychiatric goal established by the multidisciplinary team, in order that a judicious approach may be made to obtain maximum utilization of the patient's assets for performance in a job or in a sheltered environment in the community. By reviewing treatment progress notes, he is aware of the response of the patient to rehabilitation medicine activities and initiates modifications and changes whenever necessary to insure that the rehabilitation significance of the treatment desired by the physician is understood and applied in the various therapies. He renders practical rehabilitation counseling when the patient faces serious rehabilitation problems by establishing a favorable patient attitude toward treatment and by motivating the patient to the desired level of cooperation and effort. He collaborates with psychology personnel in the effective integration and implementation of rehabilitation activities to validate vocational goals and to provide testing and evaluation of the patient under simulated work conditions in rehabilitation medicine.

The coordinator is a permanent member of the medical rehabilitation board, which provides a top-echelon team approach to the patient's difficult treatment and rehabilitation problems. The coordinator's participation in this evaluation board is especially significant in terms of his total knowledge of the rehabilitation spectrum and the job demands and possibilities of community employment, as related to the mental and physical capacities of the patient measured and tested in the various therapies. The medical rehabilitation board is dependent upon him to administer its operations in accordance with intrahospital and agency procedures.

The coordinator frequently encourages therapists to engage in research projects and studies, rendering consultative and collaborative assistance in organizing their efforts. Because of his close contact with all administrative and professional personnel and his knowledge of appropriate procedures, the coordinator is able to obtain the necessary authorization, funding, space, equipment, supplies and, what is perhaps of equal importance, the cooperation of hospital staff. He coordinates the efforts of therapists participating in research studies in order that significant data may be obtained on the effectiveness of treatment approaches used in rehabilitation medicine.

In some hospitals, he serves as coordinator of the advisory council responsible for directing rehabilitation services for patients with psychiatric disorders. The council, which functions as a coordinating and advisory body, has interdisciplinary representation from such specialties as psychiatry, nursing, rehabilitation medicine, social work, psychology, chaplaincy and voluntary service.

As a Personnel and Fiscal Manager

To afford the most effective treatment in rehabilitation medicine, the coordinator studies the workload of each of the component therapies, developing plans for the most efficient utilization of available personnel, space and equipment. He serves as an adjuster to achieve an equitable distribution of all these resources to be directed toward the fulfillment of the service mission. This represents a professional function requiring the coordinator to possess a comprehensive knowledge of the needs, objectives and working procedures of all service components as well as the philosophy of the daily operational details involved in what is called "administration," but which in actual practice is really an extension of medical decisions in accordance with the policy guidelines laid down by the physician.

In directing and supervising the efforts of the paramedical personnel in the rehabilitation service, the coordinator is required to become expert in personnel management. He is closely involved in the recruitment of new employees, their processing in collaboration with hospital personnel specialists and their subsequent indoctrination and training in all aspects of rehabilitation medicine.

The coordinator keeps abreast of all pertinent hospital regulations, bulletins and other sources of information issued not only locally, but also by higher authorities within the agency or by the Civil Service Commission. He is responsible for promoting intraservice and intrahospital communication of all information pertaining to the rehabilitation program.

The coordinator develops operational procedures for the service to guide personnel on matters pertaining to health and sanitation standards and on matters related to compliance with fire, safety and disaster programs established by the hospital and agency.

As a fiscal manager, the coordinator occupies the unique position of exercising overall control of all funds for the service, working in conjunction with the assistant hospital director and the chief fiscal officer of the hospital. He is responsible for planning and developing the annual budget for the rehabilitation medicine service, allocating funds to each component for the various programs and maintaining an efficient accounting system for all expenditures. A significant aspect of his function as a fiscal manager is his ability to obtain an adequate share of funds for rehabilitation programs. In this regard, he is required to establish sound working relationships with management officials who control hospital funds and to whom he is accountable for their proper and economical utilization.

As a Public Relations Officer

The function of the coordinator as public relations officer for rehabilitation medicine should not be minimized. He must always be prepared to provide information to other members of the hospital staff, students, visitors, news media, relatives of patients and government officials on all phases of the operations of the service. For this purpose, he develops visual aids in the form of charts, diagrams or statistical data to assist him in this important role.

Rudman[6] emphasized the important role of imagery: "It behooves us without being ostentatious to make known to other hospital employees and community members some of our significant or unique accomplishments so that others may become better informed about our work and also share in our successes."

The coordinator establishes and maintains close working relationships with educational institutions, research organizational and public and private agencies concerned with rehabilitation, particularly those interested in employment in industry and sheltered workshops. He promotes a broad interest among community groups in the rehabilitation services offered by the hospital. He plans, supervises and, very often personally participates in orientation programs for volunteer organizations and community industries, aiming at enlisting their support of rehabilitation-oriented programs. The coordinator is closely involved in establishing affiliations with educational institutions for student training programs and maintaining close relationships with local and national health agencies and with all professional organizations in the field of rehabilitation.

The Coordinator as a Management Official

The coordinator is frequently relied on by top management on the local level as well as by higher echelons in the VA Central Office, Washington, D.C., to assume responsibilities in a wide variety of tasks for which his professional and administrative expertise are required. He may serve as fund raiser, as a member of hospital planning and training committees or as an advisor and consultant on special projects. Many VA coordinators have become involved in management functions as administrative assistant to the chief of staff, as staff assistants to the hospital director or as hearing officers for the Civil Service Commission. Some coordinators have attained the rank of assistant hospital director and director in VA.

Summary

The position of medical rehabilitation coordinator was created in VA psychiatric hospitals after World War II. He became the professional associate of the physician in charge of the rehabilitation medicine service, which today includes as many as seven or more major paramedical specialties in most hospitals. Similar developments took place in rehabilitation centers, community agencies and hospitals. In these facilities, the same or additional paramedical disciplines were included under the direction of the medical rehabilitation coordinator, with different titles used to designate the position.

The coordinator filled the need for leadership and coordination of the various specialists in order to achieve teamwork in rehabilitation. Initially, the role of the coordinator was considered by many physicians to be that of the nomedical partner managing the administrative matters of the program. In time, the position of coordinator in psychiatric hospitals evolved into full collaboration with the physician in many facets of the treatment program and into full participation as an intermediary between therapist and physician on psychiatric matters. The scope of the coordinator as a nonmedical expert in psychiatric rehabilitation was augmented by the application of the man-on-the-job principle.

Additional scope and dimensions have recently been added to the responsibilities of the coordinator following the restructuring of some VA psychiatric hospitals into two or three functional programs. Under this arrangement, the coordinator is likely to be designated to head the industrial (vocationally oriented) program, accruing additional professional responsibilities.

Other major responsibilities of the coordinator include his role as rehabilitation specialist, personnel manager, fiscal manager, public relations officer and managment official.

REFERENCES

1. Brent, S. Z.: Personality integration: A concept of rehabilitation of the disabled. *Am J Phys Med, 37*:7, 1956.

2. Hamilton, K. W.: *Counseling the Handicapped in the Rehabilitation Process.* New York, Ronald, 1950.
3. Knudson, A. B. C.: A Progressive Medical Leader Credits Associate. *Information Bulletin,* Department of Medicine and Surgery, VA IB 10-41; 1953, p. 11.
4. Meislin, J.: The role of the physical medicine rehabilitation coordinator in psychiatric hospitals. *J Am Corr Ther Assoc, 4*:25, 1951.
5. Metcalf, S. E.: The Functions of the Executive Assistant as a Coordinator, *Newsletter,* Association of Medical Rehabilitation Directors and Coordinators, Inc., 1953.
6. Rudman, S.: The importance of imagery in physical medicine and rehabilitation service. *Rehabil Ther Bull, 18*:4, 1968.

Section IX

ROLE OF VOLUNTEERS

Chapter 16

VOLUNTARY ACTION FOR THE MENTALLY DISABLED

HARRIET H. NAYLOR

POPULARIZED VOLUNTEERING IS REGARDED as a mixed blessing by many professionals in the field of mental health. In hospital and community mental health programs, as volunteering becomes the "in" thing to do, all sorts of people offer help, and most staff are unprepared to use it well. Some staff members misled by myths about volunteers, feel that their professional practice is in danger of being vitiated by lowered standards of dilettante or ignorant laymen. Some feel that their jobs are in jeopardy from highly qualified people who may be seeking to demonstrate competence in order to be hired. Others appreciate the potential value in this additional help and are secure enough to make the best use of the wide range of talent available from private citizens willing to give their time. With enthusiasm, they plan for assignments, orientation and training to give volunteers know-how and confidence to contribute appropriately. Such initial time investment pays real dividends in volunteer time contributed later which frees the paid staff for technical and diagnostic activities. Most important, practice without volunteers deprives patients of relationships valuable in their recovery and deprives staff of allies in the community who would go to bat for beleaguered budgets for essential staff skills.

Opportunities for creative and meaningful service attract volunteers and give them a chance to relate to others in ways they may not enjoy vocationally or in their ordinary life situations. Many a volunteer finds that he really did make enough difference to keep alive the latent rescue fantasy which probably motivates many volunteers in the first place. When a patient makes real progress because of a volunteer's help, this is the most gratifying form of thanks to the volunteer.

Volunteering is being accelerated nationally by the National Center for Voluntary Action with its network of local voluntary action centers and such legislation as Title I in the Elementary and Secondary Education Act and the Harris amendments to Social Security. Volunteers are making possible many community activities in mental health and retardation services. Competition is growing keener. The ranks of traditional, predictable types of volunteers are decreasing, while at the same time new kinds of persons are emerging as volunteers, stimulated by the urgency of today's problems. Everybody wants to *do* something. Students want to apply their ideals. Senior citizens do not want to waste their life wisdom after retirement. The disadvantaged want to improve service delivery and make services relevant to the needs they understand so well.

Convinced that mental as well as physical health is a basic human right, concerned citizens want to extend this right to all persons. Some gain support for appropriate services and serve on boards of voluntary associations organized to interpret. Some work one-to-one in direct service. A distinction is made between service volunteers and policy makers, and between governmental and private services. Consumers and their lay advocates participate in policy development and planning. Service roles are more directly involved with the victims of handicaps, but sometimes are devoted to functions removed from them, like fund raising.

Direct firsthand response from patients motivates volunteers and deepens their commitment; they find themselves encouraging people to utilize services and mobilizing the resources of the community to meet their needs.

The NIMH study, *Nonprofessional Personnel in Mental Health Programs,* documents the value of volunteer and paraprofessional to supplement staffing in mental health programs. Its typology of functions reflects new roles: *caretaking,* such as feeding and escorting patients, not only in hospital settings but in the community and at the volunteer's own home; *social sustenance:* personal, continuing relationships between friends or with a foster grandparent who encourages efforts toward self-help, independence and competence; *professional assistants* who serve within a discipline as an extension of professional time and effort by volunteers, such as a case aide under a caseworker, or a medical aide. *Bridging* volunteers use and develop community resources and offer developmental experiences outside the institution which give patients courage to enter the mainstream of community life.

In addition to these four functions the author sees another called *advocacy,* for volunteers. Concerned citizens accomplish wonders as pleaders for the mentally handicapped because they are perceived by both patients and the public as free from paid job interests, professional status needs or clinical perspectives. Volunteers can cut through red tape and influence important decisions and individuals, such as a patient considering whether to use a service or a county legislature considering the community mental health center budget. The volunteer advocate speaks more freely than paid staff, as a participating citizen and a potential consumer.

It takes secure administrators to share with the public their problems as well as their successes. Special events to which the public is invited usually show only the pleasant aspects of facilities and programs which send potential volunteers home again assured everything is going so well that they are not needed. One could enlist powerful advocates for adequate staffing and for the initiation or continuation of experimental programs, if private citizens understood these needs. Volunteers speak to budget makers and legislators about the impact on the mentally handicapped people they know personally, which gives their cause authenticity. Comprehensive health planning needs such informed, concerned citizens to speak for the mentally handicapped who cannot speak for themselves.

One block to accepting volunteers is the uneasy idea within professions that the public expects them not to need help, that they ought to be able to do the job alone. The unique value of unpaid staff is not explicit in most academic curricula, nor in many intern or preceptorship experiences. Yet active practitioners face a need for help and it is readily available from potential volunteers in most practice settings. Professional education at every level from basic professional education throughout in-service and continuing education opportunities, in professional association conferences and mixed staff groupings, should build realistic expectations about the use of volunteer manpower, as unique and valuable, rather than as a threat to standards or to jobs.

Training and supervision for volunteers must be tailored to the volunteer perspective, not simply to meeting the staff's need to exercise authority by telling them what to do. Volunteers face a variety of claims on their time and a network of obligations in their homes and communities. Through what professionals teach, they develop interest and concern and an active desire to give their time to the programs. Training must not destroy volunteer spontaneity and common sense, but should give confidence in one-self and in readily available help. Progress to more important responsibilities comes as volunteers demonstrate competence and willingness for deeper involvement. Progress can be toward administrative roles, such as taking on new volunteers as apprentices, training new staff members to work with volunteers or to recruit more volunteers and community support. One of the most coveted volunteer jobs in one system is that of "floater." Through experience in many different aspects of the programs, and floater becomes qualified as backup staffers in several areas so that no one need be disappointed if some volunteer, originally assigned, finds that his primary obligation keeps him from volunteer job. Volunteers must be deployed more frequently than paid staff for such contingencies.

Volunteer imagination and fresh perspectives enrich program development. The volunteer brings a nontechnical "human to human" perception with a neutrality invaluable to interdisciplinary teams whose other members each have special clinical or activity perspectives. The volunteer frequently understands the background of the patient, what traditions and life experiences determine the attitudes and quality of his community. This understanding leads to interpreting the patient in the context of the community who may have no roots there to staff cultural values which can vary from one block to another within a catchment area. The volunteer who really knows a program can recommend it to neighbors.

Volunteers innovate services using their knowledge of available community resources.

Volunteers come into programs not from a vacuum, but from a network of community connections to family, organizations, church and ethnic groups, etc. Thus, one volunteer converted may give a program director access to a great many influential groups in the community. Volunteers with several reference groups organize "adhocracies" to accomplish their goals by persuading fellow members of several groups to work together on a project. Members are urged to recruit volunteers by chapters of the Mental Health Association or the Association For Retarded Children. Conversely, service volunteers, aware of needs for concerted action, join community organizations with related objectives and goals. The volunteer member of an association is a two-way link for that association with the service where he volunteers. Casual advocacy among members of the association is influential because it is authenticized by first-hand testimony of the volunteer. Nothing reinforces credibility like knowing the speaker. Volunteer action centers taught to understand the needs of the mentally handicapped are important allies in communities. Service organizations such as JC's, PTA's and Veterans Auxiliaries have specific interest in mental health and retardation. Their local branches recruit for and support services whose goals, accomplishments and potential they understand and believe in.

Volunteering helps most individuals as much as it enriches the recipients of services for which they give their time and effort. In volunteering, people discover skills and capacities they did not know they had. The right to volunteer, to be on the giving end, should be extended to all and should not be only a privilege for persons who are already quite advantaged. Varied and appropriate service opportunities are needed for patients and their families, so that young people can work with younger people and so that people can work together on projects to discover commonality with others quite different from themselves. Nonprofessional manpower can extend and reinforce the work of professionals and can free professionals for practice where their full qualifications are essential. Volunteers benefit the mentally handicapped and also help themselves develop social equilibrium; in this sense, volunteering is primary prevention for volunteers. The delinquent boy feels better about himself by helping patients in a state hospital; the senior citizen slows senescence while his love and skill move retarded children to achieve levels of competence which they probably would not otherwise even attempt.

Mental health parallels health concepts of prevention. At the primary level, volunteering maintains and develops social competence. Secondary prevention maintains and develops strength to reduce crisis or acute illness among volunteers. They help patients preserve and enhance self-concepts, retain connections with home and community during residential care and offer activities to preserve ability not damaged by the illness. Tertiary prevention, to limit disability and reduce chronicity, is especially dramatic with the long-term resident of an institution.

Remotivation and habilitation involve simple life skills taught by volunteers to supplement and reinforce staff efforts to develop social awareness and competence. Skills in coping and normal living can be taught with little special training, in rehabilitation. Parties, so valuable for the mentally handicapped, wherever possible should be a result of *their* planning with volunteers, rather than unexpected events which may not fit well with the rest of their treatment program.

Most professions have goals for service which could be reached more quickly with help to follow through after the diagnostic and prescriptive process is completed. The volunteer helps people test themselves by responding like a practical, warm human being, not like a clinician with discipline and restraint. Self-perceptive understanding may be the most valuable kind of social sustenance which a volunteer can offer. Teaching living skills, stimulating practice, encouraging forays into familiar settings and helping people develop independent judgment all are gratifying functions for volunteers. Succeeding steps include developing job openings, finding living arrangements and giving the former patient confidence to join organizations and moving into interests on his own.

Good experience with staff partners makes volunteers articulate advocates of standards for trained staff, for program experiments and for projects at budget hearings. Volunteers recruit staff to "their" programs by demonstrating support and interest and to disciplines by enthusiasm for professionals they have known. Volunteers, accustomed to working in committees, have had more experience with shared decision-making than many people in professions allied under a medical technocracy.

Their participation as equals, with their unique perspective to contribute, helps keep plans realistic and relevant. One such coordinated effort involves a state hospital, a community clinic, a mental health chapter and a YWCA in one community. Patients move from an in-hospital group into a community social group living in a protected residence from which individuals spin off as regular members into interest groups as they resume normal life, all with volunteers and staff helping. Such partnership between volunteers and staff means dominance by neither, but rather mutual respect, trust and liking: a *we,* not *they,* tone. Common goals, clear and congruent, make the difference, with free communication horizontally as well as vertically, informally as well as formally. Training of staff and volunteers together builds this kind of teamwork, with periodic review of the staff, complementary volunteer roles and open opportunities for movement and advancement for both.

Where recognition for staff means salary raises and promotions, for volunteers it takes a variety of forms. Seeing patient progress is the most important factor in their staying with a job. To be entrusted with greater responsibility is another. Some volunteers say being counted on by patient and by staff is what keeps them coming. Explicit thanks as well as implicit should be expressed by the top leadership of a program. Parties for volunteers' families; letters to employers; and records on services for college applications, employers or teachers all recognize volunteer effort. Telling other people whose feelings are significant to the volunteer means a great deal to the volunteer, as does whatever is done for him directly or tangibly with pins or certificates to acknowledge his special characteristics, abilities and contributed time.

Good administration of volunteer services centralizes administrative leadership and decentralizes supervision on the job. To humanize services, volunteers help the staff to see the patient first as a person, as well as from staff members own special and different perspective. Volunteers can offer human, spiritual and aesthetic experiences which service budgets can never cover. People with mental handicaps need the creativity and fresh viewpoint of volunteers. Volunteers need a chance to be involved, to be needed, to do important work and to be valued. If staff want their input, then they will have to be sure they are the kind of people who give volunteers support and a chance to earn appropriate recognition. There is great work to be done together.

REFERENCES

Arthur, Julietta K.: *Retire to Action.* N.Y., Abingdon, 1969.

Feeney, Helen M., and Stenzel, Anne: *Training Volunteers.* New York, Seabury, 1968.

Naylor, Harriet: *Volunteers Today, Finding, Training and Working with Them.* Dryden Associates, Box 363, Dryden, N.Y. 1972.

Newman, Joseph: People helping people, U.S. Volunteers in Action. *U.S. News and World Report,* 1971.

Section X

STATE, VETERANS ADMINISTRATION AND COMMUNITY MENTAL HEALTH PROGRAMS

Chapter 17

THE MENTAL HOSPITAL

HYMAN PLEASURE

THROUGHOUT THE GREATER PART of recorded history, the role of the medical man in the care and treatment of the mentally ill has been a minor one. The mentally ill in the isolated instances where care was sought, were more likely to be taken to the clergyman than to the physician. Moreover, so poor was the knowledge of medicine in all fields, including mental illness, that it is problematical whether the ministrations of its practitioners were more effective than the clergy's. The violently insane were generally treated as criminals, while the harmless were disposed of in the same way as other paupers; and in colonial times and long after, pauperism was looked upon as merely a lesser type of crime. In 1725 a law in Rhode Island empowered the towns to erect a house of correction "for rogues, vagabonds and to keep mad persons." The law establishing the first prison in Connecticut in 1727 specifically described its use for "persons under distraction"; and in New York Province, the first institution of this type built in 1736 was to serve "as a poor house, workhouse and house of correction" and had special dungeons in the cellar for the "unruly insane." The workhouse or almshouse as distinguished from the house of correction first appeared on the American scene late in the eighteenth century but did not come into general use until the end of the colonial era.[2] Doctor Benjamin Rush, a leader in psychiatry during and after the Revolution said, "Terror acts powerfully on the body through the medium of the mind and should be employed in the treatment of madness."[4]

In England at the same time, asylums for the special care of the mentally ill were springing up and were hailed as great reforms, but John Conolly, the famous English advocate of nonrestraint wrote "they were but prisons of the worst description. . . . Terrible attendants armed with whips were free to impose manacles, and . . . uncleanliness, semistarvation, a garrote and unpunished murders . . . were the characteristics of such buildings throughout Europe." In Paris the Bicêtre for men and the Salpêtrière for women were alternately called prisons, or hospitals for the mentally ill. It was there that Phillipe Pinel in 1792 introduced a method of treatment called "moral treatment" which opened a new era. Prior to his day, the treatment was sternly repressive and custodial. It was Pinel who proved the fallacy of harsh treatment. At the Retreat in York, England, William Tuke in 1796 emphasized the noninstitutional character of his buildings and stressed the family environment emphasizing employment and exercise. Patients there were treated as guests. Chains and terrorization were strictly forbidden, although mechanical restraint, such as straitjackets and solitary confinement, was not abolished. The medicine of the time was generally distrusted and bloodletting was abolished.[2]

Although the eighteenth century was the worst in the history of the mentally ill as far as repressive confinement and prolonged physical and mental tortures were concerned, it was also the period of enlightenment which culminated in the French and American political and social revolutions. The so-called "Age of Reason" had its effect on the treatment of the mentally ill. In this country the first hospital accepting the mentally ill was the Pennsylvania Hospital which was opened in 1756 at the request of Benjamin Franklin. This hospital had a cellar area reserved for the mentally ill. Virginia opened the first American asylum exclusively for the mentally ill at Williamsburg in 1773. This was the only state hospital for the mentally ill in America until 1824 when the Eastern Lunatic Asylum at Lexington, Kentucky was opened. However, prior to this a special institution for the mentally ill called the Friends Asylum was opened in Philadelphia in 1817. In this institution treatment was based on Samuel Tuke's ideas as practiced at the Retreat in York. Here, moral treatment was the basis of the program, which meant that the patient was treated as a guest with dignity and respect and was given occupational and recreational opportunities. In the first quarter of the nineteenth century eight special institutions for the mentally ill were opened in this country, of which two were state operated, and in all of these provision was made for accepting poor people. Unfortunately, for reasons of economy, most poor-law officials were loath to send patients. In New York State the mentally ill were maintained in almshouses and jails for fifty cents a week, whereas at Bloomingdale (now the New York Hospital, Westchester), the fee was two dollars a week. In some states the cost was as low as twenty-five cents per week, and in others, the mentally ill were bid at auction for their labor value.

Throughout the first half of the nineteenth century, the majority of the mentally ill who had no money were not affected by the psychiatric reforms of the period. Generally, disturbed mentally ill continued to be confined to jails; chronic patients were considered incurable and were excluded from hospitals. In 1838 a report from an almshouse manager complained that in an unheated attic room unsealed against inclement weather and containing eleven beds, he had twenty-five men and two boys, and he added, "they (the insane and feeble-minded) were sent to us, and the law compelled us to receive them, but neither the law nor any authority under it provided us a place to keep them in a proper manner."[2]

About 1830, the myth of the incurability of mental illness was replaced by a new myth: that 90 percent of all mental illnesses were curable. Partly as a result of these ideas of curability and probably as a result of muckraking, which exposed the revolting situation of the mentally ill, a reform movement, led by Dorothea Lynde Dix, developed and resulted in the building of mental hospitals in many states. The first one in New York State, which was established as a result was Utica State Hospital, opened in 1843. The principles of moral treatment were instituted, and excellent results were obtained. However, the claims of cure in the hospitals far outstripped actuality, and many hospital directors vied with one another in claiming more than 90 percent recoveries. The mentally ill were brought to the hospitals in great numbers so that the facilities became overcrowded and more and more expensive. In 1845 when the period of vast immigration to this country began, large numbers of European peasants, many of whom could not speak English and who appeared to the citizens of this country to belong to a lower class, began to crowd into the state hospitals. The period of great immigration coincided with the disappearance of moral treatment.[5] The great advances in general medicine which occurred in the second half of the nineteenth century caused most doctors to lose interest in psychiatry, which remained a sort of stepchild. When the exaggerations of the myth of curability were abandoned, an overreaction again led to a belief in incurability and therapeutic nihilism. To the taxpayer it appeared wasteful to spend vast sums of money to support state hospitals for foreign indigents. It is a sad commentary that the best mental hospitals in 1850 were probably better than the average standard today. The poor record of achievement in mental hospitals can be judged by comparing the amount of improvement in general hospitals of 1850 with today's.[10]

Between 1850 and 1890 while the U.S. population grew less than three times, state hospital population grew eighteen times. The development of the state hospital concept illustrates how a system of care, which in its origins was inspired by the highest motives and was based on sincere hope, was vitiated and almost destroyed by a failure of hope of its sincerest friends, a condition aggravated by neglect from the populace it was trying to serve. This regression of quality continued in the first half of the Twentieth Century. In the period between 1929 and 1956 the state hospital population in New York State doubled, increasing by 2500 people each year. The number of patients was increasing at twice the population growth. Patients were being written off as lost causes.[4] The population in state and county mental hospitals in the United States peaked in 1955 at 560,000. The level of care in state hospitals deteriorated until the president of the American Psychiatric Association could say in 1958 that "the large mental hospital is antiquated, outmoded and rapidly becoming obsolete. We can still build them but we cannot staff them, and therefore we cannot make true hospitals of them. . . . I do not see how any reasonably objective view of our mental hospitals today can fail to conclude that they are bankrupt beyond remedy. I believe, therefore, that our large mental hospitals should be liquidated as rapidly as can be done in an orderly and progressive fashion." He went on to offer as a substitute treatment in general hospitals, in private practice and in community programs which, he said, "showed promise of replacing the state hospital."[13]

The development of community psychiatry is a story in itself, but in some cities a few general hospital services and community clinics were developed in the early part of the twentieth century. In a few places, such as Bellevue in New York City, there was a long tradition of services for mental illness but these hospitals mainly provided observation for the acutely ill and triage for great and unwieldy numbers of patients without any plan for definitive services. The idea of treatment in general hospitals received considerable impetus during World War II. A number of general hospitals began to play a role in the definitive treatment of acute episodes of mental illness, in contradistinction to the triage and screening role of such hospitals as Bellevue and Kings County which were known as "receiving" hospitals and whose main function seemed to be to refer patients to the overcrowded state hospitals. In 1954 New York State was the first in the union to pass a "Community Mental Health Services Act" which granted state funding at 50 percent of cost for community mental health programs. This was quickly and widely imitated throughout the United States and stimulated the development of community services. At first only clinics were developed widely, but later, after the Federal Community Mental Health Centers Act, which promoted a greater variety of essential services, was passed in 1963, far more support continued to be derived for these centers through this state funding than through the federal law.

Unfortunately, for the most part, community mental health programs tended to focus their attention on the milder mental illnesses, while the serious acute and chronic patients were still referred to state and county hospitals. However, as a result of advances in treatment, specifically the development of the new antipsychotic drugs in 1954, it became clear that even acute and severely disturbed patients could be quickly stabilized and referred for further treatment on an ambulatory basis. Based on this new knowledge and experience, the federal government in 1963 passed the Community Mental Health Center Act which for the first time provided major support for mental health programs from the federal government. It became obvious that the vast majority of acute episodes of illness could be quickly stabilized in an average of about nine days, and that if the community provided suitable transitional services the patient could be returned to his family and job.

Although the major mental illnesses could almost always quickly be stabilized, experience showed they would continue to cause prolonged, frequently permanent disabilities, with occasional acute symptomatic flare-ups. The significance of this for treatment programs was that it became clear that the methods and priorities used tended to exaggerate the need for costly inpatient facilities and inadequately provided for outpatient and community facilities. The goal of treatment for the mentally ill, which one hundred years ago was considered to be early detection, isolation and humane maintenance, was converted to a new goal, which was maintenance of the patient in his family and community with early detection of acute flare-ups and brief periods of intensive treatment. It became clear that long stays in the isolation of a large state hospital with sensory deprivation were responsible for many of the symptoms seen in state hospital patients. The term "social breakdown syndrome" was coined to describe these symptoms, which proved to be as stubborn as many of the chronic symptoms of mental illness itself.[6] The enthusiasm engendered by these new concepts resulted in the development of a plan in 1972 in California for complete closure of all state hospitals in five years. Even earlier in England the National Health Service had estimated that the need for beds for long-term stays in state hospitals, combined with beds for acute psychiatric patients in general hospitals, was only 0.5 per 1,000 population. Since this number of beds could easily be provided in general hospitals alone, it was planned that the state hospitals would be phased out in five to ten years.[8]

Already, both in California and England, which have begun to implement these plans, there have been numerous reports that they have been overhasty in their efforts to liquidate the state hospitals, because the community facilities which were supposed to provide services for the patients who would no longer need to be in state hospitals, were not developing in a timely way. Whenever economy-inspired or politically-inspired efforts have caused closing down of state hospital services on a massive scale, it soon became clear that they had been providing a service which was needed and which no one else was willing or able to provide. A recent article in *Lancet* stated, "The achievement of the nineteenth century was to set up asylums for the reception and care of victims of mental disorders, for whom the prison and the workhouse were alike inappropriate; it would be a sad irony if the effect of the twentieth century dissolution of the mental hospitals is merely to restore the *status quo ante*."[8]

The New York State Department of Mental Hygiene has recently issued a proposal for the future care of the mentally ill called the "Balanced Service System" (unpublished draft). This system proposes that for each one million population, services should be provided for approximately 3200 people per year, and that approximately one third of these people would need emergency stabilization, that is, a nine-day admission period in a facility for acute patients. This would require only seventy beds per million population. In view of the chronic nature of mental illness and the long-continued disabilities with recurrent brief episodes, patients who were treated should not be discharged but should be referred to social support and competency-training programs consisting of supervised residences, vocational training and sheltered workshops, all combined with medication and psychotherapy. With such a program it is estimated that the number of patients requiring continued care because of severe disability for prolonged periods in a facility like a state hospital would be so small as to require only approximately seventy beds per million population. The number of patients continuously carried under treatment in all services would be approximately 17,000 out of each million population, and the great majority would receive only enough care and treatment to maintain them in the community rather than to place them needlessly in beds.

This model omits services for alcoholics, drug addicts and children and probably underestimates the number of patients who would come annually for care in mental health facilities and the number of acute and chronic bed patients, but it seems to indicate that planning in one of our largest states seeks to phase out the state hospital. Fortunately, New York State is not trying to move precipitously into this new plan as California did, but instead will try to evolve such a program while learning by experience. Undoubtedly, there will be a phasing down of the state hospitals to a very small fraction of their current size and the development of a whole host of programs and facilities in the service areas all linked together, with patients passing freely from one to another depending on their needs. The fact that this process had started in 1955 is shown by the statistics. In that year state and country mental hospitals in the United States peaked at 560,000 and were down to 276,000 in 1972 despite general population growth and an increase of first admissions and readmissions. From 1962 to 1969 first admission rates rose from 130,000 to 164,000 and readmission from 150,000 to 216,000. These changes reflect the dramatic decline in the median length of stay in state hospitals which in New York State was eight months in 1955 and about thirty-five days in 1973. California now has only about 5400 patients in its state hospitals, a reduction of 80 percent since 1961, and plans to eliminate state hospitals entirely by 1977. At the same time the total number of patient-care episodes (inpatient plus outpatient) in the United States increased from 1,675,000 in 1955 to 4,038,000 in 1971. The number of inpatient episodes increased from 1,296,000 to 1,721,000, while the outpatient episodes went from 379,000 to 2,317,000. In relation to the population, inpatient episodes per 100,000 population went from 799 to 847, outpatient from 234 to 1,134.[3]

The locus of care apparently has been shifting from the state hospital to the community, but there was growing evidence that many mental patients were not receiving care from anyone. Former state hospital patients, subsisting on welfare, living in single-room-occupancy units, were being victimized by human predators of all types. Groups of patients residing in proprietary group homes for adults were being exploited for financial gain.[7,11] Obviously the phasing down of state mental hospitals has outstripped the ability of the community to care for the patients discharged, and contemporary bedlams are developing in the communities which are proving themselves both unable and unwilling to provide the kind of care which the advocates of the rapid liquidation of the state hospitals expected. Former mental patients are in some instances being thrust into communities where they find themselves alien and unwelcome.

Concurrent with the changes in treatment methods and attitudes which led to the changes in the locus of care from the community to the state hospitals and now back to the community again are certain concerns for the legal and civil rights of patients, which are having an important influence. Until the early nineteenth century there were no laws dealing with commitment: The indigent and dependent were treated like paupers and the disturbed like criminals. During the period of rapid growth of hospitals, a concern for the civil rights of such individuals began to appear, not because of a desire to protect the mentally ill but because there was public anxiety about wrongful commitment. During the 1870's a number of states enacted commitment laws which often involved a jury determination of insanity. This legalistic approach, patterned after the criminal-judicial model, contributed to the stigma of the state hospitals. It was not until the 1950's and 1960's that the commitment laws were decriminalized and the law began to pay more attention to the medical needs of the mentally ill.[9] This concern for the civil rights of the mentally ill has gone so far that indifference to human welfare may have been legislated. It is now impossible to obtain help for a mental patient in many jurisdictions unless he demonstrates dangerousness. What is the responsibility towards someone who is grossly disturbed but refuses help? Of course, to some so-called reformers, mental illness does not exist and is simply a form of social deviance, so that deprival of liberty by a psychiatrist for the purpose of treatment is considered a covert penal system designed to maintain law and order.[14] These reformers are trying to abolish serious mental illness by verbal magic: They believe it can be obliterated by nonrecognition.

At the same time, many courts, by use of the concept of the "right to treatment" which is a new legal doctrine holding that the courts are responsible for maintaining proper standards for involuntary patients,[1,12] and the class action, are in some instances trying to force legislatures to phase out state hospitals in favor of community programs by making the hospitals too expensive. This cost factor may have been important in the decision of the state of California to close down the hospitals as mentioned above. If so, events have forced at least a partial reversal because as recently as the December 1973 issue of *Health News* an official California State Health Department publication stated: "The (Governor) Reagan administration unceremoniously called off the precipitous shutdown of our eleven remaining state mental institutions. . . . The senseless confusion which has gripped the mental health community for too long is beginning to yield to more rational consideration." The best opinion available suggests that there must be a massive phasing down of the state hospital system as it is now and a great growth in community facilities and programs, but the first process must proceed gradually and in balance with expansion of the second process if one is to avoid some of the excesses one sees now. And it must be understood that this change is mandated because it is better for patients and not because it is cheaper.

Who will be the provider of these new community services? and what will happen to the personnel now operating the state hospitals? These two questions tend to answer one another. The state hospitals should consider themselves as a resource providing unequaled expertise and personnel and as educational, research and administrative centers with the kind of knowledge and traditions which are needed for new facilities and programs. Already many state hospitals have proved that they can serve both as mental health centers with short-term intensive care units and as extensive outreach programs and also can house special units for psychogeriatrics, adolescents, the deaf and large numbers of continued care patients who show little potential for even semi-independent self-care in the community. Those hospitals which can provide such services efficiently and effectively will be the ones, in combination with the county and voluntary agency services, who will still be providing care five years from now; those which adhere inflexibly to an outworn model will be phased out of existence. There has been little reduction in the incidence and prevalence of mental illness and in the need for mental health treatment. If the state hospitals prove that they still are vital enough as organizations to be flexible and innovative, they will continue to be part of the new mental health picture which is evolving.

Summary

This review of the role of the mental hospital in the care of the mentally ill opens with a historical analysis of the reason why the locus of care for the mentally ill shifted from the community to the mental hospital early in the nineteenth century. The causes which led to this change are well described.[1] The institution which arose, the mental hospital, was at first quite successful and performed an essential service for society.

Within a few decades, however, for reasons which are gone into in the paper but which were mainly beyond the control of the mental hospitals themselves, they began to fail in their function. Although the inadequacies of the mental hospitals became clear as early as the latter part of the nineteenth century and they were periodically attacked in the public media and even by the governmental bodies which created them and which were partly responsible for their condition, they continued to grow very rapidly, reaching a peak in size in 1955. It was not until the 1950's that a combination of new methods of treatment and a better understanding of the needs of the mentally ill suggested that the mental hospital standing alone through its own efforts should no longer be expected to serve as a total system of care for the mentally ill. It became clear that an effective system would include a large number of other kinds of facilities besides the mental hospital. This new understanding and new armamentarium of treatment have led to a change in the locus of service from the mental hospital as a remote independent institution back to the community, with the mental hospital taking its logical place as part of a community system of services.

This change has been taking place during the past twenty years, supported by community, state and federal financial aid. This change is making it possible to convert the goal of the treatment for the mentally ill, which one hunderd years ago was considered to be early detection, isolation and humane maintenance, to a new goal, which is maintenance of the patient in his family and community with early detection of acute flare-ups and brief periods of intensive treatment. The mental hospital will then play a more acceptable and limited role as one of the places where a patient needing inpatient care can receive it. It will also serve as an institution where those mentally ill who are not responsive to any kind of known treatment can receive relatively prolonged care and rehabilitation, and as the administrative, educational and research center for a large but defined service area for which it will be part of a total system of care carrying out a few of the many functions which are essential parts of a total range of services for a defined population.

REFERENCES

1. Birnbaum, M.: The right to treatment. *American Bar Association Journal, 46*:499-505, 1960.
2. Deutsch, Albert: *Mental Illness in America.* New York, Columbia U Pr, 1949.
3. Eisenberg, Leon: Mood-leveling drugs have markedly reduced the population of mental hospitals. *Sci Am, 229*:116-127, 1973.
4. Final Report of the Joint Commission on Mental Illness and Health. *Action for Mental Health.* New York, Basic, 1961.
5. Greenblatt, Milton, York, Richard H., and Brown, Esther, L.: *From Custodial to Therapeutic Care in Mental Hospitals.* New York, Russel Sage, 1955.
6. Gruenberg, E.: The Social Breakdown Syndrome in some origins. *Am J Psychiatry, 123*(12):1481-1489, 1967.
7. Lamb, H. R., and Goertzel, V.: The demise of the state hospital — A premature obituary? *Arch Gen Psychiatry, 26*:489-495, 1972.

8. Letemendia, F. J. J., and Harris, A. D.: Psychiatric services and the future: A local study in Oxfordshire. *Lancet, II:*1013-1016, 1973.
9. McGarry, A. L., and Kaplan, H. A.: Overview current trends in mental health law. *Am J Psychiatry, 130*(6):621-630, 1973.
10. Osmond, H.: Psychiatry under siege: The crisis within. *Psychiatr Ann, 3* (11):59-81, November 1973.
11. Reich, R., and Siegel, Lloyd: Psychiatry under siege: The chronically mentally ill shuffle off to oblivion. *Psychiatr Ann, 3:*35-55, 1973.
12. Robitscher, Jonas: Courts, state hospitals and the right to treatment. *Am J Psychiatry, 129*(3):248-303, 1972.
13. Solomon, Harry C.: The APA in relation to American psychiatry. *Am J Psychiatry, 115*(1) pp. 1-9: July 1958.
14. Szasz, Thomas S.: *The Myth of Mental Illness.* New York, Dell, 1967.

Chapter 18

MENTAL HEALTH PROGRAMS IN THE VETERANS ADMINISTRATION

Joseph J. Baker

The VA operates the largest health delivery system in the western hemisphere and possibly in the world. Its mental health facilities alone include eighty-four general hospitals offering psychiatric treatment, twenty-eight predominantly psychiatric hospitals, eighty mental hygiene clinics, forty-eight day treatment centers and thirty-seven day-hospitals, as well as other specialized facilities which provide treatment and rehabilitation of patients who have been disabled by their mental illness.

Mental health services in the above broad spectrum of VA facilities are provided by a large corps of psychiatrists, psychologists, psychiatric nurses, rehabilitation medicine specialists and other allied health personnel. The facilities themselves are scattered throughout the country with at least one in each state except Alaska. Many are located in large metropolitan areas where they are affiliated with most of the nation's universities and medical schools for the graduate education of professional workers in the system and for specialty training of its physicians. Other facilities are located in more rural areas where trained workers must be imported. In addition to its own full-time and part-time professional staff, the VA contracts with many consultants and other health providers for care and services to its veteran patients. Through the years, this network of VA hospitals, clinics and contract services has provided a dependable and credible range of mental health services for its constituents.

Along with the rest of the health services in this nation-wide network, mental health has been centrally administered within a department of medicine and surgery in the VA's Central Office. This vast department, which is presided over by a chief medical director, has responsibility for all aspects of patient care and for research, education and medical administration.

Each large professional service within the department of medicine and surgery has its own director, its own professional advisory committee made up of eminent practitioners and academicians and its own staff. The professional service in the central office does not control funds, and it has no line authority over operations in the field. It exerts its influence instead through its staff and advisory functions. Thus, it is much involved with monitoring treatment programs throughout the country, helping with recruitment of professional personnel, acting as advocate for worthwhile innovations and providing a visible axis about which multiple educational and research activities rotate.

The Mental Health and Behavioral Sciences Service is the professional service responsible for VA's programs aimed at prevention and treatment of mental illness. This is a multidisciplinary service and includes the heads of VA psychiatry and psychology, plus representatives from the professions of nursing, rehabilitation medicine and social work. The service is organized into functional divisions. Hence, for matters relating to the broad area of treatment, there is a multidisciplinary Division of Treatment Services. In the same manner, there is a Division of Mental Health Training and Education, a Division of Mental Health Research and a Division of Planning and Program Development.

This functional mode of organization is used by most large public mental health systems in America and, with numerous variations, has become the organizational model for mental health treatment teams in VA hospitals and clinics. The multidisciplinary input assures that strategies for improved treatment programs can be arrived at jointly and flexibly by focusing the necessary range of skills on specific problem areas. This kind of flexibility is especially important in a program that must be continuously sensitive and responsive to the changing clinical needs, life-styles and values of a nationwide constituency.

This complex of mental health services exists to serve veterans of the armed forces, with first priority being given to those who need treatment because of a condition connected with their military service. Those seeking treatment for a nonservice-connected illness must sign a statement of inability to pay for treatment before they can be admitted into the treatment system.

The philosophy which guides the operation of mental health programs within the VA has been enlightened by the same insights which have been current in the rest of America. Hence, there is an increased emphasis on rapid intensive treatment, short hospital stay with continuing treatment as necessary, on an outpatient basis. In an effort to cut down on the distressing incidence of "patienthood" and dependency on the hospital, it has vastly increased its commitment to various kinds of outpatient facilities. These include not only the mental hygiene clinic with its multidisciplinary treatment team, but also a variety of other facilities whose mission is to provide alternatives to hospital care. Its day treatment centers are operated primarily for the benefit of chronic patients, who are able, with the help of these facilities, to live in the community while participating regularly in treatment programs of the centers. These may be located in the hospital complex, but a recent study by the VA concluded that they could function just as effectively in settings remote from the hospital. As a result, it has been recommended that no new VA hospital construction include space for day treatment centers.

VA's day-hospitals, on the other hand, are designed to care for a more acutely ill clientele on a part-time basis. Because of this, such facilities require that hospital-type services be regularly available. Hence, they are located in or adjacent to VA hospitals.

The trends in VA outpatient psychiatry are shown in Table 18-I.

In addition, many thousands of patients are cared for in foster homes, halfway houses and various other settings which are designed to enable the patient to help himself and live as independently as possible. In this manner the VA program attempts to provide a range of treatment options sufficiently broad so that every patient can get treatment in a manner and in a setting that

TABLE 18-I
VA OUT PATIENT PSYCHIATRY TRENDS

	Mental Hygiene Clinics	
	FY 1965	*FY 1972*
Caseload	69,296	109,393
Visits	471,566	636,513
	Day Treatment Centers	
		FY 1972
Caseload	2,156*	3,007
Visits	184,754†	349,471
	Day Hospitals	
	FY 1969	*FY 1972*
Caseload	151	681
Patients Treated	634	2,831
Days of Treatment	15,863	74,441
	Other Psychiatric Outpatient Visits	
	FY 1969	*FY 1972*
	254,455	596,566

*9-30-66.
†FY 1965.

is appropriate to his clinical needs. This involves a clear departure from the archaic practice of reckoning all units of care in terms of beds occupied, an administrative-fiscal device which has been fairly well discredited, but which still has some proponents.

An idea of the dramatic shift in emphasis away from beds occupied to increased numbers of patients treated is shown in Table 18-II.

Based on a 20-percent systematic random sample of *patients*

TABLE 18-II
VA INPATIENT PSYCHIATRY TRENDS

	Psychiatric Hospitals		*General Hospitals*		*Total*	
	FY 1967	*FY 1972*	*FY 1967*	*FY 1972*	*FY 1967*	*FY 1973*
Beds	49,705	18,501	6,498	14,971	56,203	33,472
Average Daily Census	45,726	19,067	5,941	12,339	51,667	31,422
Admissions	42,159	49,289	28,917	72,291	71,076	128,580
Discharges	50,314	52,862	28,500	80,007	78,814	132,869
Turnover Rates	9.2	23.1	40.0	54.0	12.7	35.2
Patients Treated	106,245	69,532	36,226	92,616	142,471	162,148

remaining in the hospital on October 21, 1971, about 40,000 out of 81,150 patients had a psychiatric diagnosis. Of this latter group about 67 percent had a psychosis, with about four-fifths being classified as functional. Of 138,242 *psychiatric regular discharges* during fiscal year 1972, only about 33 percent represent the psychoses.* With its relatively static population of psychotic patients, then, and a rapid turnover of persons with other diagnoses (mostly alcoholism or neurosis), VA has a large commitment both to acute intensive treatment and to the maintenance of a therapeutic setting for chronic patients.

The proper treatment of new psychiatric patients represents a special challenge. Like those who seek help in other public delivery systems in America, the majority of veteran patients qualify as "poor" people by presently used definitions. Many of the younger ones, especially, are undereducated and have no job experience prior to induction into the service. Hence they are practically unemployable when they receive their military discharge. This fact alone complicates any existing emotional disturbance and often seems to make the difference between the person who is ready to identify himself as a patient and the one who is able to cope with his own problems. How such a troubled person is handled when he applies for mental health services becomes a matter of considerable importance. If he is routinely admitted to the hospital, the system confirms him in his role as a patient. While this may be acceptable in a person who is indeed mentally ill (as many applicants are), it is liable to set in motion a wholly inappropriate train of expectations and dependencies for one who is not. In order to avoid this, some VA hospitals have set up evaluation services in an attempt to insure that referrals are relevant and appropriate to the problem. Many hospital admissions which would otherwise have been inevitable are being avoided in this way.

Quite obviously, this kind of problem-solving approach cannot succeed without a diverse assortment of other helping facilities. The VA offers many of these under the umbrella of its own

*Data are from Ref. 5 of this chapter. Note that the number of discharges varies from Table 18-II, which contains data from different sources.

agency. It can provide education, job training and counseling where needed. It can provide many other supportive services, including family counseling when indicated, to help the veteran. It can even provide money for travel to enable the veteran to take advantage of these services. In addition, of course, VA depends on other agencies in the community to provide needed clinical services to some veteran clients. This collaboration with community agencies is desirable for many reasons. Veteran patients often come from families with multiple social problems and hospital personnel often find themselves dealing with agencies like county welfare, the county health department and the county's correctional personnel in attempting to help a single veteran patient to solve problems relating to members of his immediate family. It has been suggested that this kind of ombudsman approach to the patient's most distressing immediate problems can help to avert breakdown and the need for hospitalization.

Regardless of the alternative methods of treatment, of course, a certain number of patients need the structure and security provided by the hospital's inpatient service. Here, the patient has the benefit of all that a well-qualified staff can do for him. Not surprisingly, there is wide variance in hospital treatment programs in a system of this size. Obviously, the staffing pattern (and hence the style of treatment) at a VA hospital in a remote rural area will be substantially different from the one with graduate school affiliations in an educational center. But wherever it is located, the VA hospital is operated by trained medical administrative personnel accountable to the VA Central Office, and it recruits the ablest professional people available. Hence, for good reason, it is generally perceived as the best service of its kind locally.

In recent years, the VA has been part of the trend in American medicine toward increasing the capacity of the general hospital to deal with psychiatric patients. As far back as 1962, the chief medical director stated that psychiatric services "should be present in the great majority, if not in all, of our general hospitals."[4] All new VA hospitals built since that time have been general hospitals with psychiatric services and all have been built in close proximity to medical schools. Not only that, but many hospitals previously designated as "psychiatric" have been converted to general medical and surgical hospitals by virtue of major additions of staffs and services.

Within the hospital setting there has occurred a renewed interest in the treatment environment. All large health delivery systems must guard constantly against the bugaboo of depersonalization, coldness and lack of concern for the feelings of patients. The psychological environment created by staff attitudes affects all patients for better or worse. The VA was most recently reminded of this by Vietnam veterans who registered many complaints about hospital attitudes and rigidities. The hospital's language, its requirements for conformity, its hours and activities and recreations geared to older patients, all were strange and distasteful to the younger veterans who generally preferred to be treated like people rather than like patients and who resented and resisted regimentation or enforced conformity to unexplained and seemingly pointless regulations. After a painstaking self-examination, the VA concluded that many of these complaints were justified and that changes were needed to create a psychological climate that took into account the younger veteran's needs, values and life-style. Only in this way was it possible to enlist his collaboration in treatment. As a result every VA hospital appointed a committee of staff people and, in most cases, young Vietnam-era patients, to make appropriate recommendations. Some hospitals set up separate wards for Vietnam-era veterans; most hospitals made changes in their recreational programs, creating special opportunities for younger hospitalized veterans to pursue their own interests. In the process of looking, adjusting and changing to improve the psychological climate in the hospital, all patients benefited, not just the young ones.

The physical environment has been given renewed attention as well. The VA has been attempting to get away from the drab and colorless which characterized so much of hospital construction until fairly recently. Older hospitals, especially, are being encouraged to repaint and redecorate, to show some imagination in the use of colors and textures, to put drapes on windows, to rearrange beds and to use room dividers in large barracks-like wards in order to afford more privacy and dignity for patients.

In its concern about the psychological and physical environment within the hospital, the VA is reemphasizing the primacy of the patient and his needs. Within this climate of concern, much flexibility is possible in shaping necessary programs of treatment. The VA's drug treatment program is a case in point. From being a minor problem on the horizon three years earlier, the incidence of heroin addiction in young veterans burgeoned into emergency proportions during 1971 and 1972, calling for rather heroic measures. The Alcohol and Drug Dependence Service was established in 1971 and given the mandate to establish Drug Dependence Treatment Centers dispersed geographically about the country to meet the needs of veterans. By June 30, 1973 the VA had forty-three Drug Dependence Treatment Centers (DDTC's) located in fifty-three facilities, forty-six outpatient clinics, two satellite clinics and four outpatient fee-for-service contracts. Each DDTC provides a multimodality of treatment. Of the fifty-three facilities, fifty-one provide detoxification, fifty-three provide drug free therapy, forty-three are licensed to provide methadone maintenance, and twenty-six provide other chemotherapy. In fiscal year 1973 there were approximately 17,500 admissions for inpatient care, while outpatient visits exceeded 800,000, which is more than double the workload experienced in fiscal year 1972.

The hospital drug dependence treatment units are like nothing else within the hospital setting. Operated on the DATOP or Synanon model, many of them avoid the doctor-patient roles entirely, with therapy being pretty much the function of the whole group living experience. Here, encounters or confrontations within the unit are the rule and everyone is expected to challenge deviant behavior in anyone else. Professional staff people are not exempted from this group interaction. Instead, they are likely to be on a first-name basis with the patients and are regularly called on by the patients to explain, and defend if need be, decisions that seem arbitrary. Treatment goals of the group are things like getting one's head "straight" or getting it "off the street," learning to trust other people, learning to be responsible to the group and, ultimately, learning responsibility for oneself. Only a very flexible system can accommodate a treatment model so seemingly antiprofessional and so at odds with the usual hierarchical administrative structure of the hospital.

The effort to involve patients therapeutically takes many forms. For older patients who must remain in the hospital, the greatest therapeutic necessity, after providing for physical needs, may be to keep them engaged with the here and now. A model program of reality orientation for such patients was developed at one of VA's predominantly psychiatric hospitals, in which a deliberate attempt was made to create, and routinely use, a variety of visual and auditory reality reinforcers. Hence each day, in one way or another, the patients are made aware of the day and date, of where they are, of what they are doing and will be doing, and, as much as possible, are drawn into the planning of their own activities. Because of the remarkable success this program has had in the diminishment of confusion and disorientation, many other VA and non-VA hospitals have adopted this model.

Regressed patients, many with chronic forms of schizophrenia, make up another type of clinical challenge. For them, some VA hospitals are now using "token economy" as a technique aimed at social rehabilitation. This is a scheme whereby socially acceptable behaviors by the patient are reinforced by awarding him tokens with which he can "purchase" his meals, lodging, articles of clothing, cigarettes, toothpaste and other amenities. In this way many patients who previously were withdrawn and totally unconcerned about personal hygiene, and who in other ways showed unacceptable behaviors, have been helped to behave more compliantly and in ways less disruptive to other persons.

Another form of rehabilitative therapy for long-term, as well as acute, patients is "work-for-pay." This is akin to the token economy program, but in this case the desired behavior is useful work and the reward is money rather than a symbolic token. There are many variations. Some programs are essentially sheltered workshops within VA hospitals. In others, the hospital functions somewhat as a broker, finding jobs in the community that patients can do. Another variant finds patients involved in such diverse activities as the operation of a string of gas stations or painting and remodeling houses. There is evidence to suggest that acute patients are helped more by this type of incentive therapy than chronic ones are. As a matter of fact, the results with chronic patients tend to be rather discouraging if one is looking for total rehabilitation. However, the evidence suggests that this is a modality which helps to minimize the effects of illness and prolonged hospitalization and, therefore, that regression and withdrawal would be much more pronounced without it.

In addition to providing the important outpatient activities already described, some VA hospitals also work very closely with providers of aftercare in the community. Most of VA's predominantly psychiatric hospitals and general hospitals with large psychiatric sections have foster home programs where the staff meet at regular intervals with the men and women who operate foster homes for veterans in the hospital's service area. By keeping communication open and by indoctrinating these persons about what to expect from patients, it has been possible to reduce readmissions substantially. Other hospitals provide continuing follow-up through satellite clinics at strategic places which are serviced by itinerant professional teams at regular intervals, while still others detail professional members to live and work almost full-time in communities remote from the hospitals themselves.

The multidisciplinary philosophy which guides VA's mental health programming perceives rehabilitation not as a separate function, but as the ultimate goal for everyone involved in treatment. In the effort to interrupt or minimize the effects of the disease process, all members of the staff are seen as "therapists" or "rehabilitation workers." In reemphasizing the process of rehabilitation, VA's mental health programs have become more closely allied than ever before with VA's own rehabilitation medicine service.

REFERENCES

1. Ayllon, Teodoro, and Azrin, Nathan: *The Token Economy.* New York, Appleton, 1968.
2. Environment as Therapy (30-minute color film). Available through Pfizer

Pharmaceutical, Inc., New York, New York.
3. Folsom, James C.: Reality orientation for the elderly mental patient. *J J Geriatr Psychiatry, I* (2), 1968.
4. Middleton, William S.: CMD Letter 62-25. December 20, 1962.
5. 1972 Annual Report of the Administrator of Veterans' Affairs. Washington, D.C., U.S. Govenment Printing Office.
6. The Vietnam-era Veteran: Challenge for Change. Administrator's Seminars on Vietnam-era Veterans. VA publ. 1971.
7. Winick, W.: *Industry in the Hospital: Mental Rehabilitation Through Work*. Springfield, Thomas, 1967.

Chapter 19

THE COMMUNITY MENTAL HEALTH CENTER IN REHABILITATION

TIMOTHY B. MORITZ AND ALAN J. TUCKMAN

THE COMMUNITY MENTAL HEALTH CENTER offers a unique approach to the rehabilitation of the mentally disabled. It is a comprehensive system of diagnostic, rehabilitative, consultative, educational and preventive services designed to meet the needs of the mentally disabled patient and his family in his own community. Continuity of care to the individual and coordinated care to the family, as close to home as possible, with minimal disruption of family life are added features.

The spectrum of services provided to the community may be divided in the following manner: planning and coordination, the indirect service system, the direct service system and evaluation and feedback mechanisms.

PLANNING AND COORDINATION

The planning of the center involves professionals, consumers, related agencies and concerned citizens, together identifying and evaluating preexisting services and unmet community needs. Factors such as anticipated growth of various population groups, transportation problems impeding access to existing services, language and ethnic barriers to acceptance of effectiveness of the services must be considered. Short-term, intermediate and long-term plans are developed, including planning for space acquisition and facility development, most appropriately through rentals in the community. Priorities are established, and potential costs, revenues and funding sources identified. All of these efforts are focused on the specific catchment area for which the community mental health center is responsible.

Effective coordination of services is essential to successful center operation. Since this usually involves several previously autonomous agencies, as well as multiple units of the sponsoring agency, the task is complex and difficult. The center board and the director must have adequate authority and supporting staff to ensure this. The essential techniques include setting up uniform philosophy and policy, and developing procedures, clinical records and management information systems shared by all components. Strong leadership, continuous monitoring and effective professional and administrative supervision are vital to success. The well-coordinated system is capable of far more effective service delivery and prevention than fragmented autonomous agencies producing wasteful duplication of some services and deficiencies in others.

THE INDIRECT SERVICE SYSTEM

The indirect service system is the newest feature of the community mental health movement, distinguishing it from earlier models of mental health delivery. Subsumed under community consultation, education, liaison, outreach and prevention are services designed to reduce the incidence of emotional breakdown through intervention at stages prior to the onset of overt illness. The simplest of these, liaison with other caregiving agencies and individuals, removes the center from an isolated position in the community and brings it into the network of caregiving agencies, thus improving its availability and receptivity.

A Division of Consultation and Education (CE) is the center's direct link with the community. Although many informal channels of contact evolve between center staff and community agencies, it is generally left to CE staff to develop formal relationships with these community caregivers. Many individuals in emotional distress turn first to their closest caregiver, the clergyman, welfare caseworker, police officer, family doctor or lawyer, for assistance. It has been estimated that 71 percent of individuals turn first to these caregivers for help with emotional problems and only 29 percent seek help directly from mental health professionals.

It is therefore, incumbent upon CE staff to train these "community gatekeepers" in the identification and handling of emotional problems. In this manner, the mental health professionals' impact upon the community is many times greater than it might be in treating individual patients directly. By working through a clergyman or probation officer, many more individuals in distress can be reached. Consultation programs are developed with school staff, probation officers, judges and lawyers, police officers, jail staff, welfare caseworkers, clergy, public health nurses, general hospital emergency ward staff, physicians and social agency staff.

Consultative efforts may take various forms. Consultee-centered case consultation helps the consultant more appropriately deal with the emotional problems of his client. Program development consultation affords a consultee group the input of mental health professionals in the designing of programs for its staff and clients. Through administrative consultation, an agency director may request help in resolving problems in the functioning of the agency brought about by interpersonal staff difficulties. An important result of regularly scheduled consultative programs with community agencies is the "satellite and coordinator effect." Frequently a number of different caregiver agencies in the network will send representatives to consultation meetings of other agencies. This produces a multi-agency forum for discussions concerning the management of clients of several of the participating agencies, as well as stimulating interagency referral and liaison.

Related to consultation efforts are training programs designed for specific caregivers such as police, clergy and general physicians. These may include seminars and workshops in normal child development, psychopathology, sensitivity training and techniques in brief therapy and crisis therapy. Frequently, programs evolve, tailored to the specific needs of the caregiving group. An example of this is the development of a marital discussion group for police officers and their wives arising from the observation of the massive stress imposed upon a family by one member's entering police work and the very high divorce rate which ensues. Programs, like this one, cross over from consultation to prevention of mental illness in the caregivers themselves. The above example is one which is considered intervention with "a population at risk." These are groups who, by reason of their social, personal or vocational position, can be expected to manifest a higher incidence of emotional breakdown. Therefore, the CE service itself may assume responsibility, or may stimulate another agency or group to assume responsibility, for developing "reach-out" programs for the recently widowed, pregnant adults, recently retired, the elderly and isolated, rape victims, unmarried pregnant adolescents and young people contemplating marriage; and even a big-brother/big-sister program for children of one-parent families.

Another outreach program heavily utilized by the community is a "Hotline" telephone counseling service. Through the use of trained volunteers, an extensive crisis counseling, information and referral network may be developed.

Community education about mental illness, mental health and mental health center programs is an area which borders on public education. This is an essential service designed to improve the understanding and acceptance of mental illness and treatment by the community.

Regularly scheduled open-house activities and tours of the center, displays at shopping malls, continuing contributions to local newspapers and radio programs and regularly scheduled workshops at schools and colleges in the community, staffed by center professionals, help to reduce the mysticism and isolation of the mentally ill. By using center therapists in these programs, the therapists themselves will expand and redefine their roles in the mental health delivery system. The narrowly defined "therapist" may then view himself as the "community mental health professional," responsible not only for an individual patient, but for the continuing mental health of the entire community.

THE DIRECT SERVICE SYSTEM

The treatment services of the center may be viewed as a continuum within a delivery system designed to meet the unique needs of each community. This is a major departure from prior models of mental health treatment which provided a small number of fragmented services developed with little consideration of community needs.

Within this coordinated delivery system, distinct adult and

children's services may be defined, although there are crossovers and blurring at many points.

Adult services may be divided into psychiatric, psychosocial, social-supportive and vocational programs. In many instances the patient may avail himself of several programs concurrently or sequentially, depending upon individual needs.

While some centers require that all patients enter a single intake service staffed by representatives of various programs, providing complementary and concurrent evaluations, others have divided their intake activities and allowed entry through several portals. The latter seems the more appropriate, since an early delineation of need is naturally brought about by patients themselves and by the caregivers who refer them. Intake services for the acute emergency are part of a twenty-four-hour evaluation and crisis treatment program including brief, individual and group therapy. Mobile evaluation and treatment programs, utilizing a multidisciplinary team, are aimed at assessing a crisis situation in a family, within its natural setting.

Less severely handicapped individuals often present themselves to the outpatient clinic program for individual, group and family counseling. Here, greater emphasis is placed on the development of programs utilizing the family as the primary unit for therapeutic intervention. With the advent of more sophisticated drugs such as lithium carbonate and long-acting intramuscular phenothiazines, general and specialty medication clinics are being developed. Often patients are seen in groups to evaluate medication dosage, effectiveness and side reactions and to provide an additional socializing experience.

With increasing awareness of the epidemic proportion of the alcohol and drug problem in many communities, programs are developed to meet these needs. A comprehensive alcoholism program must include detoxification; drug treatment (disulfirm) ; and individual, family and group therapy. These services are provided on a short-term as well as a long-term basis and include twenty-four-hour inpatient, partial hospitalization and outpatient services. An intimate and well coordinated relationship with local (Alcoholics Anonymous) groups is essential. Some centers are participating in the development of alcoholism education councils. Others are experimenting with various halfway or "pretreatment" facilities, such as professionally staffed "flophouses" for the transient alcoholic, not yet ready to make the full commitment to a formal treatment program.

Drug abuse treatment service include inpatient, outpatient, detoxification and medication components similar to those provided for alcoholics. Added features may include a mechadone maintenance program; a residential treatment facility; and storefronts staffed by professionals, former addicts and drug counselors assigned to school districts and responsible to the schools' guidance department, but meeting regularly with the center's drug treatment staff.

The chronic, socially impaired individual presents to the center in diverse ways. He may have been discharged from a chronic ward of a state hospital, may be a resident of a boarding or nursing home or may have been sheltered in his family's home for many years. He may be classified as mentally retarded, elderly, socially isolated or suffering from a chronic physical disorder such as multiple sclerosis or blindness; or may have been diagnosed as having a severe adolescent adjustment reaction or chronic schizoprenia. The presenting problem though, is a social and vocational maladjustment in the community rather than a distinct psychiatric symptom; and thus, psychosocial, social supportive and vocational rehabilitation services must be developed to complement psychiatric programs.

Psychosocial programs include adult day training projects designed to teach activities-of-daily living skills, photography, writing, consciousness raising, reading, current events, nutrition, cooking personal hygiene, parent-child relations, grooming, music and art for the socially isolated. Specialty groups are designed for couples, individuals with neuromuscular disorders, the blind, boarding home residents, alcoholics and drug abusers, the mentally retarded and senior citizens.

Prevocational programs include the development of client-run food canteens and stores selling products manufactured in the program, as well as clerical and woodworking shops.

Recreational programs include sports activities, social and folk dancing, parties and trips for cultural and recreational enrichment.

A coordinated vocational program includes an evaluation and counseling service, a transitional workshop for individuals who can be expected to ultimately move into competitive employment and a long-term sheltered workshop for those too severely impaired to ever function outside of this setting.

Job placement and follow-up counseling are essential to the continued adjustment of individuals who have graduated from the program.

In an attempt at providing supervised community living facilities as alternatives to the dehumanizing effect of chronic state institutional confinement, many centers have developed, or stimulated other community agencies and groups to develop, cooperative apartments, boarding homes, adult foster homes, halfway houses, hostels and even sheltered villages. The success of these programs is often directly related to the extent of the education of the community about the mentally ill. Small, well publicized demonstration projects help to gain support for these placements.

Childrens' services are, perhaps, the greatest challenge to a community mental health center. They include the provision of evaluation services for the preschool child who presents with abnormal behavior or delayed development, as well as treatment services to meet the needs of these children. The school system's enormous resources are not available to assist these children, and services preexisting in the community are generally sparse. Problems frequently go undiagnosed and untreated, until the child reaches school. By that time, problems, which initially were easily remediable, have become chronic and refractory to treatment, hidden under layers of superimposed difficulties associated with environmental mishandling. Efforts to assist the school-age child whose problems have already become fixed are less effective and more time-consuming than early intervention techniques.

Thus, it is appropriate to focus on a child development center for preschool children, staffed with a multidisciplinary team of specialists in child development, including a child psychiatrist, neurologist, psychologist, social worker, pediatrician, nurse, speech and hearing therapist and special education teachers. Consultants are available in opthalmology, genetics, immunology, dentistry, orthopedics, physiatry and physiotherapy, as well as electroencephalography and sophisticated medical laboratories, providing genetic, endocrine and metabolic studies. Early accurate diagnosis will permit specific curative treatment in some cases, implementation of special educational and rehabilitative techniques at the time of maximum potential effectiveness in others and the minimizing of trauma to the child and family in all.

Direct services of the child development center include individual and group play therapy, drug treatment, social casework, special education techniques and specific medical therapies. The provision for therapeutic nurseries, day-care centers, respite services and home visitation programs, is highly desirable, permitting more intensive intervention and diminishing the need for residential placement. The center may offer all of these services in an integrated program, or it may stimulate their development by contract agencies. Special consultation and education programs directed at obstetricians, pediatricians, hospital nurseries, agencies serving preschool children and new parents, are critically important in the programs' early intervention efforts.

The major demands on the center for services to school-age children are for consultation to schools and for outpatient clinic services. The moderately mentally disabled child functioning in the public school system is in need of supporting services, including respite programs, summer camps and special evening or weekend recreational programs, along with parent counseling and family therapy. The center may develop therapeutic day-care and special education facilities for severely mentally retarded or emotionally disturbed children whom the school system has decided it cannot serve. These facilities, combining the resources of mental health and special education, are able to effectively meet the needs of children whose problems are too severe to be handled within existing school programs. Availability of these programs in the community allows many more families to keep their children at home and prevent their institutionalization.

Effective services for adolescents require more than the traditional outpatient clinic. Emergency treatment and crisis intervention are of critical importance, as are specialized drug abuse and alcoholism services. Adolescents who do poorly in individual and group psychotherapy may respond well to socialization programs. School dropouts may receive critical assistance from involvement in tutorial or remedial educational programs associated with vocational counseling.

The center's hospital service should be able to offer intensive inpatient treatment to children and adolescents including the provision of screening and referral services to state schools, state hospitals and other residential facilities.

The development of group and foster homes for emotionally disturbed, mentally retarded and developmentally disabled children in the community will further reduce the need for placement in large, remote institutions.

EVALUATION AND FEEDBACK

In order to truly meet its mandate as a dynamic and responsive mental health delivery system, the community mental health center must develop a comprehensive evaluation and consumer feedback mechanism.

It has been found that a number of diverse and complementary projects are necessary to assess the appropriateness and effectiveness of existing services and to plan for future activities. These programs may be divided into utilization review activities, consumer advisory boards, consumer advocate or ombudsman activities, consumer literature, patient and agency surveys, follow-up studies and program evaluation and analysis.

Utilization review, a concept practiced in medical facilities for many years, but quite new to mental health services, is the process of reviewing treatment planned and rendered. This may be performed by chart review alone or may include a discussion with the therapist, patient, patient's family member and referring agency representative. Of course, this process is carried out by a select interdisciplinary committee having a firm, defined mandate from the center director and community mental health board, with active participation of center therapists.

A consumer advisory board is an essential ingredient of consumer feedback for program review and planning. To be truly effective, the board must include patients, family members and special interest groups such as the elderly, the poor, adolescents and minorities in the community, as well as representatives from various community agencies. The board will most appropriately reflect the character and composition of the community being served.

One of the most productive consumer input activities is that performed by the consumer advocate, also known as the ombudsman, consumer liaison or consumer-center facilitator. This individual, paid by the center, the community mental health board or county government, is available to both community residents and center staff to aid in the resolution of difficulties as diverse as helping a patient air a complaint about a center staff member, facilitating the transfer of an elderly patient to a nursing home or smoothing the ruffled feathers of an ambulance corps that encountered difficulties in delivering a patient to the center.

Each center must maintain an active brochure, designed to advise the new or prospective patient of his rights and responsibilities and of the procedure he will undergo in entering the mental health system, and to describe services and terms. A prime focus of this brochure is to impart to the patient a sense of participation in his treatment and to dispel the feeling of passivity often found in the psychiatric patient entering a new and overwhelming treatment program.

Surveys of patient and referring agency attitudes about the center, patient and family evaluation of symptom relief and improved functioning at discharge and at follow-up, as well as professional judgments and objective indices, are ingredients of continuing evaluation studies of program effectiveness. These, together with cost-effectiveness and cost-benefit analysis, goal attainment evaluation, surveys of unmet needs, skewed service utilization patterns and epidemiologic studies, are essential for maintaining a relevant and appropriate delivery system.

Superceding all of these consumer feedback and program evaluation mechanisms is the need to stimulate a sense of openness and receptivity, in staff and management, to the information derived from such studies. This will ensure that the information obtained will stimulate appropriate corrective responses and optimal allocation of resources.

Summary

The community mental health center can provide a dynamic, responsive, comprehensive system of services, within which the mentally disabled can be effectively and efficiently rehabilitated to maximum potential in their own community. Closely related are the center's efforts to mobilize the community to utilize its resources to prevent mental disability and to accept the mentally disabled within it. The synergistic effect of all of this has far greater potential for the mentally disabled and for the community than efforts to provide individual rehabilitative, treatment or prevention programs in isolation.

While it may be questioned whether the community mental health center has the obligation to provide such a diverse array of services, it may be appreciated that the promoting of community mental health necessitates far greater intervention in the community than former mental health delivery systems.

REFERENCES

1. Beigel, A., and Levenson, A. I.: *The Community Mental Health Center.* New York, Basic Books, 1972.
2. Bindmen, A. J., and Spiegel, A. D.: *Perspectives in Community Mental Health.* Chicago, Aldine, 1969.
3. Caplan, G.: *An Approach to Community Mental Health.* New York, Grune, 1961.
4. Caplan, G.: *The Theory and Practice of Mental Health Consultation.* New York, Basic, 1970.
5. Cassidy, T. M., Moritz, T. B., and Block, W. E.: A suburban community responds to its drug crisis. *Med Arts Sci, 25*:43, 1971.
6. Shore, M. F., and Mannino, F. V.: *Mental Health and the Community: Problems, Programs and Strategies.* New York, Behavioral Publications, 1969.
7. Tuckman, A. J.: Disaster and mental health intervention. *Community Ment Health J, 9*:151, 1973.
8. Tuckman, A. J., and Paul, S.: Community psychiatry and traditional clinic. *NY State J Med, 73*:555, 1973.

Section XI

NONVERBAL COMMUNICATION–BODY LANGUAGE

Chapter 20

ON TEACHING COMMUNICATIVE SKILL

ALBERT E. SCHEFLEN

In the last generation the social behavior of people and other animals has come to be studied in a non-Aristotelean manner. As a consequence it has become clear that human communication involves more than the use of language to express affective states and ideation. People must know how to take location, establish postures and orientations and move together, or they will not be able to communicate, i.e. they will not be able to form and maintain human relationships. In such a case a person will become what medical and psychological people call "sick."

Those who have observed the visible behavior of communication (and watched people who have not learned it) are perplexed by the traditional approaches of psychiatry and psychotherapy. First of all, they cannot see why there is so much diagnostic mumbo-jumbo and so many multiple doctrinal schools of psychodynamic and genetic explanation. Secondly, they do not understand why clients or patients are supposed to stumble around in recollection until they discover what is wrong with them. Instead, such heretics ask a simple question: Why we do not teach children and unlearned adults what they need to know in order to be social, human beings?

This problem will be discussed here, first with a description of some of the behavior people must be able to exhibit if they are to act in a communicative way. Next will be a description of some of the weird nonverbal behavior of those people who are labelled neurotic, psychotic or defective. Last will be a discussion of what therapists can do to learn about and apply this sort of perspective.

INTRODUCTION

One must first ask what people must know how to do if they are to form and maintain social relationships. One does not yet have to care whether they have *conscious* knowledge of what to do. In fact, it is not necessary to know what people know at all, for one can take an operational position about these matters. *In some sense or other, people must know how to do that which one sees them do.*

In order to determine what behaviors are not successful in sustaining communication, one can ultimately examine communicational events that do not come off and behaviors which repeatedly fail in an event or disrupt it. But it will be wise to begin with the study of events and contributions that *do* come off by some criteria or other. So first is a description of what people do in events which are (1) considered successful by the participants and (2) come to a usual and traditional outcome.

Operational Stance

The observational process involves another relationship—a relationship between participants in a communicational event and those who are observing and describing this event. So one must also pay attention to this aspect of the subject.

What one "sees" in nature depends upon the vantage point from which he makes his observations—up on where he is stationed and what he has been trained to look for.

The reader should imagine that he has freed himself from the responsibility of diagnosing, treating or understanding the psychology of a client or subject and in fact, that he has freed himself from the task of interacting with him. Procedures used previously include sitting off at a distance and watching *some other people* relate or maybe taking a videotape or a motion picture of such an event and sitting down to study it in an unhurried and relatively detached way.

In studying communication, one concentrates on relationships and observes what happens *between and among* the people in a small group. The focus here, then, is not upon what is supposed to be happening *in* a particular participant. There is no denial of the relevancy of thoughts and feelings to the communicational process, but for the moment one should observe the process itself, seeing what the participants can perceive as a basis for their communicational experience. The concentration, then, is on what can be seen, heard and felt, rather than on inferences and theories about such matters.

WHAT PARTICIPANTS MUST KNOW HOW TO DO

If participants are to establish communicational relations, at the least, they must know how (1) to come together and establish a postural-orientational relation, (2) to carry their part in a customary and appropriate program of activity and (3) to qualify and regulate what they are doing in keeping with a variety of contexts.

Behaviors That Establish a Communicational Frame

If people are to communicate directly they must come together so that they can see, hear and maybe touch each other. To do this they may have to thread their way through other gatherings and territories. They must exchange recognition signals or greetings, form a cluster and in some measure become involved together. They must hold this postural-orientational involvement until they have finished.

Many contemporary communication theorists have come to call this a "communicational frame." Consider some of the behaviors that go into it.

MOVING THROUGH: If participants are to get there they have to move about. Often they must move through or past other gatherings, and sometimes they have to get across barriers and thresholds. In doing so they traverse owned territories.

One has to know certain rules of passage to accomplish these transits without offense. The average adult can tell something about such rules, but even if he is not articulate about the matter one can see that he moves about without raising too many eyebrows or precipitating a riot.

Elements of this complicated behavior of passage have come under study in recent years. Each involves a deference to the territories of others and a selective avoidance of interaction with strangers. Here are two examples.

Among the behaviors of territorial passage is a particular kind of postural-kinesic ritual. When passing through the property of another person or group or when passing through or near an assemblage of strangers, a person should curl and keep his hands near his body and his eyes to the front. The head is slightly lowered. One does not stride or swagger through space already claimed by others with head high, chest out and eyes staring. To do so is to challenge the right of others to be there and, thus, invite a contest of dominance or territorial defense.

By the same token people do not stride across the thresholds of others without being invited to do so. They pause at the threshold of another person's chair or room to await at least a glance of recognition and a nod of invitation. On the other hand, one does not need to stand at the threshold of his or her own territory or at the threshold of an intimate and await an invitation. One can see each of these everyday rules of territorial passage violated in bizarre ways if he will watch the transit of patients on the ward of a mental hospital.

On streets or other public places one pedestrian must pass another without behaving in a rejecting manner on the one hand, or without inviting an encounter on the other. One does so with postural, kinesic behavior that Goffman calls the ritual of "civil inattention." One glances at the other passerby for a split second and then casts his eyes down and away. And as each pedestrian does this he will briefly lower his head. To refuse the glance of attention not only risks a collision, but it seems to indicate that the other person does not exist. One sees such an omission, for instance, when a white resident passes a black one in a small town. On the other hand, the holding of the glance beyond its usual duration is tantamount to making a pass, making a pitch or otherwise requesting an encounter.

Almost everyone in a culture knows these simple behaviors. At least almost everyone uses them thousands of times each day. But a much greater complexity of unwitting skill is involved. Everyone of these rituals varies in occurrence and quality with a host of contextual dimensions. For one thing the nature of these mini-interchanges varies with ethnicity. In addition, the issue of which participant performs which elements varies with their relative class and status, with the priority of their arrivals and so on. Furthermore, density and activity will make a difference. If people are obviously busy, for instance, or if the place is very crowded, these rituals are likely to be waived altogether. Thus, one wonders how people learn these matters and can apply them in great variation in a multitude of situations which they must appraise in split seconds. Or conversely, since nearly everyone does learn all this, one may wonder how some few people do *not*.

GREETING AND RECOGNITION: When a frame is being established, the participants will exchange what Ferber and Kendon call a "distance greeting." They will approach each other and exchange a flashing of the eyebrows[4] and a display of palms. They may also offer a salutation. The exchange of such behaviors differs from the civil inattention ceremony in which such signals are avoided. In fact, these recognition signals can evoke the formation of a frame for greeting and conversation.

After the participants display palms and flash their eyebrows, they often approach to tactile distance. They greet each other in language; and in many American subcultures they will shake hands, embrace or kiss. In other traditions nodding or bowing is used, and tactile contact is avoided. Thus, a small microsequence of behavior is essential in gauging what happens next. The aversion of gaze is usually followed by passing on, while a greeting is followed by coming together. Theoretically, then, a person could avoid any encounters at all by using only the behavior of civil inattention.

There are also a great many variants of the greeting ritual and a member of any society must know each of these and when each is appropriate. Not only is greeting and recognition behavior specific in form for an ethnic tradition, it is also specific for a particular relationship. One may kiss a relative or an old friend's wife, for example, but not a relative stranger at first introduction. And the kind of kiss and the distance at which the pelvis is held distinguishes a friendly greeting from a sexual advance. In addition, the warmth and overtness of the greeting display is a statement about the quality and nature of the relationship, so that an unexpected evasion or a neglect of palm displays or touch is equivalent to a social slight or an avoidance. Similarly, an elaborate greeting performed as one enters a meeting already in progress is embarrassing and disruptive.

When an interchange of greeting behavior has been completed, the participants may pass on, but they do not do so without at least a token parting and a rationalization for not lingering longer. Often, however, those who have greeted one another will then engage in a conversation or possibly a courtship exchange. When they shift from the greeting phase to some other interaction, they will reestablish a frame for this next activity.[7] To do this they often back off a few inches, orient to each other and adopt a particular relation of postures. In doing so they build a postural-orientational frame that is appropriate to their relationship, to the business at hand, to the tradition of distances in a particular culture, to the need to acknowledge the presence of others, to the density of the place and so on.

If the participants have the same plan of interaction and come from the same background, they will adjust the dimensions of the frame almost instantly and quite automatically. But sometimes the matter is more complicated. If one person is of northern European extraction, for instance, he may stand at a distance of more than three feet for standing conversation, while the partner, of Mediterranean extraction, may stand at a distance of less than three feet for conversation. Those influenced by traditions using a large space will stand back from such a distance. A sort of dance to adjust distance may result with each participant taking personal reference to the other's proximity.

If one person has a plan for courtship in the frame he or she may stand at a distance of about two feet, while the partner, who envisions a conversation, may seek a distance of greater magnitude. Here again a phase of adjustment may take place. The courting member may be cooled off or the noncourting participant may be induced to using less space and to courting. In any case there is an appropriate context for the spatial dimension of the frame, and a socialized and acculturated person knows what this is.[5] Furthermore, such a person can pick up cues and make allowances even if his partner is of a different ethnic background.

Another dimension of the frame is the degree to which the participants orient their bodies and faces to each other. In some cultures, such as Eastern-European Jewish, an almost full face-to-face relation may be used even for casual conversation, while in other cultures, such as the American Black working class, this degree of closure of the frame is usually avoided. Otherwise a confrontation may be induced. Similarly the frame is closed by using a full face-to-face orientation in courtship and in highly intimate and secret conversations. For casual conversation the frame is left partly open. A relation of bodily orientations of maybe 45° is used. And those who are expecting others to join them or are talking as they start to move use a frame of about 90° of closure.

Thus, the interpersonal distance and the degree of face-to-face closure define certain kinds of relations and activities. They can also induce or preclude these particular activities. It is difficult to talk to a partner who stands six feet away in a relatively crowded room, and it is impossible to continue and escalate intimate conversation or courting activity at such a distance.

The frames of rapport and intimate conversation are also characterized by keeping the head up, by exchanging glances, by uncrossing the arms and, in some cultures, by touching. All in all the picture of short-distance, full vis-a-vis eye contact and uncrossed extremities is one of high involvement. Animated voicing and active facial gesticulation may also accompany this degree of involvement. Conversely, the use of maximum distance, off-angle facing, arm folding, head dropping, eye aversion, flatness of the vocal qualities and projection of the voice to the floor form a picture of low involvement. By habitually using such behaviors, a person may habitually cool interactions such as courting, rapport, intimate conversation and the like.

One should notice that a closed frame excludes those who are not "in" it. A closed frame can be adopted in order to form and maintain a dyad, and the inability to do this may prevent dyadic relatedness. On the other hand, the formation of a closed dyadic frame is impolite in a gathering and it may be tantamount to rejection of a friend who stands nearby waiting to participate. If spouses are thereby excluded for a long time a kind of micro-infidelity results. In fact those who use such frames persistently get a reputation for seductiveness. Maybe this is what they want, or maybe they *are* seductive, but it behooves them to know what they are doing.

One should bear in mind, too, that frames can be much larger than these dyadic ones. Three or four people often establish a frame for conversation in public places. In living room conversations, meetings or psychotherapy sessions six, eight or more people may take stations in a semicircle and establish a frame. Here, there will be no description of these larger frames in detail, but there is one aspect of grouping and spacing that is especially salient to this subject. In a larger gathering a central position may be taken by a few major participants, while others group themselves in a second ring of participation or otherwise take a station on the periphery. This central grouping is called the "nucleus" of the frame, and more peripheral space is known as the "region."

Ordinarily, the region is occupied by those who have supportive or ancillary roles in the activity—by those who coach, referee, mediate, audit, substitute, serve or wait. Those, in the nucleus have rights of speaking and participation which differ from the rights of those in the region. Accordingly, those who are to take an active and focal part will gravitate to the center of the conclave or maybe to a special place at one end. They do not ordinarily hang back in the region. Conversely, those who do not have the status or privilege of central participation do not barge into the nucleus uninvited. Only children or people of great status in the group can freely violate these rules of station and participation.

There is a point at which an activity comes to an end and the frame is then dissolved. The participants leave or engage in some other activity. So one who is adequately socialized knows when something is over and how to leave the frame.

Traditional Coactions and Interactions Within a Frame

When a particular kind of frame has been established, an appropriate kind of transaction will occur within it. The frame and the transaction define and maintain each other.

In any tradition there are particular kinds of transactions which the people can recognize from their component actions and stages. So unless a particular human event is extremely offbeat in form, one can identify it as a courtship, a conversation, a confrontation, a psychotherapy session, a business meeting or whatever. In these customary kinds of transactions, a particular format of actions is prescribed. The participants are expected to do a particular thing and then another and so on. Sometimes these traditional programs feature an exchange of speech behavior, sometimes a sequence of physical actions and sometimes an interchange of kinesic or body language behaviors. In actual transactions all of these behaviors occur.

In early stages of courtship, for example, an escalating degree of closure and physical closeness is seen. As postural and spatial involvement increases, a customary set of kinesic signals is exchanged. There is, at first, glancing which gradually increases to holding a gaze. Men preen their ties, coats and hair; women their sleeves, necklaces and hair. Women display their palms and raise their breasts. Both parties show an increase in bodily tonus. Pot bellies, double chins and eye bags disappear. Finally, touch may occur.

In conversation a certain participant will usually lean or sit forward a little in initiating an utterance. Speakers also place their hands in front of them or to the sides in a gesticulating position. Listeners sit back a bit, face the speaker, nod their heads from time to time or mutter something. In some cultures everyone speaks at once. In others the floor belongs to the one who is assertive or tricky enough to gain it. In British-American traditions, the speakership is rotated on a turn-taking basis.

In confrontation, involvement escalates in a manner similar to that of courtship, but the participants make displays of dominance. Their chests and jaws protrude, they glare, etc. The other kinds of customary transactions which one sees in the frames of everyday life will not be dealt with here. Instead, the point should be made that a socialized person knows and uses the repetoire of his society; the acculturated person uses those particular forms which are traditional for his background.

Metacommunicative Regulation

Ordinarily then, people establish a traditional frame and engage in a customary sequence of activity, but human behavior is not, of course, this cut and dried. As people take part in customary events, they continuously qualify, explain, apologize, vary and otherwise modify their contributions. In other words, participants behave communicatively in a customary way, but they also behave in reference to what is going on. They sometimes behave, as Bateson says, in a metacommunicative way.[1] They communicate about the ongoing process of communication.

In one form of metacommunication participants exchange signals in order to qualify their meanings. They smile, for example, to indicate that a particular statement is not to be taken as an affront. They exchange winks or eye crinkles in indicating that a particular interaction is joking, teasing or ironic. One glares as the other shrinks back for an instant if a particular statement is to be taken very seriously and regarded as an order. Or when one person acts in an offending way and *says* that he did not mean to cause offense, another can acknowledge this apology with a nod, and the program of action moves forward. So metacommunicative behavior can be linguistic, kinesic or both.

A variety of metacommunicative actions serve to control behavior or to manipulate what is going on. For instance, a frown, a glare, a display of chest or fist and a menancing step forward can monitor a behavior that is unexpected or unacceptable. A display of courtship activity can be used to induce an alliance or gain the right to speak. By the same token turning away from another participant can deprive that person of the speakership or cool off an incipient rapport.

In summary, then, the participants establish a frame and begin to carry out some sort of usual activity, but as they do so a continuous interchange of regulatory behavior maintains or alters the scene. A great many of these behaviors consist of subtle microacts which are often not within the participants' realm of consciousness. Yet if one does not recognize and use these behaviors, life can be an endless series of misunderstandings.

DEVIATIONS IN USE OF THE COMMUNICATIONAL CODE

So the use of a tradition has a certain lawfulness. There is a code of customary movement and gesture which members of particular background learn and share as they do in the case of a language. By using this code in a customary manner, people can form relationships and get across ideas. They can also manipulate the communicational system to gain power, pursuade others, elicit rejection and so on.

When one watches a familiar social event, he can observe its general progress and can see all sorts of variations and deviations. Often one can at least guess why some particular person or subgroup is doing the unexpected. But there are certain people who invariably perform in a culturally deviant way. They characteristically misperform one or many features of the code, and one may be hard pressed to see how this can benefit them.

When one observes these people, he can notice that they do not establish frames in a usual way or they do not establish them at all. They cross thresholds without invitation and walk unconcernedly through other people's turf. And they are thrown into consternation and bewilderment if these actions elicit a hostile response to the violation. Or conversely some people hang back from crossing territorial lines they are supposed to cross.

Similarly, there are people who seldom greet those they know. They look down and away when they are recognized. Yet some of these same people try to hold a gaze with the strangers they pass. As a consequence, they are often accosted by drunks or transients, and they never seem to know why this happens. Others stray through hostile territories allowing their gaze to wander. Thus, they accrue many sometimes unpleasant experiences and see the world as especially sexy or especially hostile.

Some people stand at courtship distance in every conversation without knowing it. Or they take positions so far in the region that they are left out of the central activities. Or they make endless courtship displays in all kinds of transactions, except when they are actually in a courtship frame. So they are always being invited to bed by people they should not sleep with, but they cannot consumate courtship with their mates. Some people cannot establish or hold any frame.

In conversation there are those who underproject their voices to the point of inaudibility. They look away from prospective listeners who then disassociate with them, but they misconceive the source of their rejections. They blame *what* they have said or they blame their personalities, for example. They do not realize that they have provided a signal which breaks off the conversation. There are many people who do not use the behaviors necessary to get to speak in a group. They do not sit forward. They do not place their hands in front of them in the position of gesticulation. They do not look at their prospective listeners or make an audible signal of readiness to speak. They simply try to talk from a listener's posture and never get much of a chance. Minute after minute and year after year they get angrier and angrier about the fact that no one listens to their ideas.

There are people who are always making displays of dominance or of submission. There are those who interrupt any conversation and those who stand in the region in slumped positions with their heads down, when they are supposed to be protecting their interests. And there are those who never know when an event is over. They never relinquish the floor. They cannot move from one subgroup to another. When the party is over they seemingly have no way to say "goodnight." They cannot go home. In short, these people do not seem to know the customary frames or the rules of sequencing an activity.

There are also a number of people who do not understand metacommunicative activity. They never know whether they are being courted or simply befriended. They never catch the point of a joke. They cannot tell whether they are being teased or viciously attacked. They do not pick up kinesic warnings, and they make awful blunders. And not only do they fail to pick up the signals, they also do not provide them to others. So others find them hard to be with, confusing or easily hurt.

WHAT CAN ONE DO ABOUT THIS?

The saddest thing about these people is that no one knows how to help them. If they seek medical help, nothing is found on physical examination. If they have a gross defect in speech behavior they may be referred to a speech therapist, but no one refers them to a kinesic therapist or a touch therapist or a "frame" therapist. They may spend years in psychotherapy learning about motives that lead them to social failure, but they will be very lucky to learn anything at all about *how* they fail.

As people with these problems grow up, they face an escalation of difficulty. They are doing something wrong, and no one seems able to help them see what it is. Since they have difficulty forming friends or engaging in communicative events, they withdraw from the effort. They nurse ideas about the hostility of other people and about their own inadequacies. And these statements are fed to people in every media. Maybe they have bad breath or an offensive body smell. Maybe they have an oral dependency or an unresolved Oedipus complex. They do not really want to get along with others. Maybe they are like Uncle John or Aunt Sue and hence have bad genes.

In any event, it is agreed that something is wrong with them. As their efforts at correction are unavailing, they may get crazier and crazier. This may result in a burst of frustrated violence, like Melville's *Billy Bud,* or withdrawal from social engagements in principle. Ultimately, they may end up in institutions. Yet their craziness will be explained cyclically. It will be said that they are neurotic, or whatever, because of something *within* them. This explanation will, of course, recycle the problem and divert the possibility of observation. The problem is thus "psychologized" or "biologized." A difficulty in communication has been mislocated within the body or within the mind.

There seems to be little help for most patients until the stranglehold of this Aristoteleanism is broken. One must relinquish the tendency to classify and label everyone. One must surrender the notion that events have a first, prime, real or basic cause—a cause that is located in the glands, in the genes, in the head or somewhere within the person. One must not simply assume that a person with communicational difficulty has a motive for having it. It is not simply that some initial wrong in affectivity or cognition causes a deviance in visible behavior. One has to get past a hidden belief in original sin.

The therapist who can get past this preoccupation with labeling and primary intraorganismic causes can observe communicational behavior *per se*. He can make observations for himself. Then he will spot gross deviations in his client's or his patient's participation. He can use videotape or other devices to help him, but the main thing is to know where to look.

The fantasy of the psychodynamicist is that he is looking into his patient. It seems, instead, that he is merely looking into a set of Aristotelean doctrines about people, not into a person. He can, instead, look at people and between people. Then he will see behavior and problems of behaving. He will soon be at least an amateur expert in body language, proxemics and the like. And if he is interested he can read some of the growing and now voluminous literature on the subject.

REFERENCES

1. Bateson, G.: The Message: This is play. In Schaffner, B. (Ed.): *Group Processes,* vol. II. Madison, Madison Printing Co., 1955.
2. Bateson, G.: *Steps to an Ecology of Mind.* New York, 1972.
3. Birdwhistell, R. L.: *Kinesics and Context.* Philadelphia, U of Pa Pr, 1970.
4. Eibl-Eibesfeldt, I.: *Ethology: The Biology of Behavior.* New York, HR & W, 1970.
5. Hall, E. T.: *The Hidden Dimension.* New York, Doubleday, 1966.
6. Kendon, A.: Movement coordination in social interaction. *Acta Psychologica, 32:*100-125, 1970.
7. Kendon, A., and Ferber, A.: A description of some behavior greetings. In Michael, R. P. and Cook, J. H. (Eds.): *Comparative Ecology and Behavior of Primates.* London, Acad Pr, 1973.
8. Scheflen, A. E.: *Body Language and The Social Order.* Englewood Cliffs, P-H, 1972.
9. Scheflen, A. E.: *Communicational Structure.* Bloomington, Ind U Pr, 1973.
10. Scheflen, A. E.: *How Behavior Means.* Garden City, Anch. Doubleday, 1974.
11. Scheflen, A. E.: Quasi-courting behavior in psychotherapy. *Psychiatry, 28:*245-257, 1965.

Section XII

THE RIGHTS OF PSYCHIATRIC PATIENT'S

Chapter 21

BILL OF RIGHTS*

EMPLOYMENT OF PATIENTS

THE LAW STATES THAT THE department shall encourage the employment of patients and residents as part of therapeutic, community care and release programs and that it should provide training for gainful employment.

It also mandates that patients and residents employed by a facility receive compensation in accordance with state and federal labor laws.

Sheltered workshops operated at department facilities must comply with all laws and regulations applicable to sheltered workshops operated by voluntary agencies.

The law requires that specific regulations be adopted to protect the rights of patients and residents who are involved in pre-vocational or vocational training or who are employed by a facility.

The department is currently working on the regulations which will establish guidelines to ensure that every patient's and resident's rights in these areas are protected. Although not finally decided, the regulations will probably include the following provisions. They will apply to all facilities operated by, or which require an operating certificate from, the department.

Rehabilitation Services

Each facility must provide patients and residents with rehabilitation services to optimize their physical, psychological,

*The source of this chapter is Article 15 of the recodified Mental Hygiene Law, entitled "Rights of Patients." It is reprinted with permission from *Mental Hygiene News,* published by the New York State Department of Mental Hygiene, June 21, 1974.

social and vocational development with a view to meaningful employment.

The objective is to assist every patient and resident to move as far as possible toward independent living through the development of self-help skills and social competence, including communication skills and vocational competence. These services may be rendered at the facility or in the community. Certain vocational rehabilitation services must be available. The services must be appropriate to the developmental level and in accordance with the overall service plan of each patient or resident.

Patients and residents must be involved to the fullest extent possible in the formulation of their vocational objectives and vocational service plans. Required services include vocational evaluation including written comprehensive interdisciplinary evaluation (medical, psychological, social, vocational and educational) that provides information relevant to vocational objectives and goals, written vocational objectives for the patient, a written plan to achieve those objectives including the assignment of responsibilities and a schedule for periodic review and revision.

Implementation of any plan for vocational rehabilitation services should take into consideration the developmental level of the patient and should include, but not be limited to, prevocational programs to promote work readiness including relevant vocational academic instruction; the development of work attitudes, self-help and social skills and practice in job tasks; vocational training provided through on-the-job training, transitional sheltered workshops, work-study programs and classroom training and education; vocational placement in competitive employment, sheltered workshops or trade training programs; and assistance in vocational placement including such job-related factors as living arrangements; social, recreational and religious activities; medical and educational services, transportation, and legal and financial affairs.

Documentation of the services provided, evaluation of the patient's progress and revisions of the plan must be included in the patient's clinical record.

Patients Involved in Work Activities

Patients or residents may not be required to perform any work in a facility, except in relation to their personal care and possessions.

Before engaging any patient in work activity, the patient must be given written notice and oral explanation of this provision. Patients may engage in work at the facility only in accordance with these regulations.

Any patient or resident who is engaged in training involving work, in work training or in work at a facility must be informed orally and in writing of the rate of pay, pay period, the methods of determining total pay, deductions from total pay, the reasons for them, if any, and the provisions of department regulations concerning work and work training.

PART TWO

RESEARCH IN REHABILITATION OF THE MENTALLY ILL

Chapter 22

REHABILITATION OF MENTAL PATIENTS

Howard E. Freeman

It is quite clear that the research efforts of social scientists and social psychiatrists have been a key determinant of the marked modifications in hospital treatment programs that have occurred in the past two decades or so. Those concerned with the application of social research can be most proud of the efforts of their colleagues and their role as agents of social change. Certainly, the indiscriminant use of shock therapy, the needless custodial orientation hospital personnel and the irrational long-term institutionalization of patients are conditions to be deplored and cannot be justified on either therapeutic or humanitarian grounds.

In retrospect, however, it is clear that the changes that have occurred in hospital treatment cannot be defended in terms of their efficacy. In a perhaps overly harsh critique, Perrow points out that the restructuring of the mental hospital has occurred in ways that contradict principles of effective organizational arrangements.[2] It is impossible to maintain that the goal of the hospital is to cure the mental patient or that an appropriate technology has been developed for actualizing this goal. The doors of the hospital are not one-way entrances to the community used solely by persons restored to health, individuals able to take up active instrumental roles and to assume the full responsibilities of community life. Instead they are doors used by both the sick and the healthy and revolving doors at that. The total accomplishment of the last twenty years is the transfer of the problem from the hospital to the community.*

*Much of the data and the views expressed in this paper are from the author's studies with Ozzie G. Simmons. The author will not make specific reference to this research, for it is summarized in a book they coauthored, *The Mental Patient Comes Home*. See Ref. 1.

If the goal of the hospital is merely the temporary dismisal of patients, then perhaps the problem of hospital treatment has been fairly well solved, at least for patients with so-called functional disorders. From a humanitarian point of view and in terms of manpower and economic resources, it is most reasonable to argue that the mental hospital should be looked at as a way station and that intensive treatment and rehabilitation efforts must take place in the community, not in the hospital. Current treatment programs in Great Britain, many other European countries and here in the United States are predicated on this view, and the ongoing expansion of community mental health centers undertaken in all of our states will undoubtedly result in a further emphasis on community rehabilitation programs.

Certainly, the author is sympathetic to the policy of minimizing hospital and maximizing community treatment programs. However, he is somewhat pessimistic about the success of these efforts, not because of the loci of these programs but rather because of underlying confusion in their goals and the assumptions on which they are predicted. *Rehospitalization* and *conformity to social norms* are analytically two separate issues. Programs directed at remodeling the posthospital career of the mental patient, the author contends, must be undertaken with a recognition that efforts directed at keeping the patient out of the hospital may have no impact, or indeed possibly a negative one, on his levels of work and social performance. Further, he believes that the research evidence on the posthospital experience of patients suggests that efforts directed at maximizing the patient's instrumental roles, that is, his occupational and social behavior, may not influence whether or not he will be able to remain in the community. This view is derived from the research undertaken by the author in collaboration with Ozzie G. Simmons. Their studies will be described in some detail, along with the implications for program development of these studies.

Research on the Posthospital Experience of Patients

Their position at the point of initiating their large study of 649 former mental patients dramatically illustrates how far the pendulum had swung. It has been some time since psychiatric studies of mental illness have completely ignored social and cultural dimensions. Their frame of reference, however, not only included but was dominated by these dimensions. Psychiatric status and what may be described as "medical variables" were given no place in their consideration of the posthospital experience of mental patients. The study took mental health research the full circle, but as the author will try to show, the pendulum has swung too far. Social and cultural variables are not the key, in themselves, to understanding the posthospital experience of patients. The study described here took its departure from a particular conceptual position, but the findings failed to support this position completely. An understanding of how the researchers arrived at the original position is best conveyed by tracing the development of their series of follow-up investigations of former mental patients and their families, of which this study was the third.

The Community Health Project was initiated in 1953 under a special grant from the NIMH. The initial mandate from the funding agency was general and broad, namely, to undertake a study that could provide a general framework and some working hypotheses for research on the community experiences of former mental patients. Under the direction of Ozzie G. Simmons, a team representing sociology, anthropology, psychology, social work and psychiatry developed plans for a long-term follow-up study of former mental patients, employing primarily semi-directed interviews and a case study approach that was to be supplemented by a series of cross-sectional studies.

During the initial development of the project there was a close working relationship with a pilot study of rehabilitation and rehabilitation personnel at the Boston State Hospital under the direction of Doctor Ralph R. Notman. It was an opportunity to undertake a joint survey with the Boston State Hospital Project that led to the development of the author's first follow-up study. In their study group were fifty-nine patients of varying diagnoses and ages who had successfully remained in the community for over two years. Notman and his associates were interested in knowing more about the status of this group, and the author undertook an investigation, truly exploratory in character, to assess their posthospital experience. The findings of this study, although amorphous in many respects, were striking enough to provide the direction of subsequent research and the basis for the adoption of a conceptual frame. A most relevant finding was the wide range of variation in the performance levels among patients who can leave the hospital and remain for extended periods in the community. Only about 50 percent of the patients who succeeded in remaining in the community for twenty-four months were working full-time or were responsible for the care of the home. Similarly, the social participation of the patients in the study group ranged from being highly active in both formal and informal social relationships to being as isolated and inactive as hospitalized patients in chronic wards. One finding from this exploratory investigation that had a major impact on the direction of the author's thinking was the family role of the patient in relation to his posthospital performance. He found that those patients who were high in performance, that is, who were working full-time or actively engaged in the care of the home and who had active social lives, were much more likely to be found in conjugal families or living alone than in families in which they were the "son" or "daughter." It was on the basis of this relationship, as well as certain correlations between performance levels and personality variables that the author advanced the notion of differential tolerance of deviance as an explanation for the posthospital performance of patients.

In the form originally stated, "tolerance of deviance" meant the continued acceptance of the former patient by his family members even when he fails to perform his instrumental roles. The data from the study suggested that, among any group of patients released from the hospital, there are a significant number who perform at a low level, but remain in the community, and another group who perform at a low level, but return to the hospital because their relatives are less tolerant. With this underlying notion as a departure point, the author and Simmons attempted a second investigation focused on the problem of continued acceptance of the former patient by his community associates despite his failure to perform according to the community's basic descriptions for his age and sex roles.

Since they could not test this proposition directly, they formulated a series of hypotheses, derived from their notion of tolerance of deviance, that could be tested and thus provide support for the underlying proposition. The independent variables they selected referred to structural, social psychological, cultural and attitudinal characteristics of the patients' families. In the second investigation they restricted the study group to male patients. The female informants interviewed were all relatives, predominantly the wives and mothers, of male patients who succeeded in remaining in the community since their latest release from the mental hospital some time between 1954 and 1955. Every male patient with the following characteristics was included in the potential drawing group: twenty to sixty years of age, white, native born, living in the Boston area at the time of release, hospitalized for more than forty-five days prior to release, not physically handicapped to the extent of being unemployable, not addicted to narcotics and not hospitalized primarily for acute alcoholism. By diagnosis all were psychotics with functional disorders, the majority diagnosed as schizophrenic.

The results of this study replicated the earlier findings on the relationship of posthospital performance in family settings. Again, the author found that the patients who succeeded in remaining out of the hospital for over a year were most likely to have high levels of work and social performance if they lived with their wives rather than with their parents. In addition, he found that low-level patients were more likely to reside with relatives who were "typical" in personality, at least with respect to the ideal personality stereotypes in our culture. These relatives of low-level patients tended to be authoritarian, anomic, frustrated, rigid and withdrawn, in comparison with relatives of high-level patients. Moreover, the patient who performed poorly in the community tended to have other male members available in his household to replace or supplement the patient, and the former patient who performs poorly is less likely to be looked upon by family members as a breadwinner or potential breadwinner. A direct relationship also appeared between patients' posthospital performance levels and the social class status of their families: Middle-class families, in contrast with lower-class ones, contain proportionately fewer patients who neither work steadily nor participate regularly in social activities. In addition, the author observed relationships in the predicted direction between performance levels and other variables that are thought to reflect commitments to dominant societal values. Finally, he found that low-level patients tended to reside with relatives who did not expect them to work or to participate in social activities even six months after release from the hospital. Patients with high performance levels, on the other hand, live with relatives who expect them to work and be socially active within three months after hospitalization.

The findings of this survey were consistent with the proposition that family members' tolerance of deviance played an important part in the posthospital experience of mental patients. The author and Simmons believed, on the basis of these findings, that they had gained an understanding of a *unitary* process that accounted for both success and failure of former patients, as well as for their performance levels. Their assumption was that patients who did well in respect to work and social participation stayed out of the hospital and the ones who did poorly in these respects had differential risks in accordance with the structural characteristics of their families and the social-psychological attributes of their family members. The assumption was made, of course, with very little information on patients who returned to the hospital.

The lack of information on failures, that is, patients who returned to the hospital, was a critical limitation for the position that success and failure and posthospital performance levels represent a unitary process. There were, of course, other criticisms about the author's research procedures, and thus, he felt a more refined study was needed. It is this most recent study that will be discussed next, in detail. In this study of 649 patients, the author again began with the conceptual position of differential tolerance of deviance, although certain refinements were included. The two principal innovations were procedural and methodological: Female as well as male patients are included in the study group, and a two-stage study design was employed so that *a priori* predictions could be made regarding posthospital performance. The first interview was obtained as soon as possible after the patient returned to the community. In the event that he remained in the community for a year, a second interview took place at that time. If the patient returned to the hospital during the year the second interview was obtained as soon as possible after hospitalization.

The characteristics of this study group are similar to those employed in the previous study except that female patients are also included. Each patient selected was last hospitalized in one of twelve hospitals in eastern Massachusetts and was released from the hospital during the first six months of 1959. As in the previous survey, interviews were conducted by psychiatric social workers in the home.

The major findings of this study with respect to correlates of social and occupational performance levels substantially replicate those of the previous study and point unequivocally to an association between patients' posthospital performance levels and characteristics of their family settings and family members.

The examination of the same variables, however, neither permits the prediction of the success or failure of the patients who remain in the community nor supports the author's original position that instrumental performance and community tenure are necessarily related. Rather, it appears that the success or failure of patients in remaining in the community and their levels of occupational and social performance are, to a considerable extent, *independent* of each other. The author tried to assess the reasons patients were returned to the hospital and found, most often, that it was not inadequate performance, but the manifestation of symptomatic expressions of illness, i.e. bizarre behavior, that resulted in rehospitalization. Certainly, the patient manifesting extreme symptoms is not as likely to work or to be retained on the job, and thus there is some overlap between the symptomatic behavior that typically results in rehospitalization and his performance levels. But many of the patients who returned to the hospital were performing occupationally and socially as well as those who remained in the community. The author's notion of differential tolerance and his view of the posthospital experience as a unitary process, in the face of the empirical data of this study, needed to be revised.

It is clear that two of the assumptions made on the basis of the author's earlier studies were incorrect. The first of these was the assumption that rehospitalization of the patient, typically associated with *inadequate instrumental performance by itself, does not account for rehospitalization.** Most typically, relatives' reports of reasons for rehospitalization specify bizarre behavior, and it appears that reactions to inadequate performance, if there are any, take place within the family network and that the sanctions are mainly attitudinal.

The second assumption which now seems erroneous was to regard the posthospital period as a discrete time-span in the life experience of the patient. In part at least, this view was derived from the prevailing stereotype, which the author also held, that there are clearly distinguishable boundaries between the patients pre-in-hospital and posthospital careers. As one of the consequences in new in-hospital treatment programs and of tranquilizing drugs, hospitalizations have become short, a matter of months for virtually all the patients in our study group. Another consequence of current hospital treatment programs has been to open the hospital doors in a real sense so that patients returned to the community typically precede their release by leaves, passes and off-ground privileges. Return to the community is not an event in the same sense as it is for the prisoner or for the patient hospitalized for an acute physical illness. Consequently, recidivism may not have any substantial relationship to the gross characteristics measured of the patient's posthospital setting or of his significant others, since these are not likely to be different in the posthospital period from those that prevailed in the prehospital period.

Social scientists and psychiatrists interested in cultural differ-

*See the work of Dinitz, Lefton and Pasamanick in Ref. 1.

ences have emphasized the variations in the manifestations of mental illness from one community to the next and the differential reactions of community members to a typical mode of interpersonal behavior. It could be that rehospitalization, in particular, occurs in the face of behavior that community members regard with *reasonable uniformity* as requiring the action of a formal treatment agent, the hospital. The author's study group of patients and their families was drawn from one metropolitan area, and although it is a locale with considerable diversity in social class status, religious and ethnic backgrounds and life experiences, there are also certain common factors. Despite variations in background, virtually everyone in the study group had sufficient education to be sensitive to the messages transmitted by the mass media and had exposure to the mental hygiene movement via television, magazines and newspapers. Also, the very fact that patients were once hospitalized, in comparison with those who have never received formal treatment, may well be the cutting point in respect to social differences in reaction to bizarre behavior.

Unlike work and social participation, the extreme form of symptomatic behavior which appears to be the main reason for rehospitalization of the patient may constitute a range of behavior about which there is widespread agreement regarding the action that must be taken, once relatives have been through the experience of hospitalizing a family member. Certainly, the author's notion of differential tolerance had only limited applicability in explaining patients' success and failure in remaining in the community.

The current emphasis on social deviance assumes that mental health, adjustment and rehabilitation are a single entity and patient's interpersonal behavior and their medical condition are only minimally differentiated. Both interpersonal behavior and symptomatology are looked upon as manifestations of social deviance, especially, but not only, when the physician cannot identify a definite organic basis for the condition. In the author's analysis, he found no relationship, however, between symptomatic behavior and social, cultural or interpersonal variables. Socially deviant behavior and illness as manifested in symptoms may not be either the same or even parallel phenomena, and social variables that predict social deviance may have little to do with illness. The illness itself may not be primarily related to the setting the patient returns to after hospitalization, to his characteristics of family associates or to whether or not he works or otherwise takes on an active community role.

Consistent with the data obtained, the author wants to first examine the issue of instrumental performance. It is virtually indisputable that the degree of conformity of an individual to the norms of the community is dependent upon his interaction with primary group associates and that in this respect the members of his family setting are key figures. In child-rearing, the expectations of conformity are expressed and communicated to a large degree by means of a reward and punishment system, one that includes a variety of verbal and physical cues and punishments as well as material and psychological rewards. In adult life, of course, some of the same elements remain, as is known from studies of industrial work-groups and street-corner gangs. In childhood and adulthood, however, obtaining effective social control rests on the assumption of shared expectation systems.

One of the goals of rehabilitation, that of conforming to normative standards of instrumental performance, appears to be a consequence of shared expectations. The author assumed at the beginning of his study that performance which did not meet expectations would result in exclusion; that is, inadequate performance in the face of high normative standards would evoke hospitalization. He failed to take sufficiently into account, however, that the return of the patient to his family does not constitute an interpersonal situation in which members are experimenting and innovating with different means of making known their expectations and standards of conduct. Rather it is a relatively stabilized system in which the already established shared expectations of family members constitute the main if not the only, means of control, at least for the adult members of the unit.

In part, of course, expectations of adult performance differ depending upon the position of the individual in the family. For example, expectations of spouses, by virtue of their role as marriage partners, are higher. It is, of course, the degree of exposure of the family members to the relevant value system of the larger community that determines their levels of expectations with respect to the behavior of the persons in their family settings. Consequently, the types of the characteristics that the author has found to be associated with performance levels are probably reflections of a larger system, i.e. the differential commitment to, and internalization of, the normative patterns that serve as models in urban communities. A second possibility is that the key determinant is not differential internalization, but rather the variations in the manipulative ability and skill of the relative in communicating his expectations to the patient. The types of variables found associated with performance levels appear to make sense when looked upon in the light of this interpretation as well.

Whatever the relative importance of these characteristics as reflectors of internalization of norms or as indicators of manipulative interpersonal skill, the results of this study suggest that in the posthospital situation conformity to shared expectations is not obtained by an active process in which family members continually engage in an assessment of alternative strategies, including rehospitalization. Rather it is a passive situation in which the performance level of the family member is virtually prescribed at any point in time. There are no real choices; conformity with the expectations of one's familial associates is the only alternative.

The author's data regarding posthospital expectations suggest that there are no marked shifts in the expectation system of family members subsequent to the hospital period. If there were, this would be reflected in the posthospital period by some degree of innovation and experimentation with active means for enforcing more adequate instrumental performance, in which rehospitalization would figure as one such means. But relatives have little contact, with hospital personnel, of a sort that might induce marked shifts in their expectations, and there is no evidence of posthospital contact with other professional persons at a level that might instigate change in relatives' expectation systems. Moreover, the philosophy of some contemporary mental health practitioners, who preach tolerance because they believe it leads to less stress for the patient and consequently less bizarre behavior, may actually support rather than discourage the maintenance of expectations incongruent with the norms of the community.

Apart from family members, the patient's own expectations regarding his performance may receive negative reinforcement by virtue of the emphasis that may be accorded *gradual* transition to the community in such treatment activities as day- and night-hospitals and in-hospital work programs. The author has suggested that the interpersonal process which determines the patient's conformity to norms of instrumental performance places him in a role that is more passive than active, but this does not mean that his situation is static. Interpersonal factors that do influence the expectation system—if they are truly important at the level of familial relationships between adult members—may have the effect of lowering rather than raising the shared expectations of family and patient. In part, this is because both the practitioner and the patient's family like rehabilitation with regard to performance levels to the control of symptomatic behavior. Symptomatic behavior is frequently regarded as a reaction that the patient manifests when he is unable to cope with the expectations and demands of those with whom he interacts. Treatment programs often seek to limit the demands imposed upon patients to those with which he is ready to cope. On this basis, patients who manifest symptomatic behavior or whose life history includes episodes of severe bizarreness are typically believed to be highly vulnerable to the stress of high expectations. The author's data fail to support this notion that symptomatic behavior of the patient is related directly to the expectations of those with whom he interacts. Indeed, in his data there is a correlation between expectations and symptomatology, but in the opposite direction: High expectations are associated with an absence of symptomatology.

The point which will be considered further here is the relative continuity of performance levels between the prehospital and posthospital period and hospitalization itself as rarely being a discrete segment of the life experience of the patient. First, however, the meaning of this position will be discussed with regard to success or failure. As repeatedly noted, in his studies the author has found no relationships between success and the sociocultural variables. There is no adequate information in this study on the regularity or intensity with which patients manifest symptomatic behavior, except for relatives' responses in such evaluative terms as "frequently" and "occasionally." Patients are likely to manifest bizarre behavior episodically rather than consistently. In the face of this, one alternative already mentioned is that families are rather uniformly distributed in their degree of tolerance of symptomatic behavior regardless of their sociocultural differences. Another possibility, as noted, is that the genesis of these symptomatic behaviors may be organic or intrapsychic, and thus, the patient may not appreciably respond to interpersonal control as it is exerted by family members.

At this point, it is probably just as valid to look upon the rehabilitation of the patient with regard to success or failure as essentially an issue of the control of symptomatic manifestations of illness and not of inadequate instrumental behavior. Former mental patients' conformity to occupational and social norms is, of course, just as important, if not more so, than keeping them in the community. But, if one wishes to maximize movement toward the goal of conformity to norms, he should not water down the programs because of an invalid view that tampering with the performance levels of the patient and placing high demands on him will result in rehospitalization.

Admittedly, if carried beyond reason, unrealistically high expectations may inhibit the performance of patients in their social roles and evoke behavior that appears to be a manifestation of mental illness, which would happen with anyone. On the basis of his findings, the author does *not* advocate the use of force or other authoritarian methods to obtain high performance from patients anymore than he desires a return to the educational philosophies that were prevalent prior to the days of John Dewey. But in the same manner, as it has been necessary to reinterpret the term "permissiveness" on the basis of contemporary child-rearing studies and to modify ideas on "autonomy" in order to revitalize educational programs, the author also maintains that it is necessary to redefine the views on "gradualism," "tolerance" and "expectations" in developing treatment programs for the mentally ill. A discussion of this point follows.

Implications for Program Development

As the author observed in beginning this report, research on former mental patients is a consequence of innovations in treatment practices. The need and continued quest for further changes in treatment programs are apparent in the final report of the Joint Commission on Mental Illness and Health. While the author's research does not provide him with a strong enough basis for recommending immediate and extensive modification of current psychiatric practices, his findings do need to be taken into account in program development and in experimental and demonstration studies.

Hospital personnel and community mental health practitioners are faced with the problem of conflicting obligations in according relative priority to the issues of instrumental performance on the one hand and remission of symptoms on the other. This conflict is, of course, not unique to the mental health practitioner, but occurs in virtually all of the practices of medicine. Perhaps the point may be made most easily by an analogy. The physician treating a patient with a stomach ulcer may advise him to leave his job and take an extended rest or vacation. Although this may indeed be indicated medically, it can result in economic deprivation for the patient and his family and a corresponding change in their style of living. In the actual case, the physician is likely to compromise on a recommendation which takes into account both the patient's medical and social needs. This conflict is frequent and more intense in current mental health treatment programs and in the release practices of hospitals.

A predominant orientation of hospital personnel is to treat symptomatology, and the question of social needs is handled by reinterpreting inadequate instrumental behavior as an integral part of the condition of illness. Such behavior, however, is in significant part a function of lifelong socialization experience and is analytically distinct from illness. In the psychiatric profession, treatment based on "insight," if the practitioner is psychodynamically oriented, or on drugs and shock therapy, if he is more physiologically oriented, is not necessarily aimed at inducing changes in performance potential. Few physicians would contend that shock treatment is conducive to better work performance, or drugs to greater social participation, and most psychoanalysts would not feel comfortable in using measures of instrumental performance to assess the outcome of their therapeutic endeavors. But they would contend, or at least it is often implied, that improvement in the patient, as measured by their psychiatric criteria, eventuates in more effective instrumental performance. According to the author's findings, however, this is questionable.

One position mental health practitioners could adopt is to limit their goals to remission of psychiatric symptoms and to exclude from their purview any concern with levels of instrumental performance. Medical practitioners are confronted, however, in the treatment of all illnesses—physical as well as mental—with the realities of the "sociological:" demands of their patients and patients' families. Getting well in the medical sense is, of course, of interest to the patient and his family, but illness and wellness in their eyes are likely to be regarded as primarily affecting the prerequisites for instrumental activity. This is one factor that may account for the intrusion of concern on the part of mental health practitioners with instrumental performance.

If, however, the mental hospital and particularly community mental health programs are to play a major role in social control as well as in the treatment of illness, then, with respect to the value accorded instrumental performance in our society, the key emphasis must be placed on modifying the patient's expectation system in the direction of greater conformity to the normative demands of the larger community. The risks in doing this would be great, if in fact such attempts at modifying expectations had direct consequences for the patient's psychiatric state. The author's findings, as noted, suggest that this linkage is minimal, however, and that current notions of permissiveness and reduction of stress need to be reexamined, both with respect to in-hospital and posthospital programs. This orientation can be quite compatible with the conception of the hospital as dedicated to humanitarian therapeutic care and would not require a return to traditional custodial care.

If conformity to normative demands is to be achieved, the transitional programs now in vogue, such as bridges between hospital and community, in the rehabilitation process may require substantial reorientation. For example, one risk incurred in those halfway houses which advocate gradualism is that they may constitute, as a consequence, "low expectation" settings. Programs that serve transitional functions may be needed, but are likely to be effective only to the extent that they consistently orient toward instrumental performance the patient who can potentially respond to such expectations. Low expectations simply support socially deviant instrumental performance and reinforce the patient's failure to perform in ways defined by the instrumental role expectations of the larger society.

Perhaps even more important than transitional programs, which serve only a relatively small proportion of former patients, is the provision of permanent posthospital settings for patients as alternatives to the ones from which they were hospitalized. If modification of patients' low expectations is the desired goal, perhaps the only feasible approach is to relocate them into residential settings that are oriented to higher levels of instrumental performance than those from which they came. There is little point in raising the patient's self-expectations during hospital treatment with regard to instrumental performance levels if he is returned to a family that does not expect him to perform instrumentally. Organizing transitional programs oriented to high expectations and shifting patients into new settings in the posthospital period would, of course, impose heavy responsibilities on the hospital. As the author's findings indicate, the patient's relationship with the hospital is minimal once he leaves his bed. If hospitals are to take the role of agents of social control, they will have to develop and maintain extensive procedures for follow-up relationships with former patients.

It is not, of course, the hospital's responsibility alone to carry forward such a modified program. Not only is there minimal post-hospital contact between hospital and patient, but he is ignored by community agencies as well. The point being made is not unique to mental patients, but applies generally to the set of conditions that the community seems to impose on all persons defined as markedly deviant. The same issues are involved in returning the delinquent, the criminal and other deviants to their previous environments and are equally problematic for the former patient. If the author is correct in his interpretation that the primary means of social control for the patient are his own expectation system and those of persons significant to him, then effective social control calls for radical alteration of the low-level patient's life situation, including detachment from settings that only reinforce low expectations.

This interpretation also raises some points about the strategy currently employed in the allocation of treatment resources for different kinds of patients. From the point of view of potential instrumental performance, most effort probably is expended currently on those patients who have the highest expectations. From the standpoint of social control, i.e. conformity to instrumental norms, there is little need to devote major attention to those patients whose prehospital careers and community settings suggest that they are likely to resume adequate levels of instrumental performance. If mental hygiene clinics accept former patients at all, these are the ones on their treatment rosters. It may actually be a disservice to involve them in the follow-up relationships with these hospital or community agencies whose present orientations are toward reduction of stress, which may lower rather than raise the patient's expectations. The more logical approach in such cases would be to adopt the physician's orientation to acute disease, namely, that when the condition has been treated, the patient's relationships with medical personnel should be severed. The author would suggest that if the hospital and the community mental health practitioner assume responsibility as agents of social control, their resources should be diverted mainly to those patients whose return to the community sends them to settings highly tolerant of deviant instrumental performance, and all available effort should be applied toward redirecting such patients into settings more in accord with the prevailing community norms.

If the emphasis is to be on social control, however, it must be acknowledged that this can be achieved only with great difficulty and extensive reorientation of both administrators and practitioners in institutions and in community programs. If the author's findings on families have relevance for professional-patient relations as well, a critical message to be communicated is that high expectations of instrumental performance must constitute the key orientation in interpersonal relations between staff and patient while he is in the hospital and between community practitioner and patient afterwards. The hospital would have to place its emphasis on the return of patients to either productive non-kin settings or to families with high expectation systems. Moreover, if community agencies are to play a more substantial part in aftercare programs, they would have to modify many of the basic orientations of their current programs from ideals of tolerance to the value and merit of conformity to the normative standards of the community.

In seeking to clarify the dual orientation that most practitioners now hold, the author submits that, if the mental health specialist is concerned solely with the treatment of psychiatric symptoms, practitioners must forego the rationale that treatment directed at symptom remission also maximizes the performance potential of the patient. If symptom remission is the only goal of treatment, it seems clear that the alternative is to provide, in the community, other persons whose primary responsibility is the movement of patients toward higher instrumental performance in accordance with the community's norms. Although there may be convincing arguments for the development of such a new group of professionals or the separation of treatment for norm conformity from that for mental illness, current efforts are directed at the integration of various professions and, thus, this idea is unrealistic. Therefore, it is necessary for mental health practitioners to be concerned with a two-fold problem. In the first place, there is truly the illness problem, and there, the professional group must be dedicated to its treatment. But the other issue is that large numbers of persons fail to contribute to the productivity of the larger community and represent, because of their limited contribution, a serious social problem as well.

In view of the substantial discrepancy between the community's standards regarding the productivity of the individual and the low levels that characterize the instrumental performance of so many former mental patients, the community is confronted with a problem in which the issue of instrumental performance and its social control is to be judged by policy rather than by psychiatric criteria. It is for this reason that the author is concerned with the distinction between the need for treatment of mental illness, on the one hand, and the need for promoting conformity to the community's standards regarding role performance on the other. When statements are made that one out of every seven men were judged to be mentally or emotionally incapable of serving effectively in the armed forces and almost this number cannot support themselves in times of peace, the observation is not based primarily on an image of large numbers of persons being actively ill in the sense of manifesting bizarre behavior, but rather being passive in the face of demands made on them by the larger community. The cost, in these terms, may be too great a luxury for a responsible democracy.

The issue here is that the sociological and psychiatric rehabilitation of mental patients may indeed need to be the goal of different types of programs. There is no question but that mental illness is clearly a phenomenon that places an individual in an aggregate whose identity is dependent not only on his behavior but on the response of community members to the way he acts. The point to be emphasized, however, is that membership in such an aggregate does not restrict the individual to being deviant solely in the ways that identify him as mentally ill. To be specific, inadequate instrumental performance may not connote "sickness" among former mental patients any more than it does among other community members. The author would contend that the distinguishing characteristic of the mental patient is his symptomatology. It is symptomatic behavior that evokes response from community members at least on a formal level. When one is concerned with aggregates of social deviance other than mental patients, does he seek to account for deviance in the same terms as when considering mental patients? Why attempt to explain inadequate instrumental performance differently for mental patients than for everyone else in the community? In order to understand the posthospital fate of the mental patient, it is essential that the analytic distinction between behavior during illness and instrumental behavior be kept clear and that the issues related to the illness not be confused with those related to inadequate instrumental role performance.

The point needs to be extended further. Structural arrangements for both in-hospital and community programs being what they are in this country, hospital personnel and community practitioners must face up to their dual tasks—treating an illness and obtaining conformity with social norms. Work programs are numerous, but work programs for what? Are they to be conceived as adjuncts to therapies and treatment plans that are primarily oriented toward symptom remission? If they are, the author contends that mental health practitioners, if only because there are no others available or willing to take on the task, are neglecting their responsibility as agents of social control. In addition to being concerned with work *in* mental illness, it is necessary to consider the problem of work *among* the mentally ill. In the extreme, particularly in community programs, it seems the mental health practitioner might almost want to forget that he is dealing with former patients, but rather, that somehow or other he has come into contact with a group of individuals who have a high risk of being inadequate workers (as if, say, he was dealing with the residents of a housing project with a large number of persons on welfare). What the author pleads against is the rationalization of work programs on the grounds that they are efficacious in reducing the rehospitalization rate or in getting people out of the hospital faster and into model programs on this view; he argues that there is sufficient justification for programs of work on the grounds that conformity to instrumental norms is also a proper responsibility of the mental health practitioner and that the practitioner should emphasize adequate work performance because of the value attached to it by community members.

This orientation toward work programs would result in substantively different efforts than are now being undertaken, particularly in the posthospital treatment of the patient. For example, it would require a shift in populations on the part of community clinics or at least an increase in clients to include former patients other than those who drop in for counseling on the way to or from work; it would require the relocation of more patients to nonfamily settings and the reorientation of existing halfway houses and other intermediate settings, rather than the pleading with relatives to be more understanding; it would require more role-playing programs on matters of finding a job and relating to supervisors, rather than group therapy sessions devoted to working out oedipal problems; it would require telephone services and persons to wake up patients and see that they got to work on time, instead of visiting nurses who drop around to see if the patient is taking his pills or cutting his toenails; and it would require a different commitment on the part of practitioners and lay persons influential in the mental health movement.

This paper began with the author's suggestion that he is discouraged about current community mental health efforts and does not believe that moving the hospital to the community is the solution; what he believes is the answer is the view that persons hospitalized are more than patients: They are people. We have a responsibility to be concerned about them in other ways than their symptom remission or their rehospitalization rates, and these should not be the only criteria to justify programs of work, etc. that maximize normative behavior.

REFERENCES

1. Freeman, Howard E., and Simmons, Ozzie G.: *The Mental Patient Comes Home*. New York, Wiley, 1963.
2. Perrow, Charles: Hospitals: Goals, structure and technology. In March, James (Ed.): *Handbook of Organizations*. New York, Rand, 1965.

PART THREE

ROLE OF PSYCHOPHARMOCOLOGY IN REHABILITATION

Chapter 23

PSYCHOTROPIC DRUGS IN THE REHABILITATION OF MENTAL PATIENTS

NATHAN S. KLINE AND LESLIE BAER

THERE IS NO LACK OF information about drug usage for the physician. A number of textbooks on psychopharmacology are in existence and most of the medical journals contain articles about the use of psychotropic drugs by the family physician or general practitioner. At another level there are at least a few books dealing with psychotropic drugs which are written for the lay public (including one on depression by one of the authors[1]). Almost totally lacking is any systematic source of information for the nonphysician who has to deal with psychiatric patients. This article is written to attempt at least in part to fill the gap.

General Remarks

It is truly unfortunate that the word "drug" carries with it the connotation of an undesirable substance producing an abnormal state, the consequences of which are addiction, dependence and social undesirability. This has resulted in a very substantial number of patients discontinuing treatment prematurely or even refusing to accept such treatment because they do not wish to become drug addicts. This is particularly true in respect to psychotropic drugs since the drugs which are abused usually have as the basis for such abuse the psychological effect produced.

No one would consider insulin a drug for which addiction or dependence could develop. Yet, someone would be likely to consider one of the phenothiazines, which are just as essential for preserving psychological integrity as is insulin for maintaining normal endocrine function, as a completely different case. Unfortunately, this attitude toward psychotropic drugs pervades not only the patient population but the general public and the nonphysicians working with patients, as well as a substantial part of the medical profession and even a frighteningly large number of psychiatrists. If ever there were an example of the *word* distorting the *reality,* this is it.

Efforts to substitute such terms as "pharmaceutical" or "medication" present supreme examples of why the Anglo-Saxon argot has managed to triumph over not only Latin but the derived Romance languages. It is not only the preference for one syllable rather than three but the colorful and orally satisfactory nature of the word "drug" itself. Interestingly enough, the original meaning was simply "dry," related to the Middle Old English term "droggen" and the present-day German "trocken," both of which also mean dry. In the sixteenth and seventeenth century, transportation of any sort was exorbitantly expensive, and the only two items really worth shipping were brandy and spices. The longshoreman who had to handle the shipments needed to know which was which since a container with fluid in it would be dealt with differently than one with spices. Hence, when being shipped from the continent (usually the Netherlands), those with spices were labeled "drogge" (dry). The English, who are still not notoriously polyglot, assumed that the word "drogge" referred to the content itself rather than its dry condition. Hence, spices which included most of those substances referred to today as drugs were classified under this general heading.

The Role of Rehabilitation

Treatment is only one element in the overall process of rehabilitation, and pharmaceuticals are only one factor in treatment. Nevertheless, the revolution in the biochemical treatment of psychiatric disorders starting some twenty years ago has altered not only its own subsystem but the entire structure of psychiatric rehabilitation. The ability to treat that which was formerly untreatable as well as the capacity to evaluate the effectiveness of such pharmaceutical treatment opened up a whole new vista and challenged other areas of psychiatric rehabilitation to meet the same standards.

Since available resources are not sufficient to attempt rehabilitation of every patient by all the means possible, hard decisions have to be made as to the criteria leading to treatment or non-treatment. Before the advent of modern drugs it was an agonizing process to select the paltry few who would have the opportunity of receiving intensive psychotherapy. With the ready availability of medications, their relative cheapness and the capacity for any physician to relatively easily learn the rudiments of such treatment, it has become possible to treat virtually every patient admitted to the hospital or seen in private practice, if drugs are indicated. The substantially increased number of patients now capable of remaining outside of the hospital has placed a sizable new responsibility on those engaged in rehabilitation.

In the matter of *selection of patients for treatment,* the authors agree that almost everyone can be included. In contrast to the overall improved behavior resulting from pharmacotherapy, there still remain a group for whom psychotherapy is the method *par excellence.* For the overwhelming majority of patients, perhaps 95 percent, the addition of one treatment or another may not be totally curative, but does allow the patient to function in a participant manner.

In the "bad old days" admission to a psychiatric hospital carried with it a fairly high expectation of continued existence there. Under these circumstances efforts at rehabilitation were necessarily quite limited. Since relatively little could be done, the aspects of rehabilitation other than treatment tended to shrink. Now, by one of those eternal anomalies, the very improvement of the treatment process which has led to an expansion of its importance should have been followed by an even greater increase in other areas of rehabilitation. There should have actually been a diminution of the relative role treatment plays in the overall process of rehabilitation. The effectiveness of pharmacotherapy which makes it possible for patients both to leave hospitals and to be maintained with relatively little psychiatric attention means that the other areas of rehabilitation are in need of vast expansion. Unfortunately this has not yet occurred, although it seems inevitable. Since traditional psychotherapeutic intervention was of such limited benefit, those in rehabilitation were usually left with the feeling that they could easily keep up with the workload. At the present time with approximately half a million discharges from public mental hospitals each year, the task of rehabilitation suddenly becomes overwhelming. Further, in the long arid period, the other aspects of rehabilitation had shrunk so that treatment became almost the "all" of rehabilitation. Now that the disproportionately large role assigned to treatment is beginning to decline, a new and exciting task lies ahead.

Hypnotics and Sedatives

The appropriate medical term for sleeping medications is "hypnotic," which literally in Greek means "inclined to sleep." Since the word hypnosis (put to sleep) is much more familiar, the nonmedical reader may be confused at first by the term. The use of sleeping medications probably goes back to prehistoric times since a variety of psychological states, such as anxiety, depression, phobias, etc. can produce an uncomfortable state of sleeplessness. Not only the writings of Hippocrates but the earliest descriptions of the Incas, the Chinese and the Egyptians all describe drugs used to assist in producing sleep.

Certainly, the most ancient and widely used drug for this purpose is alcohol. Even today more people probably help themselves get to sleep with brandy, whiskey or beer than with all other sleeping medications. The barbiturates do run a close second. Incidentally, there are two stories as to the origin of the name "barbiturate." They are basically "urates" and the discovery was made by Fischer in Vienna in 1845. One version is that the identification occurred on St. Barbara's Day, hence "Barbara-urate." The alternate theory is that his mistress at that time was a waitress at the restaurant where he usually ate, and her name was Barbara.

A substantial number of the individuals who use barbiturates for sleeping medications do so habitually. Many of these are not psychiatric patients in the usual sense of the word, but suffer from mild insomnia. As far as it is known, it is perfectly safe for most of these people to go on using one or two sleeping pills of this type for an indefinite number of years. If the evening dose is omitted, many of these patients are unable to sleep. In some of them the substitution of a placebo is sufficient but there are others who are dependent on the pharmacological action of the drug. There are two circumstances which indicate real trouble is brewing: One is when the patient starts using the barbiturate during the day in order to relieve himself of anxiety or depression; two, when the dose of medication is escalated and instead of one or two doses, the patient climbs to three or four and then on upward.

In 1970 approximately $5.25 *billion* worth of pharmaceuticals were sold; about 75 percent of these were for prescription items and the other 25 percent were over-the-counter preparations. Of this grand total, 27 million went for barbiturates and 25 million for nonbarbiturate sleeping medications on prescription. Seventeen million were over-the-counter proprietary sleep-inducers, and another 5 million were "calming agents."

There are more than two dozen separate barbiturates on the market and more than fifty preparations which contain barbiturates in addition to other substances. Phenobarbital is still widely used in the treatment of epilepsy, and some of these preparations are used during the daytime for sedatives, but in general the recommended use is as sleeping medication.

Some of the barbiturates have short periods of effectiveness, some long, and some fall between. As a help to the lay reader, the major barbiturates are listed below by both their generic and trade names with indication as to whether they are long, short or intermediate in periods of action. In addition, there is a listing of some of the commercially available preparations which contain barbiturates in addition to other substances. (Tables 23-I and 23-II).

Although many individuals could use a small dose of barbiturate every night for most of their lives without any harm, there are others who find it necessary to keep increasing the dose until it reaches dangerous levels. A particular problem arises when pa-

TABLE 23-I
BARBITURATES

ALLOBARBITAL	intermediate	DIAL
AMOBARBITAL	intermediate	AMYTAL® (Lilly)
APROBARBITAL	intermediate	ALURATE® (Roche)
BARBITAL	long	VERONAL
BUTABARBITAL	internal	BUTICAPS®, BUTISOL (McNeil)
BUTALBITAL	short	SANDOUPTAL (Sandoz), ESGIC® (Gilbert)
HEPTABARBITAL	short	MEDOMIN (Geigy)
MEPHOBARBITAL	long	MEBARAL® (Sterling-Winthrop)
METHOHEXITAL	ultrashort	BREVITAL® (Lilly)
PHENOBARBITAL	long	LUMINAL® (Sterling-Winthrop) ESKABARB® (SKF) STENTAL (Robins)
SECOBARBITAL	short	SECONAL® (Lilly)
TALBUTAL	short	LOTUSATE® (Sterling-Winthrop)
THIAMYLAL	ultrashort	SURITAL® (Parke-Davis)
THIOPENTAL	short	PENTOTHAL® (Abbott)
SECOBARBITAL + AMOBARBITAL		TUINAL® (Lilly)
BUTABARBITAL + AMOBARBITAL		BUTATRAX (Sutliff & Case)

TABLE 23-II
SOME BARBITURATE-CONTAINING PREPARATIONS

ARCO-LASE PLUS (Arco)
BANCAPS® (Westerfield)
BAR-DON® (Warren-Teed)
BELLERGAL® (Sandoz)
BENTYL® with pheno (Merrell-National)
BUFF-A COMP® (Mayrand)
BUTIBEL® (McNeil)
BUTISERPAZIDE® (McNeil)
BUTISERPINE® (McNeil)
CARBITAL (Parke-Davis)
COASTALDYNE® (Coastal)
COASTALGESIC® (Coastal)
CODEMIRAL® (Burroughs Wellcome)
DIALOG® (Ciba)
DONNATAL® (Robins)
DULARIN® TH (Dooner)
EMPIRAL® (Burroughs Wellcome)
KINESED® (Stuart)
PAMINE® (Upjohn)
PANITOL® (Wesley)
PLEXONAL® (Sandoz)
SEDADROPS® (Merrell-National)

tients abruptly discontinue barbiturates after they have been on them for a fair period of time at a fairly high level. In a quarter to a third of the patients, convulsions develop which can, of course, be fatal at times. Hence, it is usually necessary to reduce barbiturate dosage gradually or to substitute some other preparation. In more severe cases or where real danger exists, the patient is often given an anticonvulsant medication to take at the same time.

Alcohol and possibly phenothiazines and monamine oxidase inhibitors potentiate the action of barbiturates. The potentiation is not an even one since the hypnotic action is much less increased than is the effect on decreasing respiration. Alcohol is the primary offender in this respect, since for some persons it acts as a disinhibitor making them *less* sleepy. The patient then takes barbiturates in an effort to get to sleep and requires more than usual. The combination of the two drugs may cause a marked decrease in respiration without producing the desired sleepiness. At sufficiently high doses brain damage, and even death, may occur.

Alcohol and barbiturates are a dangerous combination for another reason. The patient may be partially intoxicated and his sense of time distorted. A few minutes may seem like an hour so that the dose of barbiturate is repeated long before it has a chance to act. This leads to further confusion and once again, or possibly even more than once, the dose of barbiturate is repeated with the patient losing all sense of how many times he has taken medication. There are probably a considerable number of accidental deaths of this type, which look like suicides. If the combination of alcohol and a sleeping medication is necessary, certainly the safest thing to do is to put out the maximum dose and return the bottle to the medicine cabinet or somewhere else which requires some effort to reach.

There is also evidence that barbiturates may interfere with the effectiveness of the tricyclic antidepressant drugs, and for this reason other hypnotics are usually preferable with depressed patients.

In case of a suicidal attempt, the instructions found in *Psycho-*

tropic Drugs: Manual for Emergency Management of Overdosage (MEMO) should be followed.

CHLORAL HYDRATE: One of the most rapidly acting of all hypnotics is chloral hydrate. It is available both as a fluid-containing capsule and as a fluid itself. Its rapidity of action has been immortalized in its use as a "Mickey Finn" which, when added to an alcoholic drink, produces rapid somnolence. Since the material is almost tasteless and colorless, it is difficult to detect. As with other sleeping medications, an overdosage can readily result in reduced respiration. One of the side effects of the drug which is usually overlooked is its tendency to produce flatus (gas) which at times can be both uncomfortable and embarrassing.

OTHER HYPNOTICS: A large variety of other hypnotics exists. Most of these were at first believed to be nonhabituating, but the sad reality is that most of them result in the same dependencies.

Major Tranquilizers and Antidepressants

The large-scale application of newly discovered psychotropic drugs in the last fifteen years has brought about a profound revolution in psychiatric treatment. Instead of the projected increase of 150,000 to 200,000 patients in public mental hospitals during that period, there has been a decrease of about 200,000 patients. The probability of being discharged has increased more than 100 percent since 1956. The influence of the new drugs has been even greater in the area of ambulatory private patients. For the first time, the average physician can effectively treat many of the psychiatric disorders. The emotional, mental and behavioral well-being of legions of patients has been greatly improved as a result. Substantial numbers of patients who would otherwise have had to be hospitalized are functioning effectively in their own communities.

Fifteen years is a very brief time to develop fully adequate techniques of treatment and management in a new field. This is particularly true with a continuing flow of new medications. It is especially confusing since psychiatric symptoms and categories are often not very easily identifiable and measurable. But despite the drawbacks, approximately one third of all new prescriptions written are for drugs in this area.

The effectiveness of pharmacotherapy has consequences which alter traditional attitudes and practices. It will take at least another generation for most physicians to accept the facts that schizophrenics are easier to treat than neurotics; that the majority of patients who have been in psychiatric hospitals should be referred back to their family doctor rather than to a psychiatrist or an outpatient clinic; that there is a great danger of iatrogenic habituation to sedative drugs (the so-called "minor tranquilizers") ; that the psychiatrist should be used as a specialist in any other discipline, for diagnosis and treatment recommendations in difficult cases and only occasionally for outright referral since the major treatment responsibility rests with the family doctor; and finally, that much more education is required if the drugs are to be applied to their maximum advantage. In the following pages, in addition to more formal description, there has been an attempt to suggest certain practical measures which do not always appear on drug package inserts.

The Major Tranquilizers

In high doses this group of drugs is the most effective method one has for controlling psychoses. In low doses most of the same drugs are extremely useful as antianxiety agents. These two quite different uses of the same drugs at times lead to problems:

1. Patients given the drug for its sedative properties may object because they understand the drug is for "crazy" people.
2. The regimen prescribed may be inadequate. When used as a sedative or anxiolytic agent, the response is rapid and dosage is titrated against the intensity of the symptoms. When used as an antipsychotic agent, at a dose level roughly five to ten times as great, a prescribed course of medication should be followed with little regard to severity of symptoms once the decision to treat has been made. Anything less than three months cannot be regarded as an adequate trial. The complete course of treatment should be given even though symptoms are reduced or remit.
3. At the higher dose ranges, extrapyramidal symptoms, espe-

cially the akathisia manifested by restlessness and tension, are almost routine. Failure to recognize this side effect as well as the other parkinsonian manifestations is probably the most common treatment error. Fortunately, these side effects respond well to antiparkinsonian medication.

Drugs for the Treatment of Schizophrenia

There are four groups of chemicals presently on the market which are effective in the treatment of schizophrenia. A number of other drug groups are presently on trial in the United States and, in some cases, already on the market in Europe. Not every drug is effective for every patient. Fortunately, many patients who fail to respond to one group of drugs will respond to a different group or even to another drug within the same group. The same is true in respect to side effects which vary from group to group and even from drug to drug. Although relatively few formal studies have been done on combining the antischizophrenic agents, the weight of clinical experience is that side effects can sometimes be reduced to acceptable limits and therapeutic efficacy enhanced by a judicious use of several drugs when one alone has proved unsuitable because of such side effects.

The four groups of pharmaceuticals are

1. Rauwolfia alkaloids, especially reserpine;
2. the phenothiazines: chlorpromazine (Thorazine®), carphenazine (Proketazine), fluphenazine (Permitil,® Prolixin®), mepazine (Pacatal), perphenazine (Trilafon®), prochlorperazine (Compazine®), promazine (Sparine), thiopropazate (Dartal), thioridazine (Mellaril®), trifluoperazine (Stelazine®), triflupromazine (Vesprin);
3. butyrophenones (Haldol®); and
4. thioxanthenes: thiothixene (Navane®), chlorprothixene (Taractan®).

Rauwolfia Alkaloids

The Rauwolfia alkaloids in low doses are widely used in the treatment of hypertension particularly in combination with barbiturates or other sedatives. At high doses in the treatment of schizophrenia, they have fallen into disuse, in part because of the frequency of side effects and in part because no pharmaceutical company is promoting them for this purpose. In those cases where other agents have failed, they are sometimes useful. The recommended starting dose is 5 to 10 mg intramuscularly for the first five days accompanied by 3 mg orally which is then continued for a three-month trial. Antiparkinsonian drugs should be administered routinely. Combined with a phenothiazine the oral dose alone is occasionally useful with very disturbed patients who do not otherwise respond.

The Phenothiazines

The phenothiazines are sometimes divided into three subgroups on the basis of their pharmacological action and side chains: aliphatic, piperidyl and piperazine. The aliphatic group tends to be sedative; the piperidyl, less sedative and possibly antidepressant. The piperazine group tends to activate patients. The following table lists the phenothiazines in their general order of sedative effect according to clinical reports. This ordering has not been reconfirmed in controlled studies and in any case does not take into account differences between individual patients. It should be regarded as a rough guide rather than a precise statement.

There is still dispute as to whether slow release preparations are more effective either in terms of therapy or lessening of side effects, and it is not even clear whether divided dosages are more effective than once-a-day administration. The general dose range has, however, been fairly well established. Determination of dosage form and frequency of administration should depend upon the individual case; e.g. if sleepiness proves to be a problem as a side effect, the total dose might be given at bedtime or, if the medication proves so stimulating that the patient has difficulty sleeping, it might be given in the morning. Sometimes a stimulating phenothiazine can be used in the morning and a sedative one at bedtime.

Fluphenazine is also available in the enanthate form which

TABLE 23-III
DRUGS FOR TREATMENT OF SCHIZOPHRENIA LISTED IN DESCENDING ORDER OF SEDATION — ACTIVATING PROPERTIES IN REVERSE ORDER

Tablet dosage size in milligrams	*Drug*	*Intensive treatment dose in milligrams t.i.d.*	*Maintenance dose in milligrams b.i.d., t.i.d.*
5, 10, 25	butaperazine (Repoise®)	25-50	5-10
10, 25, 50, 100, 200 (30, 75, 150, 200, 300)*	chlorpromazine (Thorazine)	150-500	50-100
10, 25 50	trifluopromazine (Vesprin)	50-150	25-50
10, 25, 50, 100, 150, 200	thioridazine (Mellaril)	200-300	20-60
10, 25, 50, 100	mesoridazine (Serentil®)	50-100	10-25
10, 25, 50, 100	chlorprothixene (Taractan)	50-100	25-50
10, 25, 50, 100, 200	promazine (Sparine)	200-600	50-100
25, 50	mepazine (Pacatal)	100-150	50-100
25, 100	carphenazine (Proketazine)	50-100	25-50
5, 10	thiopropazate (Dartal)	20-30	5-15
1, 2.5, 5	fluphenazine (Permitil, Prolixin)	2-8	1-4
2, 4, 8, 16	perphenazine (Trilafon)	4-16	2-8
5, 10, 25 (10, 15, 30, 75)*	prochlorperazine (Compazine)	50-150	25-50
1, 2, 5, 10	trifluoperazine (Stelazine)	10-20	1-10
.5, 1, 2, 5	haloperidol (Haldol)	2-5	1-2
1, 2, 5, 10	thiothixene (Navane)	10-20	5-10

*Delayed release form.

is long-acting. A single injection of 25 mg will last from two to three weeks. At times 2 to 3 cc (50-75 mg) are needed. For patients who tend to forget medication or those who are resistant and agree to use the drug but have no intention of doing so, this depot-type is of great use. The occurrence of extrapyramidal symptoms is extremely high so that initially a parenteral antiparkinsonian agent should be given and followed by oral antiparkinsonian drugs. Sometimes, after a period of weeks or months the antiparkinsonian drugs can be discontinued. The French use the drug in very much higher doses up to almost 1000 mg at a single injection, but such usage has not been approved as yet here in the United States.

There are a number of other phenothiazines on the market which are used in small doses for other purposes, but which probably act similar to the drugs just listed when used in high doses. These include trimeprazine (Temaril®) for the treatment of pruritus, methotrimeprazine (Levoprome®) for pain and acetophenazine (Tindal®) for anxiety. There are several more on the market in Europe and Canada to which reference is sometimes found in publications written in English, including thioproperazine (Majeptil) as an antischizophrenic drug and pericyazine (Neuleptil, Neulactil) for "acting out" behavior.

Side Effects and Their Management

CENTRAL NERVOUS SYSTEM ACTION: As previously indicated, extrapyramidal symptoms are a common side effect. In addition to the restlessness of akathisia, there are various dystonias, and in rare instances there is evidence of tardive oral dyskinesia occurring especially among those with some evidence of brain damage or arteriosclerosis, or among the elderly. Antiparkinsonian drugs are remarkably effective, but one should also keep in mind that the added anticholinergic action of such supplementary drugs may produce some blurring of vision especially in older patients where the muscles of accommodation are not as adaptable as in the young. Reduced gastric motility and dryness of the mouth are quite common.

Any of the antiparkinsonian agents can produce toxic states including visual hallucinations in sensitive individuals. A schizophrenic patient who has been doing well with disappearance of auditory hallucinations and delusions, but who a few weeks later begins having visual hallucinations and other psychotic manifestations, should be tested by withdrawal of the antiparkinsonian agent to see whether it is not the cause of the new symptoms. Otherwise, there is danger that increased rather than decreased medication will be used. Occasionally, such recurrences have even been incorrectly blamed on the phenothiazines themselves. Not infrequently, the dose of antiparkinsonian medication can be reduced or eliminated after the patient has been on the antipsychotic drug for a few weeks.

Other neurological side effects include a slight lowering of the seizure threshold in susceptible individuals.

As with almost any other pharmaceutical, it is possible that a particular individual will develop an allergic reaction. Photosensitivity is especially marked with chlorpromazine but is occasionally seen with other phenothiazines. Sun lotions containing para-amino benzoic acid are sometimes of help in preventing the reaction. Avoidance, or at least gradual exposure, to strong sunlight is indicated for patients on phenothiazines.

Endocrine Effects: Any of the drugs in this group can produce fairly prolonged amenorrhea which, as a rule, clears up by itself after a few months and certainly when the drug is withdrawn. No interim treatment is indicated. Lactation and breast engorgement may occur in some females and may at first lead to a suspicion of pregnancy if this action of the drug is not known. Occasionally, there is an accompanying false-positive pregnancy test, especially if urine samples rather than serum tests are used. Gynandromorphy and even lactation can occur in males as well. In occasional cases disorders of glucose metabolism (hyperglycemia, hypoglycemia and glycosuria) are reported, and care should be taken before a diagnosis of diabetes or a similar disorder is made.

Autonomic Nervous System Reactions: Some degree of dryness of the mouth is almost universal, and reduced gastrointestinal function is quite common in severe cases and may even lead to a real stasis. More rarely, there is nasal congestion and occasionally myosis or mydriasis. Glycerine-based cough drops are helpful for the dry mouth, and stool softeners rather than strong laxatives are recommended for the bowel problems. All of the adverse reactions in this group tend as a rule to be self-corrective.

With thioridazine (Mellaril), inhibition of ejaculation has been described.

METABOLIC SIDE EFFECTS: There are some patients who gain weight on phenothiazines, but it is unclear whether this is due to the drug or to increased caloric intake of the patients.

LETHARGY AND DROWSINESS: Some patients complain of lethargy and drowsiness even when drug doses have been lowered to the minimal therapeutic dose. This is more true with alaphatic phenothiazines than with other types of phenothiazines, so that either a change of antipsychotic medication is indicated or small amounts of stimulant can be added.

HEMATOLOGICAL DYSCRASIAS: A variety of blood dyscrasias have been reported. Except for agranulocytosis, it is not certain that they are truly drug-related. Should patients complain of a sudden appearance of sore throat or give other evidence of infection, a white blood count and differential should immediately be performed. It is wise to always have an hematological baseline before starting treatment in order to have grounds for comparison. Such cases, when they occur, are almost always in the second or third month of treatment. Slight depression of white blood count, if it remains within the normal range, is not a reason for discontinuing treatment unless there are actual clinical symptoms.

LIVER EFFECTS: There appears to be occasional liver sensitivity usually manifest during the first month of treatment by jaundice. Occasionally, this is partially subclinical so that, if fever with virus-like symptoms occurs, tests for abnormal liver function should be administered promptly. Almost any type of jaundice can be mimicked and extra care should be exercised before making a diagnosis which may lead to laparotomy.

CARDIOVASCULAR RESPONSES: Especially among the elderly, postural hypotension, tachycardia and even syncope in the presence of normal blood pressure and pulse rate can occur. Usually such occurrences are near the beginning of drug use, recovery is spontaneous, and there is little tendency toward subsequent recurrence. In the occasional patient in whom the reaction is severe, epinephrine should not be used as it can cause a paradoxically enhanced lowering of blood pressure. Norepinephrine is required if pharmacological treatment is indicated. Occasionally, nonspecific Q and T wave distortions are seen on the EKG.

Skin Pigmentation: After long-term usage, especially in females, reports exist of pigmentary change in exposed areas of the body which produces a darkening of the skin, sometimes to a slate grey or a purplish hue as the result of a melanin-type change in the dermis. This tends to fade after the drug is discontinued. It is found almost exclusively with chlorpromazine (Thorazine).

Ocular Changes: In patients on long-term therapy there are often minute deposits in the lens and cornea but it is highly questionable whether these are of any clinical significance. There is some evidence to indicate that they occur more frequently in those exposed to bright light.

Potentiation of Other Drugs: One of the therapeutic uses of phenothiazines is to potentiate the action of other medications, particularly depressants. Care should therefore be exercised in using depressants since a more marked reaction than is desired may result. It is probably well to start these and other drugs at a quarter to a half of their usual dose (or to reduce the dose if the patient is already on such medication). This includes most sleeping pills.

Also potentiated are anesthetics, opiate, alcohol, atropine and phosphorus insecticides.

Antiemetic Action: Since phenothiazines tend to reduce nausea and vomiting for a brief period, they occasionally may mask evidence of intestinal obstruction, brain tumor or overdosage of toxic drugs. Other evidence of these serious independent conditions usually makes them manifest, but the difference of the clinical picture because of absent emetic symptoms should be kept in mind.

Overstimulation: Some of the antipsychotic drugs, especially those at the activating end of the spectrum, occasionally produce undesirable overstimulation including insomnia. Changing the time of day of administration, combining with a sedative or a more sedative antipsychotic agent or even changing the drug may be indicated.

SELECTION OF APPROPRIATE MEDICATION

1. Once a decision has been made that a drug should be given, a full course of treatment is indicated, similar to that in digitalizing a patient. The disappearance of one or more of the initial symptoms or even complete remission of symptoms is not a reason for dropping the dosage or discontinuing the course of treatment. In general a three-month course of therapy is recommended, with gradual lessening of the dose only after that time. This is in contrast to the use of some of these same drugs for their sedative and antianxiety properties.
2. The experience of the therapist with a particular drug is a good reason for its selection, all things being equal. The physician should use new medications only if the ones with which he is familiar are not producing a satisfactory response or if the new medication has some distinct advantage.
3. The patient's favorable response, or lack of it, may point toward or away from a specific drug.
4. The degree of sedation desired, both in view of the patient's symptoms and of his occupation, and the degree of supervision and capacity to tolerate side effects are all-important in selection. Sometimes, at the beginning of therapy a very sedative drug is needed which later should be changed to a less sedative one. The same applies to activating drugs for retarded patients.

ANTIDEPRESSANT DRUGS

Classification of Depressions

Occasional depression is one of the natural conditions of existence provided the pain is not too extreme and the limitation of function not too crippling. Pharmaceutical treatment is not indicated for such existential depression. Depression can also follow from the use of drugs such as reserpine or its analogues in the treatment of hypertension, excess barbiturates and bromides, steroids (e.g. cortisone and the oral contraceptives), methenamine mandelate (Mandelamine®), as well as other substances. Viral diseases of almost any sort, operative procedures, parturition and other medical disorders such as jaundice, avitaminosis and certain types of brain tumors can also produce depression. In such conditions the primary disorder rather than depression is the main objective of therapy, although treatment of the secondary depression may be indicated. Finally, depression itself can constitute a disease entity. In view of the disagreements as to symptoms of endogenous (primary, manic-depressive) depression vs. neurotic (reactive) depression as well as the contradictory findings as to which drugs are good for which conditions, it is probably simplest at present to regard depression as a single disease entity and not attempt to differentiate the neurotic from the primary type in respect to treatment.

Differential Diagnosis

At times depression is confused with schizophrenia because of failure to take into account the frequency with which delusions and hallucinations occur in depression. Retardation can then mistakenly be diagnosed as blocking. Many drugs used in the treatment of schizophrenia will only deepen the depression, so that diagnosis here is of more than theoretical concern.

Most patients who have depression also have some degree of anxiety, and not infrequently, the depression is masked by the anxiety which is the more obtrusive symptom. Sedatives and antianxiety drugs may tend to deepen the depression. If a patient who is being treated for an anxiety state does not respond satisfactorily in a month or two, the possibility of an underlying depression being present should be examined.

Arteriosclerosis and senility are sometimes mistakenly diagnosed when the basic disorder is depression. Even more frequently, there may be minimal symptoms of such diseases of the senium which become distorted out of all proportion if they are accompanied by a depression. Relief of the depression leads to regression of the manifestations of senility and arteriosclerosis to a subclinical or even nonexistent state.

Finally, there are a series of depression-equivalents which can occur without the presence of depression itself as a symptom. Most frequently, these are psychosomatic disorders, but they can also take the form of drug dependence, phobic and obsessive reactions, compulsions and "acting out" behavior.

Treatment

Treatment alone or in combination includes (1) psychotherapy, (2) electroconvulsive therapy and (3) pharmacotherapy.

Under pharmacotherapy the two major drug groups are the tricyclics, including related drugs such as doxepin and the monamine oxidase inhibitors. In addition, the thiothixenes in schizoaffective disorders and the phenothiazines should be considered. Lithium constitutes a special case since its primary function in depression is as a prophylaxis against recurrence.

The Tricyclics

The tricyclics are so named because of the occurrence of three contiguous benzene rings with substitution of various elements into the ring and the addition of side chains. Their major *modus operandi* is probably blocking the reuptake of amines which leads to an increase in the quantity of free amines at the nerve endings, which in turn appears to facilitate neural transmission.

Not all patients respond the same way to medications, but nevertheless, the tricyclics can be grouped in general respecting their sedative qualities. This is one of the major criteria for choice of appropriate treatment. Doxepin is included, although it is not strictly speaking a tricyclic. Obviously, for an agitated or anxious depression the drugs with sedative properties are desirable, whereas for a retarded and apathetic depression the more activating preparations would be in order. Often those in the mid-range are indicated. Sedative effects are usually evident within a few hours or days, but antidepressant action more often requires two or even three weeks before the first evidence of improvement.

If either the sedative or the activating properties of the drug become a problem, the dose can be given at one time instead of being spread out through the day. This is especially useful with patients who have difficulty getting started in the morning when the activating drug may prove useful or for those with insomnia where the entire dose of a sedative-type antidepressant is useful at bedtime. Combinations of the tricyclics with each other, an activating type given in the morning and a sedative type toward bedtime, are sometimes helpful.

Combinations of tricyclics with phenothiazines are particularly useful in certain patients. The combination of perphenazine and amitriptyline (Etrafon,® Triavil®) has proved most helpful and is available in preparations of either 2 mg or 4 mg of perphenazine combined with either 10 mg or 25 mg of amitriptyline. Interestingly, there is evidence that the occurrence of extrapyramidal symptoms is less frequent when the phenothiazine is combined with a tricyclic antidepressant. On the other hand, in sensitive individuals the tricyclics given alone can also produce extrapyramidal symptoms which in turn are controllable with antiparkinsonian agents.

For all except the mildest cases or the most debilitated patients, medication should be started at 25 to 50 mg t.i.d. (except protriptyline at 5-10 mg t.i.d.). If there is no response within two weeks the dose should be doubled. If there is no response at the end of four weeks it is generally advisable to substitute a different tricyclic; and again, if there is no response within the four-week period the use of a monamine oxidase inhibitor is usually in order. Intensive treatment doses are also indicated in Table 23-IV. Maintenance dose should be continued two to six months after relief of symptoms. A decision concerning lithium prophylaxis or indefinite maintenance use should be made during this period.

Medical Conditions Requiring Caution in the Use of Tricyclics

INCREASED INTRAOCULAR PRESSURE: Because of their anticholinergic effect the tricyclics should be used with caution in the treatment of patients with glaucoma and related conditions. Although no direct evidence of such increased intraocular pres-

TABLE 23-IV
TRICYLIC AND RELATED DRUGS FOR TREATMENT OF DEPRESSION LISTED IN DESCENDING ORDER OF SEDATIVE AND ANTIANXIETY PROPERTIES

Tablet dosage size in milligrams	*Drug*	*Intensive treatment dose in milligrams t.i.d.*	*Maintenance dose in milligrams bi.i.d., t.i.d.*
10, 25, 50	doxepin (Sinequan®)	25-100	25
10, 25, 50	amitriptyline (Elavil®)	25-100	25
10, 25	nortriptyline (Aventyl®)	25-100	25
10, 25, 50	imipramine (Tofranil®)	25-100	25
25, 50	desipramine (Pertofrane®, Norpramin®)	25-100	25
5, 10	protriptyline (Vivactil®)	5-20	5-10

sure has been found with doxepin, the caution has been presumptively included on the package insert.

Urinary Retention: Some degree of sphincter spasm is fairly common, so that patients with enlarged prostate or repeated genitourinary infections should be made aware of this possibility, and patients specifically ask about this point.

Epilepsy: The seizure threshold is lowered; and for patients in whom this may be a real problem, a precautionary increase in anticonvulsant medication may be indicated.

Some Other Possible Contraindications: Hyperthyroidism is sometimes listed as a reason for avoiding these drugs, but curiously, there are some patients who fail to respond to tricyclics unless thyroid (synthetic or natural) is added. The contraindications in cardiovascular disease are so general as to be meaningless, except for avoidance in the first few weeks following acute myocardial infarct. Occasionally, the tricyclics may cause some tachycardia, and patients with cardiovascular conditions should be watched regardless of the nature of the medication added. Excessive doses in schizophrenic patients may produce reactivation of psychosis and in sensitive, anxious patients may lead to overactivity, overstimulation or agitation. Caution should be exercised with pregnant patients and those under twelve, largely because of lack of knowledge rather than any specific contraindication. A question has been raised whether these drugs should also be avoided in patients with a history of thrombophlebitis.

In theory, patients on monamine oxidase inhibitors should not be given tricyclics. This prohibition and the combination of the two drugs is discussed subsequently. The combination with thyroid medications has already been referred to. Caution has also been advised when combining with guanethidine (Esimil,® Ismelin®).

Side Effects and Their Managemnt

1. *Orthostatic Hypotension:* A 10 to 20 percent drop in systolic and diastolic pressure is not unusual in the first weeks of treatment, but as a rule pressure returns to normal by itself. Occasionally, antihypotensive drugs are indicated; or in persistent cases fludrocortisone (Florinef®) at a dose of 0.1 mg once or twice a day is helpful.

2. *Dizziness, Vertigo, Fainting, Tachycardia (Without Hypotension):* When these occur early in the course of treatment, the dosage should be halved and gradually returned to the recommended level. This is usually sufficient to relieve the side effects. If not, a different tricyclic (or doxepin) should be tried.

3. *Weakness, Fatigue, Lethargy, Drowsiness:* These effects usually wear off in the first week or two. Occasionally, a stimulant may be used but if the side effect persists longer an alternate medication should be substituted.

4. *Constipation:* To some degree, reduction in bowel activity is almost routine. As a rule the gut returns to its normal tonus within a few weeks. Agents which produce softening of the stool and/or saline cathartics such as milk of magnesia and citrate of magnesia every three to four days are in order. Mineral oil and products increasing bulk may be helpful. The usual peristaltic agents should be used with caution.

5. *Dryness of the Mouth:* To some degree, this is also a uni-

versal complaint but over a period of weeks there is some return of normal salivary flow. Glycerine-based lozenges provide some temporary relief. This is one side effect which usually persists in some degree throughout treatment with tricyclics and related compounds. If sufficiently severe, change to a monamine oxidase inhibitor may be in order.

6. *Gastrointestinal Disturbances:* These too are usually temporary, but, if they persist, trial of alternate medications is recommended.

7. *Jaundice and Liver Damage:* It is advisable to establish a baseline for both hematology and blood chemistry at the time a patient is first started on medication. The occasional jaundice or evidence of liver damage is probably not due to the medications. It is recommended that complete laboratory work be done every six months to guard against the insidious development of such conditions without awareness of the physician.

8. *Overactivity, Overstimulation, Jitteriness, Agitation:* Once these symptoms begin developing, it is unlikely that they will recede spontaneously so that either substitution or addition of a more sedative antidepressant or of an antianxiety agent should be tried.

9. *Euphoria, Hypomania, Mania:* This side effect can usually be controlled by reduction of dosage, although addition of phenothiazines may be necessary. The administration of small doses of a phenothiazine prophylactically is recommended in patients with a past history of such episodes.

10. *Hyperreflexia Tremors, Muscle Twitching, Nystagmus, Akathisia, Extrapyramidal Symptoms:* Antiparkinsonian agents are usually the best means of dealing with these sideactions, and the addition of milder phenothiazines or diphenhydramine (Benadryl®) is another possibility. Again, it should not be forgotten that the antiparkinsonian agents can produce toxic psychoses, particularly with visual hallucinations.

11. *Paresthesias, Tinnitus, Arthralgia, Neuritis:* At times high doses of Vitamins B_6 and B_{12} are of some use.

12. *Memory Impairment, Palilalia, Ataxia, Confusion, Incontinence, Toxic Delirium, Hallucinations, Coma:* Usually discon-

tinuance of medication for a period of forty-eight hours and restarting at a lower dose will give some indication as to whether this is due to drug toxicity. If the condition is of a mild degree the physician may wish to continue despite the occurrence of side effects.

13. *Seizures:* The reduction in epileptic threshold may call for the addition of anticonvulsive medication, since ordinary doses of antidepressants are still required in treatment.

14. *Headache:* This is a not infrequent occurrence when patients are starting on medication and is ordinarily controlled by common analgesics for which there is no contraindication.

15. *Blurred Vision:* In patients in the middle or older age groups, there is frequently interference with the muscles of accommodation so that near vision becomes slightly blurred. This is especially true when not only a tricyclic antidepressant, but a phenothiazine and possibly an antiparkinsonian drug are combined. There is no adequate way of handling this pharmacologically, and if the patient does not show spontaneous recovery within a few weeks, it is advisable to have him or her fitted for glasses to correct the condition as far as possible. It is often useful to mention possible occurrence so that the patient does not worry about development of brain tumor or some other serious disorder.

16. *Hematologic Changes:* There is no very substantial evidence indicating that the tricyclics are likely to precipitate such dyscrasias.

17. *Edema:* Peripheral, glottal and orbital edema have all been reported. The episodes are usually transient; and diuretic agents, if not used over too long a period of time, are helpful. In other words, treatment should be symptomatic and usually is not an indication for discontinuance of medication.

18. *Body Weight Change:* A substantial number of patients report weight gain often with the claim that they have not increased caloric intake. Frequently, however, when patients feel better they eat more heartily, often between meals and particularly at bedtime. Anorexiants should be used with caution.

19. *Appetite Change:* For patients whose appetite was poor, there should be an increase. The patient who claims to feel bet-

ter, but has not responded physiologically often constitutes more of a suicidal risk than other patients.

20. *Hyperhidrosis:* Perspiration and flushing are not at all infrequent, with episodes usually lasting from a few minutes to half an hour. Occasionally, antihistamines are of use, but often this is a condition with which the patient has to live.

21. *Skin Sensitivity:* Occasionally, in patients there is a dermatological reaction or photosensitivity. Alternate preparations should be used if the patient cannot tolerate the side effect.

22. *Dysuria:* Delayed micturition is frequent, and caution is thus advised in patients with a tendency to urinary retention or infection.

23. *Sexual Disturbances:* Occasionally, impotence and delayed ejaculation have been reported, but these are relatively rare and are usually self-limited. There is some evidence of initial increase in sperm count as well as enhanced fertility of the female, but this can be followed by a reduction in fertility (in the male) because of apparent temporary exhaustion of the germinal epithelium. The possible effect upon sterility or pregnancy should not be overlooked.

24. *Insomnia:* There is sometimes a reduced sleep need, and the patient should be reassured that it is perfectly healthy to get along with less than eight hours sleep. The compulsive taking of hypnotics to guarantee eight hours sleep is much more detrimental than helpful.

Monamine Oxidase Inhibitors

Monamine oxidase inhibitors as a rule do not produce sedation, but there are differences in potency. Isocarboxyzid (Marplan®) and nialamide (Niamid®) are relatively mild even at high doses whereas phenelzine (Nardil®) and tranylcypromine (Parnate®) are much more potent. Pargyline (Eutonyl®) is marketed for the treatment of hypertension, but it is also a potent antidepressant. It is particularly useful in the hypertensive patient who has developed a depression while on reserpine and whose high blood pressure does not respond to milder measures. Table 23-V lists drugs and dosages. As with the tricyclic antidepressants,

TABLE 23-V
MONAMINE OXIDASE INHIBITORS FOR TREATMENT OF DEPRESSION

Table dosage size in miligrams	*Drug*	*Intensive treatment dose in milligrams t.i.d.*	*Maintenance dose in milligrams b.i.d., t.i.d.*
10	isocarboxazid (Marplan)	10-30	10
25, 100	nialamide (Niamid)	100-300	50
15	phenelzine (Nardil)	15-45	15
10	tranylcypromine (Parnate)	10-30	10

initial response usually requires about three weeks, and anything less than this cannot be regarded as an adequate clinical trial. The habit of switching medications after a week or two, if they have not led to a response, is detrimental to the patient's welfare and certainly confuses the picture. However, if the patient has not begun to show response in three weeks, then a change in medication is indicated.

Medical Conditions in Which MAO Inhibitors Should Be Used Cautiously

1. *Severe Liver Disease, History of Liver Disease or Abnormal Liver Function Tests:* This is not an absolute contraindication, but it is advisable to first try tricyclics. Very many psychiatric patients show minor abnormalities if a battery of liver function tests are performed. A reading slightly outside of the usually established norms on a single test should not be a contraindication to the use of these drugs. If the deviation is more marked or occurs on several such tests it is advisable to repeat the tests since changes are frequently transitory.

2. *Cardiovascular Conditions:* Since the MAO inhibitors often induce postural hypotension, the drug should be used accordingly. A too rapid drop in blood pressure is not desirable, and hence, hypertensive patients should be started on a reduced dose. Ordinary care should be exercised, as would be the case with any cardiovascular patient.

3. *Impaired Renal Function:* Because of reduced pressure in patients who do not have sufficient urinary clearance, a check should be kept to make certain that no accumulative effect is occurring.

4. *Pheochromocytoma:* The MAO inhibitors are absolutely contraindicated in this condition.

5. *Schizophrenia:* As a rule antidepressants should be avoided in paranoid, excited or overactive schizophrenics. However, in retarded, "burnt out" or catatonic schizophrenics, the addition of antidepressants is sometimes extremely useful.

Overdosage of MAO inhibitors alone can sometimes provoke the occurrence of a florid psychosis. Antipsychotic agents should be used concomitantly if there is any question.

For patients with both depression and schizophrenia (including the schizoaffective disorders), the drug of choice would appear to be thiothixene, which has both antipsychotic and antidepressant properties. Initial dose of 10 mg q.i.d. is usually adequate, but can be increased to 20 mg q.i.d. as indicated.

6. *Epilepsy:* In seizure-prone individuals the threshold is lowered, and an anticonvulsant should be added or the dose increased if the patient is already on such medications, since treatment of the depression still requires a full dose of antidepressant drugs.

7. *Age:* Since depressions to some degree tend to be age-related, they are more frequent in older patients. There should be no absolute contraindication in respect to upper age limit of the patient. Obviously, some elderly patients are more sensitive, and their cardiovascular system does not adapt as readily so that lower doses may be indicated initially until the appropriate amount of medication can be determined. The same caution is necessary with children below the age of twelve, but there are occasions when the MAO inhibitors are indicated.

Medications and Foods That Should Be Used with Caution in Combination with Monamine Oxidase Inhibitors

1. *Fermented Products:* This particularly refers to unprocessed, highly fermented (sharp and smelly) cheeses. It is the

presence of tyramine which can cause a precipitous rise in blood pressure and even on occasion lead to cerebral vascular accidents. In addition to the sharp cheeses, beer and wine (particularly Chianti) as well as pickled herring, liver (including chicken liver), pods of broad bean, canned figs and substantial quantities of chocolate are possible sources of trouble. The fact that small amounts of these substances are tolerated may encourage the patient to move on to larger quantities. It should be emphasized that the occurrence of reactions is often unpredictable so that the patient may decide he or she is not susceptible, only to react violently after a period of apparent immunity.

2. *Tricyclic Antidepressants:* The combination of tricyclic antidepressants with MAO inhibitors is discussed below.

3. *Sympathomimetics and Other Amines:* Drugs such as phenylephrine (Neo-Synephrine®) are probably potentiated somewhat. Parenteral forms of sympathomimetics and related preparations (adrenalin, amphetamines, atropine, etc.) are as a rule *absolutely* contraindicated. Potentiation is so marked as to be capable of endangering life.

4. *Alcohol, Opiates, Meperidine (Demerol®) and Related Preparations:* These are often potentiated by the MAO inhibitors, and hence, smaller than usual doses should be tried at least initially.

5. *Antihypertensive Agents:* There is some evidence that these drugs too are potentiated.

6. *Anesthetics:* In theory, ether may also be potentiated, but can nevertheless be used with caution.

7. *Dopa, Dopamine and Tryptophane:* These agents should also be used with the greatest of caution in the parenteral form and certainly with care even orally. However, combinations of tryptophane with MAO inhibitors have been used in trials on otherwise drug-resistant patients.

8. *Over-the-counter Drugs:* Since there is a tendency to potentiation, over-the-counter preparations in general and particularly those for colds, hay fever, allergies, weight reduction and sleep should be used, with a smaller than average dose at the start.

The monamine oxidase inhibitors retard the catabolism of

the amines and hence act to increase the amount of free amine at the nerve endings. This in turn appears to facilitate neural transmission.

Combined Tricyclic and Monamine Oxidase Inhibitors

There have been reports of toxicity in combining monamine oxidase inhibitors and tricyclics. The FDA-approved package inserts recommend in all cases that the drugs not be combined. In a number of foreign countries, including England, these prohibitions do not exist, and there is some evidence that a very small dose of one combined with a normal dose of the other will enhance the therapeutic effect. It is strongly urged that FDA approval be obtained before such usage is attempted and that strict adherence to protocol and close observation of the patient be involved until one has had considerable experience. This is necessary for legal protection at the least.

How to Select an Antidepressant

Is Treatment Needed? First, consideration should be given as to whether medication is needed at all. If the condition is judged sufficiently severe to require treatment, the case for or against electroconvulsive therapy should be considered. ECT is of primary use in acutely suicidal patients for whom adequate supervision is not available.

Which Drug or Drugs? Once a decision to use pharmacotherapy has been made, the next factor to consider is whether the patient has any conditions in which the drug is contraindicated or should be used with caution.

1. Factors against tricyclic usage are thrombophlebitis, hyperthyroidism or concurrent thyroid medications, a history of glaucoma or increased intraocular pressure and certain types of cardiovascular disease.
2. Factors against the use of MAO inhibitors would be the presence of pheochromocytoma, chronic alcohol consumption, liver disorder or marked hypotension.
3. Caution is indicated for either kind of drug usage if there is a history or evidence of organic cerebral disorder, in

which case much lower than average doses should be used initially.

Prior Responses: Drugs which have worked in the past should be used again, and drugs which have failed should be avoided. At times this rule does not hold, but it should determine initial choice.

Time Between Drugs: A period of a day or two should be allowed between the administration of a tricyclic and the substitution of a monamine oxidase inhibitor. A period of five days to a week should be allowed if the patient has been on a monamine oxidase inhibitor and is to be transferred to a tricyclic. Even then, dosage of the tricyclic should be low initially.

Combination of Drugs: There appears to be free transferability between one tricyclic and another and between one MAO inhibitor and another. The MAO inhibitors can be combined safely with the phenothiazines, the butyrophenones and the haloperidals. They also seem to work well with most of the anti-anxiety drugs, although with the latter, lower than average doses can often be utilized; and if added to MAO inhibitors, the initial dose should be low.

Combinations of a tricyclic with a phenothiazine such as perphenazine and amitriptyline (Triavil, Etrafon) are also often effective. The use of two such drugs separately is an equally valid approach to the problem. There are times when a fixed ratio in a single tablet is advantageous.

ANTI-MANIC DRUGS

The drugs used for the treatment of schizophrenia, especially the sedative types, are also used in the treatment of the manic or hypomanic ("below" manic) states. Lithium carbonate is now the medication of choice but it may take from 4 to 10 days to become effective, even in doses of 4 to 8 of the 300 mg size per day. Often the addition of a phenothiazine or particularly HALDOL (haloperidol) in combination with lithium is most valuable.

REFERENCE

1. Kline, Nathan: *From Sad to Glad: Kline on Depression.* New York, Putnam, 1974.

PART FOUR

THE MENTALLY RETARDED

Chapter 24

HABILITATION CHALLENGES IN MENTAL RETARDATION

FRANK J. MENOLASCINO

OVERVIEW

THE SYMPTOM OF MENTAL retardation presents a unique challenge to the child, youth or adult so afflicted, his parents and the psychiatrist who seeks to enhance his habilitation potential. It is a major social, health and welfare challenge for our country since it represents the most frequent disorder of childhood. These implications reach beyond childhood to become one of the major roadblocks for social-vocational fulfillment of retarded citizens in adulthood. Accordingly, the implications of the symptom of mental retardation go beyond the focus of medicine and its specialties to encompass the collaborative efforts of parent organizations, social workers, educators, vocational counselors, etc. Indeed, it has been the relatively recent, clear understanding of the pressing need for this multidisciplinary approach that has brought about the many advancements in this area of human service.

National interest in the mentally retarded has had a relatively recent history. Indeed, the benchmark events of the establishment of the National Association for Retarded Citizens (NARC) in 1950 as a citizens advocacy group to spur change in the field, and President John F. Kennedy's federal mandate in 1963, can be viewed as the beginning of our nation's modern era of treatment and management for its mentally retarded citizens. For example, NARC has been a pioneer in initiating educational-vocational-residential models across our country and then prompting local, state and federal levels of government to accept these services as part of their generic aids to all retarded citizens.[2] Similarly, members of President Kennedy's Panel on Mental Retardation initially outlined what had to be done on a national scale[25] and then helped to develop the rationales for the establishment of (a) alternative models of care, (b) eleven mental retardation research facilities as resource centers for the evolution of research knowledge and (c) the twenty-one university-affiliated facilities for training professional workers on behalf of the retarded. Viewed in these perspectives, the habilitation of the mentally retarded stands today as a most exciting area for professional involvement.

WHO ARE THE MENTALLY RETARDED?

The term "mental retardation" essentially refers to the combined diagnostic criteria of impairments in intellectual ability and social-adaptive behavior. It is both a symptom of an underlying developmental disorder and an assessment of an individual's potential ability to learn. In brief, the retarded individual learns slowly, and at chronological maturity his capacity to understand and adapt to social-vocational challenges will be, to varying degrees, less than average.

Over the years, there have been many general definitions of mental retardation which have attempted to differentiate between the "intellectually subaverage" and those persons who have "normal intelligence." Unfortunately, many of the earlier definitions of mental retardation were couched in extremely negative terms. Such unfortunate misnomers as "idiot," "imbecile," "moron," "low-grade," "high-grade" and "custodial" were once, and in some cases still are, used to describe the retarded. These terms not only set the mentally retarded apart from other members of society, but also convey to most people the visions of "subhuman" status, seriously restricted ability to develop or learn and prolonged dependency, all of which may be utilized as justification for isolation from the community, custodial care and overprotection. Thus, negative "self-fulfilling prophecies" have been generated which have operated against successfully maximizing retarded persons' level of functioning. For example, once labeled as "custodial," a retarded person's living and learning environments are likely to be so structured as to reflect the predictions implied by that label, thereby precluding his developmental progress to a more advanced level of functioning. On the basis of this type of reasoning, retarded persons were frequently denied access to appropriate educational and social development programs, thereby preventing further learning and development and, thus, confirming the original negative prognosis.

This is not to say that labeling is, in itself, necessarily destructive. The process of categorization and classification is basic to clinical transactions. In theory, at least, labeling should serve as a first step toward need services. However, in the case of the retarded, professionals too often assume that once the label (e.g. "mildly retarded") has been assigned, it will result in the delivery of appropriate services. Unfortunately, in the case of the mentally retarded, these labels have too often been used as a rationale for exclusion from benefits and services which are ordinarily available to nonretarded persons.

The definition of mental retardation which is now generally accepted in the United States was adopted by the American Association on Mental Deficiency (AAMD). This definition states that mental retardation refers to significantly subaverage intellectual functioning, existing concurrently with deficits in adaptive behavior and manifest during the developmental period.[10]

The terms used in this definition may be explained as follows: *subaverage intellectual functioning*–falling below 97 percent of the population on standardized tests of global intelligence (i.e. tests which attempt to measure vocabulary, comprehension, memory, reasoning, judgment and visual-motor functioning) ; *developmental period*–from conception to about sixteen years of age; *adaptive behavior*–the ability to adapt to and control one's environment, usually defined in terms of maturation, learning and social skills. It should be noted that the AAMD definition addresses a *dual* concept of mental retardation: It is defined in terms of reduced intellectual functioning, which is associated with deficits in maturation, learning and the development of social skills.

THE DIFFICULTIES OF DIAGNOSIS

No person should be classified as "mentally retarded" until he has been evaluated by a team of qualified professionals, including representatives from the social, educational, psychological and medical disciples. Moreover, the assessment should not be considered complete unless parents or relatives have been involved in the evaluation process as significant observers and unless the person's adaptive behavior has been assessed in relation to his community and family situation, taking into account the cultural norms of his environment.

As indicated above, the diagnosis of mental retardation is made on the basis of two dimensions: (1) measured intelligence and (2) adaptive behavior. A primary tool used in the diagnostic process has been the standardized intelligence test. Tests of this type are used to sample wide ranges of knowledge and skills with the intention of comparing a person's test performance to a standard established for his age level. Basic to the use of intelligence tests is the assumption that the person taking the test has had opportunities to learn which are similar to, and share a common language and culture with, those persons on whom the test was standardized. While this assumption may seem rather obvious, it should be realized that the 1970 litigation *Dianna vs. California Board of Education* was won by the plaintiff on the grounds that some 22,000 Mexican-American children have been "entrapped" in classes for the mentally retarded because they allegedly were given culturally unfair tests in English rather than in Spanish. It is also well known, that a number of factors other than intelligence can significantly lower test scores (e.g. sensory impairments, motivation to perform well in a testing situation, anxiety associated with test taking and mental illness). Therefore, the classification of retardation should be applied only to those persons who, after a comprehensive and appropriate evaluation, continue to function at a significantly subaverage level, even after various attempts at remediation have been made.

The second criterion used in the diagnosis of mental retardation is *adaptive behavior*. It refers primarily to the effectiveness with which the individual copes with the natural and social demands of his environment and has two major facets: (1) the degree to which the individual is able to function and maintain himself independently and (2) the degree to which he meets satisfactorily the culturally imposed demands of personal and social responsibility. As in the case of measured intelligence, adaptive behavior is evaluated by comparing an individual with members of his own age group, since all behavior is evaluated in terms of whether the individual meets the standards of personal independence and social responsibility expected of his chronological age group.

It is expected that a positive correlation will exist between measured intelligence and adaptive behavior. That is, an individual who ranks relatively high in one dimension would be expected to rank high in the other area as well. Marked discrepancies between measured intelligence and adaptive behavior (e.g. an intelligence quotient within limits coupled with a subaverage adaptive behavioral level and vice versa) should cast serious doubt upon the diagnosis of mental retardation.

The Frequency of Mental Retardation

The President's Committee on Mental Retardation[25] has published the estimate that 3 percent of our nation's citizens are, at some time during their lives, diagnosed as being mentally retarded to some degree. Translated into absolute numbers, 3-percent frequency indicates that some 6.5 million children and adults are afflicted with this "developmentally delaying" disorder. Further, one in every ten Americans has a direct involvement with this problem by virtue of having a mentally retarded person in his or her immediate family. It is a disorder which handicaps twice as many children as cerebral palsy, rheumatic heart disease and blindness combined. Although this 3-percent frequency figure is consistent with the expected number of persons with IQ's of 70, it must be recalled that the clinical diagnosis of mental retardation must also encompass the dimension of adaptive behavior. Utilizing the combined criteria (assessment of global intelligence plus measurements of adaptive behavior), it becomes clear that accurate data on the exact prevalence of mental retardation are not available. For example, current evidence strongly suggests that the 3 percent estimated is conservative for children during the school years, but too high for youth and adults.[28] When the retarded reach adulthood, many become clinically invisible as they melt into general society. Indeed, it is this latter epidemiological trend which suggests that improved rehabilitation programs for the retarded can significantly affect them by initiating symptom reversal (or amelioration) and thus, can greatly facilitate his long-term adjustment potential.

Levels of Retardation

The levels of retardation are usually discussed according to degree of severity and the concomitant expected potentials for learning and general development. The levels of mental retardation are usually classified as mild, moderate, severe and profound. The mildly retarded are almost always capable of learning to do productive work; nearly all can learn academic school subjects to varying degrees and are capable, as adults, of living independently and becoming self-supporting *if* they have received appropriate care, training and other services during childhood, adolescence and early adulthood. Moderately retarded persons can almost always learn to care for themselves, to profit in varying degrees from classroom instruction and to do simple routine tasks. With an appropriate background of stimulation and training from early childhood, most are able to become at least partially self-supporting and are able to live in the community with some degree of supervision. Severely retarded persons generally require intensive services at all stages of life. They are capable of learning to care for themselves, and many can become marginally productive, as adults, under supervision in a sheltered work setting. Recent studies[1,16] demonstrate that the severely retarded are capable of performing many tasks which were previously thought to be beyond their capability. The profoundly retarded nearly always require major inputs and medical and/or nursing supervision in order to remediate physical-medical disabilities and maintain life. Many who are ambulatory can be taught some degree of self-care skill, such as feeding, dressing, etc.

The President's Committee on Mental Retardation,[24] in estimating the percentages by level (s) of mental retardation among the total population of America's retarded citizens, noted that 89 percent were mildly retarded, 6 percent moderately retarded, 3.5 percent severely retarded and 1.5 percent profoundly retarded. These percentages clearly indicate that the majority of the mentally retarded (i.e. the mildly retarded) are more like the normal population than different. Indeed, much of the focus in today's ground swell of work with the retarded is focusing on the "tougher" challenges: the moderate, severe and profoundly retarded.

Diagnostic Aspects

Since the focus of this chapter is on the treatment-management dimensions of the habilitative approaches to the mentally retarded, the diagnostic aspects will only be reviewed in synoptic fashion. The most frequent syndromes wherein the symptom of mental retardation is noted have been described in excellent reviews.[3,10,12] The etiological classification of the American Association on Mental Deficiency[10] is an accepted standard wherein the more than 350 causes of mental retardation are classified into eight distinct groupings on the basis of the known (or suspected) etiological factors and associated clinical manifestations. Table 24-I presents a synopsis of this widely utilized classification.

The diagnostic approach to deciphering the possible cause of the symptom of mental retardation must stress (a) a detailed medical history—What has been the evolution of the problem? The time of onset and the type may tip one off to the diagnosis. For example, the onset of seizures in the first six months of life is commounly noted in conjunction with intracranial hemorrhages, cerebral malformation disorders and a high incidence of associated mental retardation. At the age of two years, these disorders become far less common as etiological agents, and diagnostic entities such as febrile convulsions are more likely. The diagnostic approach should also stress (b) thorough physical, neurological and psychiatric assessment including measurement of head size and specific searching for anomalies or soft neuro-

TABLE 24-I
CAUSES OF MENTAL RETARDATION

A. Mental retardation (MR) associated with diseases due to infections: prenatal (i.e. syphilis, rubella); *postnatal* (i.e. meningitis and encephalitis).
B. MR associated with intoxication: *prenatal* (i.e. Rh incompatibility, toxemia of pergnancy); *postnatal* (i.e. postimmunization reactions, toxic substances such as lead).
C. MR associated with trauma or physical agent: *prenatal* (i.e. injury or anoxia at birth); *postnatal* (i.e. physical injury).
D. MR associated with disorders of metabolism: Inborn errors of metabolism (e.g. Tay Sach's, PKU galactosemia); *growth* (e.g. arachnoidactyly) or *nutrition* (e.g. hypothyroidism).
E. MR associated with growths: neurofibromatosis, tuberous sclerosis, brain tumor, et.
F. MR associated with unknown causes (prenatal): cerebral malformations (microcephaly), cranial anomaly, mongolism (chromosomal anomaly), hydrocephaly (Arnold Chiari and *spina bifida)*, etc.
G. MR associated with unknown causes (postnatal): Schilders disease, Merzbacher-Pelizaeus disease, etc.
H. MR associated with psychogenic factors: cultural-familial, psychosocial-environmental deprivation, psychosis, etc.

logical signs such as minimal choreoathetosis or asymmetric motor power. These should be supplemented by laboratory studies as clinically indicated. A developmental framework is most valuable in assessing both the child's interest and his atypical growth attainments. Psychiatric examination focuses on both the quality and quantity of responses in the interview and the nature of the parent-child interactional unit. Hyperactivity, distractibility, impulsiveness and emotional liability characterize the most frequent behavioral syndromes observed.[4] The psychoses of childhood, which can present clinically as pseudoretardation, are also a differential diagnostic challenge.[15] The following factors are to be especially searched for in the evaluation of possible retardation: (1) frequent history of prenatal, birth, neonatal and postnatal disorders and (2) growth and developmental slowness including retarded physical size and body stigmata, slow language development (e.g. no words by two years, no sentences by $3\frac{1}{2}$ years), motor slowness (e.g. no unsupported walking by 18 to 22 months), social-adaptive retardation (e.g. preference for play with younger children) and evidence of deficient global intelligence (primitive play patterns, inability to follow simple requests, etc).

Although the complexity of the range of possible causes of the symptom of mental retardation is rather awesome, some general principles can provide clarity in the individual case. These clinical diagnostic challenges—the different levels of mental retardation as manifest at differing chronological ages—tend to translate into three types of diagnostic approaches by which the mentally retarded are usually identified: (A) Multidisciplinary diagnostic team assessments usually confirm the diagnoses of profound, severe or moderate mental retardation in infancy and the preschool years. These infants and children tend to have early histories of high "risk" factors,[6] somatic symptoms and gross indices of slow developmental progress. (B) School tests and general underachievement usually are the cardinal signs which prompt the identification (and subsequent referral for diagnostic evaluation) of the mildly retarded. Interestingly, the symptom of mental retardation is rarely suspicioned in these youngsters before their initial school attendance and subsequent academic failure, which is the most frequent first overt sign in the mildly retarded. (C) At all chronological ages, the recognition of some degree of social inadaptability and vocational inadequacy becomes the major reason for diagnostic referral.

Elements of the diagnostic approach include a sequential personal-clinical history followed by thorough physical and neurological examinations, laboratory testing as indicated, psychological assessment and an evaluation of the family structure. Pearson[20] has provided an excellent overview of the physician's role in the diagnostic process in the mentally retarded, with especial reference to translating the findings of such studies into the actual implementation of an individualized treatment-management approach. He noted that the active implementation of habilitative programs must flow directly from the initial diagnostic assessment, lest the family request for help become a mere academic exercise which "illuminates all but helps no one," while the family is sent on a shopping tour for help elsewhere. Wolfensberger[30] has succinctly summarized this same diagnostic exercise in futility, which is all too frequently still practiced.

In brief, a thorough diagnostic study which clearly outlines the treatment-management intervention that will be needed by the individual patient directly leads to a discussion of principles for bringing these rehabilitative measures to fruition.

CONTEMPORARY HABILITATION APPROACHES TO THE MENTALLY RETARDED

Professional Attitudes: An overriding ingredient of the professional approach to meaningful habilitation of the retarded is the need for a positive attitude and respect for the personal dignity of mentally retarded citizens. Although this principle may sound like a cliché—the author believes it is at the core of any professional's stated interest to be of service to the retarded. Professionals have for too long viewed the retarded as "eternal children" or "subhumans" who have limited developmental potentials, and these negative self-fulfilling prophesies have come home to haunt professionals in the current wave of public concern, right-to-treatment litigations and the associated direct criticism of the large congregate care models of our public institutions for the retarded. All of these current public demands are tragic indictments of past and current myopic professional views of the retarded and firm reminders that retarded citizens have a God-given right to enjoy the opportunities of America. For example, most of the current texts in mental retardation list the individuals with Down's syndrome as in the severely retarded range. Yet a number of studies[16] have clearly shown that this particular group of retarded citizens tends to function in the moderate range of mental retardation. This is not a matter of semantics, but one of old views and attitudes which must be appreciated by the modern professional lest his "retardation" gets in the way of the children whom he is privileged to serve. Similarly, the concept of mental age (i.e. "He is 22 years old, but has a mental age of only 10 years") reflects a profound underestimating of the dimension of social adaptive behavior and a resultant professional attitude of hopelessness.

A number of recent events (i.e. the film, "Who Shall Survive," produced by the Joseph P. Kennedy, Jr. Foundation, 1972) have clearly addressed the issue of professional attitudes and value judgments which can literally destroy *any* habilitative approach to the retarded citizen. These issues, as they directly impinge on the professionals approach to management and habilitative efforts, were succintly presented in a recent article by Crocker and Cushna.[5] The format of their article underscores the importance of this primary principle of the need for a positive attitude in the habilitation of the retarded. These authors presented the following two-case vignette and then directly confronted the salient issues:

> Freddy is a child with Down's syndrome, whose birth had engendered an agonizing period of adaptation for his parents. As the early months of life proceeded, however, a sincere and abiding affection had developed which assured him of the necessary personal support. At six months of age this growing security was interrupted when he was suddenly found to be acutely ill with bacterial meningitis. After some days of troubled course in the hospital, he finally seemed returned to nearly the level of his pre-illness competency. At that time, as his mother sat with him on the ward, a resident covering for the evening paused to visit with her and asked how he was. The mother replied, "Considering that only a few days ago we were afraid we would lose him, he seems to be doing really well." "That's good," the doctor commented, "but for a child like him, it really doesn't matter, does it?"
>
> Karen was born with a large myelomeningocele, and hydrocephalus was already fully apparent. She was shown to her father once, on the first night, but her mother was never allowed to see her because the pediatrician felt that the mother could not accommodate to such a distressing picture. No neurosurgical consultation was held to discuss shunting of spinal fluid or repair of the meningocele (which was leaking). Separation of family involvement was enforced, but as the number of days in the hospital increased, the pediatrician came to realize that a long-term care program elsewhere would be necessary. He was very troubled to learn that transfer of the child to a public care facility was simply not a practicable recourse and that the few possible private nursing homes were priced beyond the means of the family (who had no relevant health insurance). In his frustration regarding Karen's deposition and ultimate future, he declared, "You know the whole situation is really just a matter of economics."

"It really doesn't matter." "It's all just economics." "What difference does it make?" These remarks and others like them emanating from well-trained child care specialists cry out for critical analysis.

Crocker and Cushna[5] outlined four areas in which professional decisions should be reconsidered: (1) lifesaving issues, (2) support programs, (3) studies on clinical options and (4) enrichment possibilities. They noted, that many professionals find the predicament of the mildly mentally retarded child to represent a palpable challenge; but in dealing with more severely handicapped children, for whom the "rewards" of conventional emotional response and identifiable educational prograss become less evident, enthusiasm pales. Major conflict exists regarding the justification of effortful or expensive training programs, in that they may represent excessive commitment of family resources and adaptive potential. A litany of patients exists in which vigorous programming for the seriously retarded child or conspicuous involvement of the family in obligations for the child's special care are decried as an imposed burden and disservice—the microcephalic, deaf-blind, severely spastic and overtly multihandicapped become a subculture for whom disenfranchisement and automatic inferences are the rule."[5] These authors have clearly delineated the attitudinal hang-ups of professionals in this area and succinctly outlined what can be done if and when these blind spots are resolved.

INTERPRETATION OF DIAGNOSTIC FINDINGS AND FAMILY DEVELOPMENT

Beyond obtaining evidence of impairment of function in one or more areas, the professional needs to develop special skills in evaluating the relative importance of these findings within the total clinical picture and then in actively engaging the family in a plan of treatment.[27] The interpretation of the clinical findings to the child's parents must encompass the sum total of the examination findings. Since the condition is often most confusing to parents, one should initially empathize with their perplexity and then attempt to review the various examination findings carefully (and tactfully). The interpretation interview should review both the child's developmental assets and liabilities and then ask how his developmental adjustment can be improved. To be effective, interpretive interviews must engage the family's interest and active participation. Frequently, a number of interviews are needed to involve the family adequately. Otherwise, the parents may continue to shop for diagnostic services and, thus, further delay treatment intervention.

Professionals must actively engage the family through participation as early as possible, since the family is the key to any effective treatment program. As previously noted, the professional attitudes and level of interest are of paramount importance in this endeavor; thus, future cooperation (or lack of it) may reflect one's unspoken, as well as spoken, attitudes at the time of first contact. The professional need to convey to the family his willingness to share with its members the facts he learns, not as an end in itself, but as part of the first step in treatment. Treatment plans become a cooperative process which parents and professionals work out over the course of time. In an early contact, it is wise to indicate that treatment planning rarely results in a single recommendation, but is something which may shift in focus and alter in course as the child grows and develops. Early implementation of this idea helps develop the concept of the professional who views the total child, referring to other special sources of help as indicated.

These children are different from other children, and some of these differences are subtle and perplexing to parents. Parental reaction frequently causes the child to realize he is different, without knowing in what way or what he can do about it. If the child already perceives the world in a somewhat distorted way, this weakens his anchor to reality so that normal avenues of learning and of reality testing undergo interference or even destruction. A feeling of estrangement may ensue, and increased disorganization of behavior to the point of psychosis may occur.[17]

Early interpretation to parents of these differences and of related feelings of the child is a necessary part of the treatment for these children. Because of lack of awareness of this dimension, many of these children are unprotected by well-meaning parents. Normal parental expectations for the average child may be too high in some areas for these children. Apparent inconsistencies baffle the parents, and mutual frustrations occur. These are compounded by similar reactions from the child's peers and by subsequent encounters with other adults in the child's world. These children frequently need more structure than usual for good functioning. Thus, what would be viewed as overprotection for the normal child may be therapeutic for some of these children. An example of this is the need for reduction of the number of environmental stimuli, which is frequently necessary so that the child does not become disorganized. Too many demands on his attention, whether they be people, objects or sounds, may cause a hyperactive retarded child to become so distractable he is unable to do anything effectively. The wise mother learns to let such a child visit with one friend at a time and frequently also interposes temporal and spatial controls which would not only be unnecessary, but would be considered overrestrictive or overprotective for the normal youngster. Special education teachers frequently use such environmental maneuvers so that the child may function better in his learning process.

Much has been written about the grief reactions of families who discover they have handicapped children. Such a reaction may occur in parents of children with mild retardation as they become aware their child is handicapped. Alertness to this dimension must be retained by professional evaluators of these children and must not be forgotten in interpretations to parents or in subsequent interviews. Assessment of family interaction and strengths is a necessary part of the total evaluation, since these assets are essential to plan a comprehensive treatment program. Some of the psychopathologies encountered in these families is reactive to their difficulties with the child in question. Interpretation of this may free parents from considerable guilt and permit more spontaneous involvement and active participation in treatment planning.

TREATMENT AND MANAGEMENT CONSIDERATIONS

A corollary to this principle of management is early descriptive diagnosis and early treatment based upon it. This includes clarification not only of what needs treatment, but what can and cannot be treated actively. Full discussion of these facts can assist families in establishing realistic expectations, so that mutual frustration is reduced and fewer secondary behavioral problems are encountered. A helpful professional posture when initiating treatment-management procedures for the mentally retarded is to take each patient where he is at the time of initial contact. He needs acceptance for what he is, not what he might have been without his problem nor what he might have been if therapy had been undertaken sooner. A corollary of this is awareness of the family's feelings and also ability to accept them as they are at this time. Increasing their guilt feelings is rarely, if ever, desirable in attempting to motivate them toward therapy.

A corollary here is to focus in each case on the maximization of developmental potential, a natural outgrowth of the implementation of treatment following the descriptive diagnostic formulation. It involves a different type of goal setting from the usual treatment expectation, since so often one must focus on what the child can do, rather than anticipate a "cure." The goal then becomes how to go about providing him the necessary opportunity and support to develop maximally with a minimum of obstacles.

While some crisis situations will be encountered, a majority can be anticipated and either avoided or minimized. Knowing the child's developmental level, his handicaps and strengths, plus his family situation, the professional can predict what types of developmental crises are most likely. After the initial contacts, when rapport with the family has been established, much of the work is preventive psychiatry.

An overriding challenge is the need to effectively coordinate the services needed for the child. This requires awareness of the various services available in a given community and an attitude which permits collaboration. It necessitates sharing of the overall treatment plan with the child (when appropriate), the family and community resources, with special emphasis on the family doctor and the child's teacher. Close attention to the clarity and continuity of communication is essential.

Services these children may need range from psychotherapy in selected instances to many types of specialized medical care, special education, vocational rehabilitation, residential services, etc. Psychopharmacologic adjuncts to modify overt behavioral manifestations may be useful in some patients in conjunction with the former. The advent of a wide range of psychopharmacologic agents to modify some of the accompanying overt behavioral manifestations of dysfunction in the mentally retarded,[8] has materially increased the range of active treatment for many of these youngsters. One may selectively alter the level of arousal, motor activity, convulsive threshold and mood. Since these children do not respond uniformly to these drugs, it is necessary that the clinician become familiar with a wide range of such products. Some drugs appear to have specificity in symptom management, although the use of psychopharmacologic agents is but one part of the total treatment approach to any child.

Children with mental retardation have all the problems common to childhood, plus their own special disabilities. Individual play therapy is useful with a number of these children, especially concerning feelings about themselves. Criteria for individual psychotherapy, as part of the total treatment program, do not differ significantly from selection of any child for psychotherapy.[19] At times one may not be sure whether or not a child's integrative capacities are adequate to make use of this form of treatment without a trial of play therapy or other forms of psychotherapy.

Many of the retarded are in need of "specialized" special education approaches which must often be modified for both the behavioral and integrative-cognitive problems which they so often present. At times a psychiatric-special education program has to be literally created for an individual. At other times, the professional is faced with the dilemma of the need for a special education program for retarded individuals whose deficits, though grossly understood, are not able to be programmed with available educational techniques (e.g. retarded individuals with associated central language disorders).

Proper selection of appropriate therapeutic techniques for problems encountered at different developmental levels will effectively assist the child to reach his full potential; however, none of these principles operating alone is enough. If they are combined and incorporated from the initial contact on, a major treatment program can be successfully accomplished. In this way, professionals can assist the child and his family in the ultimate goal of helping each child who has mental retardation to develop to his maximum potential.

In summary, contrary to commonly held public opinion, the treatment and management of the mentally retarded are not a hopeless cause. Today, one speaks of (1) *cure for a few*—such as special dietary management of children with inborn errors of metabolism (e.g. phenylketonuria), early neurosurgical intervention in craniostenosis (e.g. premature closing of the sutures of the skull), early diagnosis and definitive treatment of hypothyroidism, etc; (2) *treatment for many*—such as active resolution of any accompanying emotional disturbance or special sensory handicap, improvement of environmental and family living conditions and amelioration of other factors which may sometimes make a child appear retarded or make a retarded child appear even more retarded than he really is; and (3) most importantly, *habilitation for all:* The need for a strong habilitation posture towards the retarded, initially as a child and then as an adult, is the major key to modern approaches for retarded citizens. It is important to stress that twenty-nine out of every thirty mentally retarded individuals can be helped to grow and develop into useful, productive and happy members of the community, possessing a considerable degree of self-sufficiency. The retarded child and his family need early help from resource experts in understanding the nature of the handicap and need guidance as to how *both* the retarded child and his family can lead useful and happy lives in spite of this condition which delays normal development to varying degrees.

The mildly retarded, by far the most numerous group of retarded individuals, are among those to be found in programs such as Project Head Start, public and parochial special education classes, workshop-school vocational training programs, federal and state vocational evaluation and job-training programs; and among the ranks of the "hard-core unemployed." Although not often labeled as "retarded," this group of citizens has received a great deal of attention over the past decade in our nation's attempt to prepare them to function more adequately as a part of our increasingly complex society. At the present time, there are not nearly enough public-school-operated special education classrooms, community-based vocational training programs or adequate social services available to assist this type of individual in making a positive adjustment to the community, so that he can make his maximum contribution to society in a constructive and rewarding manner, and also live as independently and self-sufficiently as he is capable.

Contrasted with the mildly retarded are those citizens who are moderately retarded since they are generally recognized by the public as representing the "mental retardate" in modern society. Most often, these retarded children do not fit into Project Head Start programs. When they reach school age, they are called "trainable"; and only in the past few years have such children been admitted to public school programs in significant numbers. As young adults, there has been an absolute absence in most of our nation's communities of habilitative programs to prepare them for appropriate jobs and adult life in the community. For the moderately retarded and their families, the real crisis blooms with the advent of adolescence. Previously, the only alternatives available to parents of the moderately retarded in most communities were (A) to institutionalize the youngster at large public institutions, (B) to place him in private institutions for the very few who could afford them or (C) to have the youngster sit unproductively at home. For the parents of such children, the prevailing unavailability of services, coupled with an increasing degree of turmoil within their own families and an overriding sense that they were not "doing the right things" for their child, often leads to institutionalization (by default) as the only available alternative. Those adolescents who are moderately retarded desperately need prevocational training services, workshop training programs, supervised living facilities within the community and opportunities for employment as adults in wide variety of service occupations and some industrial enterprises. The picture becomes slightly brighter with each passing year for preschool and school-aged moderately retarded children. The current frontier is the development of adequate and appropriate services for America's adolescents and adults who are moderately retarded.

The *severely retarded* now have access to virtually *no* community programs in most areas of the nation. If a severely retarded child (or adult) cannot be cared for in the family home, the only alternative now available for the overwhelming majority of such families is public or private institutional care. Nationally, about 40 percent of the residents at public institutions for the mentally retarded are classified as severely retarded. Those who function at the severe level of mental retardation need and can benefit from developmental day-care services during their preschool and school-aged years, access to long-term sheltered workshop programs as adults and supervised living facilities (e.g. group-living homes) within the nation's communities. Group-living homes, or "hostels," for six to eight persons each are greatly needed across the nation to serve the severely retarded who, for a variety of reasons, cannot remain in their family homes.

In general, the profoundly retarded are, at the present time, committed to institutions within a few months after their birth or upon the diagnosis of the profound degree of their retardation. It is interesting to note the logic—or lack of logic—in our society's methods for dealing with the most unfortunate and multiply handicapped of developmentally disabled infants and children. The traditional logic has been that in order to serve those who need intensive medical and nursing supervision (the profoundly retarded), a practice has been made of sending them to relatively small communities, where most of America's large state institutions are located. These remote locations make it extremely difficult to attract qualified medical and nursing personnel to most such institutions. This procedure is followed, rather than retaining these children in our metropolitan-area centers, which are the focal points of the most sophisticated medical services now available in the nation. This logic is both myopic and appallingly inappropriate for the all too apparent needs of such children. Many of the profoundly retarded, even those who are currently termed "bed-care cases," *can* develop a repertoire of self-help skills for daily living with resultant improvement in their overall ability to function, *if* they are given adequate care, medical-habilitative service training and personal attention during these crucial, early developmental years of their lives. Some of those now considered "bed-care cases" will have an enhanced potential for developmental maximization, with appropriate pediatric rehabilitation services, in becoming at least partially independent of the confines of a crib or hospital bed.

Lastly, it should be stressed that society has not fully utilized the potential of its retarded citizens who are of employable age. The U.S. Department of Labor, in its most recent annual publication (1972), endorsed the estimate that (1) 87 percent of our 6.5 million mentally retarded citizens are potentially capable of entering the *competitive* labor market; and (2) 10 percent, or approximately 650,000, have capabilities to work gainfully in sheltered environments with adequate vocational habilitation training, assistance and support.[23]

Truly, there is quite a way to go in ongoing efforts to provide habilitative services for all mentally retarded citizens.

A CONTEMPORARY SYSTEM OF COMMUNITY-BASED SERVICES FOR THE RETARDED

An example follows of how the previously delineated treatment-management needs for the retarded are provided via a full spectrum of services which are located in the retarded individual's home community. This example will underscore the contemporary trend to provide services for all retarded citizens, based on a positive ideological-attitudinal framework which incorporates the previously noted principles of treatment and management.

The Eastern Nebraska Community Office of Retardation (ENCOR) was established on July 1, 1970, as a joint venture between five counties in the eastern portion of the state. The purpose of this cooperative agreement was to provide a comprehensive continuum of services at the local level so that no retarded person should ever have to leave the ENCOR region to receive the services he needs. The ENCOR area, although it is the smallest of the six state regions in geopolitical size, contains over one third (approximately 520,000) of the state's population and almost one half of the state's children. Although small in size, the distribution of population within this area presents a relatively great challenge for service delivery since over two thirds of the region's population is in one metropolitan area, Omaha (population/square mile is 1203.2), while the remainder of the region is relatively sparsely populated, either in a rural (with 32/square mile in one county) area or within three other smaller cities in the region.

The agreement under which ENCOR was created emphasized the intention of the five counties to create a regional administration to provide services which were not or could not be provided by other agencies or organizations for their mentally retarded citizens. Accordingly, ENCOR was created as an agency designated to fill in the gaps between existing and needed services. The administrative structure is through the county government with one representative from each of the five counties comprising the Governing Board which maintains complete authority over all ENCOR transactions.

It is important to note that all of the initial and ongoing planning activities and service efforts that underlie ENCOR came through combined efforts of parent and professional involvements and have been accomplished since July 1, 1970. In its short existence, ENCOR has gained wide support from citizens, the parents of the retarded and local and state public officials. All services within the ENCOR system operate according to the principle of *normalization.* This principle is central to the major underlying ideology of service delivery in ENCOR. The principle of normalization states that human management practices should enable a deviant person to function in ways considered to be within the acceptable norms of his society and that the means employed to reach this goal should be as culturally normative as possible.[31] Actively utilizing this principle, ENCOR is to fully develop a system of services which will provide the opportunity for an optimal life for all the retarded citizens in its five counties. ENCOR currently serves approximately 1,200 individuals of all ages.

To accomplish the task of providing services for all ages and all needs of the mentally retarded, the following five divisions comprise the ENCOR system of services:

Educational and Developmental Services

ENCOR provides developmental and educational services for all retarded children who are excluded from the public schools because of their retardation. These programs for young children are vitally important and are, therefore, staffed with highly trained individuals who are intensively developmentally oriented. Children receive services within these programs to bring their self-help skills and preacademic abilities to a level where the public schools will accept them. Included within the developmental programs are speech therapy, physical therapy, and social services—all working very closely to help the individual develop at the fastest rate possible.

Vocational Services

When a child leaves the educational and developmental services of ENCOR, he may move directly into a public school program or into competitive employment, or may need special training through ENCOR's Vocational Services Division. Within this division many facets of vocational training are provided, depending upon the needs of the individual. After an intensive evaluation which pinpoints his strengths and weaknesses, a program for each individual is developed. The child may then go into vocational and social training for employment, or he may pass into the work activities unit, which is an extended training program. ENCOR also provides minimally supervised employment in industry through specialized work stations in various industries in the communities. In these settings, vocational training is provided right in the midst of the industry or business in which the individuals seeks employment. Thus the work station in industry is the optimum of normalization. The Vocational Services Division also provides vocational placement and follow-up, as well as related classes to provide training in those skills necessary to the world of work (e.g. basic reading, arithmetic, use of a telephone, etc.). In addition, home economics and social skills training are provided in night courses, so that no interruption in the work training occurs during the day. ENCOR also collaborates with the local vocational-technical schools in providing basic education for those adults wishing to further their academic skill level.

Residential Services

Residential services are provided for persons of all ages within the ENCOR system. The services provided include children's residences (small family-like homes), adult residences, family living residences, adult-training residences, adult board and room facilities (minimum supervision residences), coresident apartments (staff supervised) and supervision of independent living arrangements. In addition, the residential services provided by ENCOR include a behavior shaping residence and a developmental maximization unit.

The adult and child residences provided by the ENCOR system operate on the belief that to allow for optimal growth, development and acquisition of skills necessary for future independent living, each resident should be accorded the opportunity of any other citizen in having a family (or its surrogate substitutes) and a home within the community. ENCOR attempts in every way to follow the same family patterns of living as are experienced by other citizens. For instance, there are usually seven to nine adults (age eighteen and over) in each adult residence. These are adults who have mastered general self-help skills and who can be trained for partial or full self-support in either business or sheltered conditions. Initially, all of these adults attend the ENCOR vocational services centers while living in an adult residence. In time they may move into board and room facilities, staffed apartments or independent dwellings, depending on need, ability and circumstances—just as typical adults in society do.

Behavioral shaping residences are provided within the ENCOR system for individuals who need short-term intensive training (24-hour service) to attain those skills and competencies necessary to return home from an institution or to be able to take better advantage of another ENCOR residential training environment.

Lastly, a developmental maximization unit provides for those individuals who are the most complex to serve. These are severely or profoundly retarded individuals who are multiply handicapped and who usually comprise the maintenance-of-life cases in institutions for the retarded. This developmental maximization unit focuses on developing self-help skills and competencies within these severely handicapped individuals that are necessary for moving them into child development programs in the community and associated residential settings. Although this program is operated in a medical setting (i.e. a hospital) to provide for the medical and physical needs of these children, it is attractively decorated and intensively child-development-oriented so as to facilitate movement into other programs.

Family Resources

Four major services are provided in this division of ENCOR: (A) *Community support services* include developmental recreation, transportation and volunteer services. Transportation services are coordinated and provided for retarded citizens attending ENCOR or public school programs when these clients are too severely handicapped or their families are unable to manage alone. In addition, the transportation services extend to public transportation utilization training for adults, to enable them to utilize public transportation to move about the community. Volunteer services involve the active recruitment, training and supervision of volunteer manpower. (B) *Adult guidance services* include intake and referral services, as well as counseling, guidance and accompanying services to assist families in seeking out, attaining and coordinating needed services—whether they be generic or through the ENCOR system. (C) *child guidance services* include guidance and counseling services that focus on families of retarded children, crisis assistance services and developmental home placements. Crisis assistance services are available to all clients and their families. The major role of this service is to provide emergency or crisis care for persons who have sudden difficulties in maintaining themselves in their homes or in independent living situations. This includes crisis relief for parents of the retarded via part-day and/or full-time residential care and training. The service also provides crisis counseling, homemaker services and part-day babysitting. For example, where there is a death, divorce or major illness in the family; a mother who is having a baby; a family moving or attending to out-of-town business; or a parent (or entire family) taking a much-needed vacation, crisis assistance services may be used. Developmental homes are similar to foster homes, but differ in that long-term placements are emphasized and training for developmental home parents is required. (D) *The supportive services* component focuses on providing an active coordination of medical, psychological, therapeutic (speech, physical therapy, etc.), home training and health care needs for all clients. Once again the programmatic rationale in this area is not the provision of services, but the coordination to the highest degree possible of existing community services—while teaching individuals to utilize what is available within the community.

Central Services

The Central Services Division of ENCOR provides not only internal operation (overall agency coordination, supervision and program planning), but also provides evaluation and planning, public education and information services, bookkeeping and accounting. The public education and information services maintain a continuous liaison with the public and active news dissemination through the communication media.

In summary, ENCOR provides a comprehensive system of services to meet the needs of any retarded individual within its five-country area. Such a system is not the usual fragmented array of programs, but rather a coordinated system which is capable of developing any service (or series of services) that is needed for any one person. Such a unique approach to services for the retarded has been very successful and has gained wide support not only from the general public and parents of the retarded, but also from public officials who monetarily support the program's operation. Many individuals have passed through the ENCOR programs into public schools and into competitive employment. Similarly, many individuals who were served as adults in the vocational training center or were supported through the Family Resources Division of ENCOR are now living independently as contributing taxpaying citizens leading full and happy lives, in contrast to what once was the bleak future of institutional life for them.

The author believes the ENCOR system of services, as just reviewed, represents a meaningful and workable alternative to institutional care for the retarded and provides an opportunity for developmental maximization and personal-social fulfillment amidst normalizing programs and facilities that are located in their home communities. In brief, it is a model of "putting it all together" as to the total rehabilitative needs of the mentally retarded.

CURRENT-FUTURE NATIONAL TRENDS IN HABILITATION OF THE MENTALLY RETARDED

Many of the current trends in habilitation efforts on behalf of the mentally retarded will have major repercussions on future patterns of professional service. Accordingly, five current trends which are most likely to have major roles in shaping the public and professional postures towards the mentally retarded in the future will be focused on here.

National Trends in Residential Services

On the national scene the last two decades have produced a series of major legislative bills on behalf of the retarded, and mental retardation has been a topic of active interest and involvement by our last three presidents. Local and state governments, especially in the current era of "right to education" and "right to treatment" litigations, have taken a second hard look at providing services for the retarded, with or without the spur of the national Revenue Sharing Act. The current ferment has been admirably aided by the November 1971 benchmark statement by President Nixon, via his "President's Committee on Mental Retardation." President Nixon's statement embodies a rather clear current trend which the author feels will have major positive repercussions in habilitative efforts on behalf of the mentally retarded. This formal statement, which has been nicknamed the "deinstitutionalization statement," invited all Americans to accept the following two major goals: (A) to reduce by one half the occurrence of mental retardation and (B) to enable one third of the retarded persons in public institutions to return to useful lives in the community.

To fulfill its presidential mandate, The President's Committee had to consider: (A) At that time, there were approximately 186,700 mentally retarded citizens in large public institutions. (B) The rate of admission to these institutions was 15,000 and the discharges 14,700 in 1970. In 1971, the discharges were greater than the admissions—the first time this trend has been reversed in many decades. Accordingly, to reduce by one-third (62,000 citizens) the number of retarded citizens who were then institutionalized in public facilities, the following three national goals are important: (A) continuing to reduce admissions by offering to parents of the retarded alternative developmentally oriented services and residential placements, (B) increasing self-help capabilities and job-ready skills of current institutional residents via highly skilled programs of service and training and (C) increasing community-based residential placement opportunities by spurring the establishment of community facilities. These facilities would have to be developed with close attention to quality standards.

Table 24-II illustrates the past, current and possible future national guidelines that flow from President Nixon's mandate to the President's Committee on Mental Retardation.

Accordingly, it is clearly evident that the old professional

TABLE 24-II

NATIONAL RESIDENTIAL TRENDS IN MENTAL RETARDATION

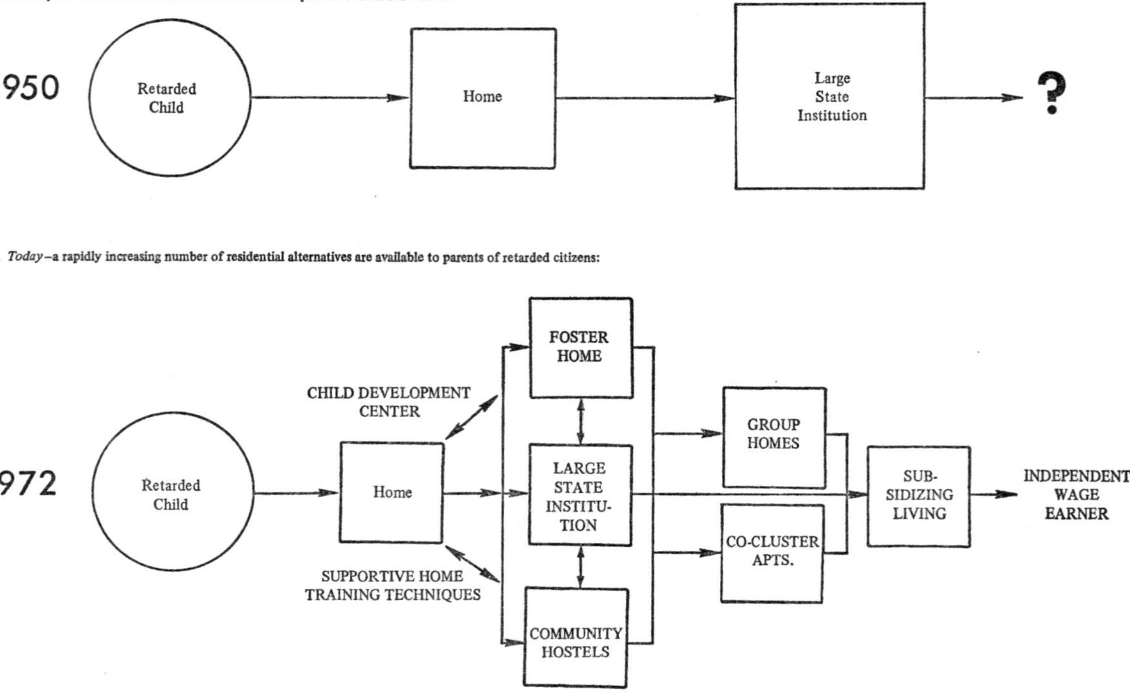

view of sending the retarded away from their home communities to "be with their own kind" will go the way of the old tuberculosis sanatorium approach. In its place there is rapidly arising a system of community-based services for the mentally retarded which, with active liaison with parents and advocates of the retarded, will provide many exciting challenges and complementary support for more early and aggressive habilitation efforts on behalf of our mentally retarded citizens!

The major public advocacy organization on behalf of the mentally retarded is the National Association for Retarded Citizens (NARC). During the last twenty-three years, this organization has displayed an outstanding record of public service in the areas of public education, initiation of service programs, research into basic and applied areas that aim at prevention, and governmental affairs. Two of their major thrusts in the 1970's are the development of home training techniques that will aid parents in helping their children within the primary home and their recent clarion call (see Appendix A) for a renaissance in residential services. Indeed, the initiation of community-based residential services for the retarded has become an "obsession" with NARC units across the country, it currently has the same vigor that the opportunity centers had in the 1960's, and there is every reason to believe that this new thrust will have the same legislative repercussions (i.e. the mandatory education laws in all of our states).

In summary, *both* of these major national trends—the President's committee mandate with its direct bearing on federal funding patterns and the reprecussions of the NARC policy statement as to the wishes of the consumers—acting in concert will, the author feels, finally "turn the corner" *away* from the large public institution as the major available resource for serving our retarded citizens. During the transitional period between institutional-based and community-based programs and services, it would appear judicious for local and state public officials to closely scrutinize and demand that the allocation of any public funds be consistent with the previously noted national trend—lest they continue to support ideologies and/or enlarged facilities that are clearly on their way to historical oblivion.

Legal Rights of The Retarded

One must be fully aware of what has occurred in regard to the recent legal movements on behalf of the mentally retarded. The changes which have come about in the last three to five years have been truly remarkable. On the basis of these changes, here are some predictions as to what current-future trends will bring for the retarded by the end of this decade: In the 1970's, a *legal move* concerning the retarded will accomplish three major goals: (1) The first and current trend is one of recognition. It is being recognized more and more that the Bill of Rights is a part of the Constitution which actually applied to mentally retarded citizens as well! Indeed, there *will* be a time when "right to education" and "right to treatment" suits will no longer arise. In essence, the current litigation in these areas will eventually rediscover the full recognition of mentally retarded citizens concerning their personal and civil rights. (2) The second major goal will be implementation. There will be a direct remedy to the recognition of the above-noted rights of the retarded. For example, in Nebraska, the "right to treatment" suit, with particular reference to the least restrictive settings, has a remedy for the recognition of the rights of the retarded that will result in the implementation of the ENCOR model of services as the affirmative answer to their needs. Accordingly, the implementation phase of the major legal thrusts in the 1970's will bring about the changes ordered by the judiciary, replete with state-national legislative changes and actions in each state. In this regard, it is heartening to note that the President's Committee on Mental Retardation, in its report entitled "MR 72: Islands of Excellence," strongly reinforced President Nixon's deinstitutionalization statement of 1971 with regard to the current tidal wave in our country toward community-based programs. The implementation of the current recognition of the rights of the retarded will carry with it many affirmative remedies that will establish and, indeed, act upon the rights of the retarded to normalized programs in the mainstream of society—programs with a developmental model based in the God-given right of every individual to grow to the best of his ability. This *implementation* phase will embrace the veiw that has been very basic to this country in its commitment to provide an opportunity for all of its citizens.

(3) The last goal is acceptance of the retarded. Yet, those in NARC have done a great deal in the last twenty-three years in regard to the acceptance of mentally retarded citizens; the recent litigation across our country, with its phases of *recognition* and *implementation,* will eventually bring the *full acceptance* of the retarded in regard to their integration into our social, educational and vocational mainstreams. Yet, there will be some major problems in completing this goal in regard to fully accepting the retarded in the community–such as the problem in Nebraska (Bellevue), which was a chronic societal problem dealing with deviancy.

These three legal trends of recognition, implementation and acceptance of the retarded present major challenges to the professionals in our country. For example, there are currently twenty-four lawsuits across the nation regarding the recognition phase of the rights of the mentally retarded as full fellow citizens. The implementation phase is just beginning as a tidal wave across our country, and the nation is moving very rapidly toward community-based programs. Lastly, the acceptance of mentally retarded citizens as fellow human beings who have the right to enjoy fully their "God-given rights will literally bring about a rediscovery of the very humanity that our forbears had in their initial pushes for the mentally retarded.

A Renaissance of Psychiatric Interest in the Mentally Retarded

Since the latter third of the nineteenth century, the relationship between emotional disturbance and mental retardation has been of interest to workers in both the mental illness and mental retardation fields. Initially, their interest was meager, with preponderant focus on a possible interrelationship between the poorly understood psychoses of childhood and manifestations of the social adaptive repercussions of mental retardation–the latter being uniformly viewed as fixed sequelae of a central nervous system disorder. This minimal professional interest continued until the following events occurred: (1) Nomenclatural clarifications of the etiologies which produce the symptom of mental retardation eventuated in a sharp focus on the similarities and the difference between mental retardation and mental illness; (2) some consensus came about in the definition of emotional disorder (e.g. an abnormality of behavior, emotions or relationships, which is sufficiently marked and/or prolonged as to handicap the individual and/or distress his family or the community and which continues up to the time of assessment); (3) research efforts in the biomedical, educational and psychosocial determinants of mental retardation attracted ever increasing numbers of investigators to study behavioral characteristics of the retarded; and (4) citizen groups (e.g. NARC) joined forces with professionals to demand that more scientific attention (as well as financial support) be focused on research dimensions of the psychosocial adjustment potentials of the retarded.

Recent contributions to the interrelationships between mental retardation and emotional disorder have reflected this renaissance of professional interest. Indeed, the overwhelming bulk of literature on this topic has appeared since 1960. There are a number of major issues and problems relevant to the relationship(s) between emotional disturbance and mental retardation. The definition of mental retardation and the associated nomenclatural system of the American Association on Mental Deficiency (AA MD) underscore the presence of subaverage intellectual functioning and the associated deficits in adaptive behavior. However, the majority of the disorders listed as capable of producing the symptom of mental retardation are more descriptive of syndromes, rather than specific etiological-diagnostic entities (especially in AAMD categories VII and VIII). Add to this uncertainty of primary causes the problems of clinical description, and the result is a major area of possible clinical confusion: symptomatic behavior which can be produced by a variety of causes. For example, the origin of a given child's hyperactivity may range from motoric expressions of anxiety to manifestations of cerebral dysfunction. Similarly, a shortened attention span may be the end product of a range of determinants from an inadequate relationship with the mother in infancy (suggesting that the mother was unable to operate as a selective stimulation barrier for the child) to defective midbrain screening of incoming stimuli. Thus, the symptomatic nature of mental retardation, in association with possible multifactorial causes for any given behavioral manifestation, increases not only the vista of etiological causation, but also the possibilities for more specific treatment intervention in these complex developmental disorders of childhood.

Accordingly, the relationship between emotional disturbance and mental retardation has had a long and colorful history. The two have been thought of as distinct, coexistent and inseparable entities. Though many aspects of these relationships remain obscure, there have been a number of cogent attempts at viewing the possible interconnections and descriptive delineations of what has actually been experienced in the clinical encounters with mentally retarded citizens whose lives also display indices of an emotional disturbance.[29] These efforts have provided some diagnostic clarity to that they serve as guidelines for therapeutic interventions which are more consistent with past, current and possible future trends in this area.

Historically, the diagnosis of emotional disturbance directly implied a notion that behavior occurred as a reflection of vague internal processes (intrinsic factors) within the organism. However, for the last three decades there has been increasing emphasis directed to the major limitations that are present in the individual environment (extrinsic factors) and their possible role in initiating atypical and abnormal behavioral patterns of response. Yet, the intrinsic and extrinsic points of view are not contradictory, but rather, are tangible elements of the same problem which must be directly confronted when viewing the diagnostic and treatment intervention approaches to the coexistence of emotional disturbance and mental retardation. Interestingly, the recent emphasis upon extrinsic factors has been accompanied by a specific applied technology of treatment intervention[9] which may provide the means to more meaningful investigation of these "unquestioned answers to unanswered questions."

Although many new questions and tentative answers are frequently postulated on this particular aspect of the retarded, the radical nature of the proposals are only superficial because the basic question—as it has always been—is a human one: the age-old question which affects those who are vulnerable and dependent and seek help from those who can give it if they are willing. For example, it is known that many mentally retarded citizens, by virtue of their poor self-image and low status in pursuing self-identity in a democratic world, are prone to error and anxiety. Similarly, the inefficient nature of their performance in this world of competition has all too often been evident and subsequently has dehumanized them as to social perception and roles. Indeed, an *apartheid* approach to the mentally retarded has been reached wherein people are seemingly more comfortable with the intrinsic (physical) components of the mental retardates' illness, but still reject them as to their social-vocational potentials. Tragically, this apartheid is often even more apparent among those who may have reinforced the negative image of the retarded via dehumanization and personal degradation although they are often unaware of their acts. There is developing a refreshing approach to this topic which is in keeping with the mounting wave of enlightened programming for the mentally retarded that is sweeping across the country at this time doing away with hollow professional promises of the past, so as to make the very labels "dehumanization" and "degradation" a sign of historical oblivion on the part of those who verbalize or act out their tragic implications.

Research

The nation has recognized the necessity for continuing programs of research, both basic and applied, in the field of mental retardation. Basic research is necessary because the fundamental mechanisms that produce large individual differences in intellectual development and in the efficiency of learning are not understood. Continuing *basic research* is essential in such areas as genetics, biochemistry, cell physiology, metabolism, developmental psychology, learning, motivation, sensory and perceptual processes and brain-behavior relationships. Understanding of such basic systems is necessary before one can truly understand the developmental deviations that may relate to them. On the other hand, the direct study of mental retardation can lead not only to better understanding of this condition, but frequently also to more general understanding of human development.

Applied research is necessary because there is an accumulation of basic knowledge, the application of which to the development of retarded persons has not yet been carefully specified. Technologies must be developed, evaluated, revised and disseminated to make use of existing knowledge toward improving the quality of life for retarded citizens. Untested methods abound for the care, treatment, education and habilitation of retarded persons. Consumer services are not always equipped to distinguish between proven and untested methods. Given limited resources, it is most efficient to insist upon small-scale testing of service systems before implementing such strategies widely.

Interestingly, research endeavors in mental retardation received their greatest impetus for growth from the major public advocacy group for the mentally retarded, NARC. The members of NARC are mostly persons who have daily concern for the care, treatment, education and habilitation of retarded children and adults. In its first two decades (1950-1970), through its dedicated efforts to initiate general research interest in the field of mental retardation via its "Pennies for Research" financial and public information programs, the thrust of these efforts helped to provide the impetus for the establishment of a national network of research endeavors. For these reasons, NARC has now focused its primary emphasis on applied research with respect to the direct use of its own limited funds. At the same time, it has engaged its governmental affairs section actively in other areas such as federal and state governments and private foundations, so as to more energetically request that they assume and extend their current-future responsibility for the support, by the state and federal levels of government, of basic research in mental retardation and retarded aspects of human development. It appears that this public advocate, research professional relationships, will continue to grow as a "noble conspiracy" to spur the further development of basic and applied research endeavors in the field of mental retardation.

A Personal Reflection on the Dignity of Risk

It may initially appear rather odd to the reader to note the title of this current-future trend in the habilitation of the mentally retarded. Yet, the author believes it points to a growing trend among professionals in mental retardation—especially among the "young turks" (and some of the not-too-young turks). Increasingly, one notes direct confrontation between statements about the potential of retarded citizens and the "weasel words" professionals utilize as rationalizations for why this potential cannot be consummated for the individual patient. In the past, treatment failures were readily explained by reference to vague etiologies *within* the patient (i.e. "Brain damaged—what can you do for them?" "You can't fight the genes."). Today one can witness a refreshing (and humbling) trend which causes professionals to ask themselves where they may have failed the retarded. In no instance is this professional self-confrontation more clearly evident than in the issue of exploring the developmental horizons of the retarded individual by joining as his professional-personal advocate in providing opportunities for growth wherein *normal* risk-taking behaviors are involved. In a provocative article, Perske[22] clearly underscored the role of risk-taking behavior as a prerequisite for all human psychosocial development, whether in retarded or nonretarded individuals. He directly notes the "dignity of risk" has been traditionally avoided for the retarded and replaced by a protective-dependent approach which tends to stilt their personality-developing potential.

For example, the professional person (or organization) working with the mentally retarded child or adult assumes certain responsibilities *to* and *for* the individual. Among these are the responsibility to protect the individual from accident or injury or from undertaking courses of action that would be harmful to his well-being. However, the degree of protection must be at an optimal level, since overprotection is as harmful as underprotection. Too great a degree of protection leads to an overly restrictive environment, deprives the individual of freedom and pleasure and inhibits opportunities for growth and development. On the other hand, the foregoing cannot be used as a rationalization for underprotection or for a *laissez-faire* attitude toward possible risks. One must strike a balance and in doing so recognize that a limited, but only a limited, number of accidents are bound to occur. In establishing the level of protection needed by each individual, general rules or policies are of considerable help. However, whatever these policies may be, they do not substitute for the evaluation of the needs of the particular person and common sense, together with the professional judgment of the person responsible for his care. For example, the open group home in the community does add some risks, but these are more than outweighed by the advantages. What risks there are are minimized, though not eliminated, by individual attention to the needs of each patient.

Rather than become obsessed with whether or not restrictions are a major focal point in the management of the retarded, it is noted here that guidelines and regulations are not substitutes for evaluation, judgment and responsibility on the part of the attending professional (s). This very openness of an increasing number of professionals to accept a portion of the risk-taking behaviors necessary for the retarded in their ongoing efforts to learn and develop personal dignity is a major current-future trend. Unlike the official societal diagnostician of the past or the custodial gatekeeper, professionals are sharing risks with retarded citizens in a mutual effort to further understand what *can* be accomplished if negative attitudes are replaced with actual transactions, destructive labels exchanged for acceptance of the retarded as fellow citizens, etc. This wave of shared responsibility for all of our fellow citizens strongly underscores the professional's role as an advocate to provide and obtain the currently unavailable components of a total spectrum of habilitative services for the retarded.

Summary

Current trends in habilitation of the mentally retarded have been reviewed within the combined contexts of the past and possible future implications. The active role of the mental health professional in these humanistic endeavors has been underscored.

The habilitation of the mentally retarded is currently a most challenging and personally rewarding area of professional participation.

APPENDIX A

NARC RESIDENTIAL SERVICES AND FACILITIES COMMITTEE

A resolution of the National Association for Retarded Citizens in annual delegate convention assembled, urging the governments of the states to establish small, community-based, homelike residential facilities for the mentally retarded.

Whereas, the subject of optimum residential services for the mentally retarded is currently receiving high-priority national attention; and

Whereas, it is recognized as the normal and desirable right of handicapped persons, including the mentally retarded, to live their lives as normally as possible, surrounded by the everyday community and integrated with that community life; and

Whereas, recently established accreditation standards, the expert opinions of leading professionals in the field of mental retardation and the President's Committee on Mental Retardation, and a landmark decision of the United States District Court, Middle District of Alabama, reflect that existing residential facilities are frequently inadequate, inhumane, isolated, substandard and misdirected; and

Whereas, it will be a function of the government of each state to reach decisions about replacement residential facilities and to implement these decisions within their state; and

Whereas, no such state government should undertake decision making affecting the mentally retarded without giving full consideration to the recommendations of those persons who can best speak for the mentally retarded,

Now, therefore *be it resolved* by the National Association for Retarded Citizens:

That the National Association for Retarded Citizens recognizes that the public interest requires that additional residential facilities for the mentally retarded must be constructed, purchased or leased.

Be it further resolved that the National Association for Retarded Citizens recommends that such residential facilities be community-based and be integrated into the mainstream of community life.

Be it further resolved that the National Association for Retarded Citizens recommends that such residential facilities consist of small living units, each replicating a normal home environment to the closest extent possible.

Be it further resolved that the President of the National Association for Retarded Citizens be requested and instructed to send a copy of this resolution to the governor of each of the fifty states, a copy to the president of each state and local unit of the National Association for Retarded Citizens and copies to such other persons as he may deem advisable.

(Passed at 1972 National Convention of the NARC)

REFERENCES

1. Bijou, S. W.: Behavior modification in teaching the retarded child. In National Society for the Study of Education: *Behavior Modification.* Chicago, U of Chicago Pr, 1973.
2. Boggs, E. M.: Federal legislation. In Wardis, J. (Ed.): *Mental Retardation: An Annual Review,* vol. III. New York, Grune, 1971.
3. Carter, C. H.: *Medical Aspects of Mental Retardation.* Springfield, Thomas, 1965.
4. Chess, S.: Emotional problems in mentally retarded children. In Menolascino, F. J.: *Psychiatric Approaches to Mental Retardation.* New York, Basic, 1970.
5. Crocker, A. C., and Cushna, B.: Pediatric decisions in children with serious mental retardation. *Pediatr Clin North Am, 19:*413-414, 1972.

6. Denhoff, E.: *Cerebral Palsy: The Preschool Years.* Springfield, Thomas, 1967.
7. Eyman, R. K., O'Connor, G., Tarjan, G., and Justice, R. S.: Factors determing the residential placement of mentally retarded children. *Am J Ment Defic, 76*:692, 1972.
8. Freeman, R. D.: Psychopharmacology and the retarded child. In Menolascino, F. J. (Ed.): *Psychiatric Approaches to Mental Retardation.* New York, Basic, 1970.
9. Gardner, W. I.: Use of behavior therapy with the mentally retarded. In Menolascino, F. J. (Ed.): *Psychiatric Approaches to Mental Retardation.* New York, Basic, 1970.
10. Grossman, H. J. (Ed.): *Manual on Terminology and Classification in Mental Retardation,* rev. ed. Washington, D.C., American Association on Mental Deficiency, 1973.
11. Group for the Advancement of Psychiatry, Committee on Child Psychiatry: *From Diagnosis to Treatment: An Approach to Treatment Planning for the Emotionally Disturbed Child.* New York, 1973, no. 87.
12. Hillard, L. T., and Kirman, B. H.: *Mental Deficiency,* 2nd ed. Boston, Little, 1965.
13. Joint Commission on Accreditation of Hospitals: *Standards for Community Agencies,* Chicago, 1973.
14. Kennedy, J. F.: *Message of the President of the United States Relative to Mental Illness and Mental Retardation.* Washington, D.C., House of Representatives Document No. 58, 1963.
15. Menolascino, F. J.: The description and classification of infantile autism. In Churchill, D. W., Alper, G. S., and DeMeyer, M. K. (Eds.): *Infantile Autism: Proceedings of the Indiana University Colloquim.* Springfield, Thomas, 1971.
16. Menolascino, F. J.: Developmental attainments in Down's syndrome. *Ment Retard, 12*:13, 1974.
17. ———: Primitive, atypical and abnormal behavior in institutionalized mentally retarded children. *J Autism Child Schizo,* (Brit) 3:3, 1973.
19. Menolascino, F. J., and Bernstein, N. R.: Psychiatric assessment of the mentally retarded child. In Bernstein, N. R. (Ed.): *Diminished People.* Boston, Little, Brown, 1970.
18. ———: *Psychiatric Approaches to Mental Retardation.* New York, Basic, 1970.
20. Pearson, P. H.: The physician's role in diagnosis and management of the mentally retarded. *Pediatr Clin North Am. 15*:835, 1968.
21. Pearson, P. H., and Williams, C. E. (Eds.): *Physical Therapy Services in the Developmental Disabilities.* Springfield, Thomas, 1972.
22. Perske, R.: The dignity of risk and the mentally retarded. *Ment Retard, 10*:24, 1972.
23. President's Committee on Mental Retardation: *MR 71: Entering the*

Era of Human Ecology. Washington, D.C., U.S. Government Printing Office, 1972.

24. President's Committee on Mental Retardation: *MR 72: Islands of Excellence.* Washington, D.C., U.S. Government Printing Office, 1973.
25. President's Committee on Mental Retardation: *A Proposed Program for National Action to Combat Mental Retardation.* Washington, D.C., U.S. Government Printing Office, 1963.
26. Robinson, H. B., and Robinson, N. M.: *The Mentally Retarded Child: A Psychological Approach.* New York, McGraw, 1965.
27. Solomons, G., and Menolascino, F. J.: Medical counseling of parents of the retarded: The importance of a right start. *Clin Pediatr (Phila), 7*:11, 1968.
28. Tarjan, G.: Rehabilitation of the mentally retarded. *JAMA, 187*:867, 1964.
29. Webster, T. G.: Unique aspects of emotional development in mentally retarded children. In Menolascino, F. J. (Ed.): *Psychiatric Approaches to Mental Retardation.* New York, Basic, 1970.
30. Wolfensberger, W.: Embarrassments in the diagnositc process. *Ment Retard, 3*:29, 1965.
31. Wolfensberger, W.: *The Principle of Normalization in the Human Services.* Toronto, National Institute on Mental Retardation, 1973, 1972.

PART FIVE

COMMUNITY SOCIO-VOCATIONAL PROGRAMS FOR MENTALLY DISADVANTAGED

Chapter 25

PSYCHIATRIC REHABILITATION AT FOUNTAIN HOUSE

JOHN H. BEARD

The Early Beginnings

FOUNTAIN HOUSE IS A NONPROFIT, voluntary organization established in 1948 for the purpose of facilitating the community adjustment of psychiatric patients following their discharge from public and private mental institutions.

Its founders were a small group of mental patients at Rockland State Hospital and two volunteers from the community, Elizabeth K. Schermerhorn and Hetty H. Richard. As a group they held in common the belief that many of the obstacles which confront patients in leaving the hospital and in rebuilding their lives in the community could be overcome or at least alleviated, if the patients themselves could come together, share their problems and be encouraged to provide each other with mutual help and assistance.

Originally known as the WANA Society, an acronym for "We Are Not Alone," vigorous and successful efforts were made to hold patient meetings in mental hospitals, in rooms made available by churches and by the YMCA, in coffee shops or automats and, when weather permit, on the steps of the New York Public Library at 42nd Street and Fifth Avenue. A one-page tract, tightly printed on both sides, was distributed widely on hospital wards and at community meetings, to welcome the newcomer—who would be known as a "member" and not as a "patient"—and to reaffirm the commitment of WANA to provide aid and assistance to mental patients so that they could leave the hospital, find a place to live, secure assistance from public welfare, find employment and alleviate their feelings of loneliness, isolation and alienation.

Each month the membership of WANA grew, along with increasing support from the professional community and from private citizens, whose interest and financial support made possible not only the creation of a sustaining organizational structure, but also the purchase of a brownstone in the spring of 1948 which would serve as a permanent clubhouse for the WANA membership and its expanding club activities. The homelike, noninstitutional quality of the brownstone, located on West 47th Street in the Times Square area of New York City, was fully in keeping with the nonclinical atmosphere which the new organization wished to convey and provide to all of its members. Also, the renewing quality of a small fountain in the patio of the clubhouse suggested that a new name, one such as "Fountain House," would not identify the special reasons for which the organization was established and which brought its membership together.

Rehabilitation Services

Over the past twenty-five years the original objectives of Fountain House have determined the design of the rehabilitation services which have been developed. In brief, all of the services of the agency relate to a cluster of community adjustment problems which typically confront psychiatric patients, usually diagnosed as schizophrenics, who have either spent many years in mental hospitals or undergone multiple hospitalizations and who have been unable to achieve or maintain a successful social and vocational adjustment in the community.[8]

Over the past decade, increasing numbers of such patients have been discharged to the community, greatly reducing the population of state mental hospitals. The transition, however, from hospital to community is one which is causing major concern throughout our nation. Articles in major newspapers, from new York to Los Angeles, are bringing to the attention of the public the plight of the severely mentally ill when placed in the community. Unemployed and financially dependent, they live in housing which is often grossly inadequate. Medical care and supervision are frequently lacking, social isolation is severe, and simple social-recreational opportunities are almost totally absent.

Adverse reaction, often organized and at times militant, arises when there is a heavy concentration of the mentally ill in a small neighborhood area where large numbers of patients live in boarding houses or in hotels. Such accommodations are viewed as a poor substitute for mental institutions, particularly when peculiar and bizarre behavior is observed by the public. Understandably, the question is asked, "Should not the mentally ill be placed in psychiatric hospitals where they can receive the care and treatment they require?"

At issue, of course, is the need to provide rehabilitation facilities within the community, so that the severely disabled mentally ill can develop their potential for community living. Various rehabilitation models, such as Fountain House, have been developed to guide and assist in the achievement of this objective. However, financial resources must be available; and there must also be a strong commitment to the view that the severe disability of the mentally ill is due in large measure not only to the process of illness, but to a host of factors external to the patient factors which can either intensify or minimize disability.

A Program of Reaching Out

Rehabilitation services at Fountain House are not confined to the clubhouse facility or to the programs it operates in commerce and industry. For example, when patients are rehospitalized, contact is maintained through hospital visits and regular mailings. Similarly, when individuals suddenly withdraw from the facility or become "dropouts" shortly following intake, reaching out efforts, through home visits by both staff and members, are promptly initiated. In almost all instances, it is found that the sudden withdrawal of a member is not a decision to reject the service, but rather an inability to become an active participant. Home visits are almost always welcomed and usually lead to the individual's reentry.

Members of Fountain House have clearly demonstrated that they can be extremely effective in conducting home and hospital visits. In so doing they illustrate the significant role which patients themselves can play in the delivery of mental health services. In view of the magnitude of the need, reliance solely on professional staff or other mental health personnel to reach out inevitably results in a failure to provide service. Studies conducted at Fountain House and in other facilities demonstrate repeatedly the high dropout rate of new applicants following intake—as high as 40 to 50 percent make fewer than ten visits. Programs of reaching out, therefore, are essential and can significantly reduce nonparticipation. Through such efforts, needed rehabilitation services can be provided to disabled individuals who would otherwise remain in the community without assistance.

The Apartment Program

The primary reason for the establishment of an apartment program in 1957 was the dire need by many members of Fountain House for more decent and adequate housing. There were patients at Fountain House who, while still in the hospital, were coming to the clubhouse during the day and returning to the hospital at night, having no home to return to. There were also members who lived with their families in suitable housing, but whose community adjustment was impaired, due to the family environment. And there were many members who lived in lonely single rooms, often in deteriorated tenement buildings, where the weekly rental fee was low, usually provided by the Department of Social Services.[7]

The apartment approach of Fountain House was simply to go out and secure a lease of its own, decorate and furnish the apartment through contributions from the community and then make the apartment available to two or three Fountain House members who could share the modest monthly rental, as well as day-to-day housekeeping tasks.

The apartment program therefore served those members who could not secure a lease on their own because of unemployment, a lack of references and impaired self-confidence. In a Fountain House apartment, however, two or three members could live together. By pooling their limited resources, members could attain more adequate housing than they otherwise could by living alone. Over the years, some forty apartments have been established throughout New York City, and 90 percent of the annual rental cost is assumed by the member residents; the deficit is a result of occasional vacancies. Members may remain in the apartments as long as they wish and, if they prefer, may take over the lease from Fountain House when it expires.

The apartment program is not viewed as a significant therapeutic experience in and of itself. The purpose is simply to provide more decent housing at minimal expense. The apartment program, however, is conducted as an integral part of rehabilitation services, not as an isolated program, unrelated to the larger rehabilitative environment. Each week apartment residents and staff hold small group meetings, often in each other's apartments, to discuss housekeeping problems or other difficulties which require attention.

By design, each apartment provides accommodations for an overnight guest, so that patients still in the hospital can visit Fountain House on an overnight basis and be introduced to the rehabilitative environment, prior to discharge.[1]

As increasing numbers of psychiatric patients are leaving the hospital, the need for more adequate housing is of crucial importance. An arrangement whereby patients can share an apartment, closely related to a mental health or rehabilitative facility, can not only provide better housing to the returning patient, but also can facilitate the individual's involvement in needed rehabilitative services.[18]

The Prevocational Day Program

There are many tasks which need to be performed each day at Fountain House in operating the clubhouse, and the help and assistance of each member are not only needed, but reflect the basic philosophy underlying "membership" at Fountain House. Regardless of the level of disability, it is believed that each member has a contribution to make, one which will be valued and appreciated by the others. The opportunities to contribute are many and varied, with respect to a specific task, as well as to the level of responsibility one can assume.

In brief, the day program has been structured around those activities which clearly reflect essential clubhouse functions.[13] For example, a cleaning service is not utilized at Fountain House. From a prevocational point of view, it is believed extremely helpful for members and staff to assume responsibility for the day-to-day cleaning and household tasks and to do so by working together, side by side. And a great deal of housekeeping has to be done, particularly in the new five-story clubhouse, dedicated in 1965. There are many stairways and halls, a large living room, a library and a dining room which also serves as an auditorium. There is a full-floor clerical office, a music room, a beauty parlor, intake-reception areas, a TV room, the women's sewing area, the game room, the fifth-floor snack bar and the outdoor patio. Administrative areas are also part of the clubhouse, and all the members and staff in administration share in housekeeping responsibilities.

Another prevocational activity relates to the buying, preparation and serving of food, either in the snack bar or in the dining room, where some 250 noonday meals are prepared and served each day. In another area, the many and varied clerical needs of the clubhouse are handled. Members assume responsibility for the busy switchboard. A daily newspaper and a monthly magazine must be prepared. Reports need to be typed and mimeographed, and there is much correspondence to be handled each day.

Members and staff also operate a thrift shop around the corner from Fountain House, working together on the truck, picking up donated merchandise, sorting and pricing in the small warehouse and, in the shop itself, selling directly to the public.

Other day program opportunities include welcoming new members and visitors at the front door and giving tours through the facility. There are also coats to be checked, member deposit and loan accounts to be handled and apartment rental payments to be received. Attendance records must be maintained, and help is needed for research calculations and bookeeping procedures. The IBM keypunch and sorting machines must also be operated.

At Fountain House such activities are viewed as ideally suited for the prevocational rehabilitation of the severely disabled psychiatric patient. All of the tasks need to be done, and they could not successfully completed without the help and assistance of day program members. The staff, therefore, experience a great deal of appreciation for the significant contribution which members in the day program make, and recognition is expressed in many ways.

Both staff and members become engaged in a process where important shifts begin to occur with respect to their concept of disability. Staff become more aware of the social and vocational potential of the disabled psychiatric patient, while the individual member discovers personal abilities and talents which lead to greater social effectiveness and more meaningful work productivity.

In structuring the activities of the day program, staff are organized into six smaller groups or units, each consisting of four to six workers. The units are differentiated on the basis of their responsibility for specific activity areas i.e. the thrift shop, the snack bar, the clerical office, the kitchen-dining room, administration and education and research. Each unit has rehabilitative responsibility for a group of members, ranging from fourteen in the administrative area to 128 in the clerical office. In essence, each unit is a smaller Fountain House, having its own responsibilities for each of the services provided by the agency. In addition to operating its own day program area, each unit maintains apartments in the community, provides transitional employment in industry, reaches out to dropouts or rehospitalized members and also takes responsibility for a portion of the evening and weekend social-recreational program.

In summary, the activities performed in the day program are done by members and staff working together. They have selected activities which have a clear relationship to the basic operations and functions o f the clubhouse. Members are encouraged to explore and choose the activity area which is of interest to them and to assume a level of responsibility which can be successfully handled. In most instances, members view their participation at Fountain House as a natural process. They are members of a club, and as members they voluntarily provide help and assistance. They do not usually view themselves as undergoing an organized, consciously directed rehabilitation process. For many, Fountain House assumes the role of an extended or substitute family.

Transitional Employment

Each weekday approximately 200 Fountain House members go to work, on a half-time basis, in some forty-four New York City business firms.[20] There are well-known department stores, such as Sears, Macy's and Alexanders. Some work in banks—Manufacturers Hanover, Chemical and Chase Manhattan; others in life insurance companies—Royal Globe, Mutual of New York, and Equitable; and others in advertising companies—Benton and Bowles and Young and Rubicam. There are also a number of smaller firms, like stationery stores and messenger services. Transitional employment[4] in all of these firms is either on an individual or a group basis.* All members receive the prevailing wage scale, and annual earnings in 1974 will approximate $400,000.

In the securing of job placements, it was not necessary to first engage in an educational process. Fountain House simply sought entry-level employment, usually jobs where the employer normally experiences a high turnover. The arrangement with the employer was not complicated. A job position would remain filled, being rotated among members of Fountain House every four to six months. Normal production standards would be maintained, and other job requirements would be met. A staff worker would first perform the job for a few hours or a few days, and on group placements a staff worker would always be present with the ten to twelve members on placement.[5,9] Little difficulty was found in securing such job opportunities from commerce and industry.

As indicated, in initiating a new job placement, a staff worker first performs the job before a member goes on placement. All of the staff assume this responsibility from time to time, including the secretarial and administrative personnel.[3] The objective is to thoroughly understand the requirements which must be met when the member is on placement. The staff also want to experience and evaluate the work environment in which the member will be placed. As most transitional placements represent entry-level employment, requiring little training or skills, staff are usually able to learn the job quickly and secure the approval of the employer to

---

*Two grants from the Social and Rehabilitation Service, Department of Health, Education and Welfare, Washington, D.C., made possible the development of transitional employment at Fountain House. A three year grant in 1964, #RD 1281-P, was for the purpose of creating individual placements in commerce and industry; and in 1972, a three year Projects with Industry grant, #26P-60310, made possible the establishment of group placements.[19]

proceed with the new placement. There have been some instances, however, where it was necessary to assign a second or third staff worker before the employer was assured that the staff was capable of doing the job satisfactorily.

By design, individual staff in each of our six rehabilitation units not only initiate job placements, but are given continuing responsibility for their managment and supervision. The implications of this procedure are very specific. The worker who initiates a placement tends to want it to succeed. A more personal sense of responsibility is taken in maintaining good relationships with the employer. The worker also wants to properly orient and train the new member going on placement to maximize job success. As the worker has personally performed the job and has direct access to it, prompt on-the-job assistance can always be provided to the member whenever difficulties arise.

Most importantly, as replacements are regularly needed to maintain an individual or group position, the worker is placed in the situation of needing members to fill vacancies when they occur. This is generally a new experience for the worker and even more so for the member who, all too often, has come to accept vocational disability and is not used to the idea of being needed to fill a real job, with regular pay, in industry.

For a member to be successful when he goes on a job placement, it is essential that basic work habits, the ability to accept supervision and to get along with others and the motivation to try transitional employment be strengthened as much as possible. There is no formula, of course, to accomplish these objectives. Certain factors are present, however. In the prevocational day program, the member receives a great deal of support and encouragement. It is a positive environment, one which utilizes and appreciates whatever help and assistance the member is able to offer. The member is given recognition and approval for participation and for the development of better work habits.

Members already on transitional employment serve as examples to fellow members and play a major role in motivating others to undergo the experience of being employed in a normal place of business. Through group discussions and videotape presentations, they are able to discuss openly those aspects of the job which are of special concern. The boss is described, as well as other employees; the work performed is outlined in detail; and special features such as free meals, paid holidays and other such benefits are always stressed.

Members on placement are also able to help reduce the newcomer's fear of failing on a job placement. At Fountain House, a failure on a job placement does not result in a member's isolation and rejection. Many members go on to three, four or even more placements before achieving independent employment. Failure, therefore, is considered as a step one must often take in overcoming disability.

Vocational disability, therefore, is not viewed as a condition which resides solely within the psychiatric patient. It is believed that much of the disability is due to factors external to the patient, the removal or modification of which will increase and enhance the individual's vocational adjustment. In the field of physical rehabilitation, it is clear that architecture, for example, can either retard or facilitate the mobility of the physically disabled, as does the presence or absence of various prosthetic devices.

Similarly, many barriers exist in society which not only prevent the psychiatric patient from making a productive contribution, but are largely responsible for the patient's designation as being vocationally disabled. The ability to pass a job interview, for example, is not necessarily correlated to the patient's ability to perform a job satisfactorily. Transitional employment in commerce and industry is an example of a social device which circumvents a series of barriers which all too often prevent employment of many psychiatric patients who have the capacity to perform gainful employment. The creation of additional social devices can further remove other barriers which currently prevent the return to productive employment of mental patients defined as vocationally disabled.

A Social and Recreational Program

On Wednesday, Thursday and Saturday evenings and Sunday afternoons, some 200 to 300 Fountain House members attend the clubhouse for social and recreational purposes. The program presents a variety of opportunities in response to individual needs and interests. The living room is a place to sit by oneself or to chat with others. Reading is available in the library, and many members enjoy the music room. The snack bar is always open and is extremely popular, and a cup of coffee can still be had for five cents. The game room is favored for bridge, pinochle, chess and checkers, and the television room is usually filled.

More organized activities are also provided, such as the poetry group, the sewing class, the dramatics club, the cooking class and the current events group which meets in the classroom. Photography is popular, and a well-equipped darkroom is available. The choral group meets on Wednesday evenings and the creative writing group on Thursdays. Movies, as well as hobby talks by staff, members and visitors are regularly scheduled. On Saturday nights, there is usually a dance, live music being provided by volunteers from the community or by the small Fountain House combo. The dramatics group presents its plays in the spring and fall, and the member talent show is greatly enjoyed by all. Free tickets are available weekly to members for Broadway shows, the Philharmonic, the opera and other cultural and entertainment events. As Fountain House is open throughout the year, holidays become special events, especially Thanksgiving, when the staff and their families assume responsibility for serving some 300 full-course dinners to the membership.

The evening social programs of Fountain House serve various groups of members. For some, it is an initial point of entry into the rehabilitation process, frequently leading to full-time involvement in the vocationally oriented day program. For those who are fully employed, it represents an important sustaining influence, particularly when full-time employment is first secured and the member is abruptly separated from the day program. Most of the members who are active in the day program look to the evening recreational activities as a primary source of pleasure and relaxation. Also welcomed are those members who have made a marginal adjustment in the community and are unemployed and financially dependent, but who reject involvement in more intensive rehabilitation efforts.

Evenings at Fountain House are also an ideal time to hold various kinds of weekly group meetings. On Thursday evenings, meetings are held for members who live in Fountain House apartments. On Wednesday evenings, members on transitional employment come together to have dinner and to meet in small groups to discuss their work experiences, and similar meetings are held for those members who are nearing the point of independent, full-time employment. Small group meetings are also held for members who have just obtained jobs of their own. It is essential, therefore, that the work schedules of staff include assignments in the evening program, if contact is to be maintained with members whose lives have become more independent and who are no longer available for daytime involvement.

The evening program of Fountain House is not viewed as a rehabilitation service which, by itself, will significantly modify or influence the social and vocational recovery of severely disabled psychiatric patients. Essential purposes are served, however; and the author believes that the program enables many of the members to alleviate their frequently intense feelings of social isolation and alienation and is, therefore, an important component of the rehabilitation services at Fountain House.

Comments of Fountain House Members

Each weekday some 400 men and women attend the Fountain House Day Program. From 200 to 300 members attend the Evening and Weekend Program, and over a period of a month, approximately 1000 individuals utilize the services of the agency.

The preceding material has described the objectives of Fountain House, its organizational structure and the rehabilitation services which are offered. However, Fountain House is essentially a place of people, all engaged in a variety of activities and having their own views, feelings and interpretations as to what has been difficult for them following hospitalization and what they believe is helpful to them at Fountain House in alleviating or overcoming such difficulties. A survey of the Fountain House membership directed itself to their views, feelings and impressions; and their responses are summarized within the following categories, each of which concerns a significant aspect of the rehabilitation process.

First of all, Fountain House was regarded as a place where one's life could begin again:"It's a start, that's what Fountain House is. I think it's a place where you can get your life moving again. For me, it started me on my way. You cannot get anywhere unless you first get established. It's simple, Fountain House is like having a bottom to one's life. It's something you sort of build on."

The opportunity to come to Fountain House was viewed as an alternative to loneliness, isolation and having no place to go:

> Just coming to Fountain House, that's what counted, not being alone all the time. When you are alone and doing nothing, you feel more nervous. Isn't that true? Before I came to Fountain House, I spent all my time staying in my room. Staying at home all day can be a drag. I was really an isolated person, without any friends. No longer do I have just four walls at home. When I stay at home I get sicker. I'm glad I don't have to hang around the streets all day long. This is the one place in the City where I can come without the fear of being isolated.

The importance of keeping busy and having things to do received frequent comment: "We keep busy here, and that's what it's all about. Keeping busy makes me feel satisfied. I keep busy here and this keeps me happy. I've got a lot of work to do here every day and this makes me feel worthwhile. We do so many different things here. Everybody needs something to do, and we are very busy at Fountain House. Here there is no busy work. Everything we do is something that has to be done."

The utilizing of one's abilities and the development of one's work skills was seen as extremely important: "Being here has certainly improved my work skills. I have learned to answer the phones. I have learned to do paperwork again. Fountain House has taught me how to run the switchboard and I've also kept up my secretarial skills. I've learned to run the cash register. I've learned that I can do a good job. I think that most of us discover talents and abilities we never thought we had."

The membership saw Fountain House as a place which both wanted and needed its members. It was a place where they were expected: "This is the only place in the city that can use me. I'm expected here every day and that's what's important to all of us. Here, you are really needed. It's a new experience for me to have something worthwhile to do every day. Here, they give you a chance to do things you never did before.

It also offered a better place to live: "When I was in the hospital

I had no home to come home to and they got me a place to live. . .I was still in the hospital when they got an apartment for me. . . Through Fountain House I got a nice apartment instead of a lonely, dreary room. I was alone in a welfare hotel; now I have an apartment and a roommate. They do this for lots of us."

Going back to work and having a job of one's own, were stressed again and again during the survey.

> This place helps you get a job of your own. Everyone needs a chance to work, to have a job of your own. Here, you have the chance to get a job. I'm going to start on a job of my own in the next few weeks. Right now they are getting me a job. They gave me two jobs, even though I messed up the first one. I got my first job last week. I have my own job and this is what counts. They gave me a job while I was still in the hospital. It's only part-time, but soon I will be working full time. I'm now working and making pretty good money. This is what counts. It helps most of us to get back to work.

Understandably, staying out of the hospital or leaving a mental institution was of prime importance:

> They help you get out of the hospital and stay out of the hospital. Coming to Fountain House is so much better than going back to the hospital again. If you are going to stay out of the hosptial, you've got to get the help you need. The important thing is the simple fact that Fountain House helps us stay out of the hospital. It's certainly kept me out of all the hospitals where I've been in the past. I'm still in the hospital and I come here every day. I believe it's cutting my stay in the hospital.

To feel more related to the world at large, to have a greater sense of the future and to anticipate a greater degree of independence were frequent points of response:

> For the first time I feel I can face the world again. It's really something to feel you are back in the world of today. It certainly helped me to feel more adjusted to the outside world. I think Fountain House also helps the outside world to accept mental patients as regular human beings.
>
> Everyone needs a future. It takes help, but we do have a future. For the first time in my life I'm looking forward to the future. What you get most here is hope for the future. All of us have a future here, because Fountain House always keeps on trying.
>
> To become more independent, that's what Fountain House helps us

to do. Some day I will be on my own and that will be wonderful. Eventually I will be on my own. There is the outlook here that some day all of us can make it on our own. I'm here because I want to be on my own and soon, I hope. I'm now thirty-one and it's about time to get away from my family and be more on my own, to live my own life.

It was expected, of course, that the comments of members would be essentially positive. The responses were being secured from individuals who were voluntarily undergoing an experience which they believed and hoped would be helpful in overcoming upsetting and painful difficulties. Many such positive views, expressed in general terms, were received: "What do I think of Fountain House? I like it. It's a pleasure for me to be here. All of us are glad to be here. I enjoy it immensely. It's a wonderful place. I appreciate Fountain House very much. For me, it's been wonderful. It's been good for almost all of us. It's pleasant to be here. I feel good being here. I enjoy Fountain House; it's my second home."

Feeling that Fountain House was helpful, however, was in most instances related to the alleviation of uncomforable and distressing feelings:

When I feel insecure, I come to Fountain House, and it helps. It helps me think less about my problems. At Fountain House I discover again and again that I'm not such a bad person after all. When I'm here, I don't feel so afraid. It's terrible to feel that way. I come here because I don't always feel human. Here, I'm not so preoccupied with myself. It's very simple, being here helps me feel a bit better.

It helped me to become more mature. I don't know how to say it, but it's given me a great sense of security. I feel like the other gentleman: We find more confidence in ourselves here. I'm getting well here. It helps me keep my mind off myself. It's helped me to believe in myself. I'm coming out of myself. It's helped me to try again and again. It's helped me find my way clear in things. It's helped me in lots of ways. It's helped me make a success of myself. Fountain House has made me feel like a grown-up and when I feel like a grown-up, I feel free. I want to make a success of myself.

Fountain House helps me in many respects. It helped me become more self-reliant. It's helped me become more established. It's helped me get some self-confidence.

It was the opportunity to be with others, to be with people, which was seen as the significant factor:

> The best thing about Fountain House is that it gets people together. It's so rewarding just to be with people again. I like the chance to mingle with people. I'm with people here, and this is what helps. When you have been sick and in the hospital, it's great to be with people again. It's so rewarding to meet new people; their backgrounds are so different. Most people don't appreciate what people can mean to each other, that you belong with them, that you are important to them, not just to yourself but to others.
>
> At Fountain House, we have the chance to make new friends. I've made a lot of friends here. You make new friends here and meet with them, and you also learn from them. I don't know how to say it, but Fountain House has helped me most by giving me the chance to have friends.
>
> For the first time I think I'm learning to get along with people. I'm not so afraid to associate with people any more. I'm not so afraid that people are going to make fun of me now. It's very simple, Fountain House has helped me to relate back to the world of people again.

The helpful process was viewed as being with others, both in terms of self-help and also in terms of mutual help: "You get help here because we are all together. Here, you can help others, and this is the way you help yourself. We need each other at Fountain House because we help each other. If you want to help yourself, Fountain House is very helpful. I help myself, and this is what's important. It's simple, we're being helped to help each other. Here we learn to help ourselves and help each other."

Such were the many and varied comments of the members of Fountain House. The staff regularly seeks out their views and does so for reasons which it believes are of fundamental importance to the field of psychiatric rehabilitation.

First of all, it is essential that the severely disabled psychiatric patient experience a personally relevant link to the rehabilitation environment. Unless this occurs, the individual will simply not undergo or participate in the very services which have been designed to facilitate social and vocational recovery.

It is also essential that rehabilitative staff members who have the responsibility for the supervision and development of more effective services, acquire a deeper understanding and appreciation as to what the patient finds helpful and constructive in the rehabilitation process.

Lastly, the disabled mental patient in the community is often viewed as one whose condition is chronic and who has little potential for social and vocational improvement, so that a limited affect will be permanently reflected in the rehabilitation setting. In the author's judgment, the responses of the members were not unduly simplistic, repetitive or lacking in appropriate emotional relevance. It is the task of research, of course, to demonstrate that the services in which the patient participates do indeed facilitate social and vocational recovery and that the views and impressions of the patient accurately reflect improvement in the adjustment process.

Education and Research

In recent years, Fountain House has devoted increasing resources to the development of its education and research function. Of necessity, the primary concern in the early years was the creation of rehabilitation services which might enable the psychiatric patient to make a more successful transition from the mental hospital to the community. As the first center of its kind in the United States, Fountain House was extremely fortunate to receive private funding from individual contributors and private foundation, and also substantial financial assistance from the New York State Department of Mental Hygiene. Such funding made it possible to develop services which it was believed would be helpful to the returning patient and also to construct in 1965 a large, attractive clubhouse facility located in the Times Square area of New York City.

In these early years, an educational process was present, although not formalized. Each year many visitors who were interested in the needs of the mentally ill were welcomed to observe and study Fountain House programs; and by the middle 1960's, similar organizations were established in major cities elsewhere in the United States.[12]

Although research findings were not available as to the effectiveness of rehabilitation in facilitating the community adjustment of the disabled psychiatric patient, it was abundantly clear that more and more such patients were being discharged from hospitals and were unsuccessful in rebuilding their lives in the community. Understandably, the need to provide help and assistance preceded the process of careful evaluation and formal research. Today, however, organizations such as Fountain House are in an excellent position to conduct evaluative studies which will lead to more effective services for the severely mentally ill. Such centers can then fulfill their pilot demonstration function by providing programs of education to other facilities which also serve the disabled psychiatric patient.

The research programs of Fountain House have been designed to study problems which are believed to be related to significant issues in the field of psychiatric rehabilitation. For example, a nine-year follow-up study has been completed to determine the extent to which rehabilitation services can significantly reduce the incidence and duration of psychiatric hospitalization.[6] In this study it was found that over a nine-year period, an experimental population having the opportunity to participate in rehabilitation services had essentially the same rehospitalization rate (68%) as did a control population (74%). The length of time in the hospital, however, differed significantly—4.1 out of nine years for control subjects vs. 2.6 years for experimental subjects. When the factor of exposure to rehabilitation services is studied, however, the rehospitalization rate for those who actually underwent rehabilitation was reduced from 74 to 37 percent. Furthermore, the length of time in the hospital over the nine-year period was reduced from 4.1 to 2.1 years.[15]

Current research under way at Fountain House concerns the following issues: Can more effective methods and techniques be developed to increase the psychiatric patient's level of exposure to rehabilitation services? Can "reaching-out" teams, consisting of patients undergoing the rehabilitation process, facilitate the participation of patients dropping out of services following intake? Can audiovisual techniques, for example, as well as other communication systems which spell out the opportunities available to the disabled patient in the community, influence participation? Also under study is the extent to which transitional employment facilitates vocational adjustment and the extent to which rehabilitation services are related to long-term vocational recovery. It is also most interesting to explore the ways in which the patient can participate in the evaluation process as well as contribute knowledge and information concerning the characteristics of the "helpful person" and the qualitative content of the rehabilitation process which the patient has found useful in facilitating adjustment. More specialized issues are also under study, such as the extent to which settings such as Fountain House can effectively serve the needs of the psychiatric patient who has the added disablity of deafness.[2]

With respect to the educational function, currently some 3000 visitors a year are received at Fountain House from elsewhere in the nation and also from many foreign countries. It is important for such visitors to have the opportunity to personally observe the services of Fountain House, as such experiences can stimulate similar efforts elsewhere for the severely mentally ill, not only in the United States but in such countries as Australia,[17] Israel, Pakistan[11,14] and Poland, with which close consultative and collaborative relationships have been established, including the training of foreign staff at Fountain House.[16]

For many years, Fountain House has served the traditional function of providing placements for graduate students in the fields of social work, vocational counseling psychiatric nursing, community psychiatry and social psychology. Other training opportunities are now available at Fountain House, for such facilities as community mental health centers, sheltered workshops, state mental institutions and private mental hospitals whose administrators wish to study the services of Fountain House in the planning and organization of psychiatric rehabilitation programs within their own facility. Our program of transitional employment has been of special interest, and, from an educational standpoint, the establishment of similar programs in some fifteen other centers has been most rewarding.[10]

For many years, Fountain House looked forward to the full development of its education and research function, and was extremely fortunate to establish in 1967 the van Ameringen Center for Education and Research in honor of its late president, Arnold L. van Ameringen, who for so many years was dedicated to the field of mental health and strongly advocated the rehabilitation services of Fountain House and its pilot demonstration function.

REFERENCES

1. Bean, B. R.: Creating alternatives for optimal residential care in the community. *Proceedings of a Conference on Creating the Community Alternative: Options and Innovations,* 2nd faculty presentation. Philadelphia, Horizon House Institute, 1974.
2. Beard, J. H.: *Programmatic Research in the Psychiatric Rehabilitation of Vocationally Disabled.* New York, Fountain House, Social and Rehabilitation Project 15-P-55062, 1970.
3. Beard, J. H., and Schmidt, J. R.: The use of support personnel in the rehabilitation of the psychiatrically disabled. In Pacinelli, R. N. (Ed.): *Research Utilization in Rehabilitation Facilities – Proceedings of an International Conference.* Washington, D.C., International Association of Rehabilitation Facilities, 1971.
4. Beard, J. H., Schmidt, J. R., and Smith, M. M.: The use of transitional employment in the rehabilitation of the psychiatric patient. *J Nerv Ment Dis, 136:*507-514, 1963.
5. Brubeck, T.: They came to work. *The Social and Rehabilitation Record. 1*(8):19-22, 1974.
6. Criswell, J. H.: Community roles in psychiatric rehabilitation. *Welfare in Review. 8(1):*8-15, 1970.
7. Criswell, J. H. and Beard, J. H.: Community residential facilities for the handicapped. In Cull, J. G. (Ed.): *Administrative Techniques in Rehabilitation Facility Operations.* Springfield, Thomas, 1974.
8. Crossen, M.: Fountain House: A doorway to living in the community. *Contemporary Models in Psychiatric Care and Rehabilitation,* no. 1, 1973.
9. DeSimone, A.: Industry's commitment to VR. *The Social and Rehabilitation Record, 1*(5):23-27, 1974.
10. Fountain House: Period Reports 1-17. New York, *Fountain House,* 1974.
11. Fountain House (Lahore, Pakistan): *Fountain House: A Project of Lahore Mental Health Association.* Lahore, *Fountain House,* 1973.
12. Glasscote, R. M., Cumming, E., Rutman, I. D., Sussex, J. N., and Glassman, S. M.: *Rehabilitating the Mentally Ill in the Community – A Study of Psychosocial Rehabilitation Centers.* Washington, D.C., Joint Information Service of the American Psychiatric Association and the National Association for Mental Health, 1971.
13. Hoffman, C.: Fountain House: A place where people become "drop-ins". *Mental Hygiene News, 44*(22):4-5, 1973.
14. Majid, H., Ahmad, A., and Mahmood, S. (Eds.): *Fountain House: A Project of Lahore Mental Health Association.* Lahore, *Fountain House,* 1974.
15. Malamud, T. J., Beard, J. H., and Criswell, J. H.: *Psychiatric Rehabilitation and Long-term Rehospitalization Rates: The Findings of Two Research Studies.* New York, Fountain House, 1974.

16. Maller, S. (Ed.): *Fountain House: An Approach to Psychiatric Rehabilitation—A Brief Report on the Workshop on Fountain House Held in November 1972.* Sydney, Psychiatric Rehabilitation Association, 1973.
17. Psychiatric Rehabilitation Association: *Eighteenth Annual Report and Statement of Accounts: For Year Ended 31st March, 1974.* Sydney, *Psychiatric Rehabilitation Association,* 1974.
18. Raush, H. L., and Raush, C. L.: *The Halfway House Movement: A Search for Sanity.* New York, Appleton, 1968.
19. Schmidt, J. R., Nessel, J. J., and Malamud, T. J.: *An Evaluation of Rehabilitation Services and the Role of Industry in the Community Adjustment of Psychiatric Patients Following Hospitalization: A Demonstration Research Study.* Final Report of Social and Rehabilitation Service, Grant No. RD-1281-P, New York, 1969.
20. Social and Rehabilitation Service, Division of Research Utilization: In between jobs for ex-mental patients. In *Research for People in Need: A Special Research Report.* Washington, D.C., U.S. Government Printing Office, 1974.

Chapter 26

TRANSITIONAL AND SHELTERED WORKSHOPS FOR THE MENTALLY ILL

Bertram J. Black

The past two decades have brought about an increase of transitional and sheltered work settings in the rehabilitation of the mentally ill. No longer is it necessary, as was the case in the 1950's, to prove that patients and expatients of mental hospitals have the capacity to become productive at jobs with proper training and graduated work experience. Rather, the use of special work settings today is put forward as a necessary component to any comprehensive mental health delivery system. It is by no means clear, however, how much real understanding there is among mental health professionals as to the purpose of such sheltered work settings in the rehabilitation of the mentally ill and handicapped or in their economic place in the scheme of society.

Although there is an extensive literature on rehabilitation of the mentally ill, contributed mainly by vocational rehabilitation specialists,[5,9] little of this seems to be available in current psychiatric writings. Even when rehabilitation is referred to in psychiatry, it deals mostly with housing needs, aftercare or the group and social modalities as practiced in inpatient care or day-hospitals. Other than expressions of interest or of desire that they be established, little attention has been paid until recently to such rehabilitation resources for mental patients as transitional or permanent sheltered workshops. With the pronounced modification taking place today in treatment of the seriously mentally ill, this picture is changing. It is therefore timely to review the experience with sheltered work and consider its use in the future of mental health care delivery systems.

HISTORICAL PERSPECTIVE

The changing scene in treatment of the mentally ill has, in the past decade particularly, brought about a shift in its locus from the hospital into the community. Successful treatment, especially of the chronically mentally ill, has come to embrace concern for the patient's ability to productively perform in society, not just his ability to leave the hospital. Since productive life for most adults, both men and women these days, means earning a living, there is increasing concern of psychiatry with work ability.

The use of work tests and work settings for the redevelopment and restoration of the mentally impaired has a history as old as the mental hospital. Until very recent years patients worked in every hospital—and were generally unpaid or received token payments—contributing to the upkeep of the institution. While modern psychiatric practice has for some time frowned upon such exploitation, which was often excused under the rubric of "therapeutic work," it has become illegal under federal wage and hour laws and Supreme Court decisions. In any event, except for a large residual pool of increasingly elderly and chronically enfeebled patients, few mental hospital residents remain in the institution long enough to learn efficient maintenance or upkeep tasks. This is not to say that short hospitalization itself produces or preserves work ability. Many of the patients kept from a long hospital stay are still disabled people so far as their productive ability is concerned. It has been known for years that length of hospital stay alone has little correlation with potential for work restoration.

Using community settings for restoration of work abilities, "reablement" as the British call it and "vocational rehabilitation" as Americans refer to it, has been actively attempted in this country and abroad since the early 1950's. The first of these utilized the existing sheltered work programs serving the physically handicapped. A number of these had their origins following World War I and dealt with the orthopedically disabled. Probably the first formal use of a community workshop for the mentally ill, however, was by

Altro Health and Rehabilitation Services in New York City.[6] Altro, too, had developed after World War I, but dealt exclusively with rehabilitation of long-term chronic illnesses, namely tuberculosis and heart disease. Shortly thereafter, under the impetus of the Federal Vocational Rehabilitation Act of 1954 and the mental health project grant provisions of the Public Health Services Act of 1956,[10,12] quite a number of sheltered work programs opened their doors to referrals from the mental hospitals. The writer estimates that at present there must be at least 200 sheltered workshops in the United States giving major services to the mentally ill, probably serving some 4000 to 5000 persons. Anyone familiar with the number of adult mentally ill (more than 39,000 are still in state hospitals in New York State alone) must realize that this is meeting but a tiny fraction of the need.

NATURE OF SHELTERED WORK

Sheltered workshops have been variously classified, categorized and defined. This writer prefers to use a generic term of industrial therapy to include work settings, whether real or simulated, that are used for the rehabilitation of the mentally handicapped. In these settings a variety of rehabilitation services can be rendered, including assessment, prevocational evaluation, personal adjustment training, vocational training, on-the-job training, work activity and others. Sometimes, the same job setting is used for all of these; sometimes, separate units of the facility are utilized; sometimes, whole facilities are specialized in one or some of the modalities. Many of the sheltered work programs restrict their clientele to "transitional" uses, expecting every user to move on to the normal workaday world or be counted a failure. Some shops make place for long stay or permanent employees, now referred to in the vocational rehabilitation nomenclature as "extended care" workers. A few have been set up specifically for extended care clientel. A newer category of industrial therapy was introduced into the Vocational Rehabilitation Act of 1968 as the "work activity center."[11] This is a carefully controlled licensure by the Federal Wage and Hour Division of the Department of Labor where long-term stay may be provided with earnings under the minimum wage.

Generally speaking, sheltered workshops are small businesses. They take work tasks to be performed by their employees (the patients) and must meet quality and quantity standards acceptable to customers who are motivated by profit, not philanthropy. The special design, problems and techniques for success have been elaborated upon elsewhere.[5] Suffice it to say here that one of the reasons these facilities have not been turned to by psychiatry as much as those in the rehabilitation field have desired may be that sheltered workshop management is for the most part out of the ken of the human services. The principles of service described herein represent the writer's distillation of direct experience with Altro Workshops and the extensions of Altro into mental health settings at Bronx State Hospital and in two large comprehensive community mental health centers in the Bronx. The principles have also been confirmed through his study of many other psychiatric rehabilitation settings in this country and abroad.

Assumptions and Clientele

During the past two decades the writer has learned some things of value in designing rehabilitation services for mentally ill persons through the medium of work. Practice today is based upon three positive assumptions. *First,* most of us believe that a combination of services may be more effective in dealing with psychiatric problems than any one service alone. A combination of therapeutic corrective relationships and situational tools is being utilized more. Rehabilitation workers are not quite so prone to rely entirely upon the effectiveness of psychotherapy alone, vocational counseling alone, social casework service alone or the expectation that a change of climate or a loving family will itself cause the cure. In many areas team relationships, cooperative efforts and joint enterprises are becoming the usual rather than the unusual, and it is becoming less important who does what than what one does.

A *second* positive assumption is the frank recognition that the world of work, the vocational area, represents an area of interpersonal relationships and that frequently it is not the field of work *per se* that is important so much as those factors that have to do with the patient's ability to interrelate with other human beings.

And *third,* another assumption in the field of rehabilitation for the world of work is that the work setting itself represents health to a person with mental illness. An ability to function in the workaday world, even in a sheltered work setting, tends to preserve and strengthen those areas of the ego which may at one time have been relatively conflict-free. These are the areas pertaining to perception, cognition and the integrative functions. The work environment itself, with its task orientation, imposes some limits on the fantasy preoccupations of many patients. It helps make the "acting-out symptomatology" of the ego alien. The experience of many workshops serving severely disturbed persons is that there are no serious manifestations of aggressive acting out among the psychiatric patients over long periods of time. It is in reality as though the setting itself made such behavior off limits.

Although many patients are referred for vocational rehabilitation at a stage which still seems far away from concern with their vocational future, a good sheltered work program's focus should always be on the ultimate possibility of return to the world of work. In the most extended of sheltered workshop systems, such as in the Netherlands and the British Remploy System, some 3 to 5 percent of seriously handicapped persons a year do, nevertheless, make the transition to regular employment.

Generally speaking there are three groups of patients referred for sheltered work.

First, there are those patients for whom the hospital or other referral source believes the outcome looks good; the patients appear in good remission and in good control of their capacities. They may have marketable skills. This group generally comes to sheltered work only if they have tried it on their own and failed, if they have initially referred themselves because of their own recognition of their needs or if some unusually sensitive professional person recognizes that good work and even social adjustment in the hospital are no guarantee of the same performance outside and that an individual patient might need considerable support if he is to function in the community.

The second group of patients referred to such a program consists of those for whom the assessment is that, while not quite ready for placement on a job, their past experience in the world of work has been sufficiently successful to provide an area of health to build on. They may need further skill training counseling, help in social adjustment and job placement. There is an increasing group of referrals as the treatment institutions and agencies become more adept at assessing the real potential of patients to manage their affairs outside the hospital, and there is greater willingness to coordinate ongoing treatment regimens with the specialized rehabilitation services of the community.

The third group of patients referred for vocational services, particularly to a sheltered work setting, are those for whom the treatment institution has come to an end of its resources or a saturation of its capabilities. The workshop, then, is looked upon as a consistent acceptable structure into which to place the patient with the hope that perhaps concomitant ambulatory treatment, or just the course of maturation or time, will effect some adjustment short of return to the mental institution. Frankly, this is a terrible classification. It simply illustrates that the stage at which there are clear enough diagnostic or prognostic signs for use within the mental institution at the time of treatment for the acute phase of the illness has not yet been reached.

Assessment and Initial Evaluation

How does a rehabilitation enterprise go about considering an individual referred for services? For the purposes of clarity, separate discussions on the processes of assessment and treatment follow. Most good services operate by means of a rehabilitation team or what might be more adequately described as a shared responsibility between representatives of a variety of professional disciplines. The services take very seriously the information available to them from the source of referral, which in most instances is a mental hospital. Nevertheless, it has been found of very great value to have independent assessments of the material supplied (case histories, summaries, etc.) as well as direct observation of the patient and his behavior, from the viewpoint of the psychiatrist, clinical psychologist and social caseworker and, at times, from the vocational counselor as well. Decisions as to the deployment of the agency's resources are made in conference between these various professional specialists.

In reviewing experiences over the past two decades, there are a number of elements in the intake picture which consistently have become matters of consideration and seem to strongly affect the final assessment which decides the rehabilitation course. This listing is an important first step in the process of examination of practice, for it is against this list of items that feedback processes from follow-up have begun to throw light upon their value as diagnostic and predictive media.

The elements considered in initial assessment are the following, which have been classified into eight items, some of which overlap. These are not definitive, but are essentially descriptive, and no one item should be considered alone.

PSYCHIATRIC STATUS (PARTICULARLY DEGREE OF REMISSION) : To this end one should obtain as careful a clinical history as possible, including onset, course (especially behavior during hospitalization), symptomatology, frequency and severity of relapse and response to therapy and therapists. If, at intake, a patient seems on the verge of the impulses, unable to withstand psychological testing, his readiness for rehabilitation in the world of work is certainly questionable. On the other hand, some persons with florid symptoms such as hallucinations and paranoid delusions have been accepted, provided they are burned out or there are other factors which may indicate a more favorable prognosis. For example, Mr. G., ultimately a successful case, was accepted at a point where he still had world destruction fantasies and believed that he was a missile. Nevertheless, he had an excellent work history and manifested other ego strengths. In spite of his symptoms, after a transitional experience in a sheltered workshop, he was able to return to work and maintain himself in the community, seeing a psychiatrist intermittently and a caseworker on a regular weekly basis.

It has been learned that symptomatic recoveries which immediately follow electric shock or drug administration are not reliable indices of readiness to use rehabilitation services. It is interesting to note that the number and length of hospitalizations do not appear to be significant indices of a successful outcome of rehabilitation. It may be that length of hospitalization simply reflects the prechemotherapy era.

HISTORY OF SCHOOL OR WORK ACHIEVEMENT: Obviously, if achievement in this area has been relatively conflict-free, it is indicative of a higher level of ego integration or potential capacity than if such had not been the case. Where activity has been used as a psychological defense, one can postulate a better rehabilitation prognosis.

CAPACITY FOR RELATIONSHIPS: By definition, the clients of sheltered workshops have serious problems in interpersonal relationships, yet this must be considered relatively. One young woman with a history of poor object relations, with the delusion that she had a dwarf in her stomach and with a history of poor impulse control did have in her background a meaningful constructive relationship with a teacher; and this made it possible for her to involve herself in a therapeutic relationship with her caseworker, to accept as positive the authoritative relationship in a work situation and, ultimately, to achieve a rather high level of adjustment. The question of "who were the patient's ego ideals" frequently is helpful in the assessment process. For example, some success has been noted with depressed middle-aged men who had a background of working in their fathers' businesses, where the fathers had been economically successful.

SECONDARY GAINS: The author believes the question of secondary gains is an important clue to capacity for rehabilitation. The extent to which the illness meets the needs of other members of the family is important to know in handling the situation. Frequently, the key to successful outcome has had to be work with the family; for so long as the illness of the patient is more comfortable to the family than his health, it is difficult to achieve results. Conversely, everyone is conscious of the negative implications of otherwise socially useful instruments, such as pension plans or insurance payments, and the secondary gains of these must be clearly understood.

STRENGTH OF SYMBIOTIC TIES: In those instances where the patient has never been able to move away from his mother in any real sense, positive results are not likely to be achieved. The threat of independence carries the prospect of intolerable loss for both parent and child. Again, there seems to be a direct correlation between the patient's capacity for making independent living arrangements and rehabilitation success. Assumptions, however, as to the strength of symbiotic ties must not be made too casually. It is only after serious attempts through treatment have been made to lessen this all-embracing tie that sometimes the conclusion must regretfully be reached that rehabilitation for the world of work is not possible.

MOTIVATION: Experience has shown that a patient's expression of positive motivation for rehabilitation for the world of work is rare. Ambivalance is the rule rather than the exception. This seems to be related to the tremendous dependency needs of most of these patients, their fear of any change in their tenuous equilibrium, the threat to the psychic economy that is served by the psychotic symptoms and the fear of aggression implied in activity. Though most people have a basic drive toward health, many of the people referred for psychiatric rehabilitation seem to have this effectively masked by the need to hold on to their illnesses.

PSYCHOLOGICAL TESTING: The information available from a consistent series of tests, applied by a competent clinical psychologist who shares in the intake assessment, serves to add a dimension to understanding the applicant that might not otherwise be available. The ability of the patient to tolerate the testing is an additional clue to his ability to make use of a rehabilitation service. Interpretation of figure drawings provides some valuable clues. Psychological tests have contributed to the assessment of capacity for impulse control, understanding of defense systems and appraisal of patients' tolerance for frustrations in the workshop setting; and to some aptitude assessment.

NEGATIVE CRITERIA: At the beginning of the author's experience, he had no positive criteria for the selection of patients, but had established as negative criteria for the elimination of applicants the following. He did not take patients with histories of brain damage, narcotic addiction or such severe assaultive behavior as might constitute damage to themselves or others in the workshop setting. Occasionlly of course, even with careful screening, a patient will get through who has such a history. And occasionally too, the rehabilitation results will even be successful. For example, one very depressed schizophrenic young man was admitted and was subsequently found to be a marijuana addict. However, he smoked only on weekends, as an antidote to loneliness and depression. Since his rehabilitation, he has been working for three years, though his adjustment is tenuous. Frequently, assaultive behavior turns out to be more symbolic than real, though on occasion referral sources have withheld real histories of dangerous symtomatology, and this has never been an advantage either to the patient or to the workshop.

Responsibility for Service

The question is often raised as to who assesses what and who carries responsibility for treatment as the patients move into and beyond the workshop. The Altro experience of the actual behavior of an intake or assessment team is illustrative of what has become recognized as a productive model. A description of the patient is provided by the referring institution or agency as well as the social situation adhering, as presented by the intake social worker. This may be augmented by discussion from a representative of the referring agency. The intake psychiatrist then presents the result of his examination of the patient. This is a form of clinical evaluation plus interpretation of clinical data supplied by the referring institution, and it ends with a tentative recommendation by the psychiatrist as to acceptance or rejection of the patient.

The clinical description is then followed by the psychologist's summarization and interpretation of the results of the psychological tests, as well as the presentation and interpretation of psychological testing material which may have been supplied through the referring institution. The psychologist, too, independently of the psychiatrist and the social worker, makes his recommendation as to the acceptance or rejection of the patient.

The social worker has already indicated his opinion with regard to accepting the patient for rehabilitation. In those instances where a strong vocational component exists, the vocational counselor on the team will at this point express his opinion with regard to the feasibility of vocational rehabilitation. This may come, in most instances, from perusal of the intake or referral information. In some cases, however, either at the request of the psychiatrist, psychologist, social worker or even the vocational specialist himself, a vocational interview may be held with the applicant prior to the intake conference.

Following these formal presentations, the meeting is open to general discussion. The intake meeting is attended by the agency's chief psychiatrist, the examining psychiatrists, the social caseworker, the clinical psychologist, the vocational specialist and a representative of the administrative staff. It is difficult for the outsider to make a determination sometimes as to who is chairman of the meeting, for all members are considered to be offering contributions of equal professional merit, and it is rare that the element of arbitration has to be utilized to achieve a decision.

The functions of the psychiatrist, social caseworker and clinical psychologist (who in this agency takes responsibility for testing) need little elaboration. The vocational specialist, who cannot see every patient, can offer a valuable consultative opinion in these meetings and is particularly looked to for his judgment as to where the applicant should be placed in the shop. (A member of the administrative staff is always present at intake meetings for occasional questions of community policy, of inter-agency relationships, of public relations or of management of the symptomatology of an individual, when a decision is required as to the agency's willingness to deal with matters which are outside the clinical rehabilitation practitioner's area of authority or even of competence.)

The intake team has learned that it is important if the patient is not accepted that there be a full and careful explanation in terms understandable to the referring hospital or agency as to the reasons for reaching this conclusion. Equally important is the handling of rejection with the patient. The teams have found that in instances where it becomes necessary, they have been able to help the patient reject them so that his experience with their intake does not add to his already low self-esteem. Often he can be helped to reject them on the basis that he does not need all the specialized services. As a community-based rehabilitation program, Altro does not carry ongoing medical treatment responsibility for the patients under its care. Following the concept which has been the warp and woof of Altro's philosophy for sixty years now, ongoing medical treatment responsibility for people with chronic handicapping conditions should rest with the hospital, outpatient departments or private medical practitioners. It is vitally important to the sheltered work program to have adequate psychiatric consultation, to contribute to the psychodynamic understanding of the patient's illness and to provide a point of contact with medical personnel of other treating institutions. The field of psychiatric treatment being what it is, medical psychiatric staff is used for brief psychotherapeutic intervention where indicated in special situations and for determining when hospitalization is indicated. For the most part, however, the psychiatrists function as consultants to caseworkers, helping them to handle emergencies, exacerbations of psychiatric conditions, renewed flare-ups, etc. They carry a teaching responsibility; they assume responsibility for control of chemotherapy. In large cities it is not unusual for patients to have access to a number of medical institutions, each of which might be prescribing different tranquilizing drugs. Finding psychiatrists who are able and willing to work in a rehabilitation type of setting has not been easy. Such a psychiatrist must be not only a good clinician, but a good consultant and a good teacher of others.

As is true of most rehabilitation settings based in the community, in which the emphasis is on preparation for the world of work, the primary professional discipline which deals most intensively with the patient is that of rehabilitation counseling. In the Altro setting, the rehabilitation counselors are social caseworkers and graduates of schools of social work, with training and experience in the field of medical, psychiatric or family casework. Each patient is assigned to a caseworker who sees him regularly once or twice a week during the period at the workshop. In the assignment of patients to the caseworkers, serious consideration is given to the matching of the client or patient with the caseworker. Some elements considered are the client's need for mothering, the need for strong feminine or masculine identification, the capacity of the worker to sympathize and understand the culture of the client, personal traits of the worker such as humor and intellectual interests, the capacity for maintaining distance or offering closeness and the capacity to fill gaps in areas of the patient's greatest deprivation.

The role of the vocational counselor is a highly specialized one. Though in New York City there is cooperation from such agencies as New York State Employment Services, and voluntary employment and guidance agencies, the inclusion of a vocational specialist on the staff provides knowledge specific to the world of work. As noted above, the vocational specialist helps in the placement of patients at the workshop. He also takes responsibility for evaluative procedures at the workshop and participates in vocational assessments with the assistance of the workshop foremen and management. Relationships with specialized vocational agencies are further enhanced by the presence of a vocational counselor on the staff.

Nurses at the workshop with industrial and psychiatric experience are important members of the team. They are the professional people who are at the workshop at all times and who have regular opportunity for observation of the behavior of the patients. They also assume the functions of an industrial nurse, such as concern with attendance, first aid and drug administrations. They participate in evaluation conferences. The shop personnel, foremen and supervisors are not professionals, but are skilled workmen in their respective fields.

Extensions of the Altro Workshops into Bronx State Hospital have brought variations of the same structure, though the principles remain intact. Since the patients, whether of inpatient or outpatient status, are in active psychiatric treatment, a direct liaison program is maintained between the sheltered workshop and the treatment service. The liaison staff are rehabilitation assistants, who maintain communication lines and serve as intake guides to other rehabilitation resources. A similar program has been developed for the Soundview-Throgs Neck and the Lincoln Comprehensive Mental Health Centers.[8]

These programs, Altro Workshops and its satellite sheltered workshops avoid attempting to solve an enigma that has puzzled mental health professionals and all but destroyed a number of former rehabilitation ventures. The question is whether modern psychiatric treatment does or does not embrace rehabilitation, since in many minds the goals are identical. One could just as easily take the position that good rehabilitation includes good treatment. The fact is that with medically chronic illness, the goal of treatment is to alleviate symptoms while the goal of rehabilitation is to help the patient to function socially even though his symptoms cannot be relieved. Both approaches are necessary, and it matters little which is considered precedent.

Treatment Techniques

Professional techniques should rest upon a base of psychodynamic understanding, therapeutic empathy, a holistic view of the patient in his milieu (familial, social and vocational), and the use of practical concrete services as required. Treatment of the schizophrenic first and foremost involves an emotional commitment. The techniques used have been described in previous articles in greater detail.[2]

A few of these are

1. handling of resistances,
2. reality testing,
3. the educative process,
4. helping the patient live with his symptoms—encapsulating the illness,
5. continuity of service after the workshop and
6. service to families.

As noted above, the sheltered workshop is a valuable therapeutic tool provided its inherent qualities are constructively and creatively utilized.

1. Enabling the client to use the workshop frequently necessitates handling of resistances at least sufficiently to permit a beginning involvement in the work setting. Conflicts, conscious and unconscious, take many forms and are defended against in numerous ways. Among the most frequent is denial of illness, appearing in many guises. This is hardly surprising in many people who are not in touch with their feelings at all and for whom the threat of facing the underlying rage and anxiety is overwhelming. Sometimes, people have marketable skills and high IQ's. Often, these persons do not see the need for any transitional workshop experience. Therefore, why enter a workshop program at all? Efforts have to be directed towards helping the patient make some degree of acknowledgment of his illness, while concomitantly offering ego support. Other patients express resistance by withdrawal. They may be unable to get up in the morning, even with an alarm clock. One cannot, of course, help such a person, unless he can be reached through some form of communication. Techniques of handling

initial resistance are often predicated upon the counselor's conviction as to the value of rehabilitation and his capacity to transmit this. The right of self-determination is part of modern social philosophy, but self-determination must be predicated on emotional readiness to make decisions and to accept the end results. The person with overwhelming anxiety, ambivalence in every area and intense confusion is often not in a position to do this and may need to "borrow our egos and supergos" awhile in order to move at all.

2. Reality testing is a most familiar function of all professional services. In the workshop setting, one can realistically appraise achievement in production and at the same time have objective observation of interpersonal phenomena. One knows when a foreman is really overdemanding; getting too close, fearful or resentful of the patient; or conversely, overprotective or distant. One is also apt to know when other patients are provocative. One can set limits as one way of bringing reality into focus. This is emotionally therapeutic in defining ego boundaries and in controlling aggression.

3. All therapy is an educational process in that one learns the recurrent patterns that produce difficulties and hopefully learns how to deal with them. On a simple level, many of the patients need to be taught some of the elementary ways of coping with daily problems. For one patient, this may mean learning how to order a meal in a restaurant; for another, it may mean structuring the use of money and time; for still another, it may be reviewing study methods. Some patients even have to be taught when to smile, when to ask a question, etc.

4. Helping the patient live with his psychosis is frequently a necessary goal, though with some patients, one can be more ambitious toward basic personality changes. Involved in this is teaching the patient the danger signals and offering him active emotional support to sustain him while he learns to understand the events which may precipitate difficulties and his usual destructive mode of coping with them.

5. Continuity and availability of service through the post-workshop period and job adjustment are basic principles of rehabilitation service. For some individuals it is imperative that they have access to the helping person at points of crises, whether on week-

ends, nights or whatever. This does not mean, however, perpetual giving, which for many would not be helpful.

6. The role of the family in relation to vocational rehabilitation requires a book in itself. As the root source of problems in interpersonal relationships, no adequate assessment of personality and vocational potential can ignore a consideration of the family's role. In some situations one can easily point to the direct relationship between vocational choice and performance and familial factors. Direct contact with families at the point of intake should be part of good vocational rehabilitation policy. Family contact certainly enhances diagnostic appraisal of the interactions directly observed.

Changes in family equilibrium occasioned by the increasing independence, autonomy and health of the sick person whose illness served a purpose in the family homeostasis often produce a problem in work adjustment.

Parental and sibling transferential manifestations, in terms of expectations and distortions in relation to the boss and other employees, are ever present. Often these distortions can be handled sufficiently, though indirectly, to permit the patient to remain on the job.

In relation to families the usual focus is on the problem of patients as adult children. Equally important are the problems of patients who are expected to carry on their roles as parents. There is some evidence pointing to the need for more thoughtful consideration of the factors which make it impossible for some women to reassume the role of mother though they may be vocationally rehabilitated and may function fairly successfully. The responsibility for their children should not be forced upon them by the community. The psychiatrist should share in making decisions in these areas.

During these past years the writer has learned some specific things about the sheltered workshop setting and the rehabilitation values that can be expected from its use. He believes these are worth mentioning at this point because, with the growth and the development of sheltered work programs across the country, there will be more and more opportunity to utilize such resources. Five benefits (among many) that the sheltered work setting can offer are

1. An opportunity to manipulate closeness and distance in the work setting. In an early paper on the Altro experience, Doctor Leopold Bellak and the writer referred to Shopenhauer's parable of the porcupines, who, in hibernation, cannot get so close that they prick each other, nor yet so far apart that they freeze. This porcupine distance can almost be measured for certain patients. It cannot ordinarily be surmised easily, but in the sheltered work setting where observation offers an opportunity for testing limits, some fine clues on this score may be obtained for vocational placement planning.[1]
2. The workshop offers an opportunity for gratification and security through earning. Of course, real work on the outside does too; but many patients are not, at the beginning, ready to take their place in the normal workaday world.
3. The work setting may be used for reality testing in a way that would not be allowed in normal work settings. The patient does not risk being fired if he overreacts to set limits.
4. There is an opportunity to examine transference manifestations in a relatively safe environment. It is less anxiety-provoking in the course of therapy to look at one's attitudes and behavior in relation to fellow employee than directly in relation to the therapist whom one cannot afford to alienate.
5. Demonstrable achievement in terms of productivity and constructive modification in interpersonal relationships strengthen the ego. The workshop provides opportunities for skill training and the development of good work habits.

After a relatively short period at a sheltered workshop, there is an unusual amount of information available as to the ability of the patient to function in various ways, his relationships with other workers, the symptoms which remain or have vanished and his attitude toward the work setting. Those from the field of vocational rehabilitation are familiar with the term "personal adjustment training," the process of preparing a patient for work habits and acceptable social behavior. A sheltered workshop is constantly involved in personal adjustment training, either formally or informally. The writer has already mentioned utilization of the workshop as a holding center, a structured setting in which to place the patient while continuing with other therapeutic intervention or awaiting development of plans: those under way in the rehabilitation setting or in cooperation with other agencies.

CONTINUITY OF CARE

Some positive assumptions which are basic to the provision of rehabilitation services for the world of work have been considered. There are, however, some problems of the therapeutic continuum in society which carry with them negative assumptions. These constitute areas which need some serious consideration in future planning for more adequate rehabilitation of the mentally ill. The first of these is an assumption, strongly held in the field of the helping professions, that if a person has a need and a resource exists in the community to meet this need, some intangible magnetic force will bridge the gap and draw them together. In the writer's experience, he has been impressed by the fact that, if such a force does in fact exist, it is of the magnetic variety that both attracts and repels. The writer is continuously appalled at the way patients habitually fall between the cracks of excellent available services. He can only suggest some of the reasons why this is so. In spite of the existence of resources, there is frequently a lack of knowledge of one or the other. Secondly, there are cumbersome processes of referral. Thirdly, there are a number of professional barriers to easy use of referral sources. Some of these stem from staff shortages, but often they stem from inadequate training or countertransferential phenomena. For example, very frequently the level of the IQ, the vocational skills or the sociocultural background are treated as isolated elements, and plans are made in relationship to them rather than giving them their proper perspective in relation to a wider array of factors.

Many persons in the field speak of the need for an intergrated continuous service and frequently indulge in a kind of magical thinking, not too different from that of the schizophrenic, that because they talk about this comprehensive service, it automatically exists. Paper programs are easily achieved, but some questions must be asked: How many agencies make their services available to the chronically mentally ill after six months or a year? How often are cases closed because the patient appeared to be getting along after a brief period of one or two months? Who stands by when a crisis occurs after two years have gone by? No agency can be everything to everyone, and perhaps one has to face the fact that certain structures can be available only for certain time periods. At the same time wishful thinking will not achieve integrated continuous service. Serious consideration must be given to whether the same teams or the same professional groups can achieve the responsibility for integration or continuity; and how, if different resources are needed at different periods, the necessary bridges can be achieved so that for the patient in the community, real continuity does exist. The writer has been increasingly impressed with the economy of continuity in service. He has found that a readiness to be available during crises paid off in the long run. He has seen patients who decompensate (some after one year, some after five or six), who again require only a few weeks of intensive service to enable them to go on at a fairly acceptable level of performance in the community. The cost of achieving an understanding between the rehabilitation agency and the resource that makes such short-term treatment available is not great.

The positive assumption, enunciated earlier in this paper, that a combination of services is often more effective than one alone does not happen to be very widely held outside of the rehabilitation field itself. It becomes discouraging at times to discover that colleagues in the profession and among the agencies are too frequently concerned with the question, "To whom does the patient belong?" rather than "Is the patient being served?" The assumption that if the patient has a meaningful relationship with one therapeutic intervener he is satisfactorily taken care of, is more widely held than the assumption that more than one kind of service may be necessary at the same time. Within the hospital this takes the form of an assessment that so long as the patient is showing up for psychotherapeutic sessions, there is no need for any other service to him. In the community it means that if the patient is being cared for adequately in a mental health center, one need not be concerned as to how he is getting along in the world of work.

Another assumption frequently made is that the available knowledge of treatment techniques that exists is actually being applied. Some time ago an eminent scientist made the observation that even in the realm of theoretical physics, the greatest need is not for more knowledge but for more constructive application of what is already known. There is a huge gap to be filled between the principles and understanding that have been developed, for example, in psychoanalytically oriented treatment approaches and their use in the routine decisions often made about an individual's vocational direction. Fortunately, some music played by ear is good, but the talent necessary for playing by ear is not easily transmittable. Professional concepts, on the other hand, can be taught. One area in which this gap can become excrutiatingly clear is in dealing with the younger patient. Many are too prone to translate the concept of rehabiltation for the younger person into the term "habilitation" and to believe they have accomplished something. What is badly needed is to transpose the dynamic and conceptual understanding with regard to educational and psychological maturation and to evolve the techniques based upon this understanding towards the treatment and rehabilitation of the younger patient. Demonstrations have shown that the transitional sheltered workshop can be of great value with this age group.[3]

Rehabilitation workers must set in motion the processes that will help them learn the outcome of the service and provide the feedback from experience. Follow-up must be thought of not only in its research sense but in terms of learning what is the minimal amount of necessary service from the community that will enable patients to retain the positive effects of the rehabilitation services that have been rendered them.

Experience with rehabilitation of long-term chronically ill people for the world of work has led the writer to voice two hypotheses that bear testing. One of these is that continuity of care requires a follow-up for years after service has been given. Whether by letter, telephone call or a friendly visit, some structured service should be available on a consistent basis so that the ex-patient is not "lost" by the very society that has expended so much in treating him in the first place. Such a follow-up is necessary to head off the crises that inevitably occur where chronicity exists. Years ago, Doctor Howard Rusk used the concept of maintaining an umbilical thread to the patient in dealing with physical impairments. In rehabilitation of the tubercular, the writer spoke of "a stitch in time" saving nine. Even though such a plan may seem repugnant to advocates of civil rights for patients, it should be tried as one part of the community continuum to maintain rehabilitation for the mental patient who has achieved it.

The second hypothesis has to do with the concept that a number of services are better than a single one in rehabilitation of the mentally ill. Agencies, both public and private, have great difficulties in cooperating together. Too many threats to differing goals, priorities, standards and methods of operation exist. The old saw of "I'll coo and you operate,"" or vice versa, always seems to hold. It may be that a solution could be found in the real estate principle of the condominium: There could be a sharing only in the limited area of overlap, without threats to the inviolability of the basic structures of the agencies.

THE FUTURE OF SHELTERED WORK

Though the growth in the number of sheltered workshops has seemed abysmally slow to those concerned with psychiatric rehabilitation, the interest in them has never wavered. Now, with the pressures to move increasing numbers of patients out of state hospitals and into a community network of mental health care, the interest in sheltered workshop development appears to be on the verge of a boom—a boom, that is, if two obstacles can be overcome. One of these is the availability of personnel trained in sheltered workshop supervision and management; the other is the dampening effect of an inflationary economy upon the opening of any new small businesses.

The first of these, availablity of trained personnnel, was well on the way to solution under the stimulation of federal funding to a number of university rehabilitation counselor training centers. Now that federal support for training is diminishing, state and local mental health and rehabilitation funding will have to be used if specialized staffing is to be available. In state hospital and community mental health center staffing, the categories of mental health aide or assistant can be used for sheltered workshop supervisory personnel. Management personnel will require a combination of business experience and on-the-job training.

The second obstacle relates to availability of work to be done, its marketing and sales. Some subsidy from government will always be required, for sheltered workshops exist for other reasons than making a profit. It will always take imagination and initiative to procure the kind of work at which mental patients can be productive and at prices that allow for fair remuneration in accord with federal and state wage and hour laws. That this can be done is attested to by the workshops now performing even in a tight business market.

One interesting possibility for developing industrial therapeutic settings of the transitional sort is organizing units of a regular business or industry. This has been done in England;[5] it is being tried to a limited extent in New York. A comprehensive rehabilitation center known as Fountain House, discussed in the preceding chapter, has a cooperative program in the clerical trades with two department stores. In these, as in the British factories, groups of patients perform normal work in a unit under joint supervision by the regular foreman and special staff from the rehabilitation program. Industry spokesmen are not usually enthusiastic about such a scheme. They find it more acceptable either to make a financial donation to charity or to supply work to an entirely separate sheltered workshop under nonprofit or governmental auspices.

Industrial physicians point to the disadvantage of labeling certain employees or potential employees by having such a unit of "foster work" in the plant. While labeling is a real danger in dealing with psychiatric patients, it has long seemed that a greater danger exists for the mental patient who has no transitional opportunity to the workaday world. The social institution of work cannot easily be incorporated into the healing institutions without violating the culture and mores of earning a living. The closer transitional and extended care work can be to the normalcy of the job world, the greater its benefit in developing productive participation in our society.

REFERENCES

1. Bellak, Leopold, Black, Bertram, J., Lurie, Abraham, and Miller, Joseph S. A.: Rehabilitation of the mentally ill through controlled transitional employment. *Am J Orthopsychiatry, XXVI*(2), April 1956.

2. Benney, Celia: Casework and the sheltered workshop in rehabilitation of the mentally ill. *Social Casework, 51*(11), November 1960.
3. Benney, Celia, Black, Bertram, J., Franke, Hilde, Gresben, Sherman P., and Lehman, Ethna: Facilitating functioning of mentally ill young adults. *Social Casework, 52*(7), July 1971.
4. Benney, Celia, and Waltzer, Shirley: Treatment of the ambulatory schizophrenic in a rehabilitation center. *Ment Hyg, 42*(3), July 1958.
5. Black, Bertram J.: *Principles of Industrial Therapy for the Mentally Ill.* New York, Grune and Stratton, 1970.
6. Black, Bertram J.: The protected workshop. *Rehabilitation of the Mentally Ill.* Washington, D.C., Publication No. 58, American Association for the Advancement of Science, 1959.
7. Black, Bertram J.: The workshop in a changing world; the three faces of the sheltered workshop. *Rehabil Lit, XXVI*(8), August, 1965.
8. Black, (Bertram J., and Kase, Harold M.: *Vocational Rehabilitation Services in Comprehensive Community Mental Health Centers.* New York, Altro Health and Rehabilitation Services, 1973.
9. Nelson, Nathan: *Workshops for the Handicapped in the United States.* Springfield, Thomas, 1971.
10. Public Law 113, 78th Cong.
11. Public Law 391, 90th Cong.
12. Public Law 911, 84th Cong.

PART SIX

THE CHALLENGE OF THE ALCOHOLIC PATIENT

Chapter 27

REHABILITATION OF THE ALCOHOLIC*

SHELDON ZIMBERG

Extent of the Problem

IN THE U.S. DEPARTMENT OF Health, Education and Welfare report to the Congress, *Alcohol and Health,*[5] it was noted that alcohol is the most abused drug in the United States. Further, it was observed that alcoholism has reached major proportions and was increasing in prevalence. There are estimated to be about 95 million drinkers in the United States, and of these about 9 million men and women are alcohol abusers. This represents 5 percent of the adult population.

Only 3 to 5 percent of the alcoholic population are represented by the most visible alcoholics, the homeless public intoxicants in the skid rows across the country. Most alcoholics are working or homemakers. It has been estimated that up to 5 percent of the nation's work force are alcoholic individuals and that almost another 5 percent are serious alcohol abusers.

Alcohol is a major factor in highway deaths among drivers and pedestrians. In a recent year alcohol played a role in the deaths of 28,000 people.

Alcoholism has a major effect on the economy. It is estimated that it costs about $10 billion a year due to lost work and accidents in business, industry, government and the military.

Public intoxication accounts for one third of all arrests reported annually in this country. If such alcohol-related offenses as

*Although the scope of this volume did not allow inclusion of a chapter on the rehabilitation of drug abusers, many of the concepts pertaining to the rehabilitation of the alcoholic apply to those disabled by drug addiction. (Editor)

driving while intoxicated, disorderly conduct and vagrancy are included, the proportion of alcohol-related arrests would be between 40 and 49 percent. Thus, a major proportion of law enforcement time and court involvement in a fruitless effort of dealing with the public manifestations of alcoholism has little impact on the problem of alcoholism itself.

It has recently been reported that about 50 percent of the homicides committed in New York City have involved a situation where either the victim, the perpetrator or both were under the influence of alcohol at the time the violence occurred.

Alcoholism is a significant problem in marital discord, contributing to at least 20 percent of the divorces in the United States. The effect on the family of the alcoholic, particularly on the children, can be devastating.

Thus, the effect of alcoholism in our society is enormous and goes far beyond the individual with the alcohol problem.

Resistances to the Provision of Services to Alcoholics

In view of the enormous extent of alcoholism in our country, and the disability, death, social disruptions and impact on the criminal justice system, it seems paradoxical that so little effort and resources are devoted to the treatment of this condition. Considerable resources in health, social welfare agencies, police and courts are expended in the dealing with the consequences of this condition, but little with the condition itself.

The question that arises is why does such a situation exist? Why are medical students intrigued by the pathophysiology of Laennec's cirrhosis and why do they totally reject the person who has a diseased liver? Several explanations appear relevant to understand this syndrome of massive denial of responsibility toward helping the alcoholic who may appear at any agency or be the neighbor down the street or the fellow employee in the next office.

The first factor is the great amount of ambivalence toward drinking in our society. This ambivalence resulted in the enactment of Prohibition, forbidding the sale of alcoholic beverages, and its subsequent repeal. The existence of ambivalence toward drinking in a society seems to be related to a high prevalence of alcoholism.[8] This ambivalence produces strong polarities of feelings toward alcohol abuse. There is the tendency among abstainers to label as alcoholics those individuals who consume even modest amounts of alcohol. For those who drink regularly and are so-called "social drinkers," the line between alcohol use and alcohol abuse is often quite blurred. Since most of the adult population does drink alcohol and the cocktail party is an institutionalized part of American society, the evaluation of someone else as an alcoholic puts one's own drinking practices on the line. Rather than do that, it is less anxiety-provoking not to make such an evaluation in a social or professional relationship.

A second factor that seems to be operative is the belief that alcoholism is not really an illness, but is somehow a moral weakness and that those who succumb to this weakness are inferior people. They are labeled and stigmatized as "bums" with the stereotype of the skid-row homeless man. Many persons have had encounters with the homeless public intoxicant, and the most common reaction to such individuals is not to see them at all, to treat them as nonpersons. The image of the alcoholic, thus, becomes the skid-row derelict. Individuals who are abusing alcohol but are still working, living with their families and riding on the commuter railroads everyday do not appear to be derelicts, and therefore, they are not alcoholics. The fact is that only about 5 percent of alcoholics are skid-row individuals. The most common place to find an alcoholic is on one's own street. Doctors try to protect their patients and social workers, their clients, by not telling them they have a drinking problem because to do so would label them as "bums." Of course, the alcoholic is usually the last person to find out he has a drinking problem and the protective efforts to avoid confronting him only feed into his or her denial of the problem.

The third factor that seems to operate is the belief that alcoholism is an untreatable condition. Evidence exists, however, that treatment can be effective for many patients.[3,4,6,7,9] The self-help program of Alcoholics Anonymous that exists on an international basis is an example of an effective approach for many alcoholics. Treatment success has been reported as low as 4 percent for programs serving skid-row alcoholics to as high as 80 percent for industrial alcoholism programs where the individual's job is dependent upon his recovery from the drinking problem. Thus, alcoholism has been truly characterized as *the most treatable of untreated diseases.* The basic lack of education in the professional schools about alcoholism and the lack of knowledge of the existence of effective treatment approaches coupled with the large number of alcoholics encountered in health professionals' activities serves to make this a problem area that is better not seen, to avoid a great deal of anxiety.

Developing Comprehensive Treatment Services

Alcoholism is a complex disease whose etiology is not understood. Authorities generally agree that three factors are involved in the production of alcoholism, namely, sociocultural attitudes toward drinking and drunkenness, psychological factors and physiological factors which may be genetically determined. This illness is a chronic illness with a high potential for relapse. In this respect, it is quite similar to schizophrenia, cardiovascular disease or diabetes. The basic difference, of course, in relation to these other chronic diseases is the conscious, although compulsive, consumption of an external substance. If there were no alcohol, there would be no alcoholism. However, this fact alone does not completely separate alcoholism from other chronic disorders because the uncontrolled and compulsive use of alcohol is itself an integral part of the pathogenesis of the disease, just as an uncontrolled reaction to stress may precipitate an attack of diabetic acidosis in a diabetic.

Besides being a chronic disorder, alcoholism is a condition that exists in various stages of severity. Table 27-I shows criteria that approximately define levels of alcohol abuse on a six-point scale. This scale has been found useful to roughly gauge the degree of alcohol abuse and to measure changes in severity that might occur through treatment. Therefore, alcohol abuse is not an all-or-none phenomenon, but one of degree. The less severe the condition, often the greater the degree of treatment success.

TABLE 27-I

Scale of Alcohol Abuse

None	Drinks only on occasion, if at all.
Minimal	Drinking is not conspicuous, occasional intoxications (up to four per year). No social, family, occupational, health or legal problems related to drinking.
Mild	Intoxications occurring up to once a month, although generally limited to evening or weekends; and/or some impairment in social or family relations or occupational functioning related to drinking. No physical or legal problems related to drinking.
Moderate	Frequent intoxications, up to one or two times per week; and/or significant impairment in social, family or occupational functioning. Some suggestive evidence of physical impairment related to drinking, such as tremors, frequent accidents, epigastric distress, loss of appetite at times. No history of DT's, cirrhosis, nutritional deficiency, hospitalizations related to drinking or arrests related to drinking.
Severe	Almost constant drinking (practically every day). History of DT's, cirrhosis, chronic brain syndrome, neuritis or nutritional deficiency. Severe disruption in social or family relations. Unable to hold a steady job, but able to maintain himself on public assistance. One or more arrests related to drinking (drunk or disorderly). One or more hospitalizations related to drinking.
Extreme	All of the characteristics of severe impairment plus homelessness and/or inability to maintain himself on public assistance.

The most widely accepted criterion of treatment success is abstinence from alcohol with improvement in an individual's social, vocational and physical health status. Some authors have felt that a return to social drinking may be possible for some alcohol abusers.[10] This may be true; however, it is currently impossible to predict which alcoholic individual could return safely to the social use of alcohol without resort to compulsive loss of control dirnking. Since most alcoholics have the illusion that one day they can return to social drinking, such a goal held out to patients would encourage their belief that eventually they will be able to continue their drinking. Such an attitude is part of the psychological pattern of the chronic alcohol abuser and is characterized by "going on the wagon" periodically. Therefore, to hold out such an expectation to patients is telling them what they want to hear and is antitherapeutic. For all practical purposes, abstinence must remain the goal in the treatment of the alcoholic.

The writer will not attempt to discuss the various forms of therapy that exist in the treatment of the alcoholic or to evaluate their effectiveness. A booklet on *Alcoholism Treatment and Rehabilitation: Selected Abstracts*[1] has been prepared by the National Institute of Alcohol Abuse and Alcoholism and presents material in this area. However, the writer will present a model describing the service components of a comprehensive approach to the delivery of alcoholism treatment and rehabilitation services which recognizes the large extent of the problem, the chronic nature of the condition and various levels of severity that will be encountered.

A comprehensive program for the treatment of the alcoholic should be based on the public health model of primary, secondary and tertiary prevention of disability. This means that efforts should be directed at establishing methods of preventing the development of new cases of alcoholism as a primary preventive approach; of diagnosing and treating alcoholics as early in their illness as possible as secondary prevention; and on the tertiary level, of minimizing the illness of severely disabled alcoholics through rehabilitation and supportive approaches.

The area of primary prevention is important in an illness like alcoholism. An experiment in primary prevention took place in the United States through Prohibition. Although that approach produced a large illegal network of manufacture and sale and a great amount of associated criminal activities, the incidence of cirrhosis of the liver declined during the years of Prohibition. However, this approach was abandoned as unworkable.

Other approaches to primary prevention need continued research to determine their potential effectiveness. Studies on predictive factors among the young that may contribute to alcohol abuse included the history of having an alcoholic father and/or mother, deviant behavior in other areas of life, parental rejection and deprivation, impulsivity and alienation from family, friends or society. Young people known to have such a history might be involved in counseling programs designed to help them avoid the use of alcohol. However, such an approach would require major efforts at screening potential alcoholics and the development of massive services. Efforts in the drug abuse field have not been very productive to date.

There is more and more evidence that a genetic factor may be involved in the development of alcoholism. If this evidence is supported by additional data, the use of genetic counseling and early intervention to prevent the development of alcoholism in later life might be indicated.

It has been noted that some cultures that use alcohol have low rates of alcoholism compared to others.[8] Research to determine what sociocultural factors contribute to low rates of alcoholism might be useful to change social practices and attitudes toward drinking in a given society. High rates of consumption of alcohol have been noted to be associated with high rates of alcoholism. Efforts to decrease consumption of alcohol through increase of taxes on alcoholic beverages, reduction of hours for the sale of bottled alcohol and shorter hours for bars to be open should also be explored for possible impact on the rate of alcoholism.

Such approaches to primary prevention are important in understanding the epidemiology of alcoholism and may contribute to reduction in the number of alcoholics in a community.

In the area of secondary prevention, early treatment of an alcoholic and the availability of 24-hour emergency services are necessary parts of this approach. In alcoholism, as in other chronic disorders, recognizing the condition early in its course generally leads to a better prognosis. In this area of early recognition, massive educational efforts for health professionals, business and industrial groups and community service agencies are essential to overcome the resistances described above. Alcoholism programs in industry have been particularly successful in treating alcoholics through the alcoholic's fear of losing his job.

The area of secondary prevention should include the availability of 24-hour emergency services including, in particular, medical services, since serious medical problems often are to be found in alcoholic individuals. Detoxification services for individuals who show alcohol withdrawal symptoms, who have a potential for alcohol withdrawal symptoms or who desire detoxification from alcohol are a necessary part of an alcoholism treatment program. The presentation of an alcoholic in a crisis is often the most strategic time to engage the individual in a treatment program. Thus, 24-hour-a-day crisis intervention services are essential to meet the needs of alcoholics.

Outpatient clinics and partial hospitalization programs are other essential components of a comprehensive alcoholism program. Such ambulatory programs should be staffed with an interdisciplinary treatment team including a psychiatrist, an internist, a social worker, a psychologist, paraprofessional alcoholism counselors, nurses, vocational counselors and activities therapists. Recovered alcoholics are particularly effective on the staffs of such services. Such programs should offer a variety of treatment services including individual and group therapy, the use of disulfiram (Antabuse®) and involvement of the families of the alcoholics in an ongoing treatment process. The services should be available and supportive on a long-term, rather than short-term, basis, because of the chronic nature of alcoholism.

Residential treatment in the form of halfway houses and hospital rehabilitation units should be available to provide patients with an alcohol-free environment for an extended period of two weeks to four months after detoxification. Many patients need such an intensive rehabilitation program because of the long duration of their condition, their resistance to ambulatory approaches or their need to be removed from severe environmental stresses.

The third area of rehabilitation involves the prevention of chronicity and efforts to reduce disability from the effect of alcoholism. This effort is needed for chronic deteriorated alcoholics who cannot be maintained in the community. The development of congregate living facilities which are supportive and protective treatment environments is necessary for this group of alcoholics for long-term stay. Periodic evaluation of these patients should be part of the program to avoid their becoming "back ward" cases.

Alcoholics Anonymous (AA) fellowship is an extremely useful therapeutic approach for many alcoholics. The widespread availability of AA meetings and the use of sponsors make AA an effective form of crisis intervention. Alcoholics who get involved in AA have a lifelong resource of support and involvement to help them live without alcohol one day at a time.

Vocational rehabilitation is a necessity for many alcoholics. This is particularly true for the socioeconomically deprived alcoholic, that is, people living in poverty not as a result of their drinking, but drinking to excess often as a reaction to the lack of opportunity. The availability of a job, job training and education can serve as a powerful incentive to remain abstinent from alcohol.

Programs should be developed for special subgroups of alcoholics to be found in a community. Such subgroups include young alcohol abusers, multiple drug abusers and elderly alcohol abusers.

Increasingly, adolescents are presenting themselves at emergency services with evidence of alcohol abuse. This phenomenon seems to be widespread and may be part of the trend noted as the decline in new cases of opiate use. Alcohol abuse is often a part of the complex clinical picture of the adolescent period. In a small proportion of cases, where the clinical evidence for a diagnosis of alcoholism is clear, treatment in an alcoholism facility may be appropriate. In others the treatment is best accomplished in a program for adolescents with consultation services provided by alcoholism personnel.

Multiple drug abuse is increasingly seen among patients coming into treatment for alcoholism. There are several distinct classes of multiple drug abusers:

Group I: Alcohol plus soft drugs, including sedative-hypnotics, minor tranquilizers and amphetamines

Group II: Alcohol plus opiates, including heroin and methadone

Group III: Alcohol plus other drugs, including LSD and other psychotomimetic drugs

Although those in the first group may differ clinically from other alcoholics and the psychopathology may be more serious, they should be treated in alcoholism treatment settings. Those in the second group are a specialized subgroup and should have specialized services including psychiatric treatment; they are not candidates for treatment in alcoholism services. Patients on methadone maintenances who abuse alcohol present a separate syndrome with a distinctive clinical picture and management of these patients is extremely difficult. They require specialized treatment in a setting staffed with mental health professionals where they could receive both their methadone and treatment for the alcoholism.

The third group consists largely of the younger drug abusers. Such youngsters should be managed in similar fashion to the young alcohol abuser.

Another group that has been observed to have a significant alcohol problem is elderly people. A prevalence study on alcohol abuse was conducted in the Washington Heights section of Manhattan.[2] It was found that age groups with the highest prevalence of alcoholism were the forty-five to fifty-four age group and the sixty-five to seventy-six age group. The highest prevalence rate was noted to be among elderly widowers. Treatment efforts with the elderly alcoholics have been found by the author to be particularly effective. Such efforts have included the use of socialization and group techniques, as well as use of antidepressant medication where clinical depression was noted.

The Treatment Process of the Alcoholic

The treatment process of the alcoholic is a long-term process. Alcoholism is a chronic illness with a high potential for relapse. As in other such chronic disorders, continuous care is required in some cases for the duration of the individual's life. AA is particularly well suited to provide this supportive treatment for an indefinite duration. All an individual has to do is to attend meetings and follow through with the "twelve-step" procedures. However, professional intervention during the beginning stages of treatment often is necessary. This is particularly true for making a complete physical and psychosocial evaluation of a patient.

Alcoholism often coexists with other problems, including psychiatric disorders, drug abuse and frequently physical problems.

Counseling or more intensive psychotherapeutic approaches, particularly group therapy under the guidance of experienced professionals in the alcoholism field, is necessary during the beginning stages of treatment. Acquainting the alcoholic with the physical effects of alcohol on his body and the effects on his ability to perform necessary functions should be part of this effort. The use of Antabuse to produce a deterent effect in regard to drinking is also an effective approach.

Several principles are important in the treatment of an alcoholic individual. The first is that the drinking itself must be terminated if therapy is to be at all effective in achieving rehabilitation. A common mistake mental health professionals make is viewing alcoholism as a symptom of underlying psychopathology or personality disorder and attempting to treat the underlying disorder. Such efforts are doomed to failure. The first step is to achieve sobriety for the patient through detoxification, to maintain sobriety through intensive directive counseling or psychotherapy and to use Antabuse. A patient who continues to drink will not be responsive to counseling or psychotherapeutic approaches.

The second principle in treating the alcoholic is understanding the transference the alcoholic will often establish with a counselor or therapist. This transference will be very intensive and characterized by a great amount of dependence coupled with hostile, manipulating and testing behavior. Thus, a great deal of ambivalence will be noted in the transferential relationship. The alcoholic will be dependent, but at times will act in a grandiose way, believing he can control his drinking as well as his life when the evidence is obviously to the contrary. Thus, massive denial is utilized by alcoholics to avoid facing their problems and their inability to handle alcohol. The use of skillfully applied group therapy can dilute this intensely ambivalent transferential relationship to a therapist and can create the possibility for more effective interpersonal relationships.

The third principle in the treatment of the alcoholic is understanding the countertransference that may develop in a therapist in response to provocative behavior and drinking of the patient as testing of his continued interest. Because of this type of testing behavior, the treatment of an alcoholic can be felt to be frustrating and unrewarding. However, the therapist must recognize that he is not omnipotent in regard to the alcoholic's drinking. He cannot, and no one can, stop an alcoholic determined to drink. A therapist can only provide the means to assist the alcoholic in achieving sobriety and cannot force him or seduce him into refraining from drinking. Only the patient's conscious efforts can achieve this for himself.

Recognizing this reality, the therapist must impose limits on the behavior of the patient and conditions under which treatment can continue. If the patient cannot meet these conditions at a particular point in time, treatment should be discontinued, but the door should be left open in the future to renew the efforts to achieve sobriety as the first step in the treatment process.

The treatment of an alcoholic has been observed to progress through several stages. The first stage involves the situation where the alcoholic cannot drink. This situation exists when there is external pressure on the patient to stop drinking, such as the threat of losing his job or of his wife leaving, or with the use of Antabuse. In a sense the alcoholic is forced to stop drinking at least for a short time. His attitudes toward drinking and the denial of drinking as a serious problem have not been changed. The alcoholic has stopped drinking not because he sees it as necesary, but because someone else does. This situation is by its nature very unstable and can easily lead to a return to drinking or can lead, through counseling and/or AA involvement, to a stage where the alcoholic "won't drink." This stage is where the controls on the compulsion to drink have become internalized and there is no longer a serious conscious conflict about whether to drink or not. At this stage, the individual's attitude toward the necessity of drinking and the deleterious consequences in resuming drinking are apparent. He has experienced a considerable attitudinal change toward drinking. The conflict about drinking is still present, but at an unconscious level. Evidence of the continued existence of this conflict is present in terms of fantasies of the patient and in dreams. This stage is the level many AA members have achieved, is a reasonably good stage of recovery and is fairly stable, only occasionally leading to a slip after years of sobriety. The third stage of recovery involves the situation where the alcoholic "does not have to drink." This stage can only be achieved through insight into the individual's personality problems and conflicts and through their resolution to a major degree. The habitual use of alcohol at this stage can be understood as a way of dealing with the individual's conflicts, and through their resolution the individual has achieved more adaptive ways of coping with internal and external problems. This stage can only be achieved through psychotherapy and self-understanding. It is a stable stage so long as the alcoholic refrains from drinking. The ability to refrain from drinking is relatively easy to maintain at this stage.

The last stage of recovery is a theoretical stage and involves the situation where "I can return to social drinking." Undoubtedly, a small percentage of alcoholics can achieve this stage, but at the present level of knowledge it is impossible to predict which alcoholic this might be. All alcoholics believe during the initial stages of recovery that they can return to controlled drinking. Therefore, for all practical purposes abstinence should be a necessary goal in the treatment of *all* alcoholics. Alcohol is not necessary to life, and it is quite possible to live without consuming alcohol. This fact should be part of the attitudinal change an alcoholic experiences during the process of recovery.

Alcoholism is a treatable condition with the techniques available. Recoveries have been produced in 60 to 80 percent of patients in some industrial alcoholism programs. As knowledge about the etiology of alcoholism increases and further evaluation of currently utilized treatment approaches tailored to specific subgroups of the alcoholic population is carried out, the success rate will be improved.

REFERENCES

1. *Alcoholism Treatment and Rehabilitation: Selected Abstracts.* Rockville, National Institute on Alcohol Abuse and Alcoholism, 1972.

2. Bailey, M. B., Haberman, P. W., and Alksne, H.: The epidemiology of alcoholism in an urban residential area. *Q J Stud Alcohol, 26:*19, 1965.
3. Davis, W. W.: Practical experience with an alcoholism program in industry. *Ohio State Med J, 66:*814, 1970.
4. DeVito, R. A., Flaherty, L. A., and Mozdzierz, G. J.: New dimensions in the treatment of alcoholism. *Ill Med J, 135:*389, 1969.
5. *First Special Report to the U.S. Congress on Alcohol and Health.* Washington, D.C., U.S. Department of Health, Education and Welfare, December, 1971.
6. Kamner, M. E., and Dupong, W. G.: Alcohol problems: Study by industrial medical department. *NY State J Med, 69:*3105, 1969.
7. Mann, G. A.: An alcoholic treatment center in a community general hospital. *Hosp Prog, 50:*125, 1969.
8. *Manual on Alcoholism.* Chicago, American Medical Association, 1973.
9. Mellon, L. J.: How Boeing handles alcoholism. *Industrial Medicine, 38:* 317, 1969.
10. Pattison, E. M.: A critique of alcoholism treatment concepts with special reference to abstinence. *Q J Stud Alcohol, 27:*9, 1969.

PART SEVEN

PSYCHOSOCIAL ASPECTS OF REHABILITATION OF THE PHYSICALLY DISABLED

Chapter 28

PSYCHOSOCIAL ASPECTS OF PHYSICAL DISABILITY

Jerome Siller

It is the purpose of this chapter to briefly characterize important aspects of the psychosocial situation of persons with physical disabilities. A wide range of considerations helpful to orienting oneself to the rehabilitation needs of the physically disabled will be presented. Specific topics considered include the origins and extent of disability conditions; the relationship of disability to chronicity, aging, multihandicaps and poverty; the identification of aspects of impairment particularly salient to the psychosocial condition; the personal impact of disability; immediate and long-term reactions to traumatization; a statement of rehabilitation focus; client-professional interactions; and a high-lighting of the social situation of the disabled.

Since the term "physical disability" subsumes many conditions and includes states which range from relatively trivial functional and cosmetic deficits, e.g. color blindness, to severely incapacitating and highly visible ones such as some cerebral palsies, facile statements of high generality are inappropriate. However, a body of literature and clinical experience does justify examining some recurrent reactions and situations facing persons with chronic physical conditions acquired either adventiously or as a result of birth processes.

Physical disabilities generally are differentiated from other types of conditions, such as psychosomatic ones, in that the sole cause is disruption of the sensory and/or motor capabilities of the person, and all social and psychological consequences stem from this physical base. When the central nervous system is involved, as in the case of cerebral palsy, cognitive elements may also intrude. Other conditions such as burns and scarring are considered to be physical disabilities because of their high cosmetic impact even though no physical function may be involved.

Barker and his associates have introduced the now widely used term, "somatopsychology," to describe the social-psychological consequences of disablement: "The somatopsychological relation . . . is concerned with those variations in physique that affect the psychological situation of a person by influencing the effectiveness of his body as a tool for actions or by serving as a stimulus to himself or others."[1] Somatopsychological analysis stresses that reaction to physical disability and to persons with a physical disability is a function of interpersonal interactions and societal prescriptions and not of intrinsic psychological factors as might be assumed by those oriented toward various forms of *somatotypology*. The stress upon dynamic interactions and fluid, evolving situations amenable to change and modification is the very basis for the rehabilitation orientation.

ORIGINS AND EXTENT

The causes of physical disabilities include such factors as genetics, fetal insult, the birth process, anoxia, infections and disease, dietary deficiencies, accidents and injuries and radiation effects. Although the same physical condition may result from a variety of causes, the impact upon the person and family may differ appreciably because of specific origin. For example, a war amputation creates a very different social and financial climate from the same amputation incurred through carelessness.

Estimates of the extent of disability are very approximate. In general, as compared to psychiatric conditions and social disabilities, physical disabilities appear to have a low profile. However, data from the Bureau of Education for the Handicapped and other sources indicate that defects in hearing, vision and speech and crippling conditions among children from birth to nineteen years of age probably well exceed 3 million in the United States alone. Among adults, estimates include such totals as amputation,

400,000; auditory defects, 15 million (of which 4½ million are judged to be seriously handicapped); visual disabilities, from 350,000 to 2 million; hemiplegia, 1 to 4 million; cardiovascular impairment, 10 million; arthritis and rheumatism, 11 million; and cerebral palsy, 550,000. Still more could be added for such conditions as muscular dystrophy, poliomyelitis, facial disfigurement and tuberculosis.

Even a casual tally of the above figures indicates that by numbers alone physical disabilities are so common as to directly or indirectly affect just about everyone in the country. Interestingly enough, though, physical disability as a generalized phenomenon seems to receive comparatively little professional attention outside of the physical medicine area. Rehabilitation in the psychosocial sense has a dedicated but small number of primary specialists, and recruitment of personnel generally is difficult. Discussion of some implications of this state of affairs follows.

CHRONICITY, AGING, MULTIHANDICAPS AND POVERTY

General discussions of the disabled and the bulk of the research literature tend to use as their model the reasonably young person impaired in a single modality. The developing picture of the disabled individual as he actually is, is that of an older person, usually with more than one serious physical condition, who is in a dismal financial situation. Rehabilitation directed toward psychosocial aspects might seem of low priority or even irrelevant considering the overwhelming financial, medical, housing and other immediate needs confronting so many.

Having a chronic condition frequently means that an entire way of life must be modified, possibly even radically. Social, vocational and even personal habits and goals must be predicated upon a new and probably more difficult base. Performing one's lifelong work or even simple activities of everyday living may no longer be possible, or possible only with fantastic dedication from self, family, friends and others. For those less grievously affected, adjustments may be simpler and life-styles less changed. In all instances the permanence of the disability (or more serious deteriorating conditions) necessitates a total adjustment in relationship to self and others. Unfortunately, this total adjustment often takes place in nonsupportive or even hostile environments as described below.

For the aged, increasing physical incapacitation, multiple handicaps and dire socioeconomic straits are an everyday reality. Data[40] on blindness, for example, indicate that about one half of the blind population are elderly and that the incidence among nonwhites in this group is two to three times as great as among the white population. For those over sixty-five, estimates have been made that over 75 percent have multiple impairments. (The American Foundation for the Blind is an excellent source for up-to-date authoritative data on these matters.) A substantial percentage of disabled persons thus exists within the poverty level and is subject to the various agencies servicing the poor (welfare, Medicare, etc.). The demoralization, degradation, frustration and resistance to interacting with these various welfare systems undoubtedly are important factors in deterring persons from fully utilizing available rehabilitation resources.

One might note that even when a person is more affluent, the financial impact of disability can be great. Beyond the financial there is the subjective experience for the elderly of awareness of body breakdown and the imminence of death. In later discussions of the psychosocial situation of the disabled, it will be well to remember that for young and old, subjective reactions to disability are highly conditioned by factors such as those above, as well as by the interpersonal and intrapsychic ones stressed below.

Rehabilitation generally is oriented toward helping persons change so that they can cope better with the environment. Although as Keith[30] points out, the conception of the rehabilitation center as presently constituted must be altered so that the disabled person becomes better equipped to deal with environments other than those of the hospital.

By rotating the axes and attacking the environmental forces that turn medical conditions of disability into psychosocial conditions of handicap, radical changes in the situation of the disabled can result. Later, certain environmental supports underlying attitudes toward the disabled by the general public and by professionals themselves will be considered. At this point let it suffice to say that rehabilitation of the physically disabled in all respects would be materially advanced by a public policy that supported financial, medical, architectural, housing and employment possibilities in a manner that was consistent, dignified and respectful of the humanity of the persons involved. Public agencies such as the Social Rehabilitation Service of HEW and the U.S. Office of Education have served important functions in this regard in the past. However, considerably more needs to be done.

This writer sees a danger present in confusing rehabilitation and welfare goals. Both are necessary and mammoth public assistance programs should not swallow up the rehabilitation and habilitation efforts which are directed toward helping persons achieve higher levels of functioning.

ASPECTS OF IMPAIRMENT SALIENT TO THE PSYCHOSOCIAL SITUATION

In this section, a number of elements that can exert decisive influence upon the psychosocial situation of the disabled will be reviewed briefly. Obviously, the factors to be discussed do not operate automatically or have inevitable impact. The individual factors viewed clinically can serve to orient one as to determining forces in an individual's condition and life. For research purposes they can serve as independent or control variables in a variety of studies. The following list is based upon unpublished lecture material of the writer and material by Freeman[20] and Nagi[41] and includes etiology, age at onset, degree and quality of limitations, onset and duration of the condition, course and cosmesis.

1. *Etiology:* The origin of the condition can present a salient stimulus to the person and to others. Thus, conditions that are fortuitously arrived at differ from those induced by carelessness, just as both differ from "heroic" circumstances. A familial stress may be imposed if assumptions are made as to neglect or genetics. Guilt feelings by the parents can thus be part of the family dynamics.

2. *Age at Onset:* Differing effects may be assumed depending

upon the time in the life cycle that a condition arises. Sensory impairment, for example, very early in life makes for a qualitatively different developmental situation than does the same disability after skills and cognitions have been developed. Socially, occurrence of a condition at one age may be more intrusive than at other ages. A distinction between congenital and adventitious origins of impairments often is stressed. Freeman[20] notes that congenital defects are more likely to produce diffuse personality alterations, and acquired disabilities to produce acute disturbances. Siller,[51,52] in a similar tone, associates congenital conditions with pervasive characterological adjustment patterns, and traumatic conditions with more focalized patterns following the sequence of trauma → anxiety → defense. In one study of child amputees, adjustment patterns of those with congenital conditions were rated better than for those of traumatic origin.[51]

3. *Degree and Quality of Limitations:* The effectiveness with which one may deal with the physical demands of the environment or processing of information is significantly determined by this element. Disabilities vary greatly in the degree to which loss of function is involved, and even within a particular disability persons with identical physical conditions show grossly different personal effectiveness. For children the consequences of severe disability can be particularly profound in that contact with the environment may be reduced, with adverse results for cognitive and social development.[20] The isolation of many disabled, of all ages, is frequently noted. Television can become an important socialization tool for such persons. Sullivan's[58] notion of consensual validation seems particularly applicable here. Where there is limited access to the usual social correctives of one's behavior and thinking, an additional burden is imposed upon the child's developmental possibilities.

Two further points will suffice here. First, to date, no convincing evidence exists indicating that severity of a condition is related to psychological maladjustment. Lowenfeld's[37] often quoted statement to the effect that "blindness creates problems *sui generis* only in the area of cognitive functions and mobility" generally can be applied to all disabilities. It cannot be over-stressed that somatic abnormality as a physical fact is not linked in a direct and clear-cut way to psychological behavior, i.e. whatever psychological consequences appear are mediated by many internal factors.

The second and final point relates to the particular difficulty that persons retaining a partial function, such as weak vision, have in adapting themselves to the need to relinquish the nonfunctional remnant.[8,27]

4. *Onset and Duration of the Condition:* Disabilities vary greatly in suddenness of onset, antecedent conditions and expected direction. Opportunities to deal with the stress of the situation obviously differ greatly and are reflected in the manner in which persons manage. Since chronic rather than acute conditions are being considered here, all are presumed to require permanent adjustments.

5. *Course:* Freeman[20] observes that disabilities may remain stationary, be progressive, improve or be episodic with periods of normality. Additionally, central nervous system involvement may directly impair coping mechanisms, integration, thinking and emotional control. Disabilities that are stationary in nature (e.g. blindness, deafness, amputation) offer a stable base upon which to predicate the future and, to that extent, make coping easier. Progressive conditions such as muscular dystrophy and other degenerative diseases pose the problem of uncertainty and continued demoralization. Improving conditions, such as some cases of mild brain damage and cerebral palsy, leave residuals (real or feared) and a sense of vulnerability. Episodic disabilities, such as seizures and diabetic conditions, create uncertainty and can be particularly bothersome if they intrude into a relationship where it was not known that the situation existed. Not unexpectedly, persons with such ailments may find it expedient to develop pervasive protective systems, such as withdrawal, designed to avoid such experiences.

6. *Cosmesis:* The appearance and visibility of a condition may be a prime determining factor in social consequences of a disability. The tremendous social relevance of facial disfigurement in particular, but also of most any disfigurement, has been amply

documented.[25,38,55] In this context, even extremes in height and weight become disabilities, as do speech and coordination difficulties.

The concept of noticeability in disability has received particular attention with respect to the use of protheses by amputees. Dembo and Tane-Baskin,[13] in studying the noticeability of a cosmetic glove indicate that noticeability depends upon the "intensity" of the situation, that is, upon the closeness of the amputee's social and physical contact with others at any particular time. The writer, building upon the Dembo and Tane-Gaskin study, has suggested that at least three important considerations may be involved in judgments of an amputee's appearance: the actual appearance of the prosthesis apart from its functioning (the static factor), the naturalness with which the prosthesis is used (the dynamic factor) and the intensity of the amputee's situation (the situational factor).[57] Treatment personnel in prosthetics may place greatest emphasis upon the appearance of the limb itself; the amputee may base his impression more upon the other two considerations. Although developed within the frame of reference of prosthetics for amputees, the above classification might have more general utility in specifying components of visibility in disability.

The importance of the cosmetic aspect of disability as a force in interpersonal experiences has already been referred to. Its impact upon the self-image of the disabled and upon familial interactions and adaptations is equally profound. It is a regrettable truth that, as Alexander[62] puts it, there is an "emotional syllogism" to the effect that suffering is caused by evil.

A variety of other features might properly be discussed, space permitting, e.g. threat to life and stigma associated with the condition. However, it might be best at this point to move from the essentially objective variables so far discussed to a more subjective or psychological level of analysis and description.

THE PERSONAL IMPACT OF DISABILITY

It can be safely asserted that the psychology of an individual with a disability is in no way unique although social problems connected with stigmatization, deviance, marginality and the like do intrude. Physical injury is but another stress situation to which the person brings a repertoire of response patterns characteristic of him. Thus, all of the professionals' insights into the bases of human behavior are applicable. The more attuned one is to a psychological level of functioning and the more capable of sensing his own feelings in past stress situations, the more likely he is to be able to help such persons.

Specific conditions, of course, impose restrictions on certain functions while leaving others untouched, even though reaction to disability itself is idiosyncratic. Thus, conditions where motor functioning is limited, where incontinence is involved or where sensory disability results, in each instance present a common problem for those sharing that experience. In the remainder of this section the writer will attempt to offer some generalizations and descriptions of common reaction patterns to disability that can serve as referent points in understanding the coping behavior of the disabled. A number of descriptions of these processes have been offered in the literature.[1,4,5,9,17,23,43,47,52,55,62] What follows is essentially the present writer's clinical-psychoanalytic approach. This restriction is due to space limitations solely, since many persons from a variety of theoretical orientations have made significant contributions to the topics discussed.

Immediate Reactions to Traumatization

There is virtual agreement that traumatic disability creates a crisis situation. Several researchers have described stages within this experience.[7,11,16,49] For example, Shontz describes the adjustment process as a succession of approach-avoidance cycles with the frequency and amplitude diminishing in time. Fink indicated a four-stage process of shock, defensive retreat, acknowledgment and adaptation. Blank[5] characterizes an individual's reaction to blindness as follows: predisposing personality and character traits, illness or accident, grief reaction or depression (the predictable reaction to loss of a major body part or function, as well as to object loss), the healthy and pathologic resolutions of the mourning state and finally, success or failure of rehabilitation.

Clinically, anxiety and depression universally are identified as the primary affects associated with disability. Occasionally, these affects are displaced, delayed or otherwise disguised so that the superficial clinical picture suggests their absence. Careful and more extended observation generally does reveal their operation. To be clinically useful, however, it is necessary to determine the personalized meaning of the disability. By joining the patient at a level of specificity of affective as well as cognitive functioning, the restitutive process may be accelerated.

The importance of denial as a coping mechanism also has been stressed. What is denied mostly is functional loss or social implications rather than blatant refusal to acknowledge the event. As a temporary mechanism in a provisional or transient form of adjustment, denial can have utility. However, denial necessarily goes in the face of reality and, therefore, can intrude in the rehabilitation process if it persists and is too prominent in the defensive structure.

Hospitalization, pain, physical dependency, immobilization and even institutional rules promote regressive behavior. Reversion to infantile patterns is a common reaction to anxiety-provoking situations of all kinds. The combination of disability specific effects with generalized anxiety therefore support a climate conducive to the development of regression in the newly disabled. Fordyce (in Neff[42]) describes many ways in which behavioral modification techniques may be applied to combat such tendencies, e.g. by not reinforcing undesirable behaviors, such as attention-getting claims. For those operating within a psychodynamic framework, one attempts to recognize constructively the underlying need without reinforcing the possible pathology. In any event, by now it is clear that the institutional structure may be a major determinant in the promotion or inhibition of inappropriate regressive behaviors (e.g. Refs. 24, 29 and 31).

Grief and related mourning behavior have been described as crucial phenomena in any kind of severe disability.[5,45,52] It is generally recognized that the depression and severe grief that follow the loss of a body part or function activate mourning reactions similar to that experienced when a loved one is lost. It takes time to work out feelings towards the departed (person, function, part) and Freud[21] brilliantly described this process when he defined the "work of mourning." Siller[52] has indicated concern that rehabilitation efforts not be used to bypass the mourning stage in persons. Thus, while early fitting of prostheses for amputees, behavioral techniques and other devices are being successfully used to quicken the rehabilitation process and to make it more effective, their impact upon the vicissitudes of the mourning process must be considered. It is his belief that without respect for the need to work through the myriad of meanings involved in the loss, the "work of mourning" will be intruded upon, with the result that the emotional experience will be unexplored and unresolved and tranquilization and denial tendencies will be reinforced. By blunting affect rather than plumbing its depths, the opportunity to emerge a richer and more complex person may be sacrificed.

Long-term Reactions to Traumatization

In discussing prominent immediate reactions to disablement such as depression, grief, anxiety, denial, regression and the process of mourning, it was possible to describe most of them as almost universal, even though wide variations in extent are observed. As might be expected, considerably more individualization is seen in long-range adjustments since variations in predisability personality, ego strength and coping styles are more relevant. Depending upon the particular disability, different need systems may be intruded upon and specific unresolved unconscious conflicts activated. It is particularly important to recognize that intrapsychic and unconscious factors are of great significance in ultimate resolutions of the persons toward constructive or pathological modes of adaptation. As Blank[5] notes, even when social, financial and other external factors are favorable, as they too infrequently are, the initial helplessness and dependency require skillful and sustained aid. It is this combination of external and intrapsychic factors that must be thoroughly understood by the professional and coordinated with meaningful rehabilitation operations.

Despite the diversity of long-term adjustment patterns, six

partial modes can be noted: passivity, dependency, aggresivity, withdrawal, compensation and coping. Before describing these reactions it is well to note that the term "partial modes" is being used to describe important rather than totally definitive characterological behavioral patterns. As Shontz (in Neff,[42]) points out, the following two notions on the effect of disability on personality have been firmly discredited: (1) that specific forms of somatic disorder are associated with specific types of personality and (2) that some types or degrees of disability constitute sufficient causes of psychological maladjustment.

Passivity is a mode of adaptation to one's environment that involves backing away from it. For the disabled person such a mechanism can have utility in protecting him from embarrassing situations. It also can be adaptive in the sense that "I'm not going to initiate action because I might fail. Rather than trying and finding out that this, too, I can't do, I would rather not try too much." The writer has seen a number of disabled persons who in this manner have imposed serious limits of achievement upon themselves vocationally and socially. There is a destructive assumption made by these people that often can be challenged, particularly if professional support is available. A more profound resistance to "opening oneself up" is the affect of shame, which is discussed below.

Passivity can evoke angry reactions in professional personnel who mistakenly resent their client. Inability to accept responsibility for initiating one's rehabilitation should not be mistaken for unwillingness to be rehabilitated.

Dependency is hardly unique to disability. However, the relationship of physical dependency to emotional dependency might be confused. Obviously, serious physical conditions can impose a state of actual dependency, regardless of the particular manner in which one has resolved such matters in the past. Two general possibilities often seen are overdependence and underdependence (pseudoindependence). Overdependent behavior is seen in such operations as excessive questioning, fearfulness, looking for approval, need for proximity with others, indecisiveness and clinging. Overdependency can be seen as a sense of being overwhelmed by catastrophe, without hope of being able to grab hold of things, at least as yet.

Temporary relief from responsibility may help some of these persons to ultimately relinquish the dependency. As with so much else, timing is of the essence. Others may unconsciously welcome the dependency as relief from the need to be self-reliant and self-supportive. If the professional's values of achievement and independence are not threatened too much, such persons might become rehabilitated on their own terms.

Pseudoindependent phenomena can be seen behaviorally as expressed in obstinacy, inappropriate confidence, inability to accept appropriate offers of help and unrealistic goal setting. Because so much of reality must be denied and interpersonal situations made awkward, this mode of adaptation generally fails to be successful in the long run.

The meaning of help for the disabled has been sensitively dealt with by Ladieu, Hanfmann and Dembo.[33] Reviews of the motivation for work by the disabled have been made by Barry and his associates.[2,34]

The possibility of secondary gains to be derived from disability is obvious. Cameron and Magaret[6] have a particularly thorough discussion of invalidism and withdrawal defenses.

Aggression was singled out as one of the partial modes of adjustment for two reasons. For one, the active and sometimes even obnoxious aggressive behavior and attitudes of patients and clients often arouse retaliatory attitudes and behaviors on the part of service personnel and others. Although psychodynamically one might recognize the hostility as a fight against passivity or against a sense of devaluation, nonetheless such persons are looked on as nuisances or worse, with negative repercussions for their treatment.

A second aspect important to note is that the aggression may be expressed passively. Passive-aggressive behavior takes such forms as not taking one's medicine, misinterpreting what is said, "forgetting," doing things for "you" rather than for oneself. Hostility is expressed through spite and deviousness.

Compensatory behavior used in a broad sense can be seen as a generalized orientation, the purpose of which is to maintain feelings of significance and effectiveness. It is one of the most frequent and most effective of the restitutive mechanisms. Compensatory behavior becomes problematical mostly when it is overdone and leads to impoverishment in other aspects of functioning.

In addition to these generalized modes of adjustment, mention should be made of the two affective conditions of shame and guilt that clinically have been observed to intrude negatively upon the person's ability to constructively deal with his or her condition. Shame about one's appearance or diminished ability to function, in this writer's opinion, may be the single most noxious emotional consequence of disablement. The writer has repeatedly observed persons whose postdisablement adjustment is crucially determined by efforts to avoid the experience of shame. Patterns of social and vocational withdrawal, introversion, underachievement and the like often can be analyzed as defensive operations designed to avoid shame.

Guilt, as shown in self-recriminations, depression and masochistic patterns also is easily observed. Disability as punishment for sins is an ancient notion. Magical thinking connected with the guilt reaction is often connected with shopping around for the right doctor or prosthetist.

Beatrice Wright, a major figure in the area of the psychology of disability and rehabilitation, has long objected that disability generally has been presented from a one-sided, deficient point of view. In her major work, *Physical Disability—A Psychological Approach,*[62] and in other writings, Doctor Wright has stressed the coping aspects of disability. She properly takes to task the almost invariable manner in which the capabilities of persons with disabilities are ignored. It would seem from discussions and the literature that only loss, incapability and deficit predominate in the world of the disabled. She penetratingly points out that often the disability is background to a field of competence. That disability can promote important self-growth usually is not recognized. Using the Gestalt concept of spread, Wright[63] shows how persons tend to use one aspect of an individual—his physical condition—to make inappropriate generalizations to other aspects, such as his personality or intelligence.

In addition to the concept of spread, Wright[62] has explicated from an interpersonal-phenomenological approach important principles based upon the work of such basic contributors to the area of physical disability as Barker, Dembo, Leviton and Meyerson, as well as upon her own germinal contributions. The discussions of comparative values and assets, expectation discrepancy, containment, overlapping psychological situations, coping, succumbing and the requirement of mourning are invaluable for those who wish to understand the psychological impact of disability.

In ending this section on long-term adjustments to disability, it is strongly recommended that the coping ability of the disabled be recognized and that the proper emphasis of rehabilitation be upon this aspect. Professional and public lack of recognition of the coping capabilities of the disabled becomes a major deterrent to persons with disabilities.

A STATEMENT OF REHABILITATION FOCUS

Timing of therapeutic or rehabilitative interventions can spell the difference between effective or ineffective professional operations. The following thesis, taken from an earlier presentation,[52] is intended to supply some theoretical basis for specific dealing with the disabled:

> It is clear that an overriding problem for one who incurs a severe disability is the belief that life as known cannot continue. Among the nondisabled a primary reaction of many, asked to contemplate the possibility of crippling, is that they would rather be dead. Perhaps the fuller statement should be, "As a cripple I would no longer be my recognizable self, and therefore I am horrified at the possibility of losing my ego. For all practical purposes I would then be dead, because the self that I know would not exist."
>
> This has implications for where the focus of rehabilitation should lie. The aim is to assist the person toward reformulating a self that approves of continuing to be, despite important discontinuities with its past identity. Specifically, this means the promotion of a new self-image predicated on worth, rather than on deficiency and self-contempt.*

*Dembo and her associates' analysis of enlarging the scope of values is most relevant here. See the discussion in Reference 62.

The goal of rehabilitation, therefore, never changes – it is *always* directed toward promoting ego integrity and feelings of self-worth – but the specific operations of the rehabilitation unit must constantly shift, being coordinated with the physical, psychological and social realities of the rehabilitant. The danger arises when these operations are mistakenly identified as being the ultimate goal. Thus, one speaks of prosthetic rehabilitation, vocational rehabilitation and so on as entities real in themselves. It is my position that these are partial processes, the timing of which is governed by a strategy designed to foster the ego-integrative qualities of the rehabilitant.

This position might be made clearer by an illustration using functional effectiveness and independence training. It is natural for a person newly disabled to have great anxiety about the extent to which he will be functionally capable. Independence training in the early stages is most valuable as a prod toward the enhanced self-esteem necessary to undo the narcissistic insult generated by the disability. It is a misplaced emphasis, *at this point* in the rehabilitation regime, to be literally concerned about how well the patient is doing so far as specific functions are concerned. On the other hand, at a later point, activities daily living may very well be a specific focus and charts of progress and the like seriously attended to. Early rehabilitation should be directed to shaping basic life goals with later rehabilitation focused on providing the emotional, physical and technical resources for their accomplishment. Foremost among early rehabilitation goals would be facilitation of a restitutive orientation, so that recrystallization of the self is in terms of acceptance rather than hate. The direction of this recrystallization will be a major determinant of response to later specific rehabilitation procedures. Rejection of prosthetic restoration by certain amputees or of aids by the blind or deaf well illustrate the consequences of resolution of the self in the direction of hate. . . .

The nebulous phrase, *acceptance of loss,* might be defined in terms of the foreging discussion as being the extent to which the reconstituted self is oriented toward self-approval (i.e. recovered from the narcissistic wound) and responsive to reality (i.e. relying on protective mechanisms that are essentially no pathological).

Some of the above can be restated in more concrete and descriptive terms. Some persons are restitutively oriented following disablement, attempting to compensate for their condition. Others are not directed toward positive gratifications, seeking instead avoidance of the implications of their condition; and their primary motivation is to ward off anxiety, shame and other noxious affects. This later resolution is the basis for residual self-hate. Our job is to extend every aid possible to help the patient feel that he, as a personality, still continues. The obligation to give functional aid should be seen in the larger context of enhancing self-respect. Functional and physical progress, therefore, can be effective as ego-builders, but functional efforts in early treatment should be seen as specific strategies designed to help the rehabilitant feel that such things are possible and, thus, serve as a promise for the future. One need not be overly concerned with graphs of achievement, although they can serve as objective cues of the rehabilitant's internal state. As indicated earlier, my fear is that emphasis on function serves as a ready way of avoiding the affective implications of disablement.

CLIENT-PROFESSIONAL INTERACTIONS

Dembo advances the important notion that there are really two psychologies in working with the disabled (or, really, any client group).[12] There is the position of the researcher or professional, and there is the position of the client suffering: "The outsider is usually concerned with more inclusive units in rehabilitation matters—with abstract knowledge and theories rather than with the needs of an individual case. . . . He is removed from the problems of the individual sufferer needing help here and now."[12]

These important ingredients of distance from the phenomena (whose ache is it?) and unit of involvement (abstract laws or phenomenological experience) must account for many problems in rehabilitation. So long as a subject-object relationship dominates professional-client interactions, patterns of rehabilitation necessarily will be influenced accordingly. Observable consequences are such phenomena as status issues, regression to infantile dependent modes, transference and countertransference manifestations and, among the profesional staff, interdisciplinary strife rather than true teamwork.

Status factors play an important role in the patient-professional relationship in disability.[53] Recipients of professional services mostly are in a status position inferior to that of the deliverer of the service. Factors such as physical dependency, higher socioeconomic and educational attainment on the part of the staff and the hierarchical arrangement of rehabilitation settings all contribute to such a status differential. In addition, psychological regression to infantile dependent states stemming from the stress, physical pain and actual physical dependency promotes infantile attitudes toward authority and authority figures.

In this atmosphere of regressive transferential distortions, the unconscious response to something in the present as if it were the same as something from the past readily is engendered. Thus, the nurse can assume properties of the mother, the physician properties of the father, other clients properties of one's siblings. Such attitudes as "getting better for the doctor" or "spiting the doctor" each have the same dynamic base in dealing with the doctor as a father figure, the reaction to whom is more important than is one's own future. Many such transferences can be observed to assume a wide variety of guises in relation to professional personnel, family, institutions, etc. These factors of status differential, regression and transferential distortions are responsible for many of the complications that stand in the way of appropriate goal-directed behavior in rehabilitation.

A body of research literature is being built up demonstrating the importance of professional attitudes, the social-religious-cultural background of the professional and many other variables as influencing treatment and rehabilitation outcomes. Thus, Ford, Liske, and Ort[18] present evidence that physicians and advanced medical students may have positive reactions to chronic illness when it is felt that professional skills such as diagnosis or treatment can be exercised and when a satisfactory personal relationship with the patient can be established. On the other hand, unfavorable feelings and a tendency to avoid the situation are associated with ideas of demanding, hostile, severely disabled and hopelessly ill patients. Physical handicaps, blindness and malingering did not engage the repondents' thought or professional skill.

Certain concentrations such as physical disability, aging, dying and mental retardation generally are not areas of choice for professional involvement. The reasons for this situation are complex and include such factors as personal repugnance and a sense of futility. Professionals seem to prefer to work with those who are like themselves culturally and socioeconomically and with those whom they feel they can help. Thus, Margolin,[39] in a questionnaire survey of 535 physicians, found considerable pessimism concerning possible outcomes of rehabilitation. When actual disability is invloved, an additional pressure is introduced in the form of disfigurement; and professionals, like the rest of the community, prefer to work with the "beautiful" people, that is to say, the physically attractive, verbal, cooperative, educated individuals and, in general, those with whom an identification can be made. It is vitally important that greater recognition be made of those factors limiting free profressional involvement in physical rehabilitation and of the steps taken to counteract them. As immediate concrete steps, explorations of feelings can be done on the training and job level, and financial and other inducements can be offered on the work level.

Systematic work on professional-client relations in a rehabilitation hospital setting had been undertaken over a period of years by the late Gloria L. Leviton (in Neff.[42]) A preliminary theoretical structure was offered by Leviton utilizing the concepts of specific values, needs and beliefs of the partners that determine their views on rehabilitation issues. It was proposed that improvement in the rehabilitative professional-client relationship be made by studying the determinants underlying the divergent viewpoints.

THE SOCIAL SITUATION OF THE DISABLED

To many, the most serious handicap to successful rehabilitation often resides in the social climate of the person rather than in the physical facts of disability. Disability clearly can interfere with the assumption of ordinary social roles such as breadwinner, friend, spouse, etc. As Kutner (in Neff[42]) indicates, status of the disabled, at least in the United States, continues to have an ambivalent, though essentially negative, valuation. Jordan's[28] multinational studies seem to support the generality of the lower status position of the disabled.

Such terms as stigmatization, marginality, inferior status, minority group position and the like have been introduced in describing social-psychological consequences of disability. The assumption seems to be that the disabled are not only perceived as being different, but that this difference is "bad." Certainly, the frequent perception of the disabled is that the nondisabled are bothered by, or put down, the disabled. In at least one study it was found that this sensitivity was so great that when amputees rated how nonamputees would react to amputees, they were more critical in their actual ratings than were the nonamputees.[22]

A wide variety of techniques has been used in studying attitudes of the nondisabled toward the disabled. Various studies report rankings of disabilities along such dimensions as most to least favorable and most to least serious. For example, Tringo[59] has provided data on the hierarchy of preferences toward twenty-two disability groups. Interestingly enough, the position of disability conditions in such ranking studies is usually high and even close to the "normal" when mental retardation, mental illness, alcoholism or criminality are also included, although more severe states such as cerebral palsy or bad facial burns meet with a strongly negative reaction. Obesity regularly is one of the most severely ranked of all conditions.

Most research on attitudes toward the disabled has been of an unsystematic nature using diverse measurement induces and limited populations. Around 1960 Yuker and his associates introduced the "Attitude Toward Disabled Persons Scale"[64] which has served as a vehicle for more systematic studies. A summary of much of the work on research studies may be found in the work of Siller[55] and Yuker.[65]

Until the mid-1960's formal research assumed that attitudes toward the disabled could be measured along a single dimension such as acceptance or rejection. Around that time Whiteman and Lukoff[60,61] and Siller[54,55,56] conducted systematic programs that resulted in clear empirical evidence that the nature of the organization of attitudes toward the disabled is multidimensional. These researchers, utilizing factor analytic techniques, identified and provided measures of a number of attitudes toward the disabled that have been cross-validated in numerous studies since then. A brief description of these dimensions follows. The set of seven obtained by the Siller group is described, since they essentially include the ones described by Whiteman and Lukoff and are based on substantially larger and more varied populations.

The factorially defined dimensions were *interaction strain:* an uneasiness in the presence of the disabled and uncertainty as to how to deal with them; *rejection of intimacy:* a rejection of close, particularly familial, relationships; *generalized rejection:* a pervasive negative orientation with derogation, unpleasant personal reactions and advocacy of segregation; *authoritarian virtuousness:* an ostensible "pro-disabled" orientation which is rooted in an authoritarian context and advocates special treatment; its correlations with other disability dimensions suggest that it is a negative dimension despite its surface tone; *inferred emotional consequences:* intensely hostile references to the character and emotions of the disabled person; *distressed identification:* highly personalized reactions to disability with the emphasis on the disabled as a stimulus which activates anxiety about one's own vulnerability; *imputed functional limitations:* an evaluation of the ability of the disabled person to function in his environment.

The seven dimensions described above have been found in relation to such disabilities as amputation, blindness, deafness, obesity and disability in general. Some more specific dimensions have been found in relationship to cosmetic conditions and obesity. In general, it is believed that a valid and reliable basic taxonomy of important components of attitudes has been described by the Siller group, along with sensitive measures of these components.

The implication of distinguishing attitude structure is considerable. Although attitudes, as predispositions to behavior, can describe only part of the bases for disabled-nondisabled interactions (e.g. situational demands may override all others), by discriminating elements of these attitudes action to improve interactions can be enhanced. For example, in a number of settings the Disability Factor Scales (DFS), which is the generic name for the instruments developed by Siller and his colleagues, are being used by professionals and by trainees to sensitize themselves as to their own disability-related attitudes. Siller has suggested also that disabled persons might, by themselves and in groups with professional rehabilitation personnel, use the DFS to understand their own and others' attitudes toward the disabled. As a further development, the disabled might use the DFS material as a point of departure for developing procedures improving their coping capabilities in interactions with the nondisabled. The DFS also is uniquely suitable for use as a research instrument in the light of its efficient size, vocabulary level and extensive psychometric development.

As a rough summary of some of the findings of numerous studies dealing with attitudes toward the disabled, the following might be noted: (1) To most persons disability has little salience. However, in their responses, frequent stereotypes emerge which support the position that the status of the disabled is low and negatively tinged. (2) Wright's[62] emphasis on "salutory" aspects of disability—e.g. admiration for coping, amazement at accomplishments despite disability, better understanding of life—seems justified for at least some people. "Anormalization" (attribution of superior powers to the disabled) also appears. However, these salutory aspects of disability can also be used in the service of essentially rejecting or subordinating attitudes. (3) Attitudes toward the disabled are consistent as indicated by test-retest correlations. (4) Attitudes toward the disabled are only weakly correlated with personality variables although significant relationships with such variables as low anxiety, dogmatism, authoritarianism and alienation have been demonstrated. (5) Among demographic factors such as sex, age, education and the like, only education seems to be implicated. (6) Attitudes mostly are generalized, that is, someone aversive to one condition is likely to be aversive to others. (7) Attitudes toward the disabled are multidimensional in nature. Interdisability consistencies are greatest along the same or similar attitude components.

A significant review on nondisabled-disabled interactions has been done by Richardson[44] in which he concluded that "the kinds of people who initiate social relations with him (the disabled person) will be those who are less successful in social relations, those who hold atypical values, those for whom physical disability cues have low perceptual salience or those who like others to be dependent upon them." Obviously, a wide variety of factors enter into determining any particular interaction. Thus, in any situation, personality, socioeconomic and cultural background, religion, prior experience, specific contextual elements and the like play a role. For one person antipathy toward the disabled may be rooted in profound personality dynamics, such as those suggested by the notion of castration anxiety, while for another social learnings or religious belief may be crucial factors in acceptance or rejection. In other instances the total stimulus value of the disabled person may be so overwhelmingly favorable that the fact of disability may be trivial in the total context. Most of the work on these factors has been essentially clinical in nature, and systematic controlled research is yet to be done.

It is remarkable how little really has been done on improving the coping capabilities of the disabled in social interactions. One outstanding exception to the paucity of knowledge regarding this matter has been the work of Fred Davis[10] on deviance disavowal. Davis has examined the manner in which the visibly handicapped managed social interactions. In a brilliant analysis based upon interviews with visibly handicapped informants, Davis shows how the threat posed by the handicap to sociability is, at minimum, four-fold: its tendency to become an exclusive focal point of the interaction, its potential for inundating expressive boundaries, its discordance with other attributes of the person and, finally, its ambiguity as a predicator of joint activity. Davis then delineates in transactional terms the stages through which a sociable relationship with a normal person typically passes. These stages are designated as (1) fictional acceptance, (2) the facilitation of reciprocal role-taking around a normalized projection of self and (3) the institutionalization in the relationship of a definition of self that is normal in its moral dimension, however qualified it may be with respect to its situational contexts.

It would seem that systematic studies focusing on the mechanisms persons with disabilities use for facilitating successful interaction with the nondisabled would be a matter of high priority.

Clinical, impressionistic and autobiographical accounts of what it means to be disabled or to be the relative of someone who is disabled can be found spread out in the literature. Research studies have been directed toward the interaction and social acceptance of the handicapped child in the school situation; other studies have dealt with the vocational and employment situation and still others with familial interactions. Due to the generally scattered nature of these studies and the fortuitous nature of the sample employed, hard generalizations in these areas cannot be comfortably offered. However, one would seem justified to venture some interpretative summaries and inferences.

Personal accounts of what it means to be disabled in interaction with the nondisabled identify the particular salience that disability has for others. While in certain instances courtesy, consideration and kindness are shown, in others avoidance, curiosity and even rudeness may be demonstrated. Issues of help, status derogation, assumption of incapability and the like enter into interactions specifically because of the disability. For the involved person this means that new situations often have to be "dealt with" rather than just be "experienced." Breaking the ice and establishing oneself as a real person repeatedly need to be done. The ability to suppress anger at inconsiderateness and personal devaluation is needed, and retreat from free interactions may be employed as a solution. It would seem that extensive work on the bases for extinguishing the difficulties in interactions, and for possitively reinforcing conditions leading to favorable experiences, is needed.

In considering social interactions in the classroom, one must coordinate the special educational needs of children having sensory and other disabilities with the social climate of the school and the classroom. The writer's own attitude research clearly demonstrates that segregation of the disabled can be advocated ostensibly as a favorable action, but really serves as a means of dealing with aversive feelings. Even when a special class is contained within a regular school, whether that group is incorporated within the regular student body or not, there are variations from district to district and from school to school. In the view of many, providing special services wherever possible within the regular classroom is the preferred approach.

Specific studies of exceptional children in the regular classroom would suggest that hyperactivity and aggressive behavior are most likely to set some children off from the others. If disability interferes with group functioning it naturally imposes problems. Yet, in some classrooms truly beautiful things can occur when atmospheres are created where the human worth of everyone, disabled and nondisabled alike, is promoted and the growth of all is facilitated by appreciating and respecting individual differences. It would be most worthwhile to identify the characteristics of teachers and schools that promote such a context and to try to bring them to general attention.

Family and peer interactions with the disabled are highly variable in nature.[3,46] No small set of descriptors suffices to characterize the many kinds of interactions observed and reported. Data can be provided demonstrating no special effects or gross consequences. From a psychological point of view, a more relevant structuring of the problem might be the particular manner in which such interactions are conducted, the circumstances leading to that particular interaction and the ultimate consequences. The fact of disability must enter into all interactions. Whether an individual becomes more central or more peripheral in the family or group structure, or whether dominance patterns change, and so on, is not definable in terms of the condition alone. Certainly, the consequence may be negative, as the high rate of divorce reported for hemiplegics suggests. Resentment of extra attention awarded the disabled sibling can be a factor, etc. On the other hand, family solidarity may be enhanced as well as diminished, and social groups might define their goals only in terms that would not diminish their disabled member. Thus, although the presence of a person with a disability might require special efforts from a family or group, it does not mean that this expenditure necessarily has a negative implication for the relationship. Definition of personal, group and situational factors leading to gratifying experiences between the disabled and nondisabled should be researched. For example, might one not expect a different interaction experience in a low-anxiety, noncompetitive, cohesive group setting than if the opposite conditions prevailed?

Finally, the vocational situation of the disabled can easily be characterized by the necessity of states like New York to actually include the physically and emotionally disabled within its civil rights legislation. Deprivation of rights for equal employment opportunities abounds, and persons regularly are denied opportunities for employment in work they can perform. Sometimes this job discrimination is buttressed by architectural barriers, insurance issues and other so-called, or even real, restrictions. However, employment personnel can be influenced positively, despite their tendency to discriminate, when the applicant presents an effective and socially acceptable manner. Gradients of acceptance of different disability conditions by employers have been reported (e.g. orthopedics and cardiacs are much more acceptable than are those with epilepsy, cerebral palsy and visual handicaps). In the study just noted (Federation Employment and Guidance Service[15]) willingness to employ physically disabled applicants was associated with size of the firm, past experience with the disabled, the type of disability and the type of business. It would seem that the greater willingness of larger firms to hire the disabled might be better utilized than it has been and that financial pressure by the government should be encouraged here as it has been in respect to other equal opportunity efforts. The role of work in rehabilitation has been systematically discussed in Neff.[42]

This brief review of selected topics relevant to the rehabilitation of the physically disabled is intended to serve as an introduction to an important area of clinical application that, for a variety of reasons, seems to have remained out of the mainstream of scientific attention. As a result, systematic studies and comprehensive programs of research have been sparse, and definitive conclusions rare. Important conceptual work by a few persons like Dembo, Wright, Barker and Meyerson has provided a framework for workers. Clinical experience and impressions remain an important element in the day-to-day operations of personnel. In some settings important creative integrations of theory and practice are progressing (e.g. Diller, in Neff[42]), and in a number of places utilization of behavioral techniques for rehabilitation of the physically disabled is radically influencing procedures (Fordyce, in Neff[42]).

In closing, the writer would suggest that the rehabilitation of the physically disabled would be greatly facilitated by comprehensive and systematic research geared to the immediate needs of the disabled person. However, these efforts should be embedded in conceptualizations, based upon general principles, which self-consciously relate to general psychological and sociological knowledge so as to avoid the sterile empiricism already so prevalent in rehabilitation.

REFERENCES

1. Barker, R. G., Wright, B. A., Meyerson, L., and Gonick, M. R.: *Adjustment to Physical Handicap and Illness: A Survey of the Social Psychology of Physique and Disability,* rev. ed. New York, Soc Sci Res, 1953, Bulletin 55.
2. Barry, J. R., and Malinovsky, M. R.: *Client Motivation for Rehabilitation: A Review.* Rehabilitation Research-Monograph Series, no. 1. Gainesville, U of Fla Pr, 1965.
3. Barsch, R. H.: *The Parent of the Handicapped Child.* Springfield, Thomas, 1968.
4. Blank, H. R.: Countertransference problems in the professional worker. *The New Outlook for the Blind, 48:*185-188, 1954.
5. Blank, H. R.: Psychosocial problems of the blind and the rehabilitation system. In *Blindness and Services to the Blind.* Cambridge, OSTI Press, 1971, pp. 186-189.
6. Cameron, N., and Margaret, A.: *Behavior Pathology.* Boston, HM, 1951.
7. Cohn, N.: Understanding the process of adjustment to disability. *J Rehabil, 27:*16-18, 1961.
8. Cowen, E. L., Underberg, R. P., Verillo, R. T., and Benham, F. G.: *Adjustment to Visual Disability in Adolescence.* New York, American Foundation for the Blind, 1961.
9. Cruickshank, W. M. (Ed.): *Psychology of Exceptional Children and Youth,* 3rd ed. Englewood Cliffs, P-H, 1971.
10. Davis, F.: Deviance diavowal: The management of strained interaction by the visibly handicapped. *Social Problems, 9:*120-132, 1961.
11. Davis, F.: *Passage through Crisis: Polio Victims and Their Families.* New York, Bobbs, 1963.
12. Dembo, T.: Rehabilitation psychology and its immediate future: A problem of utilization of psychological knowledge. *Psychological Aspects of Disability, 16:*63-72, 1969.
13. Dembo, T., and Tane-Baskin, E.: The noticeability of the cosmetic glove. *Artif Limbs, 2:*47-56, 1956.
14. Diller, L.: Cognitive and motor aspects of handicapping conditions in

the neurologically impaired. In Neff, W. S. (Ed.): *Rehabilitation Psychology*. Washington, D. C., Am Psychol, 1971.

15. Federation Employment and Guidance Service: Survey of employer's practices and policies in hiring of physically impaired workers. In McDaniel, J. W.: *Physical Disability and Human Behavior*. New York, Pergamon, 1969.
16. Fink, S. L.: Crisis and motivation: A theoretical model. *Arch Phys Med Rehabil, 48*:592-597, 1967.
17. Fitzgerald, R. G.: Reactions to blindness. *Arch Gen Psychiatry, 22*:370-379, 1970.
18. Ford, A. B., Liske, R. E., and Ort, R. S.: Reactions of physicians and medical students to chronic illness. *J Chronic Dis, 15*:785-794, 1962.
19. Fordyce, W. E.: Behavioral methods in rehabilitation. In Neff, W. S. (Ed.): *Rehabilitation Psychology*. Washington, D. C., Am Psychol, 1971.
20. Freeman, R. D.: Emotional reactions of handicapped children. *Rehabil Lit, 28*:274-282, 1967.
21. Freud, S.: Mourning and melancholia. In Strachey, J. (Ed.): *The Complete Works of Sigmund Freud,* standard ed., vol. XIV. London, Hogarth, 1957.
22. Friend, E.: Social interaction of amputees and nonamputees as related to their attitudes toward amputation. Unpublished doctoral dissertation. New York, New York University, 1971, p. 41.
23. Garrett, J. F., and Levine, E. S. (Eds.): *Psychological Practices with the Physically Disabled*. New York, Columbia U Pr, 1962.
24. Goffman, E.: *Asylums*. New York, Doubleday, 1961.
25. Goffman, E.: *Stigma*. Englewood Cliffs, P-H, 1963.
26. Goldstein, Hyman: Statistical implications of the problem of geriatric severe vision impairment and blindness, 1967*.
27. Goldstein, K.: *The Organism*. New York, American Book Co., 1939.
28. Jordan, J. E.: *Attitudes toward Education and Physically Disabled Persons in Eleven Nations*. East Lansing, Latin American Studies Centers, 1968.
29. Keith, R. A.: The need for a new model in rehabilitation. *J Chronic Dis, 21*:281-286, 1968.
30. Keith, R. A.: Physical rehabilitation: Is it ready for the revolution? *Rehabil Lit, 30*:170-173. 1969.
31. Kutner, B.: Milieu therapy in rehabilitation medicine. *J Rehabil, 35*:16-18, 1969.
32. Kutner, B.: The social psychology of disability. In Neff, W. S. (Ed.): *Rehabilitation Psychology*. Washington, D. C., Am Psychol, 1971.
33. Ladieu, G., Hanfmann, E., and Dembo, T.: Studies in adjustment to

*In Reference 5.

visible disabilities: Evaluation of help by the injured. *J Abnorm Psychol, 42*:169-192, 1947.

34. Lane, J. M., and Barry, J. R.: Recent research on client motivation. *Rehabilitation Research and Practice Review, 1*:5-25, 1971.
35. Leviton, G. L.: Professional-client relations in a rehabilitation hospital setting. In Neff, W. S. (Ed.): *Rehabilitation Psychology,* Washington, D. C., Am Psychol, 1971.
36. Leviton, Gloria L.: *Rehabilitation Psychology.* In press.
37. Lowenfeld, B.: Psychological problems of children with impaired vision.*
38. MacGregor, F. C.: Some psychosocial problems associated with facial deformities. *Am Sociol Rev, 16*:629-638, 1951.
39. Margolin, R., Goldin, G. J., and Stotsky, B. H.: How the attitudes of physicians affect rehabilitation. *Am Correct Ther J, 23*:70-73, 1969.
40. Nagi, S. Z.: *Disability and Rehabilitation: Legal, Clinical, and Self Concepts and Measurement.* Columbus, Ohio State U Pr, 1968.
41. Nagi, S. Z.: Rehabilitation and visual impairments. Some issues in research and practice. In *Blindness and Services to the Blind.* Cambridge, OSTI Press, 1971.
42. Neff, W. S.: Rehabilitation and work. In Neff, W. S. (Ed.): *Rehabilitation Psychology.* Washington, D. C., Am Psychol, 1971.
43. Nemiah, J. C.: Common emotional reactions of patients to injuries. *Arch Phys Med Rehabil, 45*:621-623, 1964.
44. Richardson, S. A.: The effect of physical disability on the socialization of a child. In Goslin, O. A. (Ed.): *Handbook of Socialization Theory and Research.* New York, Rand, 1969, p. 1057.
45. Rochlin, G.: *Griefs and Discontents: The Forces of Change.* Boston, Little, 1965.
46. Ross, A. O.: *The Exceptional Child in the Family.* New York, Grune, 1964.
47. Safilios-Rothschild, C.: *The Sociology and Social Psychology of Disability and Rehabilitation.* New York, Random, 1970.
48. Shontz, F. C.: Physical disability and personality. In Neff, W. S. (Ed.): *Rehabilitation Psychology.* Washington, D. C., Am Psychol 1971.
49. Shontz, F. C.: Reactions to crisis. *Volta Review, 67*:364-370, 1965.
50. Siller, J.: The generality of attitudes toward the physically disabled. *Proceedings, 78th Annual Convention.* Washington, D. C., Am Psychol, 1970a.
51. Siller, J.: Psychological concomitants of amputation in children. *Child Dev, 31*:109-120, 1960.
52. Siller, J.: Psychological situation of the disabled with spinal cord injuries. *Rehabil Lit, 30*:290-296, 1969.
53. Siller, J.: The psychopathology of status. *Rehabilitation Counseling Bul-*

*In Reference 9.

letin, 14:102-107, 1970b.

54. Siller, J., and Chipman, A.: Factorial structure and correlates of the attitude towards disabled persons scale. *Educational and Psychological Measurement, 24*:831-840, 1964.
55. Siller, J., Chipman, A., Ferguson, L. T., and Vann, D. H.: *Studies in Reactions to Disability. XI: Attitudes of the Nondisabled Toward the Physically Disabled.* New York, School of Education, New York University, 1967a.
56. Siller, J., Ferguson, L. T., Vann, D. H., and Holland, B.: *Studies in Reactions to Disability. XII: Structure of Attitudes Toward the Physically Disabled: Disability Factor Scales — Amputation, Blindness, Cosmetic Conditions.* New York, School of Education, New York University, 1967b.
57. Siller, J., and Silverman, S.: Studies of the upper extremity amputee: VII. Psychological factors. *Artif Limbs, 5*:88-116, 1958.
58. Sullivan, H. S.: *The Interpersonal Theory of Psychiatry.* New York, Norton, 1953.
59. Tringo, J. L.: The hierarchy of preferences toward disability groups. *Journal of Special Education, 4*:295-306, 1970.
60. Whiteman, M., and Lukoff, I. F.: Attitudes toward blindness and other physical handicaps. *J Soc Psychol, 66*:133-145, 1965.
61. Whiteman, M., and Lukoff, I. F.: Attitudes toward blindness in two college groups. *J Soc Psychol, 63*:179-191, 1964.
62. Wright, B. A.: *Physical Disability: A Psychological Approach.* New York, Har-Row, 1960.
63. Wright, B. A.: Spread in adjustment to disability. *Bull Menninger Clin, 28*:198-208, 1964.
64. Yuker, H. E., Block, J. R., and Campbell, W. J.: *A Scale to Measure Attitudes Toward Disabled Persons.* Albertson, Human Resources, 1960.
65. Yuker, H. E., Block, J. R., and Younng, J. H.: *The Measurement of Attitudes Toward Disabled Persons.* Albertson, Human Resources, 1966.

Chapter 29

REHABILITATION GOALS – MYTH OR REALITY*

BERNARD KUTNER AND ARTHUR S. ABRAMSON

DISABILITY HAS RECENTLY BEEN defined by Haber and Smith[4] as "the inability to perform usual role activities as a result of a physical or mental impairment of long-term duration." The sequence of concepts in this definition is rather important since it provides clues to the mission of rehabilitation. The initial problem is that of an impairment which shall be defined as a reduced capacity to perform functional acts (i.e. walking, dressing, eating, speaking, etc.). The impairment, to qualify as a disability, must have two further characteristics: (1) It must be of long duration (either permanent or lasting an indefinite or protracted period of time), and (2) it must result in the inability to perform "usual role activities." This latter term is used to identify the individual's normal and expected social behavior (i.e. as a spouse, a parent, a worker, homemaker, friend, relative, church member, etc.).

The social components of disability have two major facets. One is the individual's own sense of inadequacy or incompetence to perform social acts. The second is the result of consensus or social prejudice. If an employer rejects a prospective employee because of his presumed inability to carry out a job or if a wife takes a job to help her husband avoid the difficulty of working with a physical handicap, the individual is *prevented* from en-

*A modified version of the keynote address presented to the Annual Meeting of the Allied Health Professions Section of the Arthritis Foundation, Detroit, Michigan, June 19, 1970.

gaging in normal role activities. The culpability of others in defining the limitations of the disabled is probably less understood than the objective physical limitations, but its net effect is to produce a social handicap superimposed upon its physical counterpart.

Thus, when an individual becomes physically impaired and, as a result of his impairment, is unable or prevented from participating in those social relationships normally expected of him, we refer to him as "disabled." These changes in role relationships have been described as "role disorders," that is, disturbances in role-taking stemming from the inability to perform functional acts.[13] Following the onset of a severely disabling condition (i.e. quadriplegia, crippling arthritis, stroke, etc.) and especially upon hospitalization, all social roles may be terminated or sharply curtailed except for two: first the sick role, then the disabled role. The sick role has been very amply described by others.[3,10] The individual is not expected to do more for himself than his physicians and members of the allied health professions expect him to do. The disabled role is somewhat different since it requires that the individual (1) make efforts to overcome his handicap by perseverance, (2) adapt to the disability, (3) compensate by use of the unaffected parts and (4) work and be socially active to some degree. Nevertheless, the disabled role (depending upon the relative degree of disability) may still include such aspects as legitimate dependency, need for physical assistance by others, retirement from gainful employment, reduced household responsibilities and a sharp curtailment of social relationships in the community.

Prolonged institutional treatment as well as protracted disability will tend to impair social functioning. It has been argued elsewhere[6] that hospitalization, by minimizing social demands upon the patient and by legitimizing highly dependent behavior, tends to exacerbate underlying dependency needs, exponentially affecting the already present changes in social roles brought on by the illness itself. Thus, extended in-hospital rehabilitation involves the simultaneous assuming of the dependent sick role and the more independent disabled role. Nearly everyone who has been a hospital patient has rankled over some of the infantalizing routines of hospital life at the very time when the acute condition has subsided and the patient is beginning to feel "normal" again. The opposed expectations of the two roles arouse frustration and conflict in the recuperating patient in whom no residual impairment is expected. But the severely disabled patient is torn between expectations to act in a "motivated" manner while undergoing feelings of dependency and self-doubt.

An examination of the rehabilitation process in the light of current understanding of disability follows. While a disclaimer must be made for those rare rehabilitation centers and hospitals whose programs are oriented differently, the central thrust of programs for the rehabilitation of the disabled is primarily the recovery of physical function. The point of departure is physical diagnosis and physical treatment. Social diagnosis and social treatment are, for the most part, distinctly secondary considerations. The psychosocial disciplines are regarded as "ancillary," associated with or allied to medicine. While lip service and slogans of "comprehensive care" and "teamwork" are legion, the field of rehabilitation medicine continues to treat the patient as an amalgamation of broken and intact parts rather than as a complete person with a partial disability. A recent study[8] of physician attitudes toward rehabilitation found (to no one's surprise) psychiatrists most interested in the psychological aspects of rehabilitation, but physiatrists and general practitioners "were most concerned with the physical aspects of rehabilitation."

A concern with medical diagnosis and with the physical aspects of therapy is consistent only with one part of the definition of disability, namely, that which deals with the improvement of functional impairments. Physical, occupational and speech therapy are the traditional disciplines concerned with the correction of physical impairments. All three disciplines include some psychosocial courses in their training programs; but just as is the case of medicine, when put to practice in the clinical setting, the psychosocial aspects of disability are made distinctly secondary to the major task of physical restoration.

The psychosocial disciplines traditionally related to rehabilitation—social work, clinical and counseling psychology, vocational counseling and, to the limited extent where it is used, psychiatry—are employed in distinctly adjunctive roles in the rehabilitation process. Each of these disciplines tends to take its cues from a circumscribed medical perspective to aid the patient in adjusting to the rehabilitation program, to deal with his family while he is in treatment and to prepare him for return to the community. While these objectives are consistent with the general intent of rehabilitation, do they, in fact, deal with the central issue of rehabilitation: restoring the individual's ability to perform normal role activities? At this point in time one can only respond by saying that they are relevant only by indirection. Garrett and Levine[2] have characterized disability as "a social problem with medical aspects." Practitioners of rehabilitation medicine deal with disability *as a medical problem with social aspects.* Can the traditional medical model of treating physical illness by primarily physical means be less applicable to the treatment of disability? The writers believe this to be true. Logically, if disability is in fact a problem of role dysfunctions brought on by physical impairment, the treatment of disability should be targeted on these role disturbances while the physical impairments are simultaneously undergoing therapy. Disability as a psychosocial problem requires a psychosocial form of intervention not *incidental* to physical treatment but *collateral* to it. Since residual disability (that is, a change in the capacity to perform certain expected roles) is a common outcome of therapy for physical impairments, it is incumbent on any rehabilitation program to provide the conceptual framework, personnel, skills, space, time and funds to carry out the appropriate therapeutic program. It is in these very areas of psychosocial therapy that many current programs are fundamentally lacking. Paradoxically, this has not proved to be a major handicap to the organization of multidisciplinary rehabilitation teams. One can conceivably establish and operate a highly successful rehabilitation program without any psychosocial team members at all. (Indeed, some programs do just that.) A truncated team consisting of physicians; nurses and aides; and physical, occupational and speech therapists can restore a considerable degree of function to hospitalized physically impaired patients. But while they may function well in the hospital, will they function well at home, in a job and in the community? There is reason to believe that, while some will, many others will not. To some extent, some patients will fail to make an adequate readaptation to life following therapy. A portion of the responsibility for this failure lies in the fact that current rehabilitation programs fail to provide the appropriate emphasis in therapy. Admittedly, there are patients who will not succeed in independent living, nor make use of skills learned during therapy, regardless of the strength or subtlety of the psychosocial input of a given program. There are others who fail because of conceptual limitations of rehabilitation programs in falsely defining the nature of "the beast." What, in fact, are the role disorders and role dislocations which have been alluded to here?

There is no question but that the American people harbor mixed feelings about the disabled in their society. They are sympathetic at the plight of the disabled, feel pity and perhaps even some guilt. At the same time, "the cripple" still is stigmatized and stereotyped irrespective of the extent of his physical impairment. The stereotype, as Beatrice Wright[14] has observed, "spreads" into other areas, even implicating the viability of intact functions. Family members, friends, associates, employers and strangers share vaguely negative feelings toward the disabled person. A host of trained observers in this field have likened the status of the disabled person to that of a minority group member. Those who feel hostility toward difference, toward weakness and toward ethnic minorities also have room for antipathy toward the disabled.[1,9]

If society is not ready to accept the disabled person to its bosom and such feelings are shared by the individual's own family, it is no surprise that the individual senses the presence of resistance to his reentry into any functionally useful roles. Indeed, very likely, he shared the ambivalence of the majority before he himself became disabled. While the attitudes of the American people cannot easily be changed more favorably toward the disabled, there are more immediate goals for change in both the individual himself and between himself and his family. Disability often entails the loss of self-esteem, social withdrawal and feelings of dependency and of rejection. Within the family, disability in one member may engender feelings of strangeness and alienation, uncertainty of behavior and even open antipathy. Since the individual may feel ashamed or embarrassed by his appearance and behavior, he may withdraw from friends, and the withdrawal may become mutual—an unspoken agreement to prevent the disability from arousing covert feelings of rejection. Hence, a frontal assault on the problem of role dysfunction would appear to entail two major efforts: (1) to strengthen the individual's inner resources (his self-esteem, decision-making ability, initiative, morale and motivation) and (2) to strengthen the relationships between the patient and his immediate family.

Conventional methods for dealing with patients who are depressed, somatically concerned, socially constricted and anxious would call for individual or group psychotherapy. In the context of a rehabilitation program, such an approach would not be economically feasible, nor would it use the unit's staff to greatest advantage. Faced with the same kind of problem—too many patients and too few staff—a good many psychiatric hospitals have turned to milieu or environmental therapy either as an adjunct to psychotherapy or as the primary treatment of choice. (See Refs. 5, 11 and 12.) Recently, one hospital attempted an experimental therapeutic community program for disabled patients.[7]

Briefly, milieu therapy engages an entire nursing unit, ward or patient population in a combined effort with staff members to deal with the myriad administrative problems common to nearly all institutions. Patients are brought together to form a governmental structure, which when combined with a parallel staff structure produces a so-called "therapeutic community." The community aspect of the program permits the patient-staff group to approach, examine, attack and solve outstanding issues identified by the group. The range of such problems may be very broad, covering such diverse areas as relieving nursing shortages, rearranging time schedules, developing a social-recreational program, making use of evening and weekend time, maintaining ward discipline (i.e. use of television, smoking areas, etc.), celebrating holidays, dealing with the dietary department, settling disputes among patients, arranging for maintenance and repair of living quarters, obtaining patient use of elevators and public canteens and a host of others. Any hospital or rehabilitation center will provide grist for the community mill since they are almost never problem-free. The involvement of both patients and staff in solving problems encourages the development of a kind of community feeling. The patients' need to *live* comfortably and staff's need to *work* comfortably gel into a community of interest and often lead to the removal of long-term grievances or chronic inequities. The therapeutic community need not be a substitute for general hospital administration nor even for the rehabilitation unit. However, it must be capable of initiating and following through to higher authority on recommendations for change. It is through this power to influence affairs and to move toward the interface between institutional and personal needs that the milieu therapy approach generates its therapeutic aspects.

The community structure of the nursing unit permits the individual to join the central group and its spin-off subcommittees. The act of joining immediately removes the patient from his isolation and his abject dependent relationship to the hospital. It inserts him into a group of peers each of whom has some form of disability that identifies and legitimizes his presence. In the writer's own experience, adults of nearly the entire age spectrum (with the possible exception of young patients who identify with their own generation), of both sexes and of varying diagnoses and disabilities, may successfully be fused into a working patient organization. The patient is made to feel accepted into the group on whatever level he is capable of functioning. Further, the patient is cast into a series of new roles, not merely that of disabled patient. Instead, he is a group member, a committee member or even an officer in the patient government. Moreover, he is given, and is expected to perform, certain functions: planning social or recreational activities, arranging meetings, setting agendas, negotiating with others, calling and writing people, meeting with staff members, supervising discipline, etc. In brief, milieu therapy involves the inclusion of the patient in roles of a socially functional nature that are not contrived but purposeful, having the potential of either success or failure. The introduction of new, even unfamiliar roles engages the patient in activities having therapeutic value: social relationships, discussion, planning, decision making and execution of planned activity. Such experiences can have the net effect of demonstrating to him that even major disability need not cut him off from meaningful social activity, that personal effectiveness is not necessarily conditioned by degree of physical involvement. Hence, severe hemiplegic patients, double amputees, arthritic patients, aphasics, etc. may find themselves acting in a normal manner vis-a-vis in social roles despite the severity of their conditions.

Participation in a therapeutic community may begin at a simple level, in very small groups. The patient may not be able to tolerate large group discussions and may even remain at this level throughout the program. Others may be given greater responsibility and may move up to committee chairman or officer. In general, the patient's own drive and involvement in the program will help determine his eventual status in the community. For some patients, even minimal participation, in pairs, may be intolerable, and they will remain passive bystanders.

The therapeutic community casts the staff member into a triangle of roles. First, he is a professional or allied health professional operating within his sphere of competence, training and skill. Second, he is a member of the "staff group" within the therapeutic community. This group has the function of planning the use of their time and skill, to feed into the orientation of the milieu program. Thus, if the group decides that a rescheduling of hours is necessary to increase the patient's opportunity to use physical skills he is learning, plans for such new schedules must be thought through. If the psychosocial program interferes with existing schedules, a decision must be made on therapeutic priorities. In brief, the milieu therapy group consisting of all staff operating within the unit is drawn into a new orbit of team functioning, a new group identity and a new group loyalty.

Third, the staff member becomes a member of patient-staff

groups, committees, etc. Here, both patients and staff are face-to-face in the unfamiliar setting of an equal-status group. The superordinate position of staff members in traditional roles is set aside, and each individual finds himself, along with patients, as an otherwise undifferentiated personality. After several weeks of embarrassed silences and false starts, the group usually begins to lose its alien character as the members warm to their tasks. In the well-functioning therapeutic community, joint committees are commonplace and the borderline between "we" (the staff) and "they" (the patients) becomes obscured. Patients may now confront the staff as persons with whom they have dealings, as their sense of distance from professionals melts away.

Of major value in the therapeutic community approach to rehabilitation is the patient's need to expend social effort. Even though the activities he engages in while a member of the therapeutic community may never again be duplicated in his experience on the outside, the effort involved in carrying out the new community roles may serve to compensate for some of the physical disabling brought about by his medical condition. In fact, the psychosocial regression following discharge may be quite profound. Hence, the in-hospital milieu program must be overcompensatory to allow for slippage in open society.

The second aspect of role dysfunction that must be dealt with while the disabled patient is held captive by the rehabilitation facility is his relationship to his family. It seems almost trite to point out that the family is the primary agency for resocialization of the patient upon his return home. Yet, the patient's family may be in no position to reabsorb him into the household. While he has been away for many weeks or months, most of the tasks he had normally performed (i.e. his social roles) may have been redistributed among others. A wife may have gone to work, or a husband may have begun to care for the home and do the domestic chores, while others may have filled in other aspects of the vacuum left by the patient. When he returns with a residual disability, some of these roles may return to him in whole or in part, or they may have become permanently lost, without suitable substitutes. It is easy for a disabled person to become an isolate in his own home, gradually sinking into dependency and chronic invalidism as a way of life. The family's involvement in the therapeutic program becomes of critical importance since family members can, through no fault of their own, make all the arduous and expensive physical training endured by staff and patient alike come to a meaningless end at the threshold of the patient's home. To sustain hospital gains and to go on from there to possible improvement and to social revitalization, family members must understand themselves, must deal with their own myths, fantasies and misconceptions concerning crippling disability and must make provision for the useful and productive inclusion of the stricken ex-patient in the family circle. This is an order of expectation that may fortuitously be attained by some, but may be well out of the reach of others.

To complete the rehabilitation of the patient while in the hospital or rehabilitation center, patients and family members should undergo a careful social diagnosis to determine to what extent role dysfunction will occur upon completion of treatment. If trouble is seen in the prognosis, it is logical that a plan for family therapy be drawn up. Currently, typical involvement of the family in the treatment process stops at a point where it should begin, with information on the need for continuance of therapeutic activity. Knowing the patient's limitations is not, however, sufficient preparation for living together. The *family unit* is disturbed when one member is disabled and a shift of roles, resulting in the patient's being left without a meaningful function or with an unsatisfactory role, requires *that the unit itself rather than the patient alone be part of the treatment plan.* Psychiatry has long since discovered the value of family therapy in the treatment of emotional disorder in one of its members. It can be of no less value in rehabilitation medicine. Family treatment should begin early in the rehabilitation process. It could take any number of forms including single family units, multiple-family therapy with either the same or a similar disability (i.e. cord-injured patients, amputees, arthritics, etc.), or in family groups with mixed disabilities. It may be conducted in individual hour-long sessions or in marathons of varying length (24, 36 or even 48 continuous hours). It could involve confrontation tactics, psychodrama or a combination of approaches. Therapy could be conducted by trained family or encounter therapists: psychiatrists, psychologists or social workers with special experience. It could also involve other staff members as part of the therapy group. The central issue of all such family therapy is the unfolding of feelings and attitudes: first, those of the patient about himself and his disability, his feelings about his family's feelings about him, his views of himself in the family constellation and his fantasies about the future. Second are the feelings and attitudes of the patient's spouse, his children and other close relatives. They, too, should be involved in family therapy. Honest and open discussion of feelings will help clear the air and undo some of the irrational bases of the family's rejection, aversion, repulsion, and avoidance of the disabled, and of the patient's own fears of rejection, self-hatred, denial and self-isolation. From such therapy, rational approaches to role-taking may be made, hopefully demoting the disability to its true status and opening new avenues for exploitation of residual skills and resources.

From all that has been said in this paper, it might be tempting to conclude that traditional rehabilitation medicine approaches the problem of therapy with its clothes on backwards. Rather, the writers would prefer to look at it as a case in which the primary mission of the field—the restoration of the patient to the highest level of physical, social and psychological functioning of which he is capable within the limits imposed by his disability—has not recently been examined with respect to its own programs for achieving this goal. With present methods, it can only remain a myth. The disciplines involved in the rehabilitation process have selected as their primary target the physical restoration of the patient. In terms of funding, staffing, space, equipment and daily work, the emphasis remains on physical medicine and not on comprehensive (including social) rehabilitation. One cannot function without the other. The results obtained by the most advanced and exquisite forms of physical restoration will go for nought if the patient has no place in life to use his newly acquired capabilities. The psychosocial approaches delineated in this paper are not necessarily a panacea for our problems, but a serious attempt to include them in the rehabilitation effort would begin to set the priorities more equitably, more logically and more therapeutically than is currently the case.

REFERENCES

1. Cowen, E. L., Bobgrove, P. H., Rockway, A. M., and Stevenson, J.: Development and evaluation of an attitudes to deafness scale. *J Per Soc Psychol, 6:*183-191, 1967.
2. Garrett, J. F., and Levine, E. S. (Eds.): *Psychological Practices with the Physically Disabled.* New York, Columbia U Pr, 1962, p. ix.
3. Gordon, G.: *Role Theory and Illness.* New Haven, College & U Pr, 1966.
4. Haber, L. D., and Smith, R. T.: Disability and Deviance: Normative Adaptations in Role Behavior. Paper read at annual meeting of American Sociological Association. San Francisco, 1969, p. 1.
5. Jones, M.: *The Therapeutic Community.* New York, Basic, 1953.
6. Kutner, B.: Milieu therapy in rehabilitation medicine. *J Rehabil, 34:* 14-17, 1968.
7. Kutner, B., Rosenberg, P., Berger, R., and Abramson, A. S.: *A Therapeutic Community in Rehabilitation Medicine.* In press.
8. Margolin, R. J., Goldin, G. J., and Stotsky, B. H.: How the attitudes of physicians affect rehabilitation. *Am Correct Ther J, 23:*70-73, 1969.
9. Noonan, R.: Personality determinants in attitudes toward disability. Abstract of doctoral dissertation. Gainesville, University of Florida, 1967.
10. Parsons, T.: *The Social System.* Glencoe, Free Pr, 1951, pp. 439-447.
11. Rapaport, R. N.: *Community as a Doctor.* Springfield, Thomas, 1960.
12. Stanton, A., and Schwartz, M.: *The Mental Hospital.* New York, Basic, 1954.
13. Weissman, R., and Kutner, B.: Role disorders in extended hospitalization. *Hospital Administration, 12:*52-59, 1967.
14. Wright, B. A.: *Physical Disability—A Psychological Approach.* New York, Har-Row, 1960.

Chapter 30

A BILL OF RIGHTS FOR THE DISABLED

Arthur S. Abramson and Bernard Kutner

Whereas, the disabled in the United States, constituting a large minority with a commonality of need and a unity of purpose, seek only to obtain for themselves what all Americans believe to be their birthright—life, liberty and the pursuit of happiness; and

Whereas, impediments and roadblocks of every nature are to be found at every hand, effectively preventing the fulfillment of life's promise for a large proportion of the disabled; and

Whereas, the American people, largely through lack of knowledge and misinformation have not as yet recognized the disabled as fellow human beings with a handicap to which all should make some accommodation, and who deserve equal opportunity as citizens; and

Whereas, the Congress of the United States and the legislatures of the various states, counties and municipalities have not as yet, by legal means, made it possible for the disabled person to attain equal access to those benefits of life enjoyed by the able-bodied, *be it resolved:*

Health — 1.

That all disabled persons be afforded the opportunity for full and comprehensive diagnostic, therapeutic, rehabilita-

---

Reprint from *Archives of Physical Medicine and Rehabilitation,* vol. 53, March, 1972. "Copyright, 1972, American Congress of Rehabilitation Medicine."

tive and follow-up services in the nation's hospitals, clinics and rehabilitation centers without regard to race, religion, economic status, ethnic origin, sex, age or social condition.

Health — 2.

That all disabled persons requiring same be given and trained to use such orthotic, prosthetic or adaptive devices that will enable them to become more mobile and to live more comfortably.

Education — 3.

That all disabled persons be given every opportunity for formal education to the level of which they are capable and to the degree to which they aspire.

Employment — 4.

That all disabled persons, to the extent necessary, have the opportunity to receive special training commensurate with residual abilities in those aspects of life in which they are handicapped, so that they may achieve the potential for entry into the labor market in competitive employment.

Employment — 5.

That all employable disabled persons, like other minorities, be covered by equal opportunity legislation so that equal productivity, potential and actual, receives equal consideration in terms of jobs, promotions, salaries, workloads and fringe benefits.

Employment — 6.

That those disabled persons who because of the severity of their handicaps are deemed unable to enter the normal labor market, be given the opportunity for special training and placement in limited work situations including sheltered workshops, home-base employment and other protected job situations.

Employment — 7.

That a nationwide network of tax-supported sheltered workshops be created to offer limited work opportunities for all those severely disabled persons unable to enter the competitive labor market.

Housing — 8.

That nationwide and local programs of special housing for the disabled be established to permit them an opportunity to live in dignity and reasonable comfort.

Architectural Barriers — 9.

That federal, state and local legislatures pass laws requiring the elimination of architectural barriers to buildings, recreational, cultural and social facilities and public places. Such legislation should include architectural standards for all new construction.

Architectural Barriers — 10.

That federal, state and local legislation be passed establishing standards and a reasonable time for modification of existing sidewalks, buildings and structures for the comfortable use of the handicapped.

Transportation — 11.

That every community, county or other legally constituted authority establish programs and standards for the creation of special transportation for the disabled including modification of existing mass transportation systems and the development of new specially designed demand-schedule transportation facilities.

Income Maintenance — 12.

That every disabled person who because of the nature of his handicap is unable to be self-supporting, be given a guaranteed minimum income not below established federal standards adequate to live in reasonable comfort and in dignity.

Institutional Care — 13.

That federal, state and local laws be enacted for the benefit of the disabled confined to any form of institution, setting minimum standards of housing, conveniences, comfort, staff and services.

Civil Rights — 14.

That civil rights legislation, national and local, be amended to include disability as one of the categories against which discrimination is unlawful.

Training — 15.

That federal and state tax-supported programs of training be established to prepare professional and nonprofessional personnel for work with the handicapped in the fields of health, education, recreation and welfare.

Research — 16.

That federal legislation be enacted expanding existing and developing new programs of research and demonstration, by grant and contract, in both basic and applied fields, dealing with the problems of disabling conditions and the disabled.

Be it further resolved that these rights, being urgent and critical to the well being of the disabled population of the United States, be given the high priority they justly deserve in the hearts, minds and programs of our nation's leaders.

AUTHOR INDEX

C

D

E

F

W

Y

Z

SUBJECT INDEX

B

C

E

F

L

M

Q

R

T

Randall Library – UNCW
RC576 .M4 NXWW
Meislin / Rehabilitation medicine and psychiatry
3049002087932